RACE,
WORK,
AND
LEADERSHIP

RACE, WORK, AND LEADERSHIP

New Perspectives on the Black Experience

Edited by

LAURA MORGAN ROBERTS

ANTHONY J. MAYO

DAVID A. THOMAS

Boston, Massachusetts

Harvard Business Review Press

The web addresses referenced in this book were live and correct at the time of the book's publication but may be subject to change.

Library of Congress Cataloging-in-Publication Data

Names: Roberts, Laura Morgan, editor. | Mayo, Anthony J., editor. | Thomas,
   David A., 1956– editor.
Title: Race, work, and leadership : new perspectives on the black experience
   / editors: Laura Morgan Roberts, Anthony J. Mayo, David Thomas.
Description: Boston : Harvard Business Review Press, 2019. | Includes index.
Identifiers: LCCN 2019002678 | ISBN 9781633698017 (hardcover)
Subjects: LCSH: African American executives. | African American leadership. |
   Diversity in the workplace—United States. | Racism in the
   workplace—United States. | Corporate culture—United States.
Classification: LCC HF5549.5.M5 R34 2019 | DDC 331.6/396073—dc23
LC record available at https://lccn.loc.gov/2019002678

The paper used in this publication meets the requirements of the American National Standard for Permanence of Paper for Publications and Documents in Libraries and Archives Z39.48-1992.

In the tradition of the African proverb, "it takes a village" to attempt the healing and restorative work of racial justice. We dedicate this book to the central members of our village—our partners and children: Darryl, Anaiah, and Isaiah Roberts; Denise, Hannah, Alex, and Jake Mayo; Willetta Lewis, Sommer, David, and Nelson Thomas.

In the spirit of Sankofa, we pay homage to the African people who first set foot on US soil exactly four hundred years ago, in 1619. We commemorate the sacrifices that were made in pursuit of the liberation of future generations of African-descended people, who would awaken the moral conscience of a nation and lead us toward a brighter future.

Contents

SECTION TWO

Comparative Studies

SECTION THREE

Phenomenological Studies
The Lived Experience

SECTION FOUR

Theorizing Black Leadership

SECTION FIVE

The Future
Lessons for the Next Generation of Leaders

Foreword

Race in Organizations:
Often Cloaked but Always Present

———————

ELLA L. J. EDMONDSON BELL
STELLA M. NKOMO

Even as we pronounce the death of race, we cannot overlook the fact that our attempts to articulate it into oblivion, to pronounce the last word on race, simply have not worked!

—*Holland (2005, p. 406)*

W e are honored to write a foreword for *Race, Work, and Leadership: New Perspectives on the Black Experience.* As senior scholars who have spent the bulk of our academic and professional lives studying race and gender in leadership and organizational life, we decided to use this space to reflect on the past, the present, and the future of race in the workplace using insights from our scholarly and practical work, as well as the contributions in this volume.

Almost thirty years ago, we were among the contributors to a special issue of the *Journal of Organizational Behavior* published in 1990 that resulted from a symposium presented at an annual Academy of Management meeting in 1987 entitled, "No Crystal Stair: Current Research on the Career Experiences of Black Professionals." The special issue documented the career challenges encountered by black professionals, which were largely absent from organizational knowledge. In his commentary article in the special issue, Clayton Alderfer (1990), the pioneering scholar of race relations in organizations, acknowledged that he was unaware of a mainstream journal on organizational behavior having ever before devoted an entire issue to the subject of race. In her introductory article as the special issue editor, Ella Bell (1990) expressed the hope that the contents would stimulate and energize the study of race in organizations. All of us who contributed articles held similar aspirations for the volume. But most of all we were hoping for change.

Our special issue has been followed by a number of important scholarly contributions that Laura Morgan Roberts, Anthony J. Mayo, and Serenity Lee summarize in their introduction to this book. All of these contributions have helped document the challenging experiences of black professionals, and many have offered suggestions for change. The last twenty-five years saw the rise of diversity officers and diversity initiatives in organizations striving for an inclusive workplace. And yes, there was some evidence of progress in the presence of black men and women in the managerial ranks of organizations, though white male managerial overrepresentation remained virtually unchanged from 1966 to 2000 (Stainback & Tomaskovic-Devey, 2009, 2012).

However, Roberts, Mayo, and Lee make two important observations in their introductory chapter about where we are today. First, race has yet to be mainstreamed in the study of organizations in a way that matches its core relevance to workplace opportunities, behaviors, and relationships. Second, the explicit discussion of race and organizational leadership is still considered taboo or irrelevant in many business circles.

As this chapter's epigraph suggests and as the chapters in this book attest, despite legislative efforts, declarations of a postrace America, and the turn to diversity as an organizational imperative, race still wields its power as a barrier to the ascendancy of African Americans to leadership positions. Race has managed to take the heat of pressures to erase it (Holland, 2005:405). In fact, recent developments in the broader society show ominous signs of its resurgence, not its demise.

Racism makes race matter (Holland, 2005). Currently, race and racism are being uncloaked in virulent expressions of white supremacy nationally and globally (Hage, 2012; Mishra, 2018; Swain, 2002). Mishra (2018) has described this phenomenon as the reawakening of a belligerent nationalism with deep historical roots. The Charlottesville march led by the alt-right in 2017 has been described as a coming-out event for those who wish to see a return to the days of the Ku Klux Klan and Jim

Crow laws. So overt have been the expressions of racism and racial harassment that African Americans have had to plead "Black Lives Matter," endure an increasing number of incidents of white people calling the police about African Americans engaging in everyday activities (e.g., swimming at a pool, barbequing at a park, selling lemonade, cutting grass, studying on college campuses, meeting in coffee shops), and tolerate being feared by whites as troublemakers and criminals (Hall, Hall, & Perry, 2016; Lowery, 2016; Patton & Farley, 2018). At the same time, there has been a rise in anti-immigrant sentiments that has been manifested in negative attitudes and restrictive immigration policies toward ethnic minorities (Hagan, Rodriguez, & Castro, 2011). Racial resentment arising from social and demographic changes has been shown to have a greater effect than economic anxiety on attitudes toward immigrants in the United States (Hooghe & Dassonneville, 2018; Miller, 2018).

Some of these phenomena are not new. The problem is that they continue to happen long after the end of segregation and declarations of a postrace America. While we can hope they are aberrations, organizations should take these developments seriously. What happens in society spills over because organizations are *in* society, not apart from it. Employees do not leave their race or racial beliefs at the entrance when they enter the workplace. A ready example is a well-publicized Starbucks incident. Two black men were arrested after employees called police to say the men were trespassing when they were actually waiting for a friend. Organizations are not immune from the troubling signs that are unfolding in societal race relations.

The Starbucks episode should make us aware of how stereotypical fears about black men may affect perceptions of them as potential leaders. However, beliefs about who can lead go even deeper than stereotyping. Roediger and Esch (2012) have traced the intimate relationship between racial beliefs and the origins of management in an industrializing America. At the time, a prevalent management practice was to rank racial groups in terms of both which jobs they were best suited for and their relative value compared to others. Blacks were only deemed suitable for the lowest and dirtiest jobs. Contemporary research has shown how the white standard for a prototypical leader limits the possibility that black men and black women will be perceived as suitable for leadership positions (Carton & Rosette, 2011; Rosette, Leonardelli, & Phillips, 2008).

Race, Work, and Leadership could not come at a better time, because too many Americans appear to believe that race and racism were somehow tamed with the breakthrough election of Barack Obama as president of the United States (Tesler & Sears, 2010), an office whose occupant has often been declared the leader of the "free world." Yet today there are only three black CEOs of *Fortune* 500 companies (after reaching a peak of twelve in 2002), and not one is a woman (Donnelly, 2018). We live in an era that seems to be a far cry from the time we could point to African American leaders like Kenneth Chenault, Ann Fudge, Richard Parsons, Franklin Raines, and Ursula Burns. While small gains have been made in the representation of African Americans in the workplace, the advancement of black men and women in management and leadership positions is stagnant (Stainback & Tomaskovic-Devey, 2009, 2012). This stagnation impedes meaningful progress toward inclusion and social justice (Abelson & Holman, 2017; Catalyst, 2017).

Roberts, Mayo, and David A. Thomas have assembled an excellent team of scholars and practitioners who provide empirical research on the impact of race on the careers and leadership experiences of black professionals in business, health care, law, and academia. The comprehensive picture provided through surveys, case studies, interviews, and archival historical data is compelling and thought provoking. The topics covered range from career pathways, authenticity, leadership obstacles, mentoring experiences, and leadership development to designing diversity initiatives. The chapters provide poignant data about the challenges and costs of not belonging to the majority group in America. Collectively, as we found in our own research over the years and as the chapters in this volume confirm, race continues to matter in the workplace.

We experienced mixed emotions while reading this book. On one hand, we are sad because we had hoped in 1990 that sharing the difficult experiences of black professionals would provide impetus for change. However, the contents of *Race, Work, and Leadership* echo many of the themes in the 1990 special issue of the *Journal of Organizational Behavior*. On the other hand, we are energized because of the apt timing of this book's publication. The stoking of fears about endangered white power and talk of white genocide by some political leaders and Far Right conservatives advance the false notion that black progress is being achieved at the expense of white people. This book counters these assertions by showing just the opposite: racial inequality in workplace opportunities for black professionals persists.

It is time to turn up the heat on race and racism if we want to cool it down (Holland, 2005). We agree with the response James Baldwin gave to a question about what black folks should do to cool the 1968 riots after the assassination of Dr. Martin Luther King Jr.: "It is not for us [black people] to cool it" (*Esquire* editors, 1968). This book should help readers understand how black professionals labor daily to persevere and excel as leaders despite the racial barriers encountered. Ending racism requires personal and institutional work not just by the people affected but also by those who participate in its continuation in overt, covert, and benign ways.

We fear that some white people, seeing the word *race* in the title, may assume the book has nothing to do with them. Ignoring it, silencing it, and calling it anything but race will not stop its significance in perpetuating racial inequality in the workplace (Holland, 2005). As DiAngelo argues in her book *White Fragility* (2018), color blindness prevents white people from grappling with how race matters not just in society as a whole but specifically in the workplace.

Now is the time for reluctant white people to find the courage to engage in real conversations about race and racism in the workplace. No doubt these will be difficult and uncomfortable conversations. *Race, Work, and Leadership* must be read from a position of open-mindedness, not defensiveness. We believe this book will benefit several audiences. Consultants in the field of diversity and race relations will find valuable material for their work. We hope academics will not only read this book to gain a deeper understanding of why race is integral to the study of organizations but also share it with students. While black professionals and managers will certainly identify with its content, it is not a book only for them. It is a must-read for corporate and institutional leaders who want to build an inclusive workplace.

Dislodging race as an arbiter of organizational experiences requires more than reading and conversation, however. Effective change requires a strong relationship between knowledge and action. Several chapters in the book provide recommendations for action. If we don't act now, thirty years from now the profile of leadership in the professions may calcify or even worsen. Changing the leadership profile of the workplace is critical to having the talent needed to address the complex twenty-first-century challenges facing organizations, both private and public. It is an undertaking that will benefit all of us. The stakes have never been higher, given today's racially charged climate.

REFERENCES

Abelson, M., & Holman, J. (2017, July 27). Black executives are losing ground at some big banks. Retrieved from https://www.bloomberg.com/graphics/2017 -black-executives-are-disappearing-from-biggest-wall-street-banks/

Alderfer, C. P. (1990). Reflections on race relations in organizations. *Journal of Organizational Behavior, 11*(6), 493–495.

Bell, E. L. (1990). Introduction. *Journal of Organizational Behavior, 11*(6), 417–418.

Carton, A. M., & Rosette, A. S. (2011). Explaining bias against black leaders: Integrating theory on information processing and goal-based stereotyping. *Academy of Management Journal, 54*(6), 1141–1158.

Catalyst. (2017). Women in S&P 500 companies by race/ethnicity and level. Retrieved from http://www.catalyst.org/knowledge/women-sp-500-companies -raceethnicity-and-level

DiAngelo, R. (2018). *White fragility: Why it's so hard for white people to talk about racism.* Boston, MA: Beacon Press.

Donnelly, G. (2018, February 28). The number of black CEOs at Fortune 500 companies is at its lowest since 2002. *Fortune.* Retrieved from http://fortune.com /2018/02/28/black-history-month-black-ceos-fortune-500/?utm_source=fortune .com&utm_medium=email&utm_campaign=raceahead&utm_content =2018030118pm

Esquire editors. (1968, July). Interview with James Baldwin. *Esquire.* Retrieved from https://www.esquire.com/news-politics/a23960/james-baldwin-cool-it

Hagan, J. M., Rodriguez, N., & Castro, B. (2011). Social effects of mass deportations by the United States government, 2000–10. *Ethnic and Racial Studies, 34*(8), 1374–1391.

Hage, G. (2012). *White nation: Fantasies of white supremacy in a multicultural society.* New York, NY: Routledge.

Hall, A. V., Hall, E. V., & Perry, J. L. (2016). Black and blue: Exploring racial bias and law enforcement in the killings of unarmed black male civilians. *American Psychologist, 71*(3), 175–186.

Holland, S. P. (2005). The last word on racism: New directions for a critical race theory. *South Atlantic Quarterly, 104*(3), 403–423.

Hooghe, M., & Dassonneville, R. (2018). Explaining the Trump vote: The effect of racist resentment and anti-immigrant sentiments. *PS: Political Science & Politics, 51*(3), 1–7.

Lowery, W. (2016). *They can't kill us all: Ferguson, Baltimore, and a new era in America's racial justice movement.* New York, NY: Little, Brown.

Miller, S. V. (2018, August). *Economic anxiety or racial resentment? An evaluation of attitudes toward immigration in the U.S. from 1992 to 2016* (Working paper). Clemson University, Clemson, SC.

Mishra, P. (2018, August 30). The religion of whiteness becomes a suicide cult. *New York Times*. Retrieved from https://www.nytimes.com/2018/08/30/opinion/race-politics-whiteness.html

Patton, S., & Farley, A. P. (2018, May 16). There's no cost to white people who call 911 about black people. There should be. *Washington Post*. Retrieved from https://www.washingtonpost.com/news/posteverything/wp/2018/05/16/theres-no-cost-to-white-people-who-call-911-about-black-people-there-should-be/?utm_term=.328cb6be1c0c

Roediger, D. R., & Esch, E. D. (2012). *The production of difference: Race and the management of labor in U.S. history*. New York, NY: Oxford University Press.

Rosette, A. S., Leonardelli, G. J., & Phillips, K. W. (2008). The white standard: Racial bias in leader categorization. *Journal of Applied Psychology, 93*(4), 758.

Stainback, K., & Tomaskovic-Devey, D. (2009). Intersections of power and privilege: Long-term trends in managerial representation. *American Sociological Review, 74*(5), 800–820.

Stainback, K., & Tomaskovic-Devey, D. (2012). *Documenting desegregation: Racial and gender segregation in private-sector employment since the Civil Rights Act*. New York, NY: Russell Sage Foundation.

Swain, C. M. (2002). *The new white nationalism in America: Its challenge to integration*. Cambridge, England: Cambridge University Press.

Tesler, M., & Sears, D. O. (2010). *Obama's race: The 2008 election and the dream of a post-racial America*. Chicago, IL: University of Chicago Press.

1

Why a Volume on Race, Work, and Leadership?

LAURA MORGAN ROBERTS,
ANTHONY J. MAYO, *and* SERENITY LEE

We had a dream . . .
That one day our sons and daughters would grow up to be
Doctors, lawyers, engineers, teachers, preachers, politicians,
    and business owners . . .
Business owners?
Yes, Business owners. With a capital B.
Because back in the day, we *were* the Capital, see?
Bought and sold per pound of flesh
Tried and tested under great duress
The great "race" started with a gun shot [bang]
Sprinting to the finish line, before the closing bell rang.
This Land is our land.
Plowed by a sacred hand.
And claimed through a courageous stand.

—*Laura Morgan Roberts, 2017*

T he foregoing poem, written by one of the editors of this volume, references the Atlantic slave trade, noting the historical (de)valuation of black bodies as capital. Blacks have been integral to the economic foundation of the United States since its inception, yet that foundation was forged on an institutionalized inequality, which continues to have debilitating effects. The social construction of blackness has been an economic tool for centuries; it has been used as a means of sourcing under- or wholly unpaid labor, rationalized by an attribution of blacks' biological inferiority. Though research has since amassed ample evidence that contradicts these essentialist notions of the superiority or inferiority of a given race (Gannon, 2016; Goodman, 2003; Kolbert, 2017), the color line persists as an enduring social issue in the United States. Over 150 years postemancipation, the wealth gap between blacks and Americans of other racial backgrounds continues to widen, with predictions that black families' median wealth will decrease to $0 by the year 2050, while white families' median wealth will exceed $100,000. There are currently no black women *Fortune* 500 CEOs, and at the sixteen *Fortune* 500 companies that share detailed demographic data, senior executive and board positions are dominated by white men (approximately 85 percent, a number that has remained consistent for decades).

On the other hand, significant advances have been made with respect to black leaders' economic influence over the past century. Most remarkably, the former president of the United States, Barack Obama, was placed at the helm of the US economy in the midst of the Great Recession and executed multi-billion-dollar stimulus packages to reinvigorate industries during financial crises. A handful of black entrepreneurs (e.g., Oprah Winfrey and Robert Smith) are among the wealthiest Americans, and though they represent the exception, their influence is nonetheless widespread as their businesses increase in value. The number of businesses majority-owned by black women grew 67 percent between 2007 and 2012, more growth than women-owned businesses as whole saw (Nielsen Report, 2017). In light of these advances, a recent study by Ernst and Young (2017) found that one-third of Americans surveyed said that the corporate focus on diversity has overlooked white men, and 62 percent of this group believe that white men are being overlooked for promotion and advancement opportunities.

A December 2017 Pew Research Center report of 1,503 adults found that racial discord has increased in the United States; a majority of respondents say race relations are generally bad, while 38 percent say they are generally good. Since May 2016, the share of Americans who say race relations are getting worse increased from 38 percent to 44 percent. The Center for the Study of Hate and Extremism at California State University at San Bernardino recently released a report stating that hate crimes have spiked in the United States for the fourth year in a row. African Americans are the most frequent targets of hate crimes overall and racial hate crimes in particular, accounting for 23 percent, while Jewish people are the most targeted religious group. According to an article in the *Washington Post*, hate crimes are grossly underreported, and 90 percent of the country's approximately sixteen thousand law enforcement agencies choose not to supply data or report no hate crimes to FBI statisticians, likely skewing the data (Hauslohner, 2018).

Notably, Ernst and Young (2017) also reported that 74 percent of respondents support an increased focus on diversity and inclusion (D&I) in today's workplaces, and 72 percent think society's focus on D&I can help companies build a better working world. Boosting women and minorities is "good business," as diversity improves the quality of decision making on complex tasks, team performance, and innovation. Yet, despite the long-standing interconnections between race, work, and leadership—and the (de)valuation of labor that has reinforced social stratification—the explicit discussion of race and organizational leadership is still considered taboo or irrelevant in many business circles.

Recent research has indicated that CEOs (and lower-level managers) who champion diversity are penalized, unless they are white males (Johnson & Hekman, 2016). A few CEOs have initiated firm-wide discussions of race, such as Tim Ryan (PWC), Michael Roth (Interpublic Group), Bernard Tyson (Kaiser Permanente), and Randall Stephenson (AT&T) (see Johnson, 2017, for other examples). Yet, among young black professionals who aspire to advance to senior leadership positions, the most frequently adopted strategy is to remain silent about race or other issues of inequality or injustice in order to avoid being labeled as an agitator (Cose, 2011). Nearly 40 percent of black employees surveyed feel it is never acceptable at their companies to speak out about experiences of bias (Hewlett, Marshall, & Bourgeois, 2017). Silence about race in the workplace compromises relationships (Phillips, Dumas, & Rothbard, 2018) and work engagement (Hewlett et al., 2017). It also feeds into a belief that meritocratic principles determine career advancement, and firms who endorse such meritocratic beliefs paradoxically practice more bias in evaluating workers (Castilla & Benard, 2010).

Our aim is to demonstrate through the chapters in this edited volume that race, and specifically blackness, is not marginal but in fact *central* to business. We acknowledge that, despite being a numerical minority in the United States (at 13.3 percent; US Census Bureau, 2017), African Americans have been integral in bringing form and flow to the industries that have shaped the US economy. This book responds to the need to explore the intersecting space within the spheres of race, work, and leadership, wherein we make tangible the contributions that black Americans have provided to the infrastructure of business. This book also highlights the very tangible ways in which black talent is being undervalued or squandered.

We focus primarily on the experiences of black leadership in the professions as "work" context—for example, we include chapters on the business of education, the business of health care, and the business practices of professional services firms (e.g., legal, consulting, and financial services). The volume includes chapters that present the realistic situation for black professionals in terms of their experience of work and advancement up the pipeline. At the same time, the volume strives to present findings and narratives that push beyond the traditional deficit portrayals of blacks to present perspectives about strength, agency, and possibility. Furthermore, this volume covers black leadership in the past, the present, and the future, primarily in the context of formalized organizations (e.g., corporations, schools, and hospitals) and, to a lesser extent, communities.

We are living in an age in which thought leadership around race, work, and leadership is desperately needed. The Black Lives Matter movement has permeated civic life and workplaces, as protesters cry for equal justice and dignity from police officers, court officials, employers, and everyday citizens (McCluney, Bryant, King & Ali, 2017; Opie & Roberts, 2017). Notably, Nike's Colin Kaepernick ad campaign (featuring the leading voice in the Black Lives Matter NFL protest movement) created $163.5 million in media exposure for Nike, and Nike's market value rose $6 billion in the weeks following the September 2017 campaign.

This volume on race, work, and leadership responds to the fierce urgency of the moment—the need to bring the best thinkers to the table to provide broader access to the widest range of innovative, grounded ideas for moving forward. This book offers entrée not only to the voices that are represented through the data we present but also to the collective wisdom of our contributors. Our authors include higher education administrators (e.g., college presidents, vice-chancellors, and business school deans), CEOs, chief diversity officers, grassroots activists, teachers, preachers, and entrepreneurs. This volume raises a platform for these voices to lend expertise on a common set of highly influential dynamics around race, work, and leadership, which heretofore have garnered limited attention in academia and the popular press. These experts provide insights on race, but they also share broadly applicable wisdom that will be helpful for a diverse group of readers interested in the dynamics of the workplace, including academics, practitioners, and managers.

This volume is unique not only because of the explicit focus on the intersection of race and business but also in part because of our composition of contributing authors. Lists of renowned thought leaders, such as those of Thinkers50 and the twenty-five most popular Ted Talks of all time, belie a disproportionate underrepresentation of African Americans and other people of color as publicly heralded experts on leadership. Of the 2017 Thinkers50 list, the majority are white men, followed by white women; only one black person was named on the list, Harvard Business School's professor Linda A. Hill (table 1-1).

Similarly, of the twenty-five most popular Ted Talks of all time, only two speakers are people of color, Pranav Mistry and Chimamanda Ngozi Adichie (table 1-2).

It is incredibly rare to find an organizational scholar of color on such mainstream lists for thought leadership in organizations and management, despite their practical expertise and scholarly accolades. Likewise, among widely known race experts, the organizational, management, and business scholars do not have prominent representation. When racially charged workplace incidents occur, black diversity scholars are rarely given voice on mainstream media platforms. Yet it is this very network of scholars and practitioners who are best equipped to provide expert advice in these situations.

Overview of *Race, Work, and Leadership*

This edited volume comprises five sections that utilize various methodological approaches to studying race. The initial impetus for this volume on race, work, and leadership emerged from a multiyear initiative to commemorate the fiftieth anniversary of the formation of the African American Student Union at Harvard Business School (HBS). This historic milestone provided an important opportunity to step back and examine the experiences of black professionals across a broad spectrum of organizations.

TABLE 1-1

Thinkers50 list (2017)

Roger Martin
Don Tapscott
Clayton Christensen
W. Chan Kim and Renée Mauborgne
Michael Porter
Marshall Goldsmith
Alexander Osterwalder and Yves Pigneur
Adam Grant
Richard D'Aveni
Rita McGrath
Daniel Pink
Erik Brynjolfsson and Andrew McAfee
Amy Edmondson
Steve Blank
Linda Hill
Eric Ries
Pankaj Ghemawat
Simon Sinek
Richard Florida
Herminia Ibarra
Vijay Govindarajan
Nilofer Merchant
Sydney Finkelstein
Hal Gregersen
Hermann Simon
Zhang Ruimin
Subir Chowdbury
Anil Gupta and Haiyan Wang
Lynda Gratton
Whitney Johnson
Jim Collins
Gary Hamel
Seth Godin
Scott D. Anthony
Liz Wiseman
Martin Lindstrom
Tammy Erickson
Stew Friedman
Erin Meyer
Susan David
Morten Hansen
Henry Chesbrough
Amy Cuddy
Jennifer Aaker
Julian Birkinshaw
Rachel Botsman
Gianpiero Petriglieri
David Burkus
Francesca Gino
Heidi Grant

TABLE 1-2

Most popular Ted Talks

Ken Robinson
Amy Cuddy
Simon Sinek
Brené Brown
Mary Roach
Julian Treasure
Jill Bolte Taylor
Tony Robbins
James Veitch
Cameron Russell
Dan Pink
Susan Cain
Pamela Meyer
Robert Waldinger
Shawn Achor
Pranav Mistry
David Blaine
Apollo Robbins
Dan Gilbert
Tim Urban
Kelly McGonigal
David Gallo
Keith Barry
Chimamanda Ngozi Adichie
Elizabeth Gilbert

With this anniversary as a backdrop, we begin the edited volume with a deep dive into the careers, aspirations, and experiences of black graduates of HBS and Harvard Law School (HLS). These chapters draw insights from two of the largest data sets of black professionals that have ever been created.

In addition to these two important data sets, the first three sections of this volume draw on a broad spectrum of quantitative and qualitative studies of the black experience. The findings, insights, and perspectives in these chapters are based on surveys of over 3,660 African American working adults, and they include comparison samples with over twenty-five thousand data points. These sections of the volume also benefit from findings that feature 140 interviews, focus groups, and case studies (table 1-3).

TABLE 1-3

Quantitative and qualitative studies of the black experience included in *Race, Work, and Leadership*

Chapter	Data	% Black	Population
Chapter 2, Gates	5 case studies	100	HBS students
Chapter 3, Mayo and Roberts	1,381 alumni	100	HBS graduates
	5,300 surveys	4	HBS graduates
Chapter 4, Wilkins and Fong	687 surveys	100	HLS graduates
Chapter 5, Washington, Maese, and McFeely	19,212 surveys	11	US adults
Chapter 6, Hewlin and Broomes	2,226 surveys	22	General US working population
	243 surveys	9	US professionals
	7 interviews	100	Lawyers
Chapter 7, Blake-Beard, Roberts, Edgehill, and Washington	201 surveys	53	US professionals
Chapter 8, Wingfield	75 interviews	80	Health-care workers: doctors, nurses, technicians
Chapter 9, Roberts, Blake-Beard, Creary, Edgehill, and Ghai	25 focus group participants	72	Highly educated health-care workers
Chapter 10, Toigo Foundation (Sims, Toigo, Allen, and Cornelius)	50 interviews	100	Finance leaders
Chapter 13, Shockley and Holloway	18 interviews	100	University faculty

Section One: History and Critical Questions in Black Business Leadership

This section opens with the transcript of a speech delivered at the HBS conference in April 2018 that commemorated the fiftieth anniversary of the founding of the African American Student Union. In this speech, Henry Louis Gates Jr. examines the actions and determination of five HBS students who courageously banded together in 1968 to fundamentally change the landscape for African Americans at HBS. Their actions are placed in the historical landscape of race relations at Harvard University and the United States as a whole. This speech sets the tone for a call to action—a call that is answered throughout this volume by various scholars and practitioners.

In chapter 3, "Pathways to Leadership," Anthony J. Mayo and Laura Morgan Roberts present a portrait of the backgrounds, experiences, and perspectives of black alumni of the HBS MBA program. With this study, HBS has allowed itself to be exposed in a way that other schools have not. Few schools make their specific racial composition data available, and if they do, they do so for compliance purposes. This unprecedented level of transparency allows Mayo and Roberts to focus on race and to do so with an historical lens, looking at the composition and experiences of black alumni over several decades.

HBS engaged in a similar process of introspection in 2012 when it celebrated the fiftieth anniversary of the admission of women to its two-year MBA program. At that time, HBS initiated a longitudinal study of the career satisfaction of its graduates, with a specific focus on the experiences of women. With this endeavor, it made itself a case study and agreed to a level of scrutiny that is often rare. This current self-examination of HBS black alumni offers a similar level of scrutiny. This willingness to be open about the specifics of its black alumni does invite potential critiques, but it also provides a forum for identifying opportunities for progress and additional research.

Chapter 3 includes two commentaries—one from Melissa E. Wooten that explores the critical and often unheralded role that historically black colleges and universities (HBCUs) play in the educational landscape. HBCUs have been strong feeder schools for both HBS and HLS students, and Wooten examines how these undergraduate institutions are evaluated by the largely white academy. The second commentary is from Arthur P. Brief, who addresses the explicit and subtle forms of racism that affect black professionals. This commentary is juxtaposed to the survey responses from black MBA alumni of HBS, who discuss the role that race has played in their careers.

In chapter 4, "Intersectionality and the Careers of Black Women Lawyers," David B. Wilkins and Bryon Fong investigate the significance of race in the careers of black lawyers. To document the achievements of HLS's black graduates, in 2016–2017 the Center on the Legal Profession surveyed virtually all living black HLS alumni about their careers since graduating from law school. As the chapter demonstrates, while much progress has been made, black HLS graduates as a whole—and black female graduates in particular—continue to face significant obstacles in their legal careers. These within-race gender differences are particularly important as women frequently formed the majority of black law school graduates at HLS and at virtually every other law school in the country. In a world in which increasingly diverse teams of lawyers must learn to work together effectively to solve problems for clients who are themselves increasingly diverse, the legal profession can ill afford to lose the talent and leadership that black female and male lawyers from HLS and other law schools have consistently displayed.

Insights from these in-depth studies of HBS and HLS alumni shed light on the persistent and seemingly intractable challenges for black professionals. Even graduating from one of the most prestigious and highly respected institutions in the world does not shield one from these obstacles to success.

Section Two: Comparative Studies

Comparative studies are one lens through which to investigate race and have been, for over fifty years, one of the most popular methods. These tend to use large data sets to identify disparities between whites and blacks. One major example of such research is the book *Breaking Through: The Making of Minority Executives in Corporate America* (1999) by David Thomas, one of the editors of this volume, with coauthor John Gabbaro. In this book, they describe what they learned from a six-year study of three companies, finding that leaders of color had to manage their careers strategically and prove their competence before gaining promotions similar to those given to their white counterparts. This book received the George T. Terry Book Award from the Academy of Management, an award that is given once every three years to honor the book judged to have made the most outstanding contribution to the advancement of management knowledge. Another contributing author to this volume, Courtney L. McCluney, coauthored a report of findings based on a large data set in collaboration with Catalyst researchers; they found that black employees experienced an emotional tax—a heightened sense of being different from their workplace peers—that diminished their ability to contribute (Travis, Thorpe-Moscon, & McCluney, 2016). The present volume enriches this body of work through the inclusion of three chapters that have gained their key insights on black engagement, connection, and authenticity in the workplace using this traditional comparative approach.

In chapter 5, "Workplace Engagement and the Glass Ceiling," Ella F. Washington, Ellyn Maese, and Shane McFeely examine the experience of black professionals as it relates to employee engagement. Many organizations use engagement as an indicator of how inclusive the work environment is, with the assumption that if employees are engaged, they also feel included on their teams and within the larger organization. The authors' research counters this assumption by examining employee engagement by racial demographics and analyzing the underlying effects that make the experience of black professionals unique from other groups. The analyses reveal that an accurate evaluation of engagement for black professionals must consider the complexity added by environmental factors such as organizational culture, employee level, and career trajectory. The authors discuss the implications of their findings for organizations looking to evaluate diversity and inclusion, and they advocate a more complex approach that builds off engagement scores but does not solely rely on them to move forward their diversity and inclusion strategy.

Research shows that individuals who perceive that they are minorities at work are likely to feel pressured to create "facades of conformity," which involves suppressing personal values and views and conveying agreement with organizational values to avoid negative publicity. However, this line of research has not systematically addressed nuanced dynamics associated with minority status related to a specific characteristic such as race, as well as the role of one's work context. In chapter 6, "Authenticity in the Workplace," Patricia Faison Hewlin and Anna-Maria Broomes explore these nuances. In a survey-based sample of 2,226 workers from various industries and corporate settings, the authors found that African Americans engage in the highest level of creating facades of conformity. In a second sample of 243 professionals, the highest degree of facade creation was in the legal sector. Follow-up interviews with seven African American attorneys illustrate challenges and opportunities associated with managing a sense of authenticity in this sector. The authors seek to stimulate future research in this arena while simultaneously challenging the way scholars and business leaders think about leveraging diversity and promoting authentic self-expression in the workplace.

This section concludes with chapter 7, which explores factors related to employee engagement, with a particular focus on the experiences of professionals from diverse cultural backgrounds. In "Feeling Connected,"

Stacy Blake-Beard, Laura Morgan Roberts, Beverly Edgehill, and Ella F. Washington review the key findings from a survey of 201 participants who attended the Partnership's annual workforce retention conference. Professionals from diverse backgrounds benefit tremendously from a cadre of supportive relationships. The impact of having supportive relationships with their managers and coworkers can be seen in participants' strong scores for job fit, career satisfaction, and organizational commitment and their reduced turnover. This study also affirms the importance of authenticity and engagement as psychological measures with real implications for the experiences of diverse professionals. The similarities and differences between racial groups are discussed. This chapter closes with implications from the research and best practices leaders should consider as they build capacity for effectively hiring, developing, and advancing diverse talent.

Section Three: Phenomenological Studies:
The Lived Experience

Phenomenological studies form the third and largest grouping of studies in this volume. Phenomenology uses a qualitative approach that emphasizes the lived experience and meaning of a phenomenon (Heidegger, 1962; McCluney, 2017). The researcher trusts the speaker to be his or her own expert on the phenomenon being discussed—in other words, the speaker is the subject, rather than the object to be studied. Ella L. J. Edmondson Bell and Stella M. Nkomo, who wrote the foreword for this volume, wrote the acclaimed book *Our Separate Ways: Black and White Women and the Struggle for Professional Identity* (2001)—using this phenomenological approach, they were able to explain how black women construct positive professional identities. The current volume contains a section of phenomenological studies to manifest and center on the black narratives that are often forgotten and marginalized, including black professionals' responses to diversity approaches, experiences of being challenged, and perspectives on facilitating organizational change. They use a variety of methodologies, including case studies, interviews, thematic analysis, narrative, and ethnography.

In chapter 8, "Views from the Other Side," Adia Harvey Wingfield examines the perceptions of diversity programs within the health-care sector. Many industries and organizations have begun to address the need to recruit and retain more workers of color. Such attempts at increasing diversity—for example, diversity trainings—are often met with pushback from white professionals, who see them as wasteful and unnecessary. But there is little study of how such diversity programs impact blacks who work in predominantly white professions or organizations. Using interviews with black doctors, nurses, and technicians, the author proposes that occupational status matters in shaping not only how health-care workers see diversity efforts but also their assessments of how these programs impact their own work and their pathways to leadership.

Laura Morgan Roberts, Stacy Blake-Beard, Stephanie Creary, Beverly Edgehill, and Sakshi Ghai continue the exploration of the health-care sector by examining the challenges of retaining and developing diverse talent. In chapter 9, "Overcoming Barriers to Developing and Retaining Diverse Talent in Health-Care Professions," the authors present the findings of an empirical study of black and Hispanic American health-care professionals' perceptions of personal and organizational factors that enable and constrain their career advancement and leadership development. The authors discuss the comprehensive insights gleaned from eight focus groups regarding facilitators of and challenges to participants' career advancement and leadership development. Several recommendations for both senior-level executives in decision-making roles and minorities who seek to advance to senior levels in health care are offered.

The exploration of the black experience continues with the Toigo Foundation's chapter 10, "From C-Suite to Startups." This chapter examines the talent "ecosystem" of African Americans that directly influences their career trajectory and leadership ascent (or, in some cases, descent), with a particular focus on careers within finance. Public recognition of the success of a very select group of prominent diverse leaders gives the impression that progress has occurred and the talent pipeline is full and thriving. Toigo has dubbed this myth the "illusion of inclusion." In reality, a huge disconnect or gap emerges when diverse talent is heavily recruited yet less robust investment is made in their retention and advancement to senior leadership within organizations or even further as business owners. This amplifies the importance of guidance and support from those who have led the journey to success.

Consistent with the data presented in section one, over the past nearly four decades, black women have increasingly pursued and earned college degrees and in numbers that surpass their representation. However, they are often not respected by their white colleagues. Chapter 11,

"Rough Waters of Resistance," addresses the issue of how black instructional coaches in K–12 schools endure implicit bias and suffer as a result. The authors, Michelle Smith Macchia and Kisha Porcher, two black senior educational consultants who work as instructional coaches, provide an illustration of how they experienced implicit bias in their schools, internalized it, and were pushed to advocacy within their consulting organization. The authors address the lack of research on how educators respond to black instructional coaches and how blackness affects an instructional coach's effectiveness, and they make recommendations for future research.

In chapter 12, "A Million Gray Areas," Kathryn Fraser and Karen Samuels, who come from different backgrounds, describe how they mutually enhanced each other's understanding of their own social identities and power constructs. Crossing paths, they found that their cultural differences bonded them together and informed how they collaborate in social justice action. They discuss how their connection is centered on Fraser's black identity and Samuels's white identity, and how they shared and endured their own oppression while educating others.

Moving to the sphere of higher education, Muriel E. Shockley and Elizabeth L. Holloway in chapter 13, "African American Women as Change Agents in the White Academy," assess the challenges facing African American women in the academy and explore the complexities of African American women scholar-activists' lived experiences as change agents in predominantly white institutions. The chapter is built around a qualitative, grounded theory study and the theoretical propositions that emerged from the experiences of African American women in predominantly white colleges. The discussion of findings reveals the ways these women embody and understand leadership and change in the academy and bears witness to and unpacks the processes that occur when African American women inhabit and lead with self in the white academy.

In chapter 14, "The Transformational Impact of Black Women/Womanist Theologians," Tawana Davis focuses on the transformational impact of leading intergroup dialogue in liberation work of the oppressed and the oppressor. Womanism is a paradigm shift wherein black women no longer look to others for their liberation but instead look to themselves. The author considers the work of Soul 2 Soul's antiracism program, which involves intergroup dialogue that raises consciousness of black struggle and resilience in the midst of oppression and offers language to address white privilege and the tools to do the work required of white people. The author explores how the leadership of black women in these spaces is pivotal for such liberation work.

In the final chapter of this section on the lived experience, chapter 15, "Psychodynamics of Black Authority," Diane Forbes Berthoud, Flora Taylor, and Zachary Green write about their experience regarding the work of a group relations conference they held in spring 2017. "On the Matter of Black Lives," an intensive experiential conference, examined leadership, authority, and identity in the post-Obama era. The conference was focused on learning about those unconscious, implicit, and often indiscernible aspects of how the matter of black lives is a part of our discourse and actions, individually and collectively. The conference was a follow-up to another group relations conference held twenty years earlier in Washington, DC, that included some of the same staff members, called "Authority and Identity: An African American Perspective." In both cases, the conference staffs were composed of only black authorities, and the purpose of the conferences was, at its core, to provide an opportunity to study authority as inhabited by black people. The authors aim to share what they learned in the design of, execution of, and reflection on this conference experience.

Section Four: Theorizing Black Leadership

Critical theory considers and challenges what we think we know. Critical theory works often challenge existing theories or assert a perspective from a set of assumptions that differ from those in the mainstream leadership literature. The chapters that take a critical theory lens in this volume make visible the experiences of black leadership and push existing theories so that they are more applicable to a diverse range of experiences, including those of African Americans. These chapters advance management theory in three main ways: by challenging historical management theories from a structural perspective, by utilizing a lens of intersectionality to bring to center the intersection of race with gender and social class, and by taking a strength and strengthening perspective, which contrasts with the typical portrayal of African Americans from a deficiency perspective.

In the opening chapter in this section, chapter 16, "Is D&I about Us?," Valerie Purdie-Greenaway and Martin N. Davidson explore the nature and efficacy of D&I programs. Companies can dramatically increase the impact of their D&I initiatives on the career trajectories of black professionals by designing for black inclusion. Such a design builds on fundamental principles of fostering an inclusive climate but incorporates a critical parameter: programs, practices, and structures that eradicate for blacks the perception that race will be a barrier to advancement. The authors examine the underlying psychological processes that make this parameter so critical for developing black leaders and suggest three practices that foster black inclusion and support the success of these leaders: explicit communication about race, building knowledge about race, and developing an organizational racial learning orientation.

Research indicates that when women and ethnic minorities are appointed to executive or corporate roles, they are more likely to find themselves on a glass cliff—in risky or precarious leadership positions that involve the management of organizations in crisis—than to find themselves in positions of stable leadership. These positions can set up women and minorities for failure, or they can be opportunities for demonstrating extraordinary leadership under pressure. To date, we know little about the glass-cliff experiences of African Americans in the corporate world. In chapter 17, "The Glass Cliff," Lynn Perry Wooten and Erika Hayes James address this gap by examining the experiences of African American CEOs. The authors seek to understand the extent to which African Americans were appointed to positions requiring crisis leadership, characterize their leadership strategies, and understand the career implications for African Americans in glass-cliff situations.

Frequently, diversity research within the organizational sciences focuses on the "case for diversity" and the organizational benefits that can accrue. In contrast, in chapter 18, "When Black Leaders Leave," Kecia Thomas, Aspen J. Robinson, Laura Provolt, and B. Lindsay Brown focus on the individual, minority group, and organizational costs of diversity loss—specifically, when black leaders leave. Black leadership is severely underrepresented across several societal domains. The norms and cultural default of leadership may contribute to creating an inhospitable and unproductive climate for black leaders that motivates their turnover. The authors discuss the consequences of black leaders leaving for black leaders themselves, for their minority followers, and for their organizations. The authors conclude with recommendations for retaining black leadership in order to avoid such negative consequences.

Although there is a growing focus on minority leadership, solely increasing the representation of underrepresented groups does not necessarily create the conditions that allow these leaders to challenge the systems of inequality that make their groups underrepresented in the first place. Black leaders face two questions: How does a minority group leader identify with and influence majority group followers, and to what extent can black leaders influence the reproduction or reduction of racial inequality? Integrating literature on leadership, identity, and identification with literature on inequality in chapter 19, "Blacks Leading Whites," Lumumba Seegars and Lakshmi Ramarajan explore the process of mutual identification between minority group leaders and majority group followers and address questions of persisting inequality as a result of these processes. The authors list four types of leaders—factionless, opposition, co-opted, and consensus—that emerge based on the process of mutual and dual identification between black leaders and the black ingroup and white outgroup and the degree to which these leaders will be likely to engage in incremental versus divergent change regarding intergroup inequality in organizations.

Despite the growth of "diversity management," D&I initiatives have not adequately hired, retained, or advanced black employees. In chapter 20, "Managing Diversity, Managing Blackness?," Courtney McCluney and Verónica Caridad Rabelo argue that D&I officers often adopt an individual approach—whereby they seek to help black employees "fit" into organizational cultures that reflect the status quo—at the expense of a structural approach, which would seek to eradicate systemic inequality in organizations and communities. The authors posit three mechanisms to explain how, in seeking to manage diversity, practitioners instead manage blackness: by adopting a (1) business case for diversity, (2) narrow imagination of black people, and (3) blanket (decontextualized) application of diversity. The authors offer an alternative perspective, intersectional justice, that accounts for history and social structures, addresses the root cause of inequality, and empowers (rather than commodifies or exploits) black communities. The authors conclude that practitioners should focus on managing injustice and whiteness rather than managing diversity, which effectively manages blackness.

In the final chapter in this section, chapter 21, "Uncovering the Hidden Face of Affinity Fraud," Audrey Murrell, Ray Jones, and Jennifer Petrie reconceptualize affinity fraud as a function of "predatory bias" that targets members of identifiable social identity groups—for example, a specific race, ethnicity, or social class—as victims of deliberate deception to secure unfair or unlawful financial gain. For example, these perpetrators enlist respected ingroup members to convince the target group that the opportunity advances identity-relevant interests. They also do not believe their own actions are criminal or biased; perpetrators of affinity fraud often rationalize their actions as an element of legitimate business practice and ignore the differential impact from targeting specific race, ethnic, or social class groups. The authors discuss key aspects of inclusive leadership that could address predatory bias and the negative impact of affinity fraud.

Section Five: The Future: Lessons for the Next Generation of Leaders

The final section of this edited volume is focused on the road ahead and the next generation of African American leaders. In chapter 22, "Ujima: Lifting as We Climb," Lynn Perry Wooten, Shannon Polk, and Whitney Williams focus on the emerging leadership journeys of millennials. For African Americans of this generation (1980–2000), their leadership journey has involved opportunities and challenges as they navigate life in a "postracial" society and live with movements such as Black Lives Matter, bans on affirmative action, and the economic shifts associated with a digital economy. Given this context, this chapter identifies four priority areas for developing the next generation of African American leaders. First, the authors argue that universities should develop the infrastructure for nurturing and developing their African American students. Second, they propose that an entrepreneurial mindset is a necessity for their success. Third, they contend that to advance issues of justice and equality, African American millennials must be empowered with the ethos to challenge the status quo and engage in collective action for positive change. Lastly, they emphasize the importance of instilling the principles of living an integrative life.

In chapter 23, the concluding chapter of this volume, "Intersections of Race, Work, and Leadership," Roberts and Mayo provide insights for understanding and enhancing the black experience. In addition, the editors summarize a series of recommendations that are beneficial for individuals trying to assert and maximize their leadership potential, for organizations trying to leverage and optimize their diverse talent, and for academics who seek to better understand the key questions that still remain about black leadership.

The bulk of our included chapters are phenomenological or theorize on the basis of qualitative data. This may be due to the fact that the numbers of black professionals (particularly those in leadership) that we seek to recruit as research participants are numerically underrepresented in the places they are being studied. Furthermore, studies that focus on a specific organization or geographic location reduce the potential sample of black professionals who are eligible participants. Organizations are often reticent to disclose demographic data to potential researchers, which creates additional recruitment challenges for targeted studies of black professionals. Further, since bodies of published work on race and the black experience at work are dispersed across disciplines, many scholars are working in parallel to lay the groundwork for theorizing from specific contexts, unaware that their counterparts in other disciplines or fields are pursuing similar questions, and thus unable to pool resources and recruitment efforts. Published management studies, in particular, have been less likely to feature isolated samples of African Americans in the top-tier journals, thus making such research findings more difficult to access once published. This volume seeks to address some of this deficit.

In keeping with the exhortation of Maxine Williams, Facebook's global director of diversity, in her 2017 *Harvard Business Review* article, we feature pieces that look beyond the limited hard data: "Algorithms and statistics do not capture what it feels like to be the only black or Hispanic team member or the effect that marginalization has on individual employees and the group as a whole" (Williams, 2017, p. 146). Williams argues that examining individual cases is, in fact, as important as aggregated data in understanding the complicated factors that shape minority employees' workplace experiences.

We hope that the chapters included in this volume bring into perspective some of those factors. We also find value in the aggregation of findings published in this volume, which point to common refrains of agency among black professionals, who face societal devaluation, potential dehumanization, and struggles for advancement alongside opportunities to build resilience, gain wisdom, and achieve collective empowerment. As we look to the future, we note that those who have blazed trails in research and practice have left evidence of tried-and-tested practices and generous guideposts in these chapters that will benefit generations to come.

REFERENCES

Bell, E. L. J. E., & Nkomo, S. M. (2001). *Our separate ways: Black and white women and the struggle for professional identity*. Boston, MA: Harvard Business Review Press.

Castilla, E. J., & Benard, S. (2010). The paradox of meritocracy in organizations. *Administrative Science Quarterly, 55*(4), 543–676.

Cose, E. (2011). *The end of anger: A new generation's take on race and rage*. New York, NY: HarperCollins.

Ernst & Young. (2017, October 6). *EY studies race, gender and exclusion: The top take-aways*. New York.

Gannon, M. (2016, February 5). Race is a social construct scientists, argue. *Scientific American*.

Goodman, A. (2003). Interview. In *Race, the power of an illusion* [Online companion to California Newsreel's documentary]. Retrieved from http://www.pbs.org/race /000_About/002_04-background-01-07.htm

Hauslohner, A. (2018, May 11). Hate crimes jump fourth straight year in largest U.S. cities, study shows. *The Washington Post*.

Heidegger, M. (1962). *Being and time* (J. Macquarrie & E. S. Robinson, Trans.) (1st English ed.). London, England: SCM Press.

Hewlett, S., Marshall, M. & Bourgeois, T. (2017, July 10). People suffer at work when they can't discuss the racial bias they face outside of it. *Harvard Business Review*.

Johnson, S. (2017, August 29). What 11 CEOs have learned about championing diversity. *Harvard Business Review*.

Johnson, S. K., & Hekman, D. R. (2016, March 23). Women and minorities are penalized for promoting diversity. *Harvard Business Review*.

Kolbert, E. (2017). There's no scientific basis for race—it's a made-up label. Race [Special issue]. *National Geographic*. https://www.nationalgeographic.com /magazine/2018/04/race-genetics-science-africa/

McCluney, C., Bryant, C., King, D., & Ali, A. (2017). Calling in Black: a dynamic model of racially traumatic events, resourcing, and safety. *Equality, Diversity and Inclusion: An International Journal, 36*(8), 767–786. https://doi.org/10.1108/ EDI -01-2017-0012

McCluney, C. L. (2017). *"Blooming where I'm planted": A phenomenological investigation of black clergywomen's marginality and leadership* (Unpublished doctoral dissertation). University of Michigan, Ann Arbor.

Nielsen Report. (2017, September 21). *African-American women: our science, her magic*.

Opie, T. & Roberts, L.M. (2017). Do black lives really matter in the workplace? Restorative justice as a means to reclaim humanity. *Equality, Diversity and Inclusion: An International Journal, 36* (8), 707–719. https://doi.org/10.1108/EDI-07-2017-0149

Pew Research Center. (2017, December 19). Most Americans say Trump's election has led to worse race relations in the U.S.

Phillips, K., Dumas, T., & Rothbard, N. (2018, March-April). Diversity and authenticity. *Harvard Business Review*.

Thomas, D. A., & Gabarro, J. J. (1999). *Breaking through: The making of minority executives in corporate America*. Boston, MA: Harvard Business School Press.

Travis, D. J., Thorpe-Moscon, J., & McCluney, C. L. (2016). *Emotional tax: How black women and men pay more at work and how leaders can take action* (Research report). New York, NY: Catalyst.

US Census Bureau (2017). Quick Facts—United States. Retrieved from https://www.census.gov/quickfacts/fact/table/US#

Williams, M. (2017). Numbers take us only so far. *Harvard Business Review, 95*(6), 142–148.

HISTORY AND CRITICAL QUESTIONS IN BLACK BUSINESS LEADERSHIP

2

A Case Study of Leading Change

The Founders of Harvard Business School's African American Student Union

HENRY LOUIS GATES JR.

I.

I am going to speak about 1968, but first, I want to take you back to the year 1900 for a moment. We tend to think of the past through our own frame of reference, more or less as a sepia version of the present. I remember reading about Harvard's time capsule, the Chest of 1900, a record of life at the university at the turn of the century, and looking for some testimony in its contents about black life on campus back then.

Remember, according to W. E. B. Du Bois, only ten black men graduated from the college between 1900 and 1904. One reference I found was a note that a white student made about his black classmate, Roscoe Conkling Bruce, "a very bright negro in college," he wrote.[1] Roscoe was the son of the first black American to serve a full term in the Reconstruction Senate, Blanche K. Bruce, Republican from Mississippi. Bruce came to Harvard from Exeter, won the Pasteur Medal for Debating and Coolidge Debating Prize, and graduated magna cum laude and Phi Beta Kappa in 1902. After extolling his fellow student's extraordinary intelligence, the writer, Harry Kellogg Durland, noted that Bruce was "singly retiring in private life," so much so that he "apparently does not see even his friends on the street if they are white men unless they first recognize him."[2] Now, we all know why Roscoe Bruce wouldn't speak to his white friends in public until they first spoke to him. It is clear that even for him, a leader of his class—in fact, the Class Day orator at commencement—visibility, for a black person at the height of the Jim Crow era, was a matter of passively being seen, not proactively being heard. He couldn't speak in public, even to his white friends, unless he was spoken to first! He could be seen, but not heard. It's important that we be reminded of these race rituals, as sad as we might find this story, both to insert ourselves more fully into the past and to chart the degree to which things racial at Harvard do change and have changed. And in 1968, black students at Harvard decided that it was long past time not only for their faces—and even more black faces—to been seen, and that their voices be heard, publicly.

In some ways, 1968 seems like yesterday for so many of us, since so much happened fundamentally to reshape our nation and the life choices for those of us in our generation in that year. But in many other ways, 1968 was a very long time ago.

Perspective matters, which makes me wonder: If MLK came back and asked you what had changed in the status and condition of black America in the fifty years since that terrible day in April 1968 when he was so brutally assassinated, what would you say? The rising role of women in general—a female historian the president of Harvard!—and of black women in the economy and leadership positions, more particularly—a black woman tenured professor at HBS [Harvard Business School]!—would have surprised him, I think. But according to our colleague William Julius Wilson, he would find the most radical transformations in the fact that since his death, the size of the black middle class doubled to 24 percent, and the size of the black upper-middle class has quadrupled, rising to 15 percent. I believe that Dr. King would find those statistics nothing short of revolutionary, considering how small the middle and upper-middle classes were when he died. (I'll return to the other side of those remarkable numbers, the nether side, near the end of my remarks, which also would have astonished Dr. King.)

But . . . as many of us in this room can vividly remember, precisely when the Black Panthers were talking about revolution in terms of burning the system down, another revolution was brewing, a class restructuring was about to occur, which William Julius Wilson calls "one of the most significant changes in the past several decades . . . the remarkable gains in income among more affluent blacks," and we can trace at least part of its roots right back to events that were unfolding on this campus and at this school.[3]

For I believe that the great insight of the founders of the African American Student Union (AASU) was that the presence and productivity of African Americans at HBS are barometers for the state of the nation as a whole and continue to serve as catalysts for growth and change at a time of promise and uncertainty in the land, both then and now. That, ladies and gentlemen, was an idea as radical as it was prescient. (And about at the same time, by the way, that seminal, visionary figure in American corporate history, Vernon E. Jordan Jr., was one of the first leaders of a civil rights organization to see its importance, too. We'll return to Vernon a bit later.)

Tracing the arc of history back to the founding of the AASU, we recall that 1968 was another year of promise and uncertainty. On one hand, we were still touched by the glowing victories of the Civil Rights Act of 1964 and the Voting Rights Act of 1965, along with the birth of the Great Society amidst a sustained postwar economic boom. On the other hand, the stalemate and death toll in Vietnam galvanized student unease and protest, while unrest in inner cities from Newark to Detroit the previous summer awakened the world to the intractable problems of social and economic injustice, as well as the fractured trust between the black community and the law, in the North as well as the South. As the Kerner Commission report on civil disorders attested, released less than two months before Dr. King was killed, a tale of two Americas was unfolding—a "nation . . . moving toward two societies, one black, one white—separate and unequal."[4]

President Kennedy had told the nation in a bold address back in June 1963, after tangling with Alabama governor George Wallace over desegregation at the state university in Tuscaloosa, that "[o]ne hundred years of delay have passed since President Lincoln freed the slaves, yet their heirs, their grandsons, are not fully free. They are not yet freed from the bonds of injustice. They are not yet freed from social and economic oppression. And this Nation, for all its hopes and all its boasts, will not be fully free until all its citizens are free."[5]

"[T]he harsh fact of the matter is that in the battle for true equality too many—far too many—are losing ground every day," Lyndon Johnson warned in his commencement address at Howard University in 1965. In laying out his broad vision for equal opportunity, or what would come to be called affirmative action, LBJ made clear that, despite the passage of civil rights legislation (a triumph he could rightfully claim), too much of black America was still "buried under a blanket of history and circumstance," going back to slavery, and that it was "not a lasting solution to lift just one corner of that blanket."[6]

Dr. King characterized this dilemma of history as the "promissory note" that the nation had issued to the formerly enslaved after the Civil War, a promissory note which had, for a century, been marked "insufficient funds." By 1968, it was well past time to deliver.[7]

II.

Into that breach stepped a handful of black members of the incoming seven-hundred-member HBS class of 1969. Five of them would change history, and it is their actions that ultimately led to the organization that we commemorate today. Arriving on campus in the fall of 1967, they each would have to answer the same question every black incoming student at Harvard had faced since Reconstruction: Would they, in the words of the great W. E. B. Du Bois (college class of 1890, PhD 1895), be "in Harvard, but not of" Harvard?[8]

To be sure, they weren't the first black students to cross the Charles River to attend the Business School. Since its founding in 1908, close to fifty African Americans had come through HBS. The first, as far as we know, was Wendell Thomas Cunningham, the son of a former slave, who earned his MBA in 1915, the same year that the infamous film *The Birth of a Nation* hit theaters, erasing in the mind of the broad American public the true legacy of Reconstruction and reinforcing the cruel, distorted color line enacted during the era of Jim Crow. Nearly a dozen black students had followed in a scattered fashion by 1930, including Norris B. Herndon, the second-generation leader of Atlanta's largest black-owned business (now Atlanta Life Financial Group). A little later, the class of 1933 counted among its graduates the pioneering educational and business leader H. Naylor Fitzhugh, who for years was a stalwart of the Howard University business faculty before becoming the first black executive at Pepsi, where he transformed their special markets business.

Fitzhugh represented a generational bridge to the group that I am calling the HBS Five, for like the Little Rock Nine before them, the five brilliant students of the class of 1969 who founded the AASU turned the late W. E. B. Du Bois's test on its head.

Whether they became "of" Harvard was beside the point. What they actually achieved was transforming Harvard so it was of them.

Their story, to model on the curriculum here, is a case study that should be read closely by anyone looking to effect change from Main Street to Wall Street.

Let me mention the protagonists in this great drama in the history of our school, one by one.

Lillian Lincoln Lambert: Lillian is a native of greater Richmond who, unlike many matriculating today, toiled as a maid and typist before enrolling at Howard, where she took a course with Professor Fitzhugh that changed her life. From there, she knew that she was equipped to aim as high as possible. Why not HBS? In the fall of 1967, Lillian became the first black woman to attend this school. Having started out in the segregated schools of the South, she understandably found the predominantly white and nearly all male Allston campus foreign. But like her classmates, she found strength in this adversity, fought to make HBS more hospitable to those black women and men who followed her, and went on to run her own building services company with some 1,200 employees.

Clifford E. Darden: To get to HBS, Clif had to drive all the way from Los Angeles, where he'd already had the experience of being one in a throng of white students at USC. He didn't stop at a Harvard MBA. He also earned his DBA here en route to an illustrious teaching career at Pepperdine.

Emmanuel Theodore Lewis Jr.: Philadelphia's own, Ted attended Washington University in Saint Louis before a stint in the Peace Corps in South America. Not only has he led a distinguished career at Accenture (Anderson Consulting), he happens to be the father of one of my dearest Harvard colleagues, and a rising star in her field of art and architectural history, Dr. Sarah Lewis.

George R. Price: Unfortunately, George R. Price is no longer with us, but while he lived, he made a difference. Also an alumnus of Cornell University's School of Industrial and Labor Relations, George worked at Levi Strauss, where he urged his company's leadership to take a stand against South African apartheid, before launching his own business, Price & Associates, in Maryland.

A. Leroy Willis: Last and anything but least, Roy Willis tested the color line in academia before ever arriving at HBS, when he forced the University of Virginia's College of Arts and Sciences to open its doors to him when he switched his major to chemistry. Roy also served in the US Army as well as in industry. And with his MBA, he focused on community economic development in nearby Roxbury. Today, he runs his own real estate consultancy on the West Coast.

Ladies and gentlemen, these were the roots that the HBS Five brought with them to campus in 1967—and the futures that sprouted before them after departing with their MBAs. In between, they studied passionately and diligently with a greater sense of mission than merely maximizing their own personal returns. Cognizant of the reality that capitalism, for all of its many blessings, produces unequal outcomes, they saw, in their enrollment, a need, according to the motto of the National Association of Colored Women, to "lift as they climbed."

They knew from their own lives the truth of something Dr. King had written that same year: "The relatively privileged Negro will never be what he ought to be until the underprivileged Negro is what he ought to be. The salvation of the Negro middle class is ultimately dependent upon the salvation of the Negro masses."[9] Which calls to mind the third thing that would have shocked Dr. King about our own times: that ours is a mix of the best of times and the worst of times. Despite the phenomenal growth of the black middle classes since his death, the child poverty rate was 38.2 percent in 2010 and hovers around 34 percent today, 33.9 percent of the prison population is comprised of black men, and "the percentage of black Americans with incomes below $15,000 only declined by six percentage points between 1975 and 2016."[10] And what about wealth accumulation? In 2016, the median wealth of white households was $171,000, ten times the wealth of black households, a larger gap than in 2007.

And that is one of the reasons why we are here today: as a reminder that we all have work to do, that none of us works for him- or herself alone but for all of us, for the larger black community and for the human community as well.

Reviewing the AASU founders' case study in innovation, institution building, and leading moral change, I can say that the first key, upon arriving on campus, was to resist the isolation of being one of six black students out of seven hundred in their class. In other words, they quickly networked to one another, as well as to their sixth classmate, Carlson Austin, who, though not a founder of the AASU, was the sixth black member of the class of 1969. And in that camaraderie, they not only found support, they found a common aspiration, rooted in the question: Why only six? Why not more?

That brought them to their second key: taking a risk. If they were going to leverage their education at HBS to effect a greater change in society, they couldn't just talk about it. They needed to act, even if that meant jeopardizing their standing at the school. The risk they took was approaching the then dean of the school, George Baker, and asking him to address the lack of support and inclusion they were witnesses to on campus. "We couldn't just sit on the banks of the Charles River," Clif Darden recalled, "and do nothing at a time when racial oppression and discrimination were still a reality in many parts of the country."[11] For Darden, Lincoln Lambert, Price, Willis, and Lewis, HBS was to be no ivory tower, and instead of hoarding the golden opportunity that had come their way, they wanted to swing the gates open wider.

Their third key was setting a goal. As it stood, they (plus Austin) represented 0.86 percent of their class. What they called for was a 10 percent representation goal—approximating the nation's African American population as a whole. And when some of the faculty resisted, by raising the red flag of quotas, the HBS Five pressed on with their goals, growing them to include not only increased representation but fellowship funding.

The fourth key was no excuses. When the HBS leadership said they'd welcome more qualified black students if only they could find them, the HBS Five—despite their full plates as MBA students—stepped up to become recruiters! Just as the abolitionist lion Frederick Douglass pushed Abraham Lincoln to allow black men to fight in the Civil War, and then recruited them when he did, these fearless students crisscrossed the country looking for the next MBA class at the nation's historically black colleges and leading undergraduate schools. While Dr. King and his allies were formulating that spring's Poor People's Campaign, the HBS Five were leading their own campaign to grow "the crossover generation."[12]

Their travels led them to the fifth key in our case study: benchmarking. If you're going to build a lasting institution, you have to scour around for successful models. And in that first academic year, they found it at UC Berkeley, where the Afro-American Student Association had quickly become a powerful voice on campus, with strong leadership and a cohesive organizational structure. It was that model that the HBS Five would bring to campus here under their first leader, Clif Darden.

From that institutional base, the AASU seized on the sixth key to their success: forging productive alliances, in this case with Dean Baker and supportive faculty members, who backed their recruiting trips and agreed to fund scholarships to make real the promise of an HBS education for those who had the potential but not the finances.

In its infancy, the AASU was essentially in the position of a startup company trying to attract venture capital from their school. That capital was inclusion, and it worked! Just look at the numbers. HBS went from having six black students in the class of 1969 to twenty-seven in the class of 1970 and fifty-eight the year after that. That's amazing.

Had there suddenly been a bumper crop of potential black business leaders? No!

These students realized that six was essentially a quota; their task—the radical task of affirmative action—was to dismantle a historically racist quota and allow talented, qualified black women and black men to compete! That is the true origin of affirmative action, and we must never allow American society to forget that. The HBS Five were dismantling a quota. And dismantle it they did.

III.

That said, it wasn't all smooth sailing in that first year.

I was a seventeen-year-old high school student in Piedmont, West Virginia, on April 4, 1968, and I can still recall so painfully what it was like to learn of the news that Dr. King had been murdered in Memphis. It was then—and remains—a break, a rip, a tear in history. That night, and in the ensuing days, all hell broke loose in 110 black communities all across America.

After the riots, all the societal ills Dr. King had been marching to solve remained with us. The difference was he was gone, and as much as his critics (and there were many) denounced him for being out of step with

Black Power and needlessly meddling in "the white man's business" of the Vietnam War, there was no doubt that his death made the air feel thinner, the landscape emptier, the hope of lasting racial peace and integration more elusive.[13]

Yet, as we mourned him, and watched his brave, dignified widow and children teach us how to endure loss, we realized we still had his words. The record of his actions. The animating force of his dream.

That animating force was felt here by the HBS Five. Clif Darden, who traveled to Atlanta for the King funeral, had actually contemplated dropping out, given the avalanche that had just hit black Americans, but then he realized, it was actually a make-or-break moment. Roy Willis felt the same. Dr. King's murder was a wakeup call to "put our MBAs on the line," he said. And Ted Lewis said this: "[F]or many African Americans, it was a very positive era in which we were living. Sometimes it was overshadowed by tragedy, but in my mind those tragedies really didn't define the era. We felt particularly emboldened—that we had nothing to lose."[14]

It's easy to miss the complexity that Ted articulates in the headlines from 1968, but it was felt—and lived—right here, which brings me to the seventh and final key in our case study of the AASU: when tragedy strikes, don't retreat. Instead, expand the mission. Be proactive. Go on the offensive. Welcome new blood. Demand more of yourself, each other, and the team.

That is precisely what the AASU did. When the next school year started, the first class hosted a welcome party for the second class. They greeted the school's first black visiting lecturer, Ulric St. Clair Haynes Jr. (later the US ambassador to Algeria) and advocated for more. They also planned for a Black Power Day, spoke out in support of Harvard hiring more minority workers for its capital projects, and called for a strike when, in 1970, a pair of black students were killed in Jackson, Mississippi. At the same time, they pressed for the creation of relevant elective courses—including one on economic development in inner cities. Looking back, Clif Darden observed, "We were the first student group at HBS formed on some basis other than professional aspirations."[15]

That basis was moral leadership. And it's a basis that has not only enhanced the black experience at HBS. It has enhanced Harvard as a mission-driven institution, while also helping to cultivate generations of

successive business leaders who have made cause and capital the foundations of their careers.

Since the AASU's founding fifty years ago, some two thousand African
American students have taken that journey across the Charles to study
at this place. The annual H. Naylor Fitzhugh Conference is a beehive
for business and other thought leaders who continue to lift as they climb.
And each generation takes up that mantle of reaching beyond one's
own professional aspirations to solve the burning questions of the day,
whether economic inequality or environmental sustainability or the
persistent disparities we see atop Wall Street and Silicon Valley.

There are too many success stories to mention everyone's name, but
let me list a select few from the 1970s and 1980s:

From Peter Bynoe (1975), the onetime part owner of the Denver Nug-
gets to star attorney Ted Wells Jr. (1976), a member of the Harvard
Corporation. From Benaree "Bennie" Pratt Wiley (1972), founder and
CEO of the Partnership, and Ann Fudge (1977), the former chairman
and CEO of Young & Rubicam Brands, to Carla Harris (1987), the vice
chairman of wealth management and senior client adviser at Morgan
Stanley, whom President Barack Obama appointed as chair of his National Women's Business Council. From Stan O'Neal (1978), who, as
Merrill Lynch CEO, became the first African American to lead a major
Wall Street firm, to Henry McGee (1979), the former president of HBO
and now a member of the faculty here. From Bayo Ogunlesi (1979), chairman and managing partner at Global Infrastructure Partners, and
William M. Lewis Jr. (1982), managing director and cochairman of
investment banking at Lazard, to Edward Lewis (1983), cofounder and
publisher of *Essence* magazine. From Raymond McGuire (1984), Citigroup's global head of corporate and investment banking, to Pamela
Joyner (1984), founding partner of Avid Partners and chair of the Tate
Americans Foundation, Deborah Wright (1984), former president and
CEO of Carver Savings Bank, and Desiree Glapion Rogers (1985), former CEO of Johnson Publications.

Ladies and gentlemen, I could go on all afternoon, since the list of
distinguished alums of this school goes on and on and on, and speaks to
a broader cross-over generation at and beyond HBS that includes the
likes of Kenneth Chenault (like Ted Wells, a member of the Harvard
Corporation), Richard Parsons, Franklin Raines, Ken Frazier, Ursula
Burns, Roger W. Ferguson, John W. Thompson, Linda Johnson Rice,
Debra Lee, Rosalind Brewer, John W. Rogers Jr., Oprah Winfrey, Sheila

Johnson, Robert F. Smith, and, most certainly, Vernon Jordan, who has done so much to integrate American corporate boards that I have hailed him as "the Rosa Parks of Wall Street."[16] (We sometimes joke that Vernon has integrated more corporate boardrooms than SNCC [the Student Nonviolent Coordinating Committee] integrated lunch counters at Woolworths throughout the South!)

Then there are the dozens of African Americans who have served in various roles on the faculty over the years, going back to Harding B. Young, a fellow in 1954–1955, just after the *Brown v. Board* decision, far too many for me to name them all.

We remember and salute each and every one, especially:

Andrew Brimmer, who taught here as visiting professor in the 1970s.

James Cash Jr., the first African American tenured professor at HBS (now emeritus).

Linda Hill, the first black woman to earn tenure at the school.

David A. Thomas, who was the first professor here to occupy the H. Naylor Fitzhugh endowed chair at HBS (now he's the president of Morehouse College); and

Tsedal Neeley, an associate professor at HBS who, I understand, will be elevated to full professor in July. Congratulations!

My friend Darren Walker, who heads up the Ford Foundation, is fond of quoting Dr. King, who said, "Philanthropy is commendable, but it must not cause the philanthropist to overlook the circumstances of economic injustice which make philanthropy necessary."[17] That is the kind of philanthropy these leaders represent, and it goes right back to the ethic Clif Darden mentioned about the founding of the AASU: to reach beyond personal or professional aspirations and to keep ever in mind that while the ranks of the black upper-middle class may have quadrupled since Dr. King's death, we still have a long way to go.

Two months before his assassination, Dr. King, in a speech he delivered in Atlanta, Georgia, taught us that "[e]verybody can be great, because everybody can serve. You don't have to have a college degree to serve. You don't have to make your subject and your verb agree to serve. You don't have to know about Plato and Aristotle to serve. You don't have to know Einstein's theory of relativity to serve. You don't have to know the second theory of thermodynamics in physics to serve. You only need a heart full of grace, a soul generated by love."[18] That is what the HBS Five so clearly understood, and that is what this celebration of the fiftieth anniversary of the birth of the AASU is all about.

IV.

The story of the HBS Five is one more reminder that we are all ultimately connected.

As Dr. Benjamin Mays, "spiritual mentor" to Dr. King as president of Morehouse College from 1940 to 1967, once declaimed, "The destiny of each man is tied up with the destiny of another. We are so interlaced and interwoven that what affects one touches all. We are all bound together in one great humanity."[19]

Proof of his prophetic words is found at the intersections of history and place, from Jamestown to Appomattox, Selma to Montgomery, Charleston to Charlottesville, Memphis to Harvard Business School.

"History is on your side. . . . Keep struggling with this faith and the tragic midnight of anarchy and mob rule which encompasses your city at this time will be transformed into the glowing daybreak of freedom and justice."[20] Those were the words Dr. King telegrammed to local black leaders in Little Rock as he, like the rest of us, watched the events unfold there.

Today, as another day moves toward night here in these United States, we again find ourselves in a struggle for freedom and justice at home and abroad. At this moment—unimaginable for most of us just a year ago—we know that we, like Dr. King, the Little Rock Nine, and the HBS Five, again have to draw a line in the sand:

We must defend the right of every American to vote.

We must defend the very affirmative action programs that launched many people of color and women of all colors into their positions of authority and power.

We must end the madness of mass incarceration and its devastating impact on the African American community.

We must fight for health care as a right for all Americans, and we must fight to keep the pipeline of educational opportunity open for the next generation, and the next. As Bill Clinton put it in 1997, "[W]e know there are still more doors to be opened, doors to be opened wider, doors we have to keep from being shut."[21]

We must defend the immigrant and the stranger, the impoverished and the forgotten, and speak sensitively and firmly to the fears of those who see globalization as a threat and who worry that the social and cultural progress of those who look different than they do will wipe away all that they have known.

And regardless of our ideological differences, we must link arms and stand—or kneel—publicly against anti-Semitism, against homophobia, against Islamophobia, against sexism, gender discrimination, and antiblack racism, and, ladies and gentlemen, against white supremacist ideology in all of its hideously ugly, violent forms. This is no time for equivocation or false equivalences. This is a time for truth.

We know that the work, begun here in 1968, is not over. We cannot allow the forces of reaction to turn back the clock on American racial relations, obliterating the heroic efforts of legions of Americans—white and black, Asian and Latino, Jewish and Christian, Muslim and Hindu, gay, straight, and trans—who risked and sometimes tragically and nobly gave their lives to make certain that the arc of the moral universe bent toward justice. Too many hands today are trying to bend that arc back, in another direction. And those of us who love truth and justice, and the principles of democracy upon which this great nation of ours was founded, must stand against those forces, just as the founding members of the HBS Five did right here in this very place.

As I hasten to close, let me express my hope that fifty or one hundred years from now, a future Lillian Lincoln Lambert, Clif Darden, Ted Lewis, George R. Price, and Roy Willis will look back on our time and say that, in this era of fracture, we showed moral leadership, that we seized our freedoms for noble ends, and that when we had the chance, we provided the inspiration for new monuments of hope to fill in a landscape for too long dominated by memorials to a poisoned past.

Ladies and gentlemen, let us seize on this anniversary to remember that we can always serve and, in serving, make a difference, even through the founding of a black student union. And let us never doubt, in these troubled times, that if we hold firm to our moral conscience and to our faith, to our shared history and the possibilities it secured for us, "the tragic midnight" of *our* time "will be transformed," as Dr. King said, "into the glowing daybreak of freedom and justice."

So it was in 1968 when the AASU was founded, so it was when Barack Obama was elected and reelected, and so it can be again.

NOTES

1. Harry Kellogg Durland, "The Chest of 1900," March 21, 1900, quoted in Ken Gewertz, "Time to Remember: 'Chest of 1900' Lets Us See the Way We Were," *Harvard Gazette*, January 18, 2001, https://news.harvard.edu/gazette/story /2001/01/time-to-remember/.

2. Durland, "The Chest of 1900."

3. William Julius Wilson, "Don't Ignore Class When Addressing Racial Gaps in Intergenerational Mobility," Brookings Institution, April 12, 2018, https://www .brookings.edu/blog/social-mobility-memos/2018/04/12/dont-ignore-class-when -addressing-racial-gaps-in-intergenerational-mobility/

4. The National Advisory Commission on Civil Disorders, *The Kerner Report*, with an introduction by Julian E. Zelizer (Princeton: Princeton University Press, 2016), 1.

5. John F. Kennedy, "Radio and Television Report to the American People on Civil Rights," June 11, 1963, https://www.jfklibrary.org/archives/other-resources /john-f-kennedy-speeches/civil-rights-radio-and-television-report-19630611.

6. Lyndon B. Johnson, Commencement Address at Howard University: "To Fulfill These Rights," June 4, 1965, TeachingAmericanHistory.org, http:// teachingamericanhistory.org/library/document/commencement-address-at-howard -university-to-fulfill-these-rights/.

7. Martin Luther King, Jr., "I Have a Dream," Address Delivered at the March on Washington for Jobs and Freedom, August 28, 1963, https://kinginstitute .stanford.edu/king-papers/documents/i-have-dream-address-delivered-march -washington-jobs-and-freedom.

8. W. E. B. Du Bois, "A Negro Student at Harvard at the End of the 19th Century," *The Massachusetts Review* 1, no. 3 (Spring 1960), 356.

9. Martin Luther King, Jr., *Where Do We Go from Here: Chaos or Community?* (New York: Harper and Row, 1967; Reprint: Boston, Beacon Press, 2010), 141.

10. Wilson, "Don't Ignore Class When Addressing Racial Gaps in Intergenerational Mobility."

11. Quoted in "AASU Founders," Harvard Business School, https://www.library .hbs.edu/hc/AASU/aasu-founders/.

12. See Henry Louis Gates, Jr., "American Beyond the Color Line," January 28, 2004, American RadioWorks, http://americanradioworks.publicradio.org/features /blackspeech/hlgates.html.

13. Martin Luther King, Jr., "My Dream: Peace: God's Man's Business," *Chicago Defender*, January 1, 1966.

14. Quoted in "AASU Founders," Harvard Business School.

15. Quoted in "AASU Founders," Harvard Business School.

16. Sujeet Indap, "Vernon Jordan: 'It's Not a Crime to be Close to Wall St.," *Financial Times*, August 17, 2018, https://www.ft.com/content/429c9540-9fd0-11e8 -85da-eeb7a9ce36e4.

17. Martin Luther King, Jr., "On Being a Good Neighbor," in *A Gift of Love: Sermons from* Strength to Love *and Other Preachings* (New York: Harper and Row, 1963; Reprint: Boston: Beacon Press, 2012), 25.

18. Martin Luther King, Jr., "The Drum Major Instinct," in *A Gift of Love*, 174.

19. Freddie C. Colston, ed., *Dr. Benjamin E. Mays Speaks: Representative Speeches of a Great American Orator* (Lanham, MD: University Press of America, 2002), 211.

20. Martin Luther King, Jr., "Dr. King Asks Non-Violence In Little Rock School Crisis," September 26, 1957, https://kinginstitute.stanford.edu/king-papers/documents/dr-king-asks-non-violence-little-rock-school-crisis.

21. William Jefferson Clinton, "Address Commemorating the 40th Anniversary of the Desegregation of Little Rock Central High School," September 25, 1997, American Rhetoric, https://www.americanrhetoric.com/speeches/wjclintonlittlerocknine40th.htm.

3

Pathways to Leadership

Black Graduates of Harvard Business School

ANTHONY J. MAYO *and* LAURA MORGAN ROBERTS

In 1968, five Harvard Business School (HBS) graduate students, including the first African American women to graduate, organized—like students on many other US college campuses during the late 1960s—to found the African American Student Union. The AASU advocated for increased representation of African American students and faculty at HBS, as well as curricular and policy changes. We used the fiftieth anniversary of the formation of the AASU as an opportunity to do a deep dive into the career paths of the school's black alumni.[1] Who are they? How have their careers unfolded? What can we learn from their specific journeys?

HBS did not track its alumni by race until the mid-1990s, and there thus was an array of opinions on the total number of black alumni of the school. To answer this question more definitively, we conducted an extensive archival research project, and through this process we found that in the 103-year time span since the first known black student graduated from HBS (Wendell Thomas Cunningham in 1915), approximately 2,300 black students have graduated from the institution. As a point of comparison, the school's total number of MBA alumni is 63,700.[2] As such, black graduates represent 4 percent of all MBA alumni.

For graduates from the classes of 1969 through 2015,[3] we compiled demographic data including gender, country of origin, undergraduate college, undergraduate major, and other advanced degrees. To assess career pathways, we conducted a comprehensive review of the work histories of graduates from the classes of 1977 through 2015.[4] Of the 1,821 black alumni from 1977 to 2015, we were able to collect complete work histories for 1,381 graduates.

This research project was conducted under the auspices of the HBS Leadership Initiative. An important book that emerged from the group's Great American Business Leaders project, one of the largest academic studies of its kind on leadership, was *Paths to Power: How Insiders and Outsiders Shaped American Business Leadership* (Mayo, Nohria, & Singleton, 2007).[5] In this book, the authors show how seven key factors (birthplace, nationality, religion, education, social class, race, and gender) influenced the composition of business leaders during the twentieth century. In particular, they outline how a group of "insiders" possessed advantages (based on the seven factors) that facilitated the challenging journey to the top while "outsiders" on those same dimensions faced disadvantages that made their path to leadership positions much more difficult. Women and people of color have historically been the ultimate outsiders in access to power, and their outsider status is still a factor today.

Paths to Power identifies four key themes that enabled access to opportunity for outsiders: place, personal networks, professional credentials, and perseverance. Place refers to business opportunities and potential. Throughout most of the twentieth century, blacks were systematically locked out of traditional opportunities. Thus, businesses designed by and for blacks provided an initial path to success, and many of those businesses were located in their home communities (Walker, 1998). Outsiders who had the means to do so found success by relocating to more hospitable environments. Access to professional networks (mentors, sponsors, etc.) was deemed especially critical for outsiders. They provided both developmental job opportunities and access to resources that were critical to success (capital, introductions, references, etc.).

In addition, outsiders relied on education to level the playing field. The authors found that blacks were far more educated than their white counterparts in the Great American Business Leaders database (Mayo et al., 2007, p. 207). Finally, perseverance was crucial for outsiders to succeed. Being locked out of traditional channels of opportunity, blacks were far more likely to found a business. In fact, every black woman who was included in the research database was an entrepreneur. There was no traditional path, and black women thus forged their own way, often creating businesses that served their own community (i.e., capitalizing on both place and perseverance).

Paths to Power also reveals that blacks who made it to the top historically were concentrated in four core industries: (1) financial services, (2) printing and publishing, (3) media and entertainment, and (4) personal care products. As noted previously, much of their success derived from creating businesses for other blacks.

One of the motivating factors in studying HBS black alumni was to compare their experiences with those of the outsiders examined in *Paths to Power*. Are they concentrated in the same industries? Did they rely on the same levers for success? Is the playing field any more level now than it was in the twentieth century? What is similar and different for black HBS MBAs?

The Numbers

Between 1915 and 1968, a total of forty-two black students graduated from HBS.[6] The representation of blacks at HBS took a major turn in spring 1968 when Clifford E. Darden, Lillian Lincoln Lambert, E. Theodore Lewis Jr., George R. Price, and A. Leroy Willis formed the AASU. Recalling his initial impressions of HBS, Darden wrote, "Imagine a Fall 1967 MBA entering class of some 700 persons of whom the overwhelming majority are white males—with a sprinkling of white females of US citizenship (approximately 38 students in total), some 45 international students and six—yes six—African Americans. Imagine a campus so monochromatic that none of the seven first-year sections that Fall could boast more than a lone student of color, and where one section was as lily-white as a debutante ball in the ante-bellum South" (African-American Student Union of the Harvard Business School, 1997, p. 13).

With the encouragement and determination of the AASU, the number of black graduates increased from five in 1969 to twenty-seven in 1970 to fifty-eight in 1971 (figure 3-1). The class of 2009 included seventy-four black graduates (about 8 percent of the overall class), which was the largest total in any graduating year in the school's history.

The mean number of black graduates has increased from thirty-seven in the 1970s to fifty-eight in the 2010s. Over the past twenty-five years, the percentage of black graduates in the MBA program has been relatively flat at about 6 percent.[7]

Women represent 35 percent of all black graduates between 1969 and 2017. While women represented only 14 percent of black graduates in the 1970s, the number of women graduates increased to 43 percent by the 2010s. In comparison, women represent 27 percent of all graduates of HBS during this same time period. The higher representation of black

FIGURE 3-1

Number of HBS black MBA alumni by class year, 1969–2017

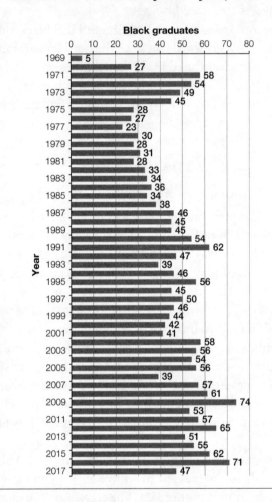

women compared to black men in the HBS classroom is consistent with the overall trends in higher education. According to Okahana and Zhou (2017), 69 percent of blacks enrolled in all graduate programs are women.

The vast majority of black graduates (90 percent) with known countries of origin were born in the United States.[8] The percentage of black graduates from the United States has decreased from 94 percent in the 1980s to 86 percent in the 2010s, while the percentage of graduates from Africa has increased from 3 percent in the 1980s to 10 percent in the 2010s.

Educational Path before HBS

In building the database of black graduates, we were interested in the educational paths that they pursued before matriculation at HBS. To that end, we were able to gather information about undergraduate colleges for 96 percent of graduates from 1969 through 2015.[9]

Undergraduate College

Over this time period, 32 percent of black graduates attended a top-one-hundred national university before coming to HBS. The next-largest concentration is graduates of Ivy League institutions, which accounts for 26 percent of all black graduates. The percentage breakdowns for black men and women are similar, though black women were more likely to attend an Ivy League college, top-one-hundred national university, or top-one-hundred liberal arts college than their male counterparts. Black men were more represented in historically black colleges and universities (HBCUs), military colleges, and other public universities.

Reflecting the initial outreach efforts of HBS, 21 percent of the graduates from the 1970s attended HBCUs (figure 3-2). In the 1980s, there was an increase in graduates from top liberal arts institutions and a corresponding decrease in graduates who had attended HBCUs (down to 8 percent of graduates). Those trends reversed in the 1990s. Graduates' educational backgrounds have been far less diverse in the past twenty years than they were in the 1970s, as a greater percentage of recent alumni attended elite undergraduate institutions. In the 1970s, Ivy League colleges, HBCUs, and top-one-hundred national universities accounted for 65 percent of all incoming students. That number increased to 82 percent by the 2010s. In addition, we see far fewer graduates from other public and private universities by the 2010s.

One Ivy League–educated alumna, reflecting on the educational credentials of her coworkers, stated, "You look around at the education of black folks versus white folks [at work]. You start to notice a pattern that all the black folks are superbly educated. The black folks went to Ivy League schools. The white folks went to possibly whatever schools they wanted to go, and so you start to see that black folks are screened much more."

Targeting alumni of HBCUs has been a part of the outreach strategy for HBS admissions since the initial request by the five founders of the

FIGURE 3-2

Undergraduate degree by decade

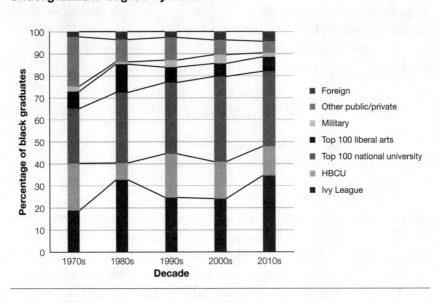

AASU to expand the number of black students in the MBA program. HBCUs such as Howard, Morehouse, Florida A&M, and Spelman were top feeder colleges for HBS in the 1970s, 1990s, and 2000s. In fact, Howard and Morehouse are included among the top ten undergraduate feeder schools for black students over the past forty years. In the accompanying sidebar, Melissa E. Wooten discusses the critical role that HBCUs play in the educational landscape, as well as the significant challenges they face in sustaining respect and legitimacy in the traditional white academy.

COMMENTARY

Melissa E. Wooten, The Struggle Is Real: Black Colleges, Resources, and Respect

Presented at the March 2018 Academic Symposium on Race, Work, and Leadership at Harvard Business School

Black colleges exist within an institutional framework that privileges white sensitivities and logics. By understanding that this framework disadvantages black colleges in similar ways across very different time periods, we can learn much about the nature and shape of white supremacy. That is, as black colleges adapt, as they push back, fight for more resources, and demand recognition for their achievements, these schools reveal how racism operates at the institutional level to consistently advantage traditionally white educational spaces.

The markers of legitimacy (e.g., endowment, enrollment, graduation rate) within higher education disadvantage black colleges. This did not happen by chance. It reflects the racially segregated institutional environment in which higher education emerged, a racially segregated system designed to favor and reward traditionally white colleges for their efforts, including those that exclude black students, intentionally or not. For instance, knowing that, on average, black students had lower ACT scores, the State of Mississippi required higher ACT scores for admission to its traditionally white colleges than it did for admission to its historically black ones (Taylor & Olswang, 1999). Despite such a dubious past, we still use average standardized test scores of first-year students to rank colleges and universities.

In response, in an environment that privileges such metrics, black college advocates find themselves pointing out the dangers of their application. Black college advocates highlight the inconsistencies in these metrics to show that no matter what, black colleges cannot win in this game, historically and contemporarily.

W. E. B. Du Bois, a graduate of Fisk University and a onetime faculty member at Atlanta University, engaged this strategy when he responded to Thomas Jesse Jones's assertion that private, black colleges provided a woefully inadequate education and produced inferior students. In assessing curriculum at black colleges, Jones criticized the schools for not abandoning classical studies in Greek and Latin. Du Bois pointed out that few white colleges had abandoned these disciplines, yet they did not stand accused of inferiority (Watkins, 2001).

Jones would have preferred that black colleges replace those disciplines and incorporate courses in economics and sociology. Du Bois pointed out the resource constraints facing black colleges as they tried to transform their curriculums to include burgeoning disciplines (Watkins, 2001). Du Bois might have also pointed out that few even recognized black colleges as the spaces where these new disciplines emerged. He established the first empirically driven department of sociology at Atlanta University, a black college. Yet the University of Chicago received credit for doing what he had already done (Morris, 2015).

One of the more recent attempts to call out the application of white logics to black colleges happened in January 2018 (Toldson, 2018). When the *Atlanta Journal-Constitution* reported that the six-year graduation rate at *many* black colleges was low, Toldson noted that the article referred to only a small proportion of black colleges. He noted how easily he identified predominantly white colleges with similarly low six-year graduation rates. He explained why graduation rates were the wrong metric for comparisons methodologically and theoretically. The small size of the black colleges highlighted in the article made "numeric calculations of their graduation rates very volatile." Moreover, the students attending those colleges, as well as those attending the predominantly white ones with similar graduations rates, most likely work full time to pay tuition and therefore would not complete college at the same rate as students who receive financial support from parents.

As the institutional environment surrounding higher education abandoned its outwardly race-conscious framework, society did not challenge the metrics associated with this system. We did not have a moment where education or legal scholars stopped to question the racially encoded assumptions baked into these metrics. Nor did we debate whether we should come up with new metrics altogether. Instead, as the institutional environment for higher education moved to an allegedly color-blind or race-neutral system, we continued to apply these metrics indiscriminately and sloppily to black colleges.

Because of this, we should understand black colleges as a case study in how white supremacy operates in higher education. As Palmer (2013) reminds us, "White supremacy is not a person or group of people, it's an ideology. . . . [W]hite supremacy encourages us to value white people, white culture, and everything associated with whiteness above the people, culture, and everything associated with people of color."

If we weren't so tethered to an institutional framework that privileged white educational spaces, we would have to continually contemplate the failures of these schools, especially as it relates to the education of black students. An analysis by the *Atlantic* showed that between 1994 and 2014, the percentage of black undergraduates at top-tier universities held flat at 6 percent (McGill, 2015). No one labels top-tier traditionally white colleges as "failing" because, more than sixty years after *Brown v. Board of Education*, the percentage of black students enrolled remains *well* below 10 percent.

Comparatively, according to the Pew Research Center, black colleges accounted for 9 percent of all black students enrolled in higher education in 2015 (Anderson, 2017). These institutions, which make up a mere 3 percent of all colleges and universities, accounted for 15 percent of the bachelor's degrees awarded to black students in 2015. They had more diversity on their campuses than many traditionally white colleges when you consider that 17 percent of students enrolled identified as something other than black in 2015.

A quick search online for "historically black colleges" will lead to more pages questioning the necessity of these schools than pointing out the foregoing realities. It does not matter that, as a group, black colleges continue to enroll a larger proportion of black students than many top-tier traditionally white colleges and have far more racially diverse campuses than many of their white counterparts. The lack of respect black colleges get for such accomplishments will remain until we change the institutional framework and force it to abandon the white logic to which it so desperately clings.

REFERENCES

Anderson, M. (2017, February 28). A look at historically black colleges and universities as Howard turns 150. Retrieved from http://www.pewresearch.org/fact-tank/2017/02/28/a-look-at-historically-black-colleges-and-universities-as-howard-turns-150/

McGill, A. (2015, November 23). The missing black students at elite universities. *Atlantic.* Retrieved from https://www.theatlantic.com/politics/archive/2015/11/black-college-student-body/417189/

Morris, A. D. (2015). *The scholar denied: W.E.B. Du Bois and the birth of modern sociology.* Oakland: University of California Press.

Palmer, N. (2013, April 8). White supremacy: Not just Neo Nazis. *Sociology in Focus.* Retrieved from http://sociologyinfocus.com/2013/04/white-supremacy-not-just-neo-nazis/

Taylor, E., & Olswang, S. (1999). Peril or promise: The effect of desegregation litigation on historically black colleges. *Western Journal of Black Studies 23*, 73–82.

Toldson, I. A. (2018, January 31). Low graduation rates aren't an HBCU thing. *The Root.* Retrieved from https://www.theroot.com/low-graduation-rates-isn-t-an-hbcu-thing-1822593343

Watkins, W. H. (2001). *The white architects of black education: Ideology and power in America, 1865–1954.* New York: Teachers College Press.

Undergraduate Majors

The vast majority of black graduates between 1969 and 2015 majored in business, economics, or some combination of engineering, computer science, and math. However, black men were more likely to be engineering, computer science, or math majors, while black women were more likely to major in economics or liberal arts studies. The number of engineering, computer science, and math majors increased from 18 percent

TABLE 3-1

Trends in undergraduate majors at HBS (%)

	1985	1985	1995	1995	2005	2005	2015	2015
	All	Black	All	Black	All	Black	All	Black
Humanities and social sciences[1]	48	55	51	29	40	35	41	30
Engineering and natural sciences[2]	31	32	25	27	31	35	38	36
Business administration	21	13	23	44	20	29	21	30
Other	0	0	1	0	9	1	0	4

1. Includes economics and government or political science majors.
2. Includes computer science and mathematics majors.

of black alumni in the 1970s to 27 percent of black alumni in the 2010s, indicating less overall diversity in majors.

To further examine the overall trends in undergraduate majors, we reviewed four class years (1985, 1995, 2005, and 2015) to compare black students with the MBA class as a whole (table 3-1). There is variability in the composition of majors in each individual class year, but overall we see a decrease in humanities and social sciences majors and an increase in business administration majors over time. There is more stability in engineering and natural science majors, which have consistently formed about one-third of the entering class. For the classes of 1995, 2005, and 2015, incoming black students were far more likely to have majored in business administration than the class as a whole.

Additional Advanced Degrees

Our analysis of the classes of 1977 through 2015 indicated that 348, or nearly 20 percent, of black alumni secured an additional advanced degree beyond the Harvard MBA. The most common additional advanced degree was another master's degree followed by a juris doctorate degree. The most common degree for this dual-degree group was a JD from Harvard Law School, which was secured by 72 black alumni. This focus on additional educational credentials is consistent with the historical analysis of black leaders in *Paths to Power*, which shows that education was used as a lever to build credibility and legitimacy (Mayo et al., 2007, p. 207).

Career Path after HBS

To better understand the career trajectories of black alumni, we examined the career choices for alumni from the classes of 1977 through 2015. The total number of alumni for this thirty-eight-year period is 1,821, and we were able to capture full employment data for approximately 1,400. We coded the industry, title, and function of every position that was held, including different positions within the same company.[10]

First Jobs after HBS

Although the numbers are small, we were interested to learn which companies were attractive as a first post-HBS employer for black alumni and how those changed over the past fifty years. The top first employers by decade are shown in table 3-2.

Similar to other graduates, black alumni shifted from working in traditional manufacturing companies such as IBM and General Motors in the 1970s to seeking employment in financial services and consulting firms beginning in the 1980s. Since the 1980s, McKinsey & Company has been a top first employer for black graduates, followed by Goldman Sachs. The number of years that black MBAs spend at their first post-HBS company has declined over the last several decades, from 9.6 and 8.6 in the 1970s and 1980s, respectively, to less than 3 in the 2010s, indicating a much higher rate of mobility.

Industry Concentrations

Approximately 35 percent of black alumni are currently working in the finance sector (figure 3-3).[11] The next-largest concentration of black alumni is those working in various professional services industries, including consulting, advertising, and legal services (18 percent).[12] Black alumni are more concentrated in these two industries relative to all HBS alumni. A comparable 2014 survey of all HBS alumni from the classes of 1982 to 2012 revealed that 27 percent and 13 percent were currently working in finance and consulting, respectively.

TABLE 3-2

Top first employers post-HBS

	1970s	1980s	1990s	2000s	2010s
1	IBM	IBM; Morgan Stanley	McKinsey & Company	Goldman Sachs	McKinsey & Company
2	General Motors	McKinsey & Company	Goldman Sachs	McKinsey & Company	Deloitte
3		Booz Allen Hamilton; Goldman Sachs; Kraft Foods	Merrill Lynch	Bain & Company	Bain & Company
4		JP Morgan; Procter & Gamble	Bain & Company; Morgan Stanley	Boston Consulting Group	Morgan Stanley
5			Booz Allen Hamilton	Procter & Gamble	JP Morgan
6			Accenture; Boston Consulting Group; Citi	Citi; JP Morgan	Boston Consulting Group
7			Donaldson, Lufkin & Jenrette; PWC	American Express Company; Merrill Lynch	

FIGURE 3-3

Industry concentrations, current employer (2017)

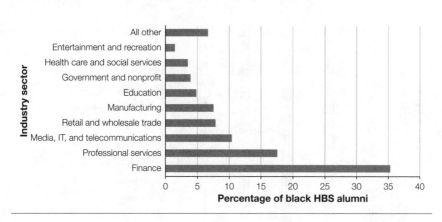

The finance industry sector is currently the top industry sector for black graduates of all decades except the 1970s (figure 3-4). Currently employed black graduates from the 1970s are more likely to work in professional services than in any other sector. The concentration of black graduates currently working in the top two industry sectors (finance and professional services) is similar for most graduating classes, though black graduates from 2010 to 2015 are more likely to work in a broader array of industry sectors, including a larger group working in media, information technology, and telecommunications.

The concentration of black HBS alumni in finance is consistent with the analysis of black business leaders in *Paths to Power* (Mayo et al., 2007, pp. 187–220). Historically, black business leaders were heavily concentrated in the insurance and banking sectors. More recently, black HBS alumni have focused their financial careers in investment management, private equity, and real estate. The paths to success for black alumni are far broader than in the past, as demonstrated by the large numbers of alumni in professional services. We see far fewer graduates focused on the publishing and entertainment sectors, and even fewer focused on the creation of black businesses for the black community. In this sense, the opportunity spectrum is much wider today for aspiring black business leaders.

While it was not surprising to find that most black alumni are currently employed in finance or professional services, we wondered whether there were specific companies that stood out as top employers. We

FIGURE 3-4

Current industry classification by class decade

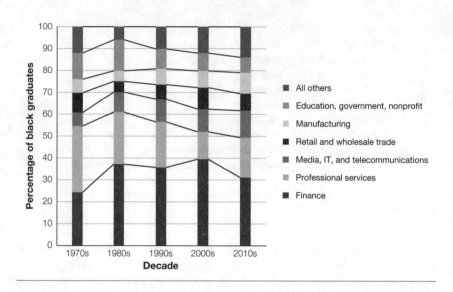

examined the current employers for 1,700 black alumni for which we
had information; the top ten current employers of black alumni are
shown in table 3-3.[13]

No one company stands out as a major employer, especially given the
overall size of nine of the top ten companies on the list. However, we
were intrigued to see that the top current employer is self-employed. Of
this group, approximately 55 percent are working as independent consultants and 25 percent are working as financial advisers or real estate
investors. Of the 92 black alumni that are currently self-employed,
69 percent are graduates from the 1990s through the 2010s.

One executive explained why he left Wall Street: "I was tired. I was
tired of having bosses. I was tired of what I considered to be unfair evaluation of performance of an African American in the professional services industry. In professional services, you are sort of good because
someone says you are good. . . . African Americans never really fare well
in that process."

Reflecting on her decision to leave corporate America, a self-employed
consultant said, "It was quite frustrating when I was told that I needed
to have more seasoning before I could get promoted. I just created a business that is $100M even though I was younger than some of the other

TABLE 3-3

Top ten current employers of black HBS alumni

Rank	Company	Number of alumni
1	Self-employed/sole proprietor	92
2	Morgan Stanley	28
3	McKinsey & Company	27
4	Google	25
5	Boston Consulting Group	13
6	Goldman Sachs	12
7	American Express Company	11
8	Bain & Company	11
9	JP Morgan	10
10	Wells Fargo	10

VPs who had done it! So why can't I get promoted? I did not appreciate what the structure said I had to go through."

Self-employment is a relatively common choice for black alumni at some point in their careers. For instance, 39 percent of all graduates from the 1970s pursued a self-employment opportunity during the course of their careers. The average duration of these self-employment positions was 11.6 years. Similarly, approximately 35 percent of graduates from the 1980s were self-employed for an average of 10.5 years, and almost one-quarter of 1990s graduates have been self-employed for an average of 7.6 years.

Functional Concentrations

Some interesting patterns emerged when we explored the functional paths that black alumni pursued in their careers. We assessed every job position to determine the primary functional concentration for each graduate. Men were more likely to pursue a functional career path in finance, and women were more likely to pursue a path in strategy or marketing.

Figure 3-5, which shows the changes in functional concentration by decade, highlights the increase and subsequent decrease in careers in

FIGURE 3-5

Functional concentrations by decade

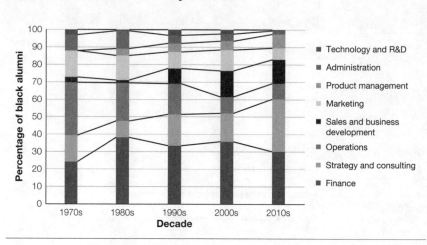

finance. This figure also showcases the drop in black MBAs pursuing careers in operations or manufacturing. While 30 percent of graduates in the 1970s pursued careers in operations, that number dropped to 9 percent by the last decade of the study. Besides strategy and consulting, the fastest-growing functional areas over time are sales or business development and product management.

Within these functional concentrations, about 38 percent of black alumni reported primarily being in a line function during their careers, and 27 percent reported being in a predominantly staff function. The other 35 percent indicated a career that included a balance of line and staff functions.[14]

Mobility

The average number of companies that black alumni have joined after receiving an MBA has been relatively steady—averaging about five for graduates from the 1970s, 1980s, and 1990s (table 3-4).

A comparable survey of all HBS alumni from 1982 to 2012 revealed some interesting similarities and differences. The number of companies that 1980s black alumni have joined after receiving an MBA is similar to the numbers for all alumni: 4.7 for blacks and 4.6 for all alumni. This similarity begins to wane with the 1990s cohort (4.7 for blacks and 4.1

TABLE 3-4

Average number of companies joined after receiving MBA

	1970s	1980s	1990s	2000s	2010s
Total	4.8	4.7	4.7	3.3	1.9
Men	4.8	4.6	4.6	3.4	1.9
Women	4.7	5.0	4.8	3.2	1.9

TABLE 3-5

Average tenure per company (years)

	1970s	1980s	1990s	2000s	2010s
Total	10.6	9.6	6.1	4.6	2.9
Men	11.0	10.2	6.3	4.7	2.9
Women	9.7	8.6	5.9	4.5	2.8

for all alumni), and by the 2000s, it is clear that black alumni are working for more firms on average than the alumni base as a whole (3.3 vs. 2.2) (Orc International, 2014).

The average tenure per company has decreased over the last forty years. Overall, the graduates from the 1970s and 1980s spent about ten years per company; that dropped to six in the 1990s and about five in the 2000s. Women tend to work for more companies, and correspondingly, their average tenure per company is lower than men's (table 3-5).

These gender differences are consistent with the overall labor force, where the average tenure for women in companies has historically been lower than men's, though that gap has been narrowing in the last few years (Hipple & Sok, 2013). There are a number of potential contextual and societal reasons for this disparity. One reason may be the increased obstacles that black women face as they try to progress in their careers. In response to increased challenges in securing internal promotions, women may be more likely to pursue lateral moves to develop expertise and social capital that will signal their leadership potential. In essence, they have to move to grow (Catalyst, 1991, 2001; Feyerherm & Vick, 2005).

Career Satisfaction

Through a series of surveys, focus groups, and in-depth interviews, we were able to gain insight into satisfaction about career progression and the factors that have contributed to or detracted from that progression for black alumni.[15] We learned that the majority of black HBS alumni are overall very satisfied or extremely satisfied with multiple facets of their careers and lives (figure 3-6). However, they reported less satisfaction with certain aspects of their careers than their white counterparts. Specifically, we found a statistically significant racial disparity (even after controlling for gender, age, marital status, parental status, industry, and firm size), such that blacks were less satisfied than whites with opportunities to do meaningful work, to realize professional accomplishments, and to combine career with personal and family life.

One alumna explained, "I have to work harder than some of my counterparts to prove myself every single day. I do benefit from the Harvard Business School brand, but I still have to overcome people's stereotypes about me, and I am not always given the benefit that white males are given, and . . . I have to prove myself before I am given trust and confidence."

Alumni were asked to reflect on the role that race and gender played in their careers. Did they consider their race an advantage, a disadvantage, or neither? Alumni answered this question from two vantage points: (1) anticipatory, when they started their post-HBS career; and (2) reflective, looking back on their actual career experiences (figures 3-7, 3-8, 3-9, and 3-10).

There were significant disparities between black and white alumni in regard to both gender and race. Similarly small percentages of black and white women expected their gender to be an advantage (about 12 percent) at the start of their careers. Black women, however, were more likely to expect their gender to be a disadvantage—62 percent for black women and 46 percent for white women.

While their responses on gender aligned with white men's, black men were even more likely to believe that their gender would be an advantage in their careers—55 percent for black men compared with 40 percent for white men. This expectation of an advantage directly contrasted with their expectations about race.

Black women expected to confront a double disadvantage in their careers—barriers based on both gender and race. A black woman described having to be cognizant to avoid stereotypes: "I think being a

FIGURE 3-6

Career satisfaction (% extremely / very satisfied)

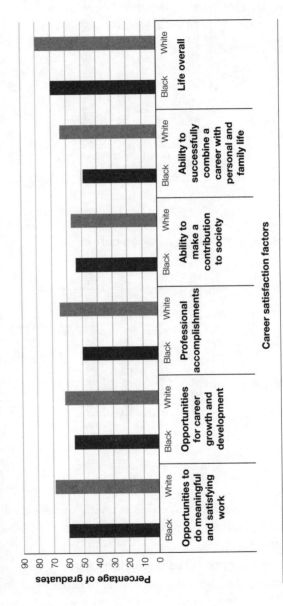

FIGURE 3-7

Impact of gender leaving HBS

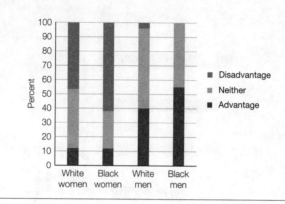

FIGURE 3-8

Impact of gender looking back on career

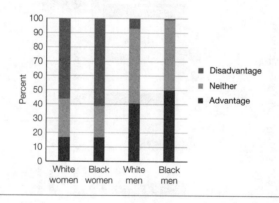

black woman, I feel like we're always trying to walk the line of not being too assertive, and not coming across angry. . . . Being one of the only black people, much less black women, and being as outspoken as I think I am, I always felt pressured to dial it back."

In contrast, black men did not expect to experience any disadvantages based on their gender (and some thought it would be an advantage), but the vast majority expected their race to be a disadvantage. A black alumnus described how he navigated his career: "In part to avoid prejudice, I opted to stay with one company so that my networks and reputation

FIGURE 3-9

Impact of race leaving HBS

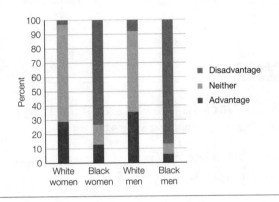

FIGURE 3-10

Impact of race looking back on career

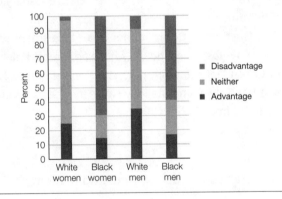

accumulated. Being presumed less competent due to ethnicity is a major startup cost that I paid once, and my networks and reputation mitigated ongoing prejudice for the most part."

Black women's expectations about their gender and race being a disadvantage seemed to be consistent with their lived experiences. They expected both to be a disadvantage and they experienced them that way. That was not the case for black men. While 86 percent of black men expected race to be a disadvantage in their careers, only 59 percent experienced it that way.

In the accompanying sidebar, Arthur P. Brief explores some of the trends in explicit and subtle racism. He further explores the impact that these forms of racism have had on the opportunity landscape for black professionals.

Arthur P. Brief, Back to the Future: A Strategy for Studying Racism in Organizations

Presented at the March 2018 Academic Symposium on Race, Work, and Leadership at Harvard Business School

What is the status of black business leadership in America? With blacks forming 12.1 percent of the labor force, the data in table C3-1 is not very comforting, with the exception of that pertaining to human resources managers.

One of several plausible explanations for the relative scarcity of black leaders is racism. The term *racism* is confusing, in part because it has changed over time and, at least theoretically, comes in an assortment of forms. First, there is the familiar *old-fashioned racism*, whose adherents believe in the biological inferiority of blacks and support strict segregation. Their number appears to have been declining steadily since the 1960s. Figures C3-1 and C3-2 depict this trend from 1972 to 2008.

TABLE C3-1

Black-white differences in managerial employment (%)

Roles	Black	White
Chief executives	3.8	90.0
General and operations managers	8.3	85.0
Marketing and sales managers	6.0	86.4
Financial managers	6.7	83.5
Human resources managers	12.3	81.7
Industrial production managers	3.8	89.5

Source: Bureau of Labor Statistics (2018).

Whites' attitudes toward racial principles

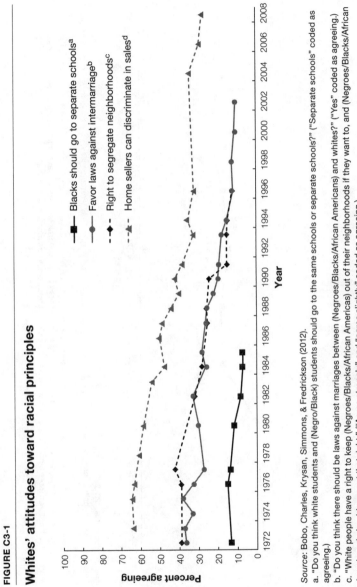

Source: Bobo, Charles, Krysan, Simmons, & Fredrickson (2012).

a. "Do you think white students and (Negro/Black) students should go to the same schools or separate schools?" ("Separate schools" coded as agreeing.)

b. "Do you think there should be laws against marriages between (Negroes/Blacks/African Americans) and whites?" ("Yes" coded as agreeing.)

c. "White people have a right to keep (Negroes/Blacks/African Americas) out of their neighborhoods if they want to, and (Negroes/Blacks/African Americans) should respect that right." ("Agree strongly" and "agree slightly" coded as agreeing.)

d. "Suppose there is a community-wide vote on the general housing issue. There are two possible laws to vote on. One law says that a home-owner can decide for himself whom to sell his house to, even if he prefers not to sell to (Negroes/Blacks/African Americans). The second law says that a homeowner cannot refuse to sell to someone because of their race or color. Which law would you vote for?" ("Owner decides" coded as agreeing.)

Whites' ratings of whites' industriousness and intelligence in comparison to blacks

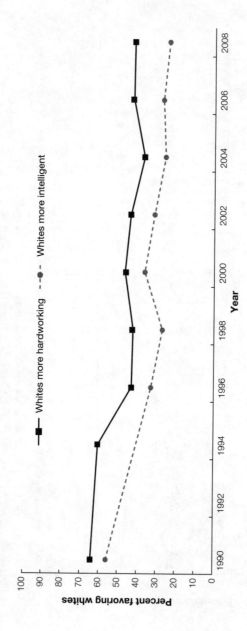

Source: Bobo et al. (2012).

"The second set of characteristics asks if people in the group tend to be hardworking or if they tend to be lazy. Where would you rate whites on this scale? Blacks?"

"Do people in these groups tend to be unintelligent or tend to be intelligent? Where would you rate whites in general on this scale? Blacks?"

The figure plots percentages of whites who rated whites higher than blacks on a given trait (industriousness or intelligence). Seven percent of whites rated blacks as more hardworking than whites, and six percent rated blacks as more intelligent.

Data from the 2016 General Social Science Survey noted that 39.8 percent of nonblack respondents reported that racial differences in inequality are due to blacks' lack of will and 6.8 percent reported that inequalities are due to the inborn disabilities of blacks. So old-fashioned racists are out there but not necessarily the problem they were.

But old-fashioned racists likely have been replaced by subtle racists. According to Dovidio, Gaertner, and their colleagues (e.g., Dovidio, Gaertner, & Pearson, 2017), racism has mutated in America since the 1960s, prompted by changes in law and social norms regarding the affirmation of egalitarian values. For many whites, not only do their stated racial attitudes appear less racist, they also have developed a private self-concept of being nonracist. Social psychologists in the 1980s began studying several forms of this new subtle racism: "symbolic racism" (Sears & Henry, 2005), "ambivalent racism" (Katz, 1981), "adverse racism" (Dovidio & Gaertner, 2004), and my personal favorite, McConahay's (1986) "modern racism," whose tenets include "discrimination is a thing of the past because Blacks now have the freedom to compete in the marketplace and enjoy the things they can afford and blacks are pushing too hard, too fast into places they are not wanted."

Now let me share with you a piece of research my colleagues and I published in 2000 (Brief, Dietz, Cohen, Pugh, & Vaslow, 2000) focusing on modern racism. The research was inspired by the case of Shoney's, a restaurant chain in the 1990s with 1,800 units in thirty-six states that was forced to pay $132.5 million for discrimination against its employees. The company from the top down believed it was good business to racially match its customer-contact employees to the customers they serve. For instance, when a store was performing under par, managers were told to "lighten up" the unit and hire "attractive white girls." Such tactics resulted in 1.8 percent of Shoney's restaurant managers being black and 75 percent of its black restaurant employees holding jobs in low paying, non-customer-contact positions (e.g., dishwasher).

We conducted two laboratory experiments using an in-basket methodology with participants playing the role of an organizational decision maker required to screen a set of job applicants' résumés and make a hiring recommendation. The participants' levels of modern racism were measured one month before the experiments in a mass testing context. In one experiment, the business justification hypothesized to release the beast of modern racism was that since the vast majority of the organization's workforce was white, so should be the new human resources manager; in the other, participants were selecting a customer representative to join a team whose members were all white, as were the team's customers. In both studies, we observed a statistical interaction between modern racism and business justifications of discrimination against black job applicants, supporting the idea that the beast of modern racism is behaviorally released by business justifications to discriminate. Importantly, these findings were constructively replicated using the IAT, an important measure of unconscious prejudice, not the modern racism scale, by Ziegert and Hanges (2005).

To me, the business justifications my colleagues and I studied represent one of likely many organizational mechanisms that link prejudice to negative outcomes (figure C3-3). I use the term *mechanism* in a way similar to how Barbara Reskin did in her 2002 presidential address to the American Sociological Association, when she spoke about ascriptive inequality. Perhaps by identifying those organizational mechanisms we can seek to modify or eliminate them, thereby allowing black leaders to blossom and flourish.

I will now move on to a second research example of organizational mechanisms. In this study, we (Roberson, Deitch, Brief, & Block, 2003) surveyed the members of a national association of black professionals employed in utilities industries to measure their solo status, experienced stereotype threat, and feedback-seeking behaviors. Let me digress a little about our sample. I have learned, after studying race for more than forty-five years, employing organizations very rarely warmly embrace race researchers for a variety of legitimate and perhaps illegitimate reasons. So, in this case, we turned to an association of black executives for our data. There are dozens of these black associations, including alumni associations from predominantly white elite universities (e.g., Harvard's and Stanford's business schools) and historically black colleges and universities (e.g., Morehouse).

Roberson et al. (2003) reasoned that black executives working as the sole (i.e., token) blacks in their work groups will experience stereotype threat and, correspondingly, engage in dysfunctional feedback-seeking behavior (e.g., indirectly seeking feedback rather than asking directly for it and discounting feedback). *Stereotype threat* is the fear of confirming a negative stereotype about one's group through one's own behavior (Steele & Aronson, 1995). It is activated in situations where the stereotype is perceived as relevant to one's performance. In fact, Roberson et al.'s reasoning was confirmed by the data they observed, thereby providing another example of an organizational mechanism, tokenism, that ties prejudice to negative outcomes.

I share this particular piece of research because I believe it demonstrates the value of getting outside the social psychological laboratory. The labora-

FIGURE C3-3

Strategy for studying racism in organizations

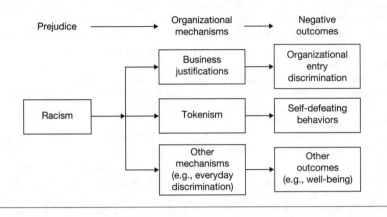

tory simply is not a rich enough context to confidently identify the relationships we did between token status, stereotype threat, and the dysfunctional feedback-seeking behaviors required of real workers in real jobs.

In some ways, the current climate in the United States is a harking back to the past. According to Bobo (2017) and others, Donald J. Trump's campaign and presidency have unleashed forces that were previously marginalized and shrinking in influence. The evidence he cites for this is drawn from the Southern Poverty Law Center, which reported that during the Trump era, the number of hate groups and hate crimes has increased dramatically. For example, hate groups during the Trump era have increased from 17 percent to 91 percent. Trump's words and deeds may be once again transforming racial attitudes in America, away from subtle racism and back to the old-fashioned kind.

REFERENCES

Bobo, L. D. (2017). Racism in Trump's America: Reflections on culture, sociology, and the 2016 US presidential election. *British Journal of Sociology, 68*(S1), S85–S104.

Bobo, L. D., Charles, C. Z., Krysan, M., Simmons, A. D., & Fredrickson, G. M. (2012). The real record on racial attitudes. In P. V. Marsden (Ed.), *Social trends in American life: Findings from the general social survey since 1972* (pp. 38–83). Princeton, NJ: Princeton University Press.

Brief, A. P., Dietz, J., Cohen, R. R., Pugh, S. D., & Vaslow, J. B. (2000). Just doing business: Modern racism and obedience to authority as explanations for employment discrimination. *Organizational Behavior and Human Decision Processes, 81*(1), 72–97.

Bureau of Labor Statistics. (2018). *Employed persons by detailed occupation, sex, race, and Hispanic or Latino ethnicity* [Data file]. Retrieved from https://www.bls.gov/cps/cpsaat11 .htm

Dovidio, J. F., & Gaertner, S. L. (2004). Aversive racism. In M. P. Zanna (Ed.), *Advances in experimental social psychology* (Vol. 36, pp. 1–51). San Diego, CA: Academic Press.

Dovidio, J. F., Gaertner, S. L., & Pearson, A. R. (2017). Aversive racism and contemporary bias. In C. G. Sibley & F. K. Barlow (Eds.), *The Cambridge handbook of the psychology of prejudice* (pp. 267–294). Cambridge, England: Cambridge University Press.

Katz, I. (1981). *Stigma: A social psychological analysis*. Hillsdale, NJ: Erlbaum.

McConahay, J. B. (1986). Modern racism, ambivalence, and the modern racism scale. In J. F. Dovidio & S. L. Gaertner (Eds.), *Prejudice, discrimination, and racism* (pp. 91–125). Orlando, FL: Academic Press.

Roberson, L., Deitch, E. A., Brief, A. P., & Block, C. J. (2003). Stereotype threat and feedback seeking in the workplace. *Journal of Vocational Behavior, 62*(1), 176–188.

Sears, D. O., & Henry, P. J. (2005). Over thirty years later: A contemporary look at symbolic racism. In M. P. Zanna (Ed.), *Advances in experimental social psychology* (Vol. 37, pp. 95–150). San Diego, CA: Academic Press.

Steele, C. M., & Aronson, J. (1995). Stereotype threat and the intellectual test performance of African Americans. *Journal of Personality and Social Psychology, 69*(5), 797–811.

Ziegert, J. C., & Hanges, P. J. (2005). Employment discrimination: The role of implicit attitudes, motivation, and a climate for racial bias. *Journal of Applied Psychology, 90*(3), 553–562.

Making It to the Top

Over the thirty-eight-year time frame of this study, 13 percent of black women (67) and 19 percent of black men (161) reached upper management (table 3-6).[16]

In analyzing the factors that contributed to success, three key areas stood out: (1) access to significant line or general management experiences, (2) global assignments, and (3) internal support systems (figure 3-11). A number of studies have shown the importance of these factors in enabling career advancement and enhancing satisfaction, as well as the detrimental impact of a lack of such factors (Bell & Nkomo, 2001; Thomas & Gabarro, 1999). Reaching the top requires access to assignments and opportunities that serve as proving grounds for increased responsibility. Black and white alumni see the tremendous potential of being tapped for positions that are considered critical in the organization. As the numbers indicate, black alumni are less likely to have been tapped for these types of assignments (especially black women), and this may contribute to a lower level of satisfaction regarding the opportunity to do meaningful work.

Equally important are global assignments, which less than 40 percent of all survey respondents received. About 26 percent of black women and 36 percent of black men had received a global assignment in their careers. The average duration of the global assignment was eighteen months for black women and twenty-eight months for black men. The majority of black men (61 percent) and black women (56 percent) believed that a global assignment improved their position in the firm. To that end, a similar percentage of black men and black women (approximately 40 percent) noted that their most recent global assignment constituted a promotion.

Black men and women were more likely to have had a formally assigned mentor than their white counterparts, but they perceived relatively less value from these organizationally imposed relationships. In contrast, informal mentorship was deemed beneficial by all groups, especially black women. One senior executive said, "A mentor helps you navigate the power structure of the firm, especially when there is no one in senior management who looks like you." A follow-up analysis of senior executive black women reinforced the importance of both key managerial assignments and the need for influential sponsors who recognize that potential and are willing to back it up (Roberts, Mayo, Ely, & Thomas, 2018).

So what has changed? In many ways, the paths of black alumni of HBS mirror the paths of the outsiders who were analyzed in *Paths to Power*. Professional credentials, personal relationships, and perseverance are still essential elements of outsiders' stories—even for Harvard MBAs. In terms of professional credentials, the majority of black alumni attended elite undergraduate institutions and majored in quantitative fields, and

TABLE 3-6

Total number of all black alumni and total number of black alumni who reached top executive positions

	1970s	1980s	1990s	2000s	2010s	Total
Black alumni	33	167	356	493	332	1,381
Women	9	61	123	199	140	532
Men	24	106	233	294	192	849
Top executive	14	48	90	68	8	228
Women	3	14	23	23	4	67
Men	11	34	67	45	4	161

FIGURE 3-11

Career enablers

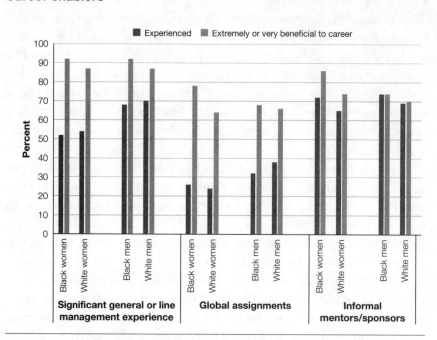

nearly 20 percent pursued an additional advanced degree. The importance of personal relationships is borne out in the surveys, as well as the in-depth study of senior black women executives. And finally, perseverance was deemed essential to both forge new opportunities (self-employment, entrepreneurship) and confront the systemic bias in business and society. Our interviews with senior black women pointed to resilience as an essential ingredient in their path to the executive level (Roberts et al., 2018).

While most contemporary research on diversity employs a multicultural lens, this study of black MBA alumni showcases the critical importance of examining race-specific experiences and the need for organizations to be transparent about their racial compositions. Race cannot be relegated to the periphery; it matters in access to opportunities and support, even for individuals who seemingly have every conceivable credential for success. One recent alumna noted, "Perhaps it sounds naïve, but [coming out of HBS] I did not expect race to have any bearing in my career. I was wrong." We hope that our initial research efforts will encourage other scholars to explore the personal and professional experiences of black leaders, and other underrepresented groups, and that the research will result in actions that ensure greater access to opportunities and wider paths to power.

NOTES

1. Throughout this chapter, we use the term *black alumni* to refer to alumni who are African American or of African descent.

2. The total alumni population, including DBA and PhD graduates and executive education graduates, living and deceased, is 113,000.

3. Gender and country of origin were also coded for the alumni of 2016 and 2017.

4. We concluded the career data analysis with the class of 2015 so that we could examine at least two years of employment post-HBS.

5. For more on the Great American Business Leaders project, see http://www.hbs.edu/leadership and the methodology chapter from Mayo and Nohria (2005, pp. 365–372).

6. The data for this chapter is drawn from an internal HBS report (Mayo & Roberts, 2018).

7. The HBS entering class size has grown from an average of 818 in the 1990s to 914 in the 2010s.

8. We were able to identify country of origin for 84 percent of all black graduates from 1969 through 2017.

9. The categories of "top one hundred national universities" and "top one hundred liberal arts colleges" were drawn from historical rankings produced by the *U.S. News & World Report.*

10. As a point of reference, when comparisons across decades are shown in this section, the 1970s includes three class years (1977 through 1979), and the 2010s includes six class years (2010 through 2015).

11. *Current position* is defined as the position that the alumnus held as of December 2017.

12. Excluding advertising and legal services, the percentage working in consulting is 16 percent.

13. While we have full employment history for 1,381 black alumni, we were able to code current employment for 1,700 of the 1,821 alumni from 1977 through 2015. This data is based on a snapshot of black HBS MBA alumni as of December 2017.

14. Data on staff versus line function is drawn from an analysis of 496 responses to a survey that that was administered to 2,000 black alumni in August 2017.

15. Survey respondents were asked to identify their race and ethnicity, and we analyzed the survey responses based on these self-selected criteria. Of the approximately 5,300 alumni who completed the survey, 4,000, or 78 percent, identified as white and 240, or 4 percent, of the respondents identified as black. Given the sample size and diversity in country of origin, we did not include comparisons between black alumni and other nonwhite alumni.

16. For this analysis, *upper management* is defined as including chairperson, CEO, president, founder, and other C-level positions (e.g., CMO, CIO, CTO, etc.). In addition, upper management also includes managing director and managing partner.

REFERENCES

African-American Student Union of the Harvard Business School. (1997). *The 25th Annual Career/Alumni Conference: Our silver past and golden future*. Boston, MA: African-American Student Union.

Bell, E. L. J. E., & Nkomo, S. M. (2001). *Our separate ways: Black and white women and the struggle for professional identity*. Boston, MA: Harvard Business School Press.

Catalyst. (1991). *Women entrepreneurs: Why companies lose female talent and what they can do about it*. New York, NY: Catalyst.

Catalyst. (2001). *The next generation: Today's professionals, tomorrow's leaders*. New York, NY: Catalyst.

Feyerherm, A., & Vick, Y. H. (2005). Generation X women in high technology: Overcoming gender and generational challenges to succeed in the corporate environment. *Career Development International, 10*(3), 216–227.

Hipple, S. F., & E. Sok. (2013). *Tenure of American workers* (Research report). Washington, DC: US Bureau of Labor Statistics.

Mayo, A. J., & Nohria, N. (2005). *In their time: The greatest business leaders of the twentieth century*. Boston, MA: Harvard Business School Press, 2005.

Mayo, A. J., Nohria, N., & Singleton, L. G. (2007). *Paths to power: How insiders and outsiders shaped American business leadership*. Boston, MA: Harvard Business School Press.

Mayo, A. J., & Roberts, L. M. (2018, April). *Spheres of influence: A portrait of black MBA program alumni* (Internal research report). Harvard Business School, Boston, MA.

Okahana, H., & Zhou, E. (2017). *Graduate enrollment and degrees: 2006 to 2016* (Research report). Washington, DC: Council of Graduate Schools, 2017.

Orc International (2014). "Career Pathways Survey 2014." Internal presentation prepared by Orc International for Harvard Business School.

Roberts, L. M., Mayo, A., Ely, R., & Thomas, D. (2018, March–April). Beating the odds: Leadership lessons from senior African-American women. *Harvard Business Review*.

Thomas, D. A., & Gabarro, J. J. (1999). *Breaking through: The making of minority executives in corporate America*. Boston, MA: Harvard Business School Press.

Walker, J. E. K. (1998). *The history of black business in America: Capitalism, race, and entrepreneurship*. New York, NY: Twayne.

4

Intersectionality and the Careers of Black Women Lawyers

Results from the Harvard Law School Black Alumni Survey

DAVID B. WILKINS *and* BRYON FONG

On January 10, 2017, President Barack Obama delivered his formal farewell address to the country in Chicago, the city that had given him his political start. In reflecting on the achievements and challenges of his two terms in office, the president paid special attention to an issue that he knew would, for better and for worse, define his presidency: race. In the simple yet elegant language that even his harshest critics have come to respect, the president said this about the state of race relations after eight years of the Age of Obama: "After my election, there was talk about a post-racial America. Such a vision, no matter how well-intended, was never realistic. For race remains a potent and often divisive force in our society. I've lived long enough to know that race relations are better than they were 10, 20, 30 years ago—you can see it not just in the statistics, but in the attitudes of young Americans across the political spectrum. But we are not where we need to be. All of us have more work to do."[1]

In this chapter, we offer a preliminary assessment of how much progress had been made—and how much work remains to be done—in a part of the American economy President Obama knows well: the legal profession. We do so by examining the careers of the black graduates of President Obama's law school alma matter in the sixteen years since the beginning of the new millennium.

To investigate the significance of race in the careers of black lawyers, and to document the achievements of the black graduates of Harvard Law School (HLS), in 2016–2017 the Center on the Legal Profession (CLP) surveyed virtually all living black HLS alumni about their careers since graduating from law school. The survey, which was officially launched in the fall of 2016, covered a wide range of issues, including law school experiences, first jobs post-HLS, current jobs, career trajectories and transitions, levels of satisfaction, and attitudes on the state of race relations. Together, the survey results offer a wealth of information about the career paths, obstacles, and successes of HLS's black graduates across more than six decades.[2]

In this chapter, we highlight data from this survey that documents the complex intersection of race and gender in the careers of HLS's black graduates. As Kimberlé Crenshaw's (HLS class of 1984) pioneering research on intersectionality makes clear, because otherwise-distinct social characteristics such as race and gender can combine and intersect in ways that produce a new category of classification with its own systems of discrimination and disadvantage, it is particularly important to highlight the role of gender and race.[3] Indeed, separate discussions about either minorities or women ignore the important reality that the majority of minority law students are women. Minority women lawyers experience many of the same issues that face white women lawyers and minority male lawyers—plus a complex set of challenges that flow from the intersection of these two forms of identity. If the legal profession and society are going to make progress on either gender or racial diversity in twenty-first-century workplaces, we all must acknowledge and better understand the importance of intersectionality in the lives of minority women lawyers. We therefore focus on the intersection between race and gender in this chapter.

HLS provides an important lens through which to study these issues. In 1869, George Lewis Ruffin graduated from HLS, becoming the first black person to graduate from any law school in the United States. In the intervening years, Harvard has graduated more black lawyers—over 2,700—than any law school in the country with the exception of the great Howard University School of Law. Among their ranks are some of the most powerful and influential lawyers in the world, including the forty-fourth president of the United States and the country's former first lady Michelle Obama (class of 1988). For this reason alone, in a profession where graduating from a top-tier law school has traditionally played an outsize role in career opportunities and success, if even these most privileged black graduates are continuing to face obstacles not encountered by their white peers, then it is very likely that issues of race and gender continue to structure the careers of black lawyers from other institutions as well.[4]

Moreover, given that our primary goal in this chapter is to understand within-race gender dynamics, focusing on the graduates of a single elite institution where black women and men enter with relatively similar credentials and have comparable experiences in law school makes it far more likely that observed differences between black women and men are the result of the "double bind" of intersectionality rather than the result of differences in qualifications. As Robin Ely, Pamela Stone, and Colleen Ammerman note in explaining the importance of their similar study of the career dynamics of Harvard Business School graduates, "Attending a top-tier business school is a reasonable indication of high levels of achievement, talent, ambition, and promise, and by looking at men and women who graduate from the same school, we had a level playing field for gender comparisons."[5] We believe the same is true for black HLS graduates. Indeed, as we will demonstrate, HLS's black female graduates enter the workforce with somewhat better credentials than their black male peers. The fact that our data also demonstrates that black women consistently tend to experience worse career outcomes than black men underscores the insight that can be derived from focusing solely on the graduates of a single top-tier school.

Finally, because HLS has graduated so many black lawyers over the last 150 years—including, since the late 1960s, a significant number of black women—our study provides a unique lens through which to examine gender differences in the careers of this important group of graduates across decades and at different stages of their careers. As the following sections demonstrate, while much progress has been made, black HLS graduates as a whole—and black female graduates in particular—continue to face significant obstacles in their legal careers. These within-race gender differences are particularly important given that for several years women have formed the majority of black law school graduates not only at Harvard but at virtually every law school in the country.

Careers in Comparison

The 2016 Black Alumni Survey was designed to be comparable to a series of other CLP career study projects. First, and most notably, the 2016 survey is a direct follow-up to the 2000 HLS Black Alumni Survey, in most cases utilizing identical questions.[6] As we discuss in more detail, because the survey questionnaires are largely identical, we can compare the responses of the more recent black HLS graduates with those of their predecessors, as well as observe how the careers of pre-2000 graduates have continued to change over time. The 2016 survey also allows us to capture the critical changes that have occurred since 2000, including the election of Obama, the nation's first black president, who is also an HLS graduate. The 2016 survey therefore includes a set of questions not present in the 2000 version, most notably on the impact the Obama presidency has had on the legal profession.

Second, the 2016 (and 2000) black alumni questionnaire shares many similar characteristics with the Harvard Law School Career Study (HLSCS), which surveyed four HLS classes: those of 1975, 1985, 1995, and 2000. Conducted in 2010 by the CLP, the HLSCS focused primarily on how gender affected the professional and personal choices of HLS graduates; the full results of the study were published in 2015 in *The Women and Men of Harvard Law School: Preliminary Results from the HLS Career Study.*[7] It is important to note that due to data limitations, specifically the relatively low response rate of minority students from the target classes, the HLSCS did not systematically address race-based issues. However, given the high comparability of the questionnaire with the 2000 and 2016 black alumni surveys, in the sections that follow, we can compare the experiences of black HLS graduates with those of the school's alumni more generally.

Finally, the results of the 2016 survey are comparable to what is known about black lawyers' careers nationally, including results from the After the JD (AJD) study.[8] AJD is a longitudinal study that tracks the professional lives of more than four thousand lawyers who entered the bar in or around the year 2000. The first wave of the study, AJD 1, was conducted in 2002–2003 and provides information about the personal and professional lives of AJD respondents two to three years after passing the bar. The second wave of the study, AJD 2, was conducted in 2007–2008 and provides data about the same respondents seven to eight years into their careers. The third and final wave, AJD 3, was conducted in 2011–2012 and provides data on these same respondents ten to twelve years into their careers. AJD findings, along with other sources of publicly available data, allow us to draw comparisons between the experiences of black HLS graduates and a national population of black lawyers.

Data and Methods: Black Alumni Survey II

Our survey sample includes 687 black HLS graduates, representing 31 percent of those surveyed.[9] For the purposes of this analysis, we focused exclusively on graduates with a JD (including joint degrees). This is due primarily to the low responses rates from LLM and SJD students, as well as the likely difference between the careers of this group and those of graduates with JDs.

As an additional check on the representativeness of our data, we conducted an analysis of respondents and nonrespondents using information from HLS records on black enrollment by cohorts and gender. Based on this analysis, and to account for any differences between the population and the survey responses, data was weighted for each cohort by gender. This weighting allows us to reach conclusions from our sample that are more representative of the population as a whole.

The majority of tables contain the following structure:

1. An **overall column** (shaded gray), which signifies all respondents in the sample

2. **Male and female columns**, which signify the responses from male and female respondents, respectively, from across the entire sample

3. **Pre- and post-2000 era columns**, which signify the responses from those who graduated from HLS on each side of the new millennium; those who graduated in 2000 are included in the post-2000 era

It is important to note that despite containing graduates from similar years, the pre-2000 era is distinct from the sample contained in the 2000 Celebration of Black Alumni (CBA) report, which surveyed black HLS graduates through 1999. While we refer to the original CBA report in our discussion, the individuals contained in the 2000 survey are not necessarily the same individuals contained in the pre-2000 era grouping of the 2016 survey. In addition, those pre-2000 graduates who participated in both surveys were at a different stage in their career when they filled out the 2016 survey. Both of these factors help explain why some of the findings contained in the full report for those in the pre-2000 era may differ from what was reported in 2000. For the sake of brevity, decade-based cohort breakdowns are not displayed. These breakdowns were, however, produced, and we refer to them when they contain important findings.

We also performed statistical significance testing on many tables. An indication of $p < .05$—denoted by * in the tables and figures in this chapter—means that we can be 95 percent confident that the observed difference between the variables in question reflects a true difference in the underlying population and not simply a sampling error. An indication of $p < .01$—denoted by ** in the tables and figures—means that we can be 99 percent confident that the observed difference between variables reflects such a true difference. The standard minimum confidence level for statistical significance for research of this kind is 95 percent.

Significance testing was run to determine whether there were statistically significant differences between men and women, between decade-based cohorts, and between eras. For example, do men present differently from women, or does the pre-2000 era differ from the post-2000 era? We have not yet conducted significant testing or other forms of regression analysis to determine whether there are interaction effects between these various groups—for example, differences between pre-2000 men and post-2000 women.

Finally, sums may not tally exactly to 100 percent due to rounding. Also, seven respondents did not identify their gender and therefore have been excluded from comparisons between men and women, but their answers have otherwise been counted in the response totals for all other purposes.

Law School Enrollment

We start our story at law school, where the ratio of black women to black men at HLS has increased significantly since gender and race numbers were first tracked in the 1980s (table 4-1). In decade-based cohort terms, more than half (54.8 percent) of the 1980s cohort were black men at HLS. With the 2000s cohort, that number had dropped to 40.2 percent. By comparison, the percentage of black women at HLS was just under half

TABLE 4-1

Distribution of gender by cohort

	Male (%)	N-Male	Female (%)	N-Female	Overall (%)	N
1980s	54.8	187	45.2	154	100.0	341
1990s	43.2	272	56.8	357	100.0	629
2000s	40.2	220	59.9	328	100.0	548
2010s	36.0	49	64.0	87	100.0	136
Overall	44.0	728	56.0	926	100.0	1,654

Note: The numbering of the tables and figures presented in this chapter does not correspond with the numbering of those presented in the full report. The full report contains additional tables and figures not presented in this chapter, thereby necessitating a renumbering process. The data contained in the figures and tables in this chapter and the full report is otherwise identical.

(45.2 percent) for the 1980s cohort; however, with the 2000s cohort, it had ballooned to 59.9 percent. This trend continues and appears to be accelerating for the yet-unfinished 2010s cohort, where the percentage of women has increased to 64 percent. Put differently, in the 2010s, nearly two out of every three black students at HLS were women.

Moreover, between 2000 and 2016, in every individual class (as separate from the decade-based cohorts just discussed) apart from 2012, the percentage of black women at HLS was substantially higher than the percentage of black men (table 4-2). Indeed, looking further back in data not shown here, apart from the classes of 1992 and 2012, black women have outnumbered black men in every individual HLS class since gender records have been kept.[10]

HLS is not alone in having higher percentages of black women than men. For instance, at Howard University School of Law, which has graduated more black lawyers than any other school, nearly two-thirds of its black students are women. National data also supports this finding. According to 2009–2013 American Bar Association data on full-time JD enrollment across all association-approved law schools, black women make up, on average, 61 percent of all black law students and black men, 39 percent. Black students constitute just 7.4 percent of all law students. Therefore, black women represent nearly two-thirds of all black law students across the United States.

TABLE 4-2

Black first-year enrollment at HLS: 2000–2016

Year	Black males	Black females	Total black enrollment	Percent black women	Overall HLS enrollment	Percent black
2000	17	36	53	67.9	556	9.5
2001	12	42	54	77.8	558	9.7
2002	20	36	56	64.3	557	10.1
2003	22	32	54	59.3	557	9.7
2004	23	34	57	59.6	558	10.2
2005	33	35	68	51.5	559	12.2
2006	26	41	67	61.2	557	12.0
2007	24	41	65	63.1	559	11.6
2008	31	36	67	53.7	566	11.8
2009	30	37	67	55.2	565	11.9
2010	26	31	57	54.4	560	10.2
2011	24	29	53	54.7	564	9.4
2012	26	19	45	42.2	559	8.1
2013	23	36	59	61.0	569	10.4
2014	16	37	53	69.8	563	9.4
2015	18	32	50	64.0	562	8.9
2016	15	18	33	54.5	563	5.9

It should be noted that the higher proportion of black female law students tracks a more general trend of increased gender parity at law schools, both at HLS and nationally. At HLS, the class of 1975 was 85 percent male and 15 percent female. In 2013, it was 52.4 percent male and 47.6 percent female. For the class of 2019, women outnumber men at time of enrollment—51 percent to 49 percent. Nationally, in 2016, the number of women JD students at American Bar Association–accredited schools was higher than that of men—55,766 to 55,059, with female first-year law students representing 51 percent of new students and male first-year law students 48.6 percent. This trend is not limited to the

FIGURE 4-1

Black first-year law student enrollment at HLS: 2000–2016

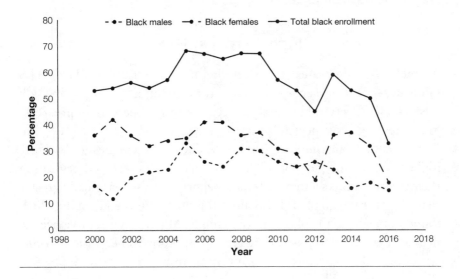

United States. In Norway, women now make up 64 percent of graduating law school classes and have made up more than 60 percent for more than a decade.[11] The case is similar in many other countries around the world. Thus, the fact that black women outnumber black men is not necessarily surprising, given the more general increase in the number of women going to law school. Nevertheless, three points should be stressed.

First, as figure 4-1 illustrates, while black women continue to outnumber black men at HLS, there has been a steep decline in the overall number of black students at the school since 2013, with a 3 percent drop between 2015 and 2016. This decline affects both black men and black women; however, in the most recent years, the greatest drop in numbers is among black women (perhaps due to their greater starting numbers). More research must be done to determine what is driving this drop at HLS.

Second, law schools and those in the profession need to be cognizant of the gender gap when it comes to black law students and, in particular, the increasingly low numbers of black men entering the profession.

Finally, precisely because substantially higher numbers of black women are graduating from law school, the profession has a serious problem as they face significant challenges arising from their race, their gender, and the intersection between the two in building successful and meaningful careers. We turn to examine this issue and the careers of black women lawyers on the basis of our survey data.

First Jobs Post-HLS

As table 4-3 illustrates, the overwhelming majority of black HLS graduates—71.9 percent—entered private practice for their first job post-HLS. This trend holds across eras, with 72.2 percent of pre-2000 graduates entering private practice as their first job post-HLS and 71.5 percent from the post-2000 era. These percentages are slightly higher than the 68 percent of black graduates who reported beginning their careers in this sector in our 2000 report. It is also marginally greater than the percentage of all HLS alumni reported in the HLSCS, which found that, across all cohorts in the sample, 61 percent went to a private firm as their first job post-HLS. Finally, as reported here, the percentage of black HLS graduates beginning their careers in private practice

TABLE 4-3

First jobs post-HLS

	Male (%)	Female (%)	Overall (%)	Pre-2000 (%)	Post-2000 (%)	N
Private practice	71.2	72.8	71.9	72.2	71.5	369
Business (practicing law)	2.4	0.8	1.6	2.7	0.0	8
Business (not practicing law)	8.6**	3.0	6.0	4.7	8.1	31
Government	7.8	6.7	7.2	8.7	5.0	37
Public interest	3.0	6.4	4.7	4.0	5.7	24
Legal services	2.7	7.2*	4.9	4.9	4.8	25
Education	2.0	2.0	2.0	0.3	4.5**	10
Other	2.3	1.1	1.7	2.5	0.4	9
Total	100.0	100.0	100.0	100.0	100.0	513

$*p < .05$
$**p < .01$

is substantially higher than the percentage reported in AJD 1, where only 57.3 percent of black lawyers were working in private law firms of any size two to three years into their careers.

When a gender variable is added, the picture becomes more complicated. Overall, male and female respondents reported entering the private sector at largely the same rate (71.2 percent of men and 72.8 percent of women). However, this overall similarity masks some interesting cohort and era differences. In the 1970s, the percentage of men entering private practice (69.6 percent) was higher than the corresponding percentage of women (40 percent). By the 1980s, however, these percentages had flipped, with 72.2 percent of men entering private practice, as compared with 85.7 percent of women in this cohort. These percentages held stable for the 1990s, with 73.7 percent of men and 85.6 percent of women entering private practice, before arriving at virtual parity for the 2000s cohort (71.9 percent men, 70.9 percent women) and then switching back to the pattern of the 1970s, where men outnumber women in private practice (this time by 82.1 percent to 63.5 percent) in the partial 2010 cohort.

The fact that the percentage of women entering private practice as their first job out of law school exceeds the comparable percentage for men is consistent with what we found in the first black alumni survey in 2000. As we reported in the study, 72 percent of the women in our sample began their careers in private practice, as compared with only 64 percent of men—a gap that was even larger (81 percent to 64 percent) for the 1990s cohort. Viewed from this perspective, the results for the post-2000 era in our current survey constitute a significant development.

Although our data does not allow us to explain these shifting patterns fully, the fact that the percentage of women who started their careers in government in the 1970s was more than three times greater than the percentage of men who did so (25 percent to 7.2 percent), while the percentage of men entering this sector is greater than the percentage of women for every other cohort except for 2010 (where no men went directly into government service), undoubtedly plays a role. At the same time, the percentage of men who began their careers in businesses where they were not practicing law is almost three times that for women whose first job was in this sector, although the percentage of women who started their careers this way has increased nearly tenfold (from 0.6 percent to 5.6 percent) between the pre- and post-2000 eras.

With respect to those entering the public interest and legal services sectors as their first jobs out of law school, the picture looks similar to what we found in 2000. In the 2000 survey, approximately 9 percent of our sample was initially employed across these two sectors. This is almost identical to the 8.6 percent of respondents whose initial job was public interest or legal services in our current sample. Moreover, there is virtually no difference between the pre- and post-2000 eras on this point, with 8.9 percent of pre-2000 era respondents and 10.5 percent of post-2000 respondents initially joining this sector.

Given all the changes in the world during the six decades covered by this study—including changes in the cost of HLS and the introduction of programs specifically designed to boost the percentage of students going into public interest and legal services—the consistency of these percentages suggests that other factors besides student debt and law school programs are influencing whether graduates begin their careers in these fields. Having said this, women continue to be more likely to start their careers in public interest and legal services jobs than men—a difference that, unlike what we found in 2000, where the difference between women and men starting in these areas had largely disappeared by the 1990s cohort, does not appear to be going away, according to our new study. This is particularly true with respect to public interest, as, shockingly, none of the men in the post-2000 era who responded to our survey began their careers in this sector.

Firm Size, First Job Post-HLS

For those black graduates who began their careers in private practice, the overwhelming majority did so by joining large law firms, with 82 percent in firms with more than 100 lawyers and 61.7 percent in firms of 251 or more lawyers (table 4-4). There is a significant cohort and era effect, with more than 92 percent of the post-2000 era starting in large law firms (82.6 percent in firms of 251 or more lawyers). Results are parallel to the 2000 report and the HLSCS.

As we found in 2000, black women are significantly more likely than men to begin their careers in the largest law firms, with 70 percent of women joining firms of 251 lawyers or more and only 53.3 percent of men joining firms of the same size—a highly statistically significant difference. Moreover, this gender difference is increasing over time. In the 1990s cohort, roughly equal percentages of women and men joined law

TABLE 4-4

Firm size (first job post-HLS)

	Male (%)	Female (%)	Overall (%)	Pre-2000 (%)	Post-2000 (%)	N
Solo	0.0	1.0	0.5	0.4	0.5	2
2–50	9.7	5.5	7.6	10.1*	7.6	28
51–100	13.6**	6.2	10.0	14.8	10.0	37
101–250	23.4	17.3	20.3	26.5	10.7	75
251+	53.3	70.0**	61.7	48.1	82.6*	228
Total	100.0	100.0	100.0	100.0	100.0	370

*$p < .05$
**$p < .01$

firms of 251 or more lawyers (similar to what we found in 2000). For post-2000 era graduates, however, women joined such firms at significantly higher percentages than men (87.5 percent women versus 76.2 percent men). It is important to note that these percentages are the inverse of those in national studies such as the AJD, where black women are shown to be significantly less likely than black men to start their careers in private firms.

The fact that black women are both graduating law school at higher rates than black men *and starting their careers in the largest law firms at higher rates than black men* is important context as we examine the percentages of black women who remain in private practice, obtain partnership, and enter firm leadership.

Current Jobs

Overall, our data shows a dramatic migration out of private practice and into other employment sectors—71.9 percent (first job in private practice) to 26.6 percent (current)—a 63 percent decrease (figure 4-2). While this finding confirms what we know about lawyers' careers over time, it should be stressed that black HLS graduates—both men and women—migrate out of private practice at much higher rates than both white and black lawyers nationally. Thus, the AJD study found that

FIGURE 4-2

Current job

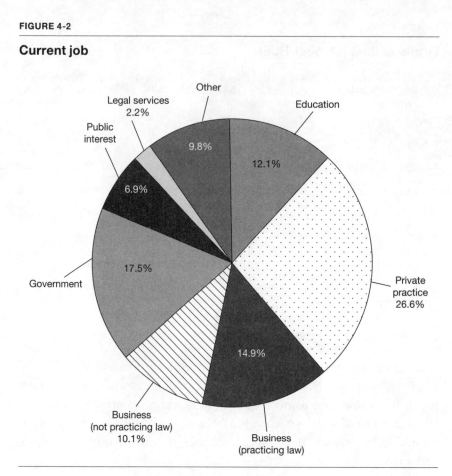

38 percent of black lawyers in private practice in AJD 1 had left the sector by AJD 3—10 percent more than the 28 percent of white lawyers who did so, but a full 22 percent below our finding here.

This, of course, raises the question of where black HLS graduates are migrating to when they leave private practice. Again, our data confirms what we know about HLS and national legal careers more generally. The largest movement was toward business (practicing law)—from 1.6 percent initially to 14.9 percent for current jobs. There was also significant migration into government (7.2 percent to 17.5 percent), education (2 percent to 12.1 percent), public interest (4.7 percent to 6.9 percent), and business (not practicing law) (6.9 percent to 10.1 percent). Legal services (2.4 percent to 2.2 percent) remained relatively stable.

TABLE 4-5

Current job

	Male (%)	Female (%)	Overall (%)	Pre-2000 (%)	Post-2000 (%)	N
Private practice	33.8**	19.6	26.6	22.5	32.2**	120
Business (practicing law)	15.7	14.2	14.9	16.1	13.2	67
Business (not practicing law)	12.9*	7.3	10.1	11.1	8.7	45
Government	15.5	19.6	17.5	16.0	19.6	79
Public interest	3.4	10.4**	6.9	7.4	6.2	31
Legal services	0.0	4.4**	2.2	0.9	4.0*	10
Education	9.9	14.3	12.1	11.9	12.4	55
Other	8.8	10.3	9.8	14.0**	3.8	44
Total	100.0	100.0	100.0	100.0	100.0	451

$*p < .05$
$**p < .01$

Adding in the gender variable, male respondents were significantly more likely to remain in private practice (33.8 percent) and business (not practicing law) (12.9 percent) as compared with female respondents (19.6 percent and 7.3 percent, respectively) (table 4-5). This difference is statistically significant. These trends remained true across the pre- and post-2000 eras. Thus, while both men and women migrate out of practice over time, women do so at greater rates than their male colleagues. Men are also more likely to be in business (not practicing law) than women. Both findings are supported by the HLSCS and the AJD study, offering evidence that these trends hold for black and nonblack populations.

At the same time, both in the aggregate and across the pre- and post-2000 eras, female respondents were more likely to be in public interest (10.4 percent) and legal services (4.4 percent) at the time of the survey than their male colleagues (3.4 percent and less than 1 percent, respectively). Women were also represented at higher rates (14.3 percent) than men (9.9 percent) in education.

Firm Size, Current Job

For those respondents who reported being in private practice for their current jobs, we see a distinct shift regarding the size of their firms relative to the size of firms reported for first jobs post-HLS. The majority of both male and female respondents who went into private law practice right out of law school joined firms of 251 or more lawyers, with only 7.6 percent going into firms with 2–50 lawyers and less than 1 percent into solo practice. By contrast, the firm size of respondents who reported currently being in private practice was bimodal (table 4-6). On the one hand, 49.4 percent reported working at firms of 251 or more lawyers. On the other hand, almost an equal percentage (41.3 percent) reported that they were either in solo practice (13 percent) or in a firm of 2–50 lawyers (28.3 percent).

This pattern is largely the result of age, with a higher percentage of respondents from older cohorts reporting that they were in solo practices or small firms, while those from more recent cohorts report being in the large law firms where they typically began their careers. Thus, respondents from the 1970s were heavily skewed toward solo practice and smaller firms (27.8 percent in solo practice and 50 percent in firms with 2–50 lawyers). The 2010s cohort, by contrast, reported 73.4 percent in firms of 251 or more lawyers, although the 23.2 percent in firms of 2–50

TABLE 4-6

Firm size (current job)

	Male (%)	Female (%)	Overall (%)	Pre-2000 (%)	Post-2000 (%)	N
Solo	13.9	11.5	13.0	24.9**	1.4	15
2–50	35.9**	15.3	28.3	33.9	22.8	32
51–100	4.9	0.0	3.1	6.2	0.0	3
101–250	6.7	5.6	6.3	6.6	6.0	7
251+	38.6	67.6	49.4	28.3	69.8**	56
Total	100.0	100.0	100.0	100.0	100.0	113

$**p < .01$

is still greater than the percentage of this cohort who started out in firms of that size. The 1980s, 1990s, and 2000s cohorts generally follow this pattern, which is clear from the era-based differences.

Respondents from the pre-2000 era reported being in solo practice 24.9 percent of the time and at firms with 2–50 lawyers 33.9 percent of the time—for a combined percentage of 58.8 percent. By contrast, 69.8 percent of respondents in the post-2000 era reported being in firms of 251 or more lawyers. All these differences are highly statistically significant.

Law Firm Partnership

Nationally, black lawyers of both genders continue to be underrepresented in large law firms, particularly among the partners in these institutions. Available data from the National Association of Law Placement underscores the extent of the problem. Thus, the average black partnership rate between 2005 and 2016 is just 1.7 percent, with a peak of 1.81 percent in 2016 and a low of 1.55 percent in 2005. As dreary as these percentages are, those pertaining to black female partners in these institutions are even worse. In 2016, for example, African American women constituted just 0.64 percent of all partners in the National Association of Law Placement sample, up only slightly from the 0.59 percent of black female partners reported in 2006. One of the goals of the survey project is to see whether black HLS graduates are doing better than the picture painted by these bleak statistics.

There are reasons to believe that black HLS graduates may indeed be more likely to become partners in law firms than these averages suggest. As indicated earlier, more black HLS graduates begin their careers in large law firms than what data from the AJD study suggests is true for black graduates nationally. Moreover, a study of all black partners listed in the 1992–1993 edition of the American Bar Association's *Directory of Partners at Majority/Corporate Law Firms* indicated that nearly half (47 percent) of all the black partners listed obtained their law degrees from either Harvard or Yale, with more than three-quarters (77 percent) having attended one of the country's twelve most prestigious law schools as ranked by *U.S. News and World Report.*[12] Anecdotal reports from interviews with black lawyers underscore that attending HLS or another similarly elite school dramatically improves a black lawyer's chances of succeeding in a large law firm—or any other sector of the legal profession.[13]

Data from our 2000 survey provided additional support for the hypothesis that black HLS graduates are making partner in larger numbers than the overall statistics cited earlier would suggest. In that study, we found that among those who were in private practice at the time of the survey, 42 percent were partners, with 37 percent reporting being equity partners. That study also revealed, however, that in one important respect the careers of black HLS graduates appeared to mirror national trends: controlling for cohort, black men were far more likely than black women to report being partners. For example, among those in the 1980s cohort who were still in private practice, 74 percent of men reported being equity partners, as compared with only 48 percent of women—although this latter percentage is still large compared to the negligible percentage of all equity partners who are African American women nationally.

Our current survey echoes these prior findings. Of respondents still in private practice at the time of the survey, 40.4 percent reported being either equity or nonequity partners in law firms (table 4-7). Not surprisingly, there is a significant era impact, with only 8.9 percent of respondents in the post-2000 era reporting being partners, compared to a stunning 72.8 percent of those in the pre-2000 era.

There is also a strong gender effect, with male respondents more than 1.5 times more likely to be made partner (47.3 percent) than female respondents (28.6 percent), suggesting that whatever the firm size, black women continue to be especially disadvantaged by the partnership process. This is particularly troubling to the extent that the majority of black

TABLE 4-7

Partnership (current job)

	Male (%)	Female (%)	Overall (%)	Pre-2000 (%)	Post-2000 (%)	N
Yes	47.3*	28.6	40.4	72.8	8.9	67
No	52.7	71.4*	59.6	27.2	91.0	46
Total	100.0	100.0	100.0	100.0	100.0	113

*p < .05

law graduates are women, and black men and women are entering law firms at largely the same rate (indeed, black women at a slightly higher rate than black men) for their first jobs post-HLS.

Moreover, in assessing these findings, it is important to remember that while many in the pre-2000 era may be partners, a significant percentage of these lawyers are likely to be partners in small or midsize firms. As we indicate shortly, a large number of the black graduates who begin their careers at the largest law firms end up leaving well before they become eligible for partnership. This impacts the foregoing finding in two important respects.

First, although the percentage of respondents from the pre-2000 era who remained in private practice and reported being partners is quite high (and considerably higher than the 42 percent who reported being partners in our 2000 survey), the actual number of lawyers in this category is relatively small since, as we also indicate later, many of the lawyers have left the private sector and now work in jobs in the public sector or have left the workforce entirely. Of the 369 lawyers in our sample who started their careers in private practice, fewer than one-third (120) were still in private practice at the time that we asked them about their current jobs.

Second, of those who were still in private practice at the time of our survey, many had migrated to small and midsize firms where they have become partners, often equity partners. As table 4-6 indicates, of those currently in private practice, 44.4 percent are in law firms with fewer than 100 lawyers, with 41.3 percent in firms of 50 lawyers or fewer. As a result, the high partnership percentages do not necessarily tell the whole story about whether black HLS graduates are making partner in large law firms in significantly greater numbers than black graduates from other law schools.

Overall partnership levels also mask important differences in the power, prestige, and pay garnered by partners who have equity in the firm and those who do not. To test whether black partners were disproportionately represented in the nonequity category, we asked those who reported that they were partners whether they had equity in their law firms (table 4-8). Nearly three-quarters (73.9 percent) answered yes, describing themselves as equity partners in their firms. Although obviously high, this percentage is still nearly 10 points below the 82 percent of HLS graduates as a whole who reported being equity partners in the HLSCS. Interestingly, a higher percentage of female respondents

TABLE 4-8

Partnership (current job, equity or not)

	Male (%)	Female (%)	Overall (%)	Pre-2000 (%)	Post-2000 (%)	N
Equity	21.1	40.1	73.9	70.6	0.0	33
Nonequity	78.9	59.9	26.1	29.4	100.0	12
Total	100.0	100.0	100.0	100.0	100.0	45

reported being equity partners (40.1 percent) than male respondents (21.1 percent); however, this difference was not found to be statistically significant, primarily because the overall number of black equity partners (thirty-three) is so small.

Firm Management

As we reported in the HLSCS, research on the legal profession makes clear that in today's law firms, making partner is just the beginning of a new competition to become a "partner with power" within the organization.[14] To that end, we asked respondents who indicated that they had been an equity partner in a law firm at any point in their career whether they had been actively involved in the management of their firm (e.g., served on a firm committee or in a leadership role, such as department chair or office head), and if so, on which committees and in which roles (e.g., member of the compensation committee, chair of the diversity committee, or office managing partner). As indicated earlier, the number of respondents eligible to respond to these questions—those who had ever been equity partners—is relatively small, with most coming from the pre-2000 era. Nevertheless, even with these caveats, the results are instructive. Overall, nearly 80 percent of respondents indicated that they were involved in firm management at some point in their careers.

A similarly large percentage of respondents reported serving on one of the eight common law firm committees—management, compensation, recruiting, associate evaluation, work assignment, diversity, ethics or conflicts, and pro bono—that we identified in the survey. Although the highest percentage of respondents reported serving on the recruiting committee (81 percent), which is not considered to be an especially powerful committee in most law firms, a significant percentage reported

serving on committees that are widely considered among the most important in law firms, including the management committee (71.6 percent)
and the compensation committee (62.1 percent). Indeed, a far greater
percentage of respondents reported serving on these important committees than on committees such as diversity (58.5 percent), ethics or
conflicts (32 percent), and pro bono (25.4 percent), which, though undoubtedly important, are not thought to produce important career
advantages.

Moreover, of those who served on the most important committees, a
very high percentage reported that they had at one time been the committee's chair. Thus, 62.1 percent of those who had ever served on the
management committee and 47.2 percent of those who had ever served on
a compensation committee reported that at some point they served as
that committee's chair. When one adds the fact that nearly two-thirds of
respondents (64 percent) reported serving as either a department chair or
the firm's managing partner, it appears that black HLS graduates have
managed to break through the "concrete ceiling" that so many black
lawyers have found in large law firms.

But just as was true with the partnership rates discussed earlier, these
percentages are likely to mask important differences. As indicated, many
of those in our sample who have become equity partners have done so
in small and midsize firms. As a result, many of those who report having served in leadership positions are likely to have done so in smaller
firms. However, three pioneers, all from HLS, have broken through the
concrete ceiling by becoming managing partners of top law firms:
John W. Daniels Jr., managing partner of Quarles & Brady, 2007–2013
(currently chair emeritus); Benjamin F. Wilson, managing partner
(2007–present) and chair (2017–present) of Beveridge & Diamond; and
Maurice Watson, chair of Husch Blackwell (2012–2018).

Moreover, regardless of firm size, the overall percentage of black
lawyers in leadership positions obscures very significant differences between the opportunities and experiences of men and women in virtually
every leadership category we investigated. Our survey found that
92 percent of all black HLS graduates to ever serve as managing partner or as a department head have been men. Similarly, 79.1 percent of
those reporting that they have been on the management committee and
89.3 percent of those reporting having served on the compensation committee are male. Indeed, these percentages hold for every committee we
identified—and become even more skewed toward men with respect to

leadership on committees. For example, 87.5 percent of all those reporting that they have chaired the management committee are men. Clearly, the disadvantages faced by black women attempting to move into leadership positions in law firms apply even to women who have obtained a prestigious law degree from HLS.

Job Changes

In addition to looking at mobility generally, the survey also attempts to track whether black HLS graduates are changing *sectors* as well as jobs. To investigate this question, we looked at the current jobs of all the lawyers who started their careers in private practice (consisting of solo practice and law firms of all sizes) and public service (including government, public interest, and legal services). Of particular interest for this chapter are those who started in private practice.

As table 4-9 demonstrates, only 28.5 percent of all black HLS graduates who started their careers in private practice were still working in that sector at the time of the survey. This is down dramatically from the 71.9 percent of our sample who began their career in this sector. Not surprisingly, there is a large era effect, with 40.7 percent of post-2000 graduates remaining in private practice, as compared to only 20.8 percent of those who graduated in the pre-2000 era, a difference that is statistically significant at the highest confidence level. Interestingly, this latter figure is also much lower than the 39 percent of graduates who started their careers in private practice who were still in this sector as of the time of our first survey in 2000, suggesting that older cohorts have continued to move out of private practice since we conducted that initial investigation.

For the more than two-thirds of respondents no longer in private practice, the most common destination for their current employment was business (practicing law), which typically means in-house legal departments (17.7 percent). This result, which holds relatively constant across both eras and cohorts (with the exception of the partial 2010 cohort, of which, not surprisingly, relatively few have moved into in-house legal departments), reflects the general trend found both in the AJD study and in the HLSCS of lawyers moving from private practice to positions in corporate legal departments. It is also consistent with what we found in 2000, where 18 percent had moved from private practice into in-house legal departments. The pattern of movement from private practice to

TABLE 4-9

Current job (initially in private practice)

	Male (%)	Female (%)	Overall (%)	Pre-2000 (%)	Post-2000 (%)	N
Private practice	36.0**	20.9	28.5	20.8	40.7**	101
Business (practicing law)	17.4	18.0	17.7	17.3	18.3	63
Business (not practicing law)	9.2	8.0	8.6	9.8	6.6	30
Government	12.8	18.7	15.7	13.0	20.0	56
Public interest	2.8	8.6*	5.7	6.9	3.7	20
Legal services	0.0	1.0	0.5	0.0	1.2	2
Education	6.5	9.9	8.1	9.6	5.8	29
Other	5.5	10.4	7.9	11.7**	1.8	28
Not in the paid workforce	9.7**	4.5	7.4	10.8**	2.0	26
Total	100.0	100.0	100.0	100.0	100.0	355

*$p < .05$
**$p < .01$

other areas (e.g., public interest, education, or business) remains remarkably stable between the 2000 and 2016 surveys, with the exception of business (not practicing law)—a category that encompasses everything from investment banking to selling insurance, although black HLS graduates are more likely to be doing the former than the latter—which actually declined as a destination of those starting out in private practice from 14 percent in 2000 to 8.6 percent in 2016.

Again there are, however, important gender differences that underscore the difficulties faced by women in general, and black women in particular, in private practice. The survey found that men are much more likely than women to still be working in private practice at the time of the survey (36 percent versus 20.9 percent), a difference that is highly statistically significant. The fact that barely 20 percent of all the black HLS women who started out in private practice remain in this sector as their current jobs will certainly come as bad news for those who seek to increase the diversity of large law firms. Conversely, black women who started work in private practice are significantly more likely than their black male counterparts to be currently working in the public interest sector (8.6 percent versus 2.8 percent), providing further support for the view that women are more likely than men to be involved in various kinds of public service, a finding supported by the HLSCS.

Race and Career Advancement

Both scholars seeking to study the legal profession and activists seeking to improve it have long struggled to understand how race affects legal careers. To investigate this critical issue, we asked questions designed to explore different avenues in which race might affect career opportunities for black lawyers. More specifically, we asked respondents to rank a set of factors internal to the workplace (table 4-10) and in the external environment (table 4-11) that other studies have suggested may influence career opportunities for black lawyers. With respect to both questions, respondents ranked the factors listed on a seven-point scale, where 1 is "not important at all" and 7 is "extremely important."

Table 4-10 examines the interaction of race with several issues that are common to the typical legal workplace. As an initial matter, this table confirms the view that the issues black HLS lawyers believe to be most important to their careers are similar to what research tells us is important to the advancement of any lawyer's career.[15] Thus, black HLS graduates ranked having an influential mentor or sponsor and gaining access to difficult or prestigious assignments as the two most important factors in their career success, and the only factors that crossed the line into being "extremely important" on our seven-point scale. Table 4-10 also underscores, however, that there are internal areas where black HLS graduates believe that race plays a distinct role in their career advancement—areas that are seen differently by women and men, and by black lawyers in the pre-2000 era and those in the post-2000 era.

With respect to gender, black HLS men were significantly more conscious about "not making mistakes," while black HLS women were significantly more focused on the "quality" of their work, concentrating on the necessity of doing higher-quality work than their white counterparts rather than simply avoiding mistakes. Female respondents were also acutely aware of the social dimensions of their jobs, paying significantly more attention than their male counterparts to networking with other

TABLE 4-10

Importance of internal career advancement opportunities

	Male	Female	Overall	Pre-2000	Post-2000	N
Access to difficult or prestigious assignments	6.1	6.0	6.1	6.2**	5.9	459
Not making mistakes	5.6*	5.3	5.5	5.6**	5.3	461
Developing a style that makes whites feel comfortable	5.7	5.6	5.6	5.6	5.6	459
Changing firms/ companies	4.3	4.5	4.4	4.4	4.3	453
Having an influential mentor or sponsor	6.2	6.4	6.3	6.2	6.4*	458
Networking with other black lawyers	4.4	4.7*	4.5	4.5	4.5	457
Practicing in a racially diverse community	4.3	4.8**	4.6	4.5	4.6	456
Working longer hours than most whites	4.7	4.7	4.7	4.8	4.6	458
Doing higher-quality work than most whites	5.5	5.8*	5.6	5.6	5.6	457
Not disclosing personal or political views	4.1	4.3	4.2	4.1	4.3	459
Socializing with white coworkers	5.5	5.7*	5.6	5.4	5.9**	460

*p < .05
**p < .01

Note: Respondents ranked the factors listed on a seven-point scale, where 1 is "not important at all" and 7 is "extremely important." The values in this table are averages of the respondents' rankings for each factor.

black professionals, practicing in a racially diverse community, and socializing with their white peers.

There were also interesting differences across eras. Black lawyers from the post-2000 period ranked having an influential mentor or sponsor and socializing with white peers as important at higher levels than their pre-2000 counterparts—though both view these factors as key. Those in the pre-2000 cohort, on the other hand, are more focused on getting access to difficult assignments and not making mistakes. Although admittedly speculative, these results are consistent with the view expressed by many scholars and diversity advocates that the battleground has shifted from combating pervasive stereotypes about black intellectual inferiority (through, among other things, doing difficult assignments and not making mistakes) to being able to "fit in" with white coworkers who can sponsor one's career.[16]

Table 4-11 applies this same kind of analysis to a range of factors external to the workplace. As this table starkly demonstrates, the most important factor that has affected the careers of the black HLS graduates in our sample is the law school's prestige. This "H-bomb effect," as one of the study's coauthors has heard countless black alumni refer to the benefit of their HLS degree, is the only factor that rises above neutrality among the list of things commonly mentioned by scholars and career counselors as being career enhancing. Even connections with HLS alumni—including black alumni—barely registers as an important career-building factor among black HLS alumni. Interestingly, while

TABLE 4-11

Importance of external factors to career advancement

	Male	Female	Overall	Pre-2000	Post-2000	N
Connections with black HLS classmates/alumni	3.0	3.1	3.0	2.9	3.3	449
Connections with other HLS classmates/alumni	3.2	3.1	3.1	3.1	3.3	448
HLS prestige	5.9	6.1	6.0	6.0	5.9	457
Employer affirmative action or diversity initiatives	3.4	3.7	3.6	3.7	3.4	450
Client-sponsored diversity initiatives	2.3	2.3	2.3	2.2	2.4	446
Bar association–sponsored diversity initiatives	1.7	1.8	1.7	1.7	1.8	449
Government minority contracting or set-aside programs	1.7	1.5	1.6	1.7	1.5	446

Note: Respondents ranked the factors listed on a seven-point scale, where 1 is "not important at all" and 7 is "extremely important." The values in this table are averages of the respondents' rankings for each factor.

employer diversity initiatives do come close to being viewed as "moderately important" by respondents, client- and bar association–sponsored initiatives and government "set aside" programs were not. This view that formal diversity and affirmative action programs have not played a significant role in advancing the careers of the black HLS graduates in our survey is consistent across eras, cohorts, and gender, and is very similar to what we found in 2000. These findings provide support for the work done by Frank Dobbin and colleagues indicating that formal diversity efforts are often largely ineffective, and sometimes even counterproductive.[17]

Satisfaction

It is the hope of every law school graduate that he or she will be able to build a satisfying career. The survey therefore asked a series of questions designed to investigate whether black HLS graduates believe that they have been able to achieve this goal. Specifically, we asked respondents to rank on a seven-point scale, where 1 is "extremely dissatisfied" and 7 is "extremely satisfied," their level of satisfaction with their current job and their decision to become a lawyer. We also asked whether, knowing what they know today, they would still attend law school. Of those who were dissatisfied with their decision to become a lawyer, we asked whether their unhappiness with the profession was due to race. Finally, we asked respondents whether they would recommend to a young person that he or she enter the legal profession, and if not, whether that decision was because of race. When taken as a whole, the data provided by these questions underscores that black HLS graduates are very satisfied with their careers, a conclusion that should not be surprising given their talent and accomplishments. The data also reveals, however, important differences in satisfaction levels across practice areas, cohorts, and eras, as well as between women and men. These differences have important implications for those seeking greater racial diversity in the legal profession.

Table 4-12 reports respondents' overall satisfaction with their careers by employment sector. As the data indicates, black HLS graduates tend to be highly satisfied with their current jobs (an overall average of 5.7), with only a modest difference between the satisfaction levels reported by men (5.8) and women (5.6). This finding is consistent with the AJD study, which found that more than 70 percent of lawyers are moderately to extremely satisfied with their careers.

TABLE 4-12

Career satisfaction (current job)

	Male	Female	Overall	Pre-2000	Post-2000	N
Private practice	5.6	4.8	5.3	5.8	4.8	102
Business (practicing law)	5.9	5.4	5.7	5.6	5.8	59
Business (not practicing law)	5.7	5.6	5.7	6.2	4.8	43
Government	5.6	5.8	5.7	5.8	5.6	74
Public interest	5.4	5.9	5.8	5.7	5.9	33
Legal services	-	5.8	5.8	6.3	5.7	12
Education	7.0	6.1	6.4*	6.4	6.4	53
Other	6.1	5.6	5.7	5.8	5.3	41
Total	5.8	5.6	5.7	5.9	5.4	417

*$p < .05$

Note: Respondents ranked the factors listed on a seven-point scale, where 1 is "extremely dissatisfied" and 7 is "extremely satisfied." The values in this table are averages of the respondents' rankings for each factor.

When we look more closely at particular employment sectors and eras, however, important differences in career satisfaction begin to emerge. While average satisfaction across all employment sectors is above 5 on our seven-point scale, private practice has the lowest average (5.3) of any sector, substantially below the levels of satisfaction reported by those in public-sector careers (which range from 5.7 for government lawyers to 5.8 for those in public interest and legal services) and in business (5.7 for both those practicing and those not practicing law)—let alone the average satisfaction level of 6.4 for those in the education sector. Moreover, the average satisfaction level of those in private practice has been steadily falling over time, with those in the post-2000 era reporting satisfaction that is a full point lower than their pre-2000 counterparts (4.8 for post-2000, 5.8 for pre-2000). Indeed, those in the most recent classes to graduate from HLS (2010–2016) expressed the lowest satisfaction with private practice of any cohort in our study (4.3), which was more than two full points below the average satisfaction of those who graduated in the 1970s (6.4). Given that the overwhelming majority of those who are in private practice in the 2010s cohort are still in large law firms, the fact that on average these graduates are barely satisfied with their careers to date does not bode well for diversity efforts in these institutions.

Perhaps most critical, the black women in our sample consistently reported being less satisfied with their careers in private practice (4.8) than their black male counterparts (5.6). Once again, women in the post-2000 cohort are even less satisfied with their private-practice careers (4.3) than their pre-2000 counterparts (5.6), who report average satisfaction levels that are close to those reported by men (5.8). Women in the 2010s cohort reported the lowest satisfaction levels (4.1) of any cohort in our study. Given that black women graduating from law school significantly outnumber black men, including at HLS, the low levels of satisfaction with private practice—and large law firms in particular—reported by HLS black female graduates post-2000 should be particularly concerning for those seeking greater diversity in this sector.

Notwithstanding these differences in satisfaction levels with their current jobs, the overwhelming majority of respondents expressed high levels of satisfaction with their decision to become a lawyer, reporting an average of 5.9 on our seven-point scale (table 4-13). As the foregoing would suggest, those in the pre-2000 era expressed significantly greater satisfaction with this decision than graduates from the post-2000 era (6.1 pre-2000, 5.6 post-2000). Men were also significantly more satisfied than women with this decision (6.1 men, 5.8 women), again particularly troubling given that black women constitute the majority of black lawyers.

When asked whether, knowing what they know today, they would still obtain a law degree, as table 4-14 documents, the overwhelming majority

TABLE 4-13

Satisfaction with decision to become a lawyer

	Male	Female	Overall	Pre-2000	Post-2000	N
Satisfaction with decision to become a lawyer	6.1*	5.8	5.9	6.1**	5.6	458

*$p < .05$
**$p < .01$

Note: Respondents ranked the factors listed on a seven-point scale, where 1 is "extremely dissatisfied" and 7 is "extremely satisfied." The values in this table are averages of the respondents' rankings for each factor.

TABLE 4-14

Would still attend law school

	Male (%)	Female (%)	Overall (%)	Pre-2000 (%)	Post-2000 (%)	N
Yes	88.7	86.4	87.7	86.3	90.0	403
No	11.3	13.6	12.3	13.7	10.0	57
Total	100.0	100.0	100.0	100.0	100.0	460

of respondents (87.7 percent) answered yes. This result is remarkably consistent over time. Indeed, those in the post-2000 era actually expressed slightly higher support for obtaining a law degree than their pre-2000 counterparts (90 percent post-2000, 86.3 percent pre-2000), with those in the 2010s cohort expressing agreement at a level that is nearly identical to the average for the sample as a whole (87 percent). Given that many in this last cohort are still in large law firms, where, as indicated earlier, many are only marginally satisfied with their careers, this underscores that the black lawyers in our sample do not conflate the value of getting a law degree with the satisfaction that they have so far found with their first legal job in a large law firm. These results are consistent with—indeed, even slightly more positive than—our findings in the HLSCS, where 85.7 percent of all HLS graduates reported that they would still obtain a law degree today.

The data tells a similar story with respect to gender. Notwithstanding the many differences in satisfaction levels—and the underlying professional opportunities that no doubt contribute to satisfaction—between women and men documented in this report and other similar studies, the overwhelming majority of black female HLS graduates (86.4 percent) would still obtain a law degree today, even knowing everything they now know about the disproportionate burdens that black women are likely to encounter in the profession. The fact that women in the post-2000 era are even slightly more positive about their decision to go to law school than their pre-2000 counterparts (87.4 percent post-2000, 85.6 percent pre-2000), and that there is only a modest decline in agreement for women in the 2010s cohort (82.4 percent), underscores that as challenging as law may be for black women, many still believe that it is a better option than the available alternatives. Moreover, even for those women and men who would not choose to go to law school today, very few reported that race would be their reason for not doing so.

Finally, we asked respondents whether they would recommend law to a young person seeking advice about potential careers. Here, the results are less encouraging for the profession (table 4-15). Although nearly 90 percent of respondents indicated they personally would still obtain a law degree, only 66.2 percent reported that they would recommend doing so to a young person seeking career advice. Moreover, as with career satisfaction in general, the percentage of those who would recommend law as a career has been declining over time. Indeed, only 57.9 percent of graduates in the post-2000 era would encourage a young person to go to law school, as compared to more than 70 percent of those graduating in the pre-2000 era, a statistically significant difference. And as was true with satisfaction generally, those in the most recent 2010s cohort reported the lowest percentage of those willing to recommend law as a career, with just a little more than half (54.6 percent) reporting that they would do so—a far cry from those graduating in the 1970s and 1980s, where, respectively, 75.3 percent and 77 percent of black graduates would encourage a young person to go to law school. Once again, this data—which is similar to what we found in the HLSCS, where more than 85 percent of respondents reported that they would still get a law degree today, but only 70 percent would recommend law to a young person—does not bode well for the profession's future.

Nor does the fact that male respondents were much more likely to recommend law to a young person (70 percent) than female respondents

TABLE 4-15

Would recommend law to a young person

	Male (%)	Female (%)	Overall (%)	Pre-2000 (%)	Post-2000 (%)	N
Yes	70.0*	62.1	66.2	70.9**	57.9	299
No	30.0	37.9	33.8	29.1	42.1	153
Total	100.0	100.0	100.0	100.0	100.0	452

*$p < .05$
**$p < .01$

(62.1 percent), again a statistically significant result. Moreover, female respondents from the post-2000 era are even less likely to encourage a young person to go into law than those in the pre-2000 era (59 percent post-2000, 64.6 percent pre-2000), with women in the most recent 2010s cohort even less likely to do so (55.1 percent). This drop over time is particularly worrisome. Although very few of those who would not recommend law to a young person cited race as the primary reason for not doing so, these results nevertheless underscore just how difficult it is going to be to make progress on achieving diversity in the legal profession if those who have arguably been among the most successful black lawyers are not enthusiastically encouraging young black women and men to follow in their footsteps.

Attitudes of Racial Progress

In addition to investigating how race and other factors have structured their individual careers, we also asked respondents to report their views about racial issues more broadly. Specifically, we asked respondents to respond to two questions, the first asking for their views about a range of issues relating to racial progress generally (table 4-16), and the second regarding what—if any—effect Barack Obama's presidency has had on opportunities for black lawyers (table 4-17). For each question, we asked respondents to rank their agreement or disagreement with particular statements on a seven-point scale, where 1 equals "strongly disagree" and 7 equals "strongly agree."

Table 4-16 reports the results for the question regarding racial progress. Overall, there are significant differences in the levels of support for the various propositions addressed in the question. The most salient finding is that African American HLS graduates believe quite strongly that black lawyers continue to face discrimination in the workplace (5.7), and that employers should engage in affirmative action to counteract this disadvantage and to promote diversity in the profession (6.1). Black men were significantly more likely to support this latter proposition than black women (6.2 versus 5.9), although support for affirmative action was high among both genders. These rankings are only slightly lower than what we found in 2000 (5.92 for discrimination, 6.3 for affirmative action), suggesting that events over the intervening sixteen years—including the election of President Obama—have not changed black HLS graduates' perception of the way race continues to structure legal

TABLE 4-16

Attitudes on racial progress

	Male	Female	Overall	Pre-2000	Post-2000	N
Law firms should engage in affirmative action	6.2**	5.9	6.1	6.1	6.0	441
Black lawyers have an obligation to use their legal skills for the black community	5.4	5.2	5.3	5.4	5.2	440
Black lawyers are doing enough to improve the black community	3.7	3.6	3.7	3.7	3.5	440
Professional opportunities for black lawyers have improved since law school	4.5**	4.1	4.3	4.7**	3.6	441
Black lawyers still face significant discrimination in the workplace	5.7	5.7	5.7	5.8	5.6	440
I am optimistic about the progress black lawyers are making in achieving professional success	4.8	4.7	4.7	4.8	4.6	436
Diversity training is an effective tool for combating the obstacles facing black lawyers	4.6**	4.3	4.5	4.5*	4.3	435
My race is an advantage in getting access to good work and/or professional opportunities	3.2	3.2	3.2	3.2	3.3	437
Black lawyers need to take more responsibility for their own careers	4.7**	4.3	4.5	4.7**	4.3	437
My racial identity has grown less important as I have progressed through my career	3.5**	2.8	3.2	3.3**	2.9	439
Progress for black Americans now depends more on economic change than on legal change	4.6**	3.9	4.3	4.4	4.1	438

*$p < .05$
**$p < .01$

Note: Respondents ranked their level of agreement with each statement on a seven-point scale, where 1 is "strongly disagree" and 7 is "strongly agree." The values in this table are averages of the respondents' rankings for each statement.

careers. Outside of this bedrock perception, attitudes about precisely how race continues to structure careers—and what to do about its continuing effects—were considerably more mixed. The only other statement in table 4-16 that elicited average agreement above 5 was that "[b]lack lawyers have an obligation to use their legal skills for the black community" (5.3), signaling broad support for what one of the authors of this chapter has elsewhere called "the obligation thesis."[18]

Although there was widespread agreement that black lawyers have such race-based obligations, far fewer respondents agreed (3.7) that black lawyers were currently doing enough to discharge this duty. Similarly, there was fairly widespread disagreement with the proposition, "My race is an advantage in getting access to good work and/or professional opportunities" (3.2), suggesting that although in results not reported here we found that black lawyers report having received projects because of their race, black HLS graduates do not view their race as having been beneficial to their careers overall.[19] Both results are similar to what we found in the 2000 report, where, on average, respondents agreed with the obligation thesis (5.23) and disagreed with the suggestion that their race has been generally beneficial to their careers (2.96).

With respect to potential solutions to the problems that the color line still poses for black HLS graduates, both self-help ("Black lawyers need to take more responsibility for their own careers") and diversity training ("Diversity training is an effective tool for combating the obstacles facing black lawyers") garnered equal levels of modest support (4.5). Interestingly, men were more likely to report supporting both self-help and diversity training than women (self-help: 4.7 men, 4.3 women; diversity training: 4.6 men, 4.3 women), as were those from the pre-2000 era when compared to those who graduated HLS in the post-2000 era (self-help: 4.7 pre-2000, 4.3 post-2000; diversity training: 4.5 pre-2000, 4.3 post-2000). Indeed, the pre-2000 cohort was much more positive about diversity training than those who responded to our 2000 survey, where the average was 4.01. On the other hand, pre-2000 respondents were more negative about self-help, where the average in the 2000 survey was 4.98. The only other important differences to note are that men are significantly more likely than women to believe that professional opportunities for black lawyers have improved since they entered the bar (4.5 men, 4.1 women), and that their racial identity has become less important during the course of their career (3.5 men, 2.8 women). There is an era effect with respect to both of these variables as well, with pre-2000 era respondents significantly more likely to agree with these statements than those in the post-2000 era (improved prospects: 4.7 pre-2000, 3.6 post-2000; race less important: 3.3 pre-2000, 2.9 post-2000). These latter results are not surprising given that post-2000 era graduates have had less time to observe these changes.

Finally, men are significantly more likely than women to believe that "[p]rogress for black Americans now depends more on economic change than on legal change" (4.6 men, 3.9 women). Men, women, and graduates from the pre-2000 era reported agreeing with this statement less than who responded to the 2000 survey, where the average level of agreement was almost 5 (4.94). This last result provides some support for the view that the economic progress that many blacks made during the Obama years has not translated into the kind of racial progress that black women in particular would like to see. This may in turn help to explain why blacks remain only guardedly optimistic about the future for black lawyers (4.7), a response that is identical to what we found in 2000.

This ambivalence is evident in respondents' views about the effect of the Obama presidency. As table 4-17 demonstrates, none of the statements about the beneficial effects of Obama's election garnered strong agreement of 5 or more on our seven-point scale, with only the statement that it "improved perceptions about the leadership potential of black lawyers" coming close to this level (4.7). Not surprisingly, those in the post-2000 era were significantly more likely to agree that Obama's election inspired more blacks to go to law school, since many of those graduating in this era may be among this group and certainly are more likely to know those who are.

None of the other three questions relating to the direct benefit of Obama's presidency for black lawyers garnered more than mild agreement, with two of the three eliciting even less support. Men, however, are significantly more likely than women to believe that the Age of Obama improved opportunities for mobility and career advancement for black lawyers, as well as perceptions about their leadership potential. This finding suggests that even with respect to what arguably has been the most historic development in black American history, the election of the country's first black president, African American women perceive that they have received fewer benefits than their black male peers. In a world in which black women are likely to constitute an even larger

TABLE 4-17

Impact of the election of the first African American president

	Male	Female	Overall	Pre-2000	Post-2000	N
Created more opportunities for career mobility and advancement for black lawyers	4.1*	3.8	4.0	4.0	3.9	438
Created a more inclusive and sensitive workplace environment	3.8	3.3	3.6	3.7	3.4	439
Inspired more black students to apply to law school	4.7	4.7	3.6	4.6*	4.8	439
Created more opportunities for young black lawyers	4.0	3.7	3.8	3.9	3.8	439
Improved perceptions on the leadership potential of black lawyers	4.9**	4.7	4.7	4.8	4.7	434

$*p < .05$
$**p < .01$

Note: Respondents ranked their level of agreement with each statement on a seven-point scale, where 1 is "strongly disagree" and 7 is "strongly agree." The values in this table are averages of the respondents' rankings for each statement.

proportion of the nation's black lawyers than they do today, this reality raises serious questions about how much progress the legal profession and the nation as a whole will make in the coming years.

What the Future Holds

In 2000, we concluded the first report on the state of black alumni by invoking the ringing aphorism typically made by presidents during the State of the Union Address—"The state of our union is good!"—to underscore that the state of HLS's black alumni at the dawn of the new millennium was good as well. Today, this conclusion still holds. HLS's African American graduates are flourishing in every sector of society, reaching unprecedented heights in law firms, business, public interest organizations, and government—including, of course, the most important political office in the free world. During the opening years of the twenty-first century, these extraordinary women and men have used their positions of power and influence to build a more prosperous, just, and inclusive America, even as the nation's age-old problem of the color line continues to shape—but never totally define—their lives and careers. The data presented in this chapter, however, also underscores that the legal profession still has a long way to go to provide an environment in which black lawyers have an equal opportunity to succeed.

Notwithstanding the considerable progress that has been made, HLS's African American graduates continue to face significant barriers in the workplace—barriers that are undoubtedly even more daunting for black lawyers who do not have the benefit of the "H Bomb" effect of graduating from HLS or another similarly highly ranked law school. The fact that our data shows that those graduating in the post-2000 era are consistently less satisfied with many aspects of their careers than their pre-2000 counterparts, and that just over half of those graduating in the new millennium would recommend to a young person that he or she obtain a law degree, highlights that these challenges will not simply dissipate with time.

This is particularly true for black women. As our data underscores, even African American women who have graduated from one of the world's top law schools continue to face a number of unique challenges at the intersection of race and gender that make it more difficult for them to build satisfying and successful careers in the legal profession than their black male peers—let alone achieve the career success enjoyed by white male and female HLS graduates. Even more depressingly, our data suggests that these disadvantages may actually be increasing as women continue to form a larger percentage of the overall black lawyer population—particularly for black women in large law firms. Indeed, the increasing obsession with short-term profits that characterizes many sectors of today's legal profession threatens to exacerbate the problems faced by black HLS graduates in the coming years. A forthcoming book based on in-depth interviews with a number of black women confirms this bleak assessment.[20]

Finding ways to move beyond this state of affairs will undoubtedly not be easy. But sixty-five years after the Supreme Court's historic decision in *Brown v. Board of Education*, it is imperative that the legal profession make it a priority to address the continuing problems faced by black lawyers in general and black female lawyers in particular. In a world in which increasingly diverse teams of lawyers must learn to work together effectively to solve problems for clients who are themselves increasingly diverse, the legal profession can ill afford to lose the talent and leadership that the black male and female graduates from HLS and other law schools have consistently displayed.

NOTES

1. Full text of Obama farewell speech available at https://www.cnn.com/2017/01/10/politics/president-obama-farewell-speech/index.html.

2. For the full report, see David B. Wilkins and Bryon Fong, *Harvard Law School: Report on the State of Black Alumni II, 2000–2016* (Cambridge, MA: Harvard Law School Center on the Legal Profession, 2017), https://clp.law.harvard.edu/assets/HLS-Report-on-the-State-of-Black-Alumni-II-2000-2016-High-Res.pdf.

3. See Kimberlé Crenshaw, "Demarginalizing the Intersection of Race and Sex: A Black Feminist Critique of Antidiscrimination Doctrine, Feminist Theory and Antiracist Politics," *University of Chicago Legal Forum* 1989, no. 1 (1989): 139–167.

4. For a discussion on the pivotal influence that law school status has on an entrant's career prospects, see, e.g., Ronit Dinovitzer et al., *After the JD: First Results of a National Study of Lawyer Careers* (Overland Park, KS, and Chicago: NALP Foundation for Law and Careers and the American Bar Foundation, 2009), 43 (documenting a statistically significant correlation between law school status and the incomes of young lawyers, with graduates of top-ten schools like Harvard earning more than 30 percent more than the graduates of law schools ranked 2-20, and more than double the average amount earned by graduates of schools ranked in the bottom category of law school rankings).

5. Robin Ely, Pamela Stone, and Colleen Ammerman, "Rethinking What You 'Know' about High-Achieving Women," *Harvard Business Review*, December 2014, https://hbr.org/2014/12/rethink-what-you-know-about-high-achieving-women.

6. See David B. Wilkins et al., *Harvard Law School: Report on the State of Black Alumni, 1869–2000* (Cambridge, MA: Harvard Law School Program on the Legal Profession, 2002), https://clp.law.harvard.edu/assets/Report-on-the-State-of-Black-Alumni-I-1869-2000.pdf.

7. See David B. Wilkins, Bryon Fong, and Ronit Dinovitzer, *The Women and Men of Harvard Law School: Preliminary Results from the HLS Career Study* (Cambridge, MA: Harvard Law School Center on the Legal Profession, 2015), https://papers.ssrn.com/sol3/papers.cfm?abstract_id=2609499.

8. To learn more about the After the JD study, see "After the JD," American Bar Foundation, accessed January 3, 2019, http://www.americanbarfoundation.org/research/project/118.

9. We thank Arevik Avedian, who performed the statistical analysis underlying this research.

10. See Wilkins et al., *Harvard Law School*.

11. See "Women in the Global Legal Profession," in "Women as Lawyers and Leaders," *The Practice* 1, no. 4 (May/June 2015), https://thepractice.law.harvard.edu/article/women-in-the-global-legal-profession/.

12. See David B. Wilkins and G. Mitu Gulati, "Why Are There So Few Black Lawyers in Corporate Law Firms? An Institutional Analysis," *California Law Review* 84, no. 3 (1996): 493–625.

13. See David B. Wilkins, "A Systematic Response to Systemic Disadvantage: A Response to Sander," *Stanford Law Review* 57, no. 6 (May 2005): 1915–1961.

14. See Wilkins, Fong, and Dinovitzer, *Women and Men of Harvard Law School.*

15. See Wilkins and Gulati, "Why Are There So Few?"

16. See David B Wilkins and G. Mitu Gulati, "Reconceiving the Tournament of Lawyers: Tracking, Seeding, and Information Control in the Internal Labor Markets of Elite Law Firms," *Virginia Law Review* 84 (1998): 581–681.

17. See, e.g., Frank Dobbin and Alexandra Kalev, "Why Diversity Programs Fail," *Harvard Business Review*, July–August 2016, https://hbr.org/2016/07/why-diversity-programs-fail.

18. See David B. Wilkins, "Two Paths to the Mountaintop? The Role of Legal Education in Shaping the Values of Black Corporate Lawyers," *Stanford Law Review* 45, no. 6 (July 1993): 1981–2026.

19. See Wilkins and Fong, *Harvard Law School*, table 27, "Received project because of race."

20. See Tsedale M. Melaku, *You Don't Look like a Lawyer: Black Women and Systemic Gendered Racism* (Lanham, MD: Rowman and Littlefield, forthcoming, 2019).

SECTION TWO

COMPARATIVE STUDIES

5

Workplace Engagement and the Glass Ceiling

The Experience of Black Professionals

ELLA F. WASHINGTON, ELLYN MAESE,
and SHANE MCFEELY

Being a Black professional in America has a unique set of challenges. Although Black professionals represent 12 percent of the US workforce, they represent 8 percent of management occupations (Bureau of Labor Statistics, 2017). Further, Blacks continue to fill a minority of senior leadership positions across every major industry in the United States: only 2 percent of *Fortune* 500 senior executives are Black (Jones, 2017); likewise, only 7 percent of senior higher education administrators (Jones, 2017) and 8 percent of leadership and board members for nonprofit organizations are Black (BoardSource, 2017).

In addition to the discrimination that some still face, because Black employees are often a minority in their workplaces, they have different experiences and quite often different outcomes from their non-Black peers (Schmitt, Branscombe, Postmes, & Garcia, 2014). Research has found differences in the Black professional experience in terms of hiring, performance ratings, promotions, and many other outcomes (Greenhaus, Parasuraman, & Wormley, 1990; James, 2000; Thomas, 2001). These experiences likely contribute to the lack of representation of Black professionals at leadership levels. However, another aspect of the experience of Black professionals that has been explored is the sociopsychological perspective. For example, studies have found that Black managers report receiving less psychosocial support in the workplace than their White counterparts (James, 2000). This chapter further examines the socio-psychological experience of Black employees through the lens of engagement.

The focus of this chapter is on the disparities in workplace engagement for Black employees. We theorize that managers' shortcomings in engaging Black professionals have contributed to these professionals' career plateaus and lack of overall satisfaction at work. This chapter uncovers how Black professionals experience employee engagement, identifies several key areas in which Black employees report a less positive work experience, and discusses recommendations for improving employee life for Black professionals.

Understanding Employee Engagement

The idea that providing employees with meaningful work that allows them to learn, grow, and ultimately obtain high performance is relatively novel. In fact, although it may be common knowledge now, the concept that employees' attitudes on the job are paramount to understanding their performance was not a topic of academic study until the 1920s when the Western Electric Company began its famous inquiry into employees' sociopsychological circumstances in the workplace (known as the Hawthorne studies) (Roethlisberger & Dickson, 1939). After decades of research on job satisfaction (Judge, Thoresen, Bono, & Patton, 2001), the conceptualization of what psychological conditions make employees productive at work gradually evolved into an understanding of employee engagement. Early definitions of engagement stem from Kahn (1990), who discussed the benefits of employees who bring their whole selves to work—physically, mentally, and emotionally. Representing the integration of management science and positive psychology, the concept of employee engagement is presently ubiquitous throughout organizational and human resource management circles.

Though there are presently several definitions of employee engagement (Kahn, 1990; Macey, Schneider, Barbera, & Young, 2011; Robinson, Perryman, & Hayday, 2004; Rothbard, 2001), most researchers' definitions of engagement use concepts such as satisfaction, involvement, and enthusiasm for work (Harter, Schmidt, & Hayes, 2002). Importantly, all definitions distinguish engagement from satisfaction, emphasizing that engagement is a unique state of investment, commitment, and motivation, whereas satisfaction is an affective state of happiness that may

TABLE 5-1

Items forming the Gallup engagement index

Satisfaction	On a five-point scale, where 5 is "extremely satisfied" and 1 is "extremely dissatisfied," how satisfied are you with [name of organization] as a place to work?
1	I know what is expected of me at work.
2	I have the materials and equipment I need to do my work right.
3	At work, I have the opportunity to do what I do best every day.
4	In the last seven days, I have received recognition or praise for doing good work.
5	My supervisor, or someone at work, seems to care about me as a person.
6	There is someone at work who encourages my development.
7	At work, my opinions seem to count.
8	The mission/purpose of my company makes me feel my job is important.
9	My associates (fellow employees) are committed to doing quality work.
10	I have a best friend at work.
11	In the last six months, someone at work has talked to me about my progress.
12	This last year, I have had opportunities at work to learn and grow.

result. Taking a formative approach to understanding employee engagement, Gallup researchers study employee engagement by assessing workers' perceptions of twelve critical elements of the workplace experience that create engagement (table 5-1). Using their responses to these items, employees are further categorized into three different groups: engaged, not engaged, and actively disengaged. Engaged workers are psychologically committed to the organization, their team, and their work. They are more productive and less likely to leave the organization. In contrast, employees who are not engaged might be productive in their roles but not committed to the organization. They might be actively looking for other jobs and are more likely to leave the organization.

Finally, actively disengaged workers are disconnected from the organization and psychologically absent from their work.

Gallup's measure of engagement is designed to address four levels of employee development needs. First, basic needs such as having clear expectations and the tools necessary to complete the job are critical to providing workers with a solid foundation in their roles. Second, engagement also encompasses employees' individual needs, such as receiving recognition for good work and feeling cared about and encouraged in their roles. Third, workers have team-related needs. They should be welcomed and comfortable in their teams and know that their ideas and opinions are contributing to organizational goals in order to feel engaged. Finally, engagement involves employees' needs for growth and development in their roles and careers within the organization. Through years of research with clients across many industries, Gallup has found that until workers have these needs met, they will not feel committed and enthusiastic about their work.

According to the recent *State of the American Workplace* report (Gallup, 2016a), using a representative sample of the working population in the United States, it was estimated that only one-third of all workers are engaged in their jobs. More than half of all workers were found to be not engaged (51 percent), while 16 percent were actively disengaged with their current role. If we look at these metrics globally, Gallup finds that only 15 percent of all workers around the world are engaged in their jobs (Gallup, 2017c). However, there are large regional differences in engagement, with East Asian countries in the single digits in terms of percentage engaged and the United States and Canada having nearly one in three workers engaged (figure 5-1).

The Benefits of Employee Engagement

As demonstrated by research in both academic and practitioner outlets, employee engagement is foundational to individual, team, and organizational success. For instance, Harter and his colleagues (Harter et al., 2002) conducted a meta-analysis at a business-unit level using the measure of employee engagement just outlined. They found that engagement at a business-unit level predicted better customer perceptions, greater productivity, and higher profit, as well as less turnover and fewer safety incidents. Additionally, Saks (2006) found that employee engage-

A crisis of engagement

Employee engagement results among residents who are employed for an employer, globally and by region
Based on data aggregated from 2014–2016 Gallup World Polls

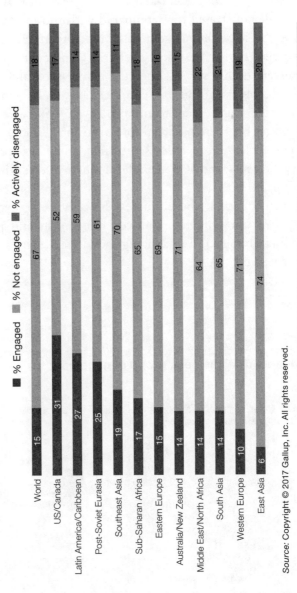

■ % Engaged   ■ % Not engaged   ■ % Actively disengaged

Region	% Engaged	% Not engaged	% Actively disengaged
World	15	67	18
US/Canada	31	52	17
Latin America/Caribbean	27	59	14
Post-Soviet Eurasia	25	61	14
Southeast Asia	19	70	11
Sub-Saharan Africa	17	65	18
Eastern Europe	15	69	16
Australia/New Zealand	14	71	15
Middle East/North Africa	14	64	22
South Asia	14	65	21
Western Europe	10	71	19
East Asia	6	74	20

ment predicted greater job satisfaction, organizational commitment, and organizational citizenship behaviors and less intention to quit the organization.

Further, a Gallup meta-analysis of over eighty-two thousand work-groups demonstrated that compared with those that are less engaged, business units with engagement scores in the top quartile demonstrate 10 percent higher customer metrics, 17 percent higher productivity, 20 percent higher sales, 21 percent higher profitability, and 41 percent lower absenteeism (Harter, Schmidt, Agrawal, Plowman, & Blue, 2016). These high-engagement teams also have 24–59 percent lower turnover depending on their base rate of turnover, 28 percent less shrinkage, 70 percent fewer employee safety incidents, 58 percent fewer patient safety incidents, and 40 percent fewer quality defects in work (figure 5-2) (Gallup, 2016a).

Taken together, these studies show that employee engagement is important not only to employee motivation and psychological in-volvement but also to improving individual, team, and organizational performance.

FIGURE 5-2

Comparison of business group engagement

When compared with business units in the bottom quartile of engagement, those in the top quartile realize improvements in the following areas:

41% LOWER Absenteeism	24% LOWER Turnover (high-turnover organizations)	59% LOWER Turnover (low-turnover organizations)	28% LESS Shrinkage
70% FEWER Employee safety incidents	58% FEWER Patient safety incidents	40% FEWER Quality incidents (defects)	10% HIGHER Customer metrics
17% HIGHER Productivity	20% HIGHER Sales	21% HIGHER Profitability	

Demographic Differences in Employee Engagement

Given the benefits of employee engagement, it is clear that a failure to engage employees puts individuals, teams, and organizations at a disadvantage. Consistently low engagement can have a negative effect on company success. Teams with low engagement are less productive, less profitable, and less likely to be loyal. This lack of loyalty to the company can cause turnover, which can cost businesses approximately 1.5 times the annual salary of every person who quits (Gallup, 2015). There are also negative impacts at the individual level from low engagement. Employees who are actively disengaged and suffering are emotionally disconnected from their work and workplace and rate their current well-being at high risk. Employees who are not engaged are also more likely to feel stress in the workplace; actively disengaged workers are more likely than engaged employees to say that they felt burned out due to work stress in the last month (50 percent versus 16 percent), that they were expected to deliver more in the same amount of time (40 percent versus 13 percent), and that they often feel rushed at work (31 percent versus 7 percent) (Nink, 2013). Thus, engagement and the absence of engagement can have important effects at the team and individual levels.

Demographic differences in employee engagement make it clear that some worker subgroups have vastly different experiences at work. For example, women in the workforce have generally been more engaged than men throughout Gallup's history of tracking employee engagement. Recent Gallup data shows that in the United States, 35 percent of female employees are engaged, compared with 29 percent of male employees (Gallup, 2016b). Additionally, Gallup has also identified generational differences in employee engagement. Specifically, millennials (individuals born between 1980 and 1996) appear to be the least engaged generation in the workforce. Only 29 percent are engaged, another 16 percent are actively disengaged, and the majority (55 percent) are not engaged, leading all other generations in this category of workers. However, there has been limited research on the racial demographic differences of workers' engagement.

Therefore, to investigate how the experiences of Black employees may differ from those of other ethnic groups, Gallup studied employee engagement in working adults in the United States[1] (table 5-2) (Gallup, 2017a). Results revealed that although there was no difference in the percentage of Black and White employees who were categorized as engaged

(33 percent) (Gallup, 2017a), a closer look at individual facets of engagement exposed that there are significant differences in the work experiences of Black employees compared with other employees. As discussed in more detail later, although there were several areas in which there were no differences between racial groups, when there were differences, Black employees scored lower on key elements of employee engagement (table 5-2). Importantly, in these areas, Black employees scored lower than both White employees *and* Hispanic employees (Gallup, 2017a), a finding that indicates that this is not simply a majority/minority discrepancy but rather a unique challenge faced by the Black employee population. Further, this finding suggests that there are differences between minority subgroups in their workplace attitudes, challenges, and experiences.

Q08. The Mission or Purpose of My Organization Makes Me Feel My Job Is Important

On average, Black employees are less likely to report that the mission or purpose of their company makes them feel that their job is important (Gallup, 2017c). Identifying with the mission or purpose of their organization provides employees with a sense of meaning in their work and a sense of belonging to a community. It is a high-level emotional need that is a critical source of intrinsic motivation for employees' commitment to their job (Campbell & Yeung, 1991). In fact, Gallup has identified that a high sense of connection to the organization's mission or purpose is associated with an increase in productivity, a 41 percent decrease in absenteeism, a 33 percent improvement in quality of work, and greater employee retention (Gallup, 2016a). Additionally, in a meta-analysis of the organizational commitment literature, Mathieu and Zajac (1990) found that high organizational commitment is associated with increased perceived competence, salary, and job level. Unfortunately, it appears that Black employees may not be benefiting from this important energizing force to the same degree as other employees and may therefore feel less emotionally fulfilled by their jobs and workplace community.

Q09. My Coworkers Are Committed to Doing Quality Work

Black employees demonstrate less endorsement that their coworkers are committed to doing quality work (Gallup, 2017c). This suggests that

TABLE 5-2

Mean difference in engagement compared to Black employees

	White	Hispanic
Grand mean	0.06	0.08
Q01. I know what is expected of me at work.	0.03	0.02
Q02. I have the materials and equipment I need to do my work right.	0.03	−0.01
Q03. At work, I have the opportunity to do what I do best every day.	0.00	0.04
Q04. In the last seven days, I have received recognition or praise for doing good work.	0.01	0.08
Q05. My supervisor, or someone at work, seems to care about me as a person.	0.07	0.09
Q06. There is someone at work who encourages my development.	0.09	0.11
Q07. At work, my opinions seem to count.	0.07	0.05
Q08.* The mission or purpose of my organization makes me feel my job is important.	0.12	0.18
Q09.* My coworkers are committed to doing quality work.	0.14	0.19
Q10. I have a best friend at work.	0.07	0.08
Q11.* In the last six months, someone at work has talked to me about my progress.	0.22	0.13
Q12.* This last year, I have had opportunities at work to learn and grow.	0.27	0.21
Satisfaction*	0.20	0.23

Source: Gallup (2017a). Results are based on a Gallup Panel web study completed by 19,212 employees, aged eighteen and older, conducted April 19 through May 7, 2017. The Gallup Panel is a probability-based longitudinal panel of US adults whom Gallup selects using random-digit-dial phone interviews that cover landline and cell phones. Gallup also uses address-based sampling methods to recruit panel members. The Gallup Panel is not an opt-in panel, and members do not receive incentives for participating. The sample for this study was weighted to be demographically representative of the US adult population, using the most recent Current Population Survey figures. The demographics of the unweighted sample are as follows: 73 percent White, 14 percent Hispanic, 11 percent Black, and 1 percent Asian. For results based on this sample, one can say that the maximum margin of sampling error is ±1 percentage point at the 95 percent confidence level. Margins of error are higher for subsamples. In addition to sampling error, question wording and practical difficulties in conducting surveys can introduce error and bias into the findings of public opinion polls.

*Indicates statistically significant and substantive differences, $p < .05$.

Black employees feel less positive about the effort, competence, and investment of their fellow team members. When employees feel part of a team that is solidly committed to quality, there is a 29 percent reduction in turnover and absenteeism, an 11 percent increase in profitability, and 6 percent more engaged customers (Gallup, 2016a). In contrast, Gallup's research indicates that Black employees are less likely to feel this sense of teamwork with their coworkers, which may adversely affect employees' commitment to their team and sense that team members are committed to high performance.

Q12. This Last Year, I Have Had Opportunities at Work to Learn and Grow

Black employees, on average, are less likely to report they have had opportunities to learn and grow in the last year compared with their White and Hispanic counterparts (Gallup, 2017c). Opportunities to learn and grow create enthusiasm and excitement for employees that motivate them to work harder and more efficiently and to generate innovation. Organizations whose employees have these opportunities also have 26 percent lower rates of absenteeism, 11 percent higher profits, and greater productivity (Gallup, 2016a). However, because Black employees' conversations with managers about growth opportunities create a sense of mutual investment for employees and leaders, Black employees are at risk for feeling that managers are less invested in their careers, as well as being less invested in their own growth in the company.

Given that Black employees may feel less connected with the mission of their organization, have a less positive evaluation of their coworkers, and perceive fewer opportunities to learn and grow at work, it is not surprising that Gallup also found that Black employees report lower levels of overall satisfaction with their workplace compared with both White and Hispanic employees (Gallup, 2017c). Furthermore, when asked how many years they intend to stay with their current employers, Black employees, on average, report intending to stay for significantly fewer years (nine years) compared with both White (twelve to thirteen years) and Hispanic employees (twelve to thirteen years).

Taken together, Gallup's findings suggest that there are important racial disparities in the workplace that may affect the degree to which Black employees feel invested and fulfilled in their working lives. The consequences of these different workplace experiences affect individual workers, teams, and organizations. Therefore, it is critical that leaders, direct managers, and individual contributors all work together to address these inequities. In the following section, we discuss the extent to which managers have a critical role in addressing engagement.

The Manager's Role in Creating Engaging Workplaces

When trying to further understand the racial disparities in engagement, our analysis looked to the manager's impact on individual and team engagement. Many of the workplace conditions that are necessary to create engaged teams should be owned by and expected of the team leader or manager. In fact, Gallup has found that as much as 70 percent of the variance in employee engagement can be traced back to the influence of the local manager (Gallup, 2015). Certainly, individual workers are not exempt from influencing their own engagement, such as finding ways to learn and grow in their roles or having positive and productive interactions with coworkers. However, team leaders are in the unique position of setting up the conditions that create enthusiasm among team members for their work. Managers who don't know how to meet the engagement needs of their team become a barrier to employee, team, and company performance. The dynamic between managers and their team is therefore critical in understanding differential engagement results across employee groups. For example, performance development best practices suggest that managers who provide frequent and meaningful feedback to employees can lead to higher-performing teams (Wigert & Harter, 2017). Yet Gallup research finds that only about one in four employees "strongly agree" that their manager provides meaningful feedback to them, or that the feedback they receive helps them do better work (Wigert & Harter, 2017).

Unfortunately, previous research has found that Black employees may receive extra scrutiny from managers, which can lead to worse performance reviews, lower wages, and even job loss (Cavounidis & Lang, 2015) and can be further disadvantaged by lack of candid feedback (Harber, 2004). White male leaders particularly struggle to provide candid feedback to diverse coworkers (Shelton & Thomas, 2013). Without adequate feedback and development, coupled with Gallup's evidence that Black employees do not feel as encouraged to learn and grow at work, it is not surprising that Black professionals trail their peers in attaining senior positions in organizations. Though discrimination and institutional barriers are often cited as drivers of racial disparities in senior management (Knight, Hebl, Foster, & Mannix, 2003; Weisenfeld & Robinson-Backmon, 2007), it is evident that poor management skills, or those that are insensitive to the unique perspective of Black employees, also help create the glass ceiling encountered by Black professionals.

Though there are racial differences in the percentage of Blacks who are promoted to management positions, in the United States, Blacks hold 8 percent of management jobs (Bureau of Labor Statistics, 2017). Our analysis further explored engagement by race for managers, given the link between engaged managers and engaged employees.[2] Gallup finds that employees who are supervised by highly engaged managers are 59 percent more likely to be engaged than those supervised by actively disengaged managers (Gallup, 2015). Consistent with the pattern for employees, Black managers were found to be less engaged than White and Hispanic managers (table 5-3). These findings suggest that even for Black professionals with upward mobility, there remain challenges with engaging them. Thus, a failure to engage Black managers is likely to have a negative impact on their teams.

Practical Recommendations

Taken together, the research discussed indicates that Black employees have different experiences with employee engagement and overall job satisfaction from their peers of other races. Furthermore, our research suggests that underlying these differences are critical discrepancies in the day-to-day experiences of Black employees in the workplace, most notably in their perception of development opportunities, including access to new learning and to discussions about their progress. To address disparities in the engagement of Black employees, managers and organizations should address the specific experiences and expectations of these employees. When evaluating disparities between Black employees and other groups, it can be tempting to focus on diversity management best practices (Kalev, Dobbin, & Kelly, 2006) and overlook the fundamentals of what drives engagement. Engagement is built through relationships with teams and managers and by having trust in the organization. Critically, diversity practices are only effective in increasing employee engagement when executed in such a way that they promote inclusion (Downey, van der Werff, Thomas, & Plaut, 2015). In light of this, we

TABLE 5-3

Mean difference in engagement for managers compared to Black employees

	White	Hispanic
Grand mean*	0.20	0.21
Q01. I know what is expected of me at work.	0.16	0.19
Q02. I have the materials and equipment I need to do my work right.	−0.03	0.06
Q03. At work, I have the opportunity to do what I do best every day.	0.03	0.03
Q04. In the last seven days, I have received recognition or praise for doing good work.	0.14	0.11
Q05. My supervisor, or someone at work, seems to care about me as a person.	0.16	0.08
Q06. There is someone at work who encourages my development.	0.33	0.23
Q07. At work, my opinions seem to count.	0.18	0.07
Q08.* The mission or purpose of my organization makes me feel my job is important.	0.28	0.42
Q09.* My coworkers are committed to doing quality work.	0.18	0.55
Q10. I have a best friend at work.	0.44	0.38
Q11.* In the last six months, someone at work has talked to me about my progress.	0.14	0.29
Q12.* This last year, I have had opportunities at work to learn and grow.	0.54	0.57

Source: Gallup (2017a). Results are based on a Gallup Panel web study completed by 2,902 managers, aged eighteen and older, conducted April 19 through May 7, 2017. The Gallup Panel is a probability-based longitudinal panel of US adults whom Gallup selects using random-digit-dial phone interviews that cover landline and cell phones. Gallup also uses address-based sampling methods to recruit panel members. The Gallup Panel is not an opt-in panel, and members do not receive incentives for participating. The sample for this study was weighted to be demographically representative of the US adult population, using the most recent Current Population Survey figures. The demographics of the unweighted sample are as follows: 74 percent White, 13 percent Hispanic, 11 percent Black, and 1 percent Asian. For results based on this sample, one can say that the maximum margin of sampling error is ±1 percentage point at the 95 percent confidence level. Margins of error are higher for subsamples. In addition to sampling error, question wording and practical difficulties in conducting surveys can introduce error and bias into the findings of public opinion polls.

*Indicates statistically significant differences, $p < .05$.

recommend focusing on creating an inclusive environment by making Black employees feel that their opinions are valued, facilitating inclusive conversations, and providing better training for managers on effective feedback and development.

First, leaders must gain knowledge of the ways in which the employee experience can be improved. One of the primary methods to understand employee perceptions across groups within organizations is simply to ask their opinions. Annual surveys, short-term pulse surveys, qualitative interviews, focus groups, and other organizational data sources are the primary tools necessary to adequately understand the needs and motivations of the workforce. These information-gathering tools should be focused not only on engagement but also on thinking more broadly about the employee experience within the organization, including feelings of inclusivity. Organizations can then use advanced analytics to understand this employee perception data on a team-by-team basis. These analyses should always include examining subgroup differences to understand different working conditions throughout the organization. Specifically, this means making sure the opinions of Black employees are being heard and responded to by leadership. Other data sources such as performance metrics, training participation, or customer metrics should also be integrated into this analysis plan. Finally, individual team leaders and managers should be provided with team-level results, feedback, and coaching on this data, what it means for their team needs, and how they should act on the data.

Second, as previously discussed, managers must take responsibility for fulfilling the needs of diverse employees in accordance with the insights provided by data analytics, as well as with the tenets of creating a fair and inclusive environment. Because team leaders control many aspects of the team's work, assignments, and definitions of success, any treatment that is preferential to one group or type of employee greatly determines employees' relative engagement in that job. Specifically, the current Gallup research identifying differences across the elements of engagement for Black versus White and Hispanic employees reveals several areas in which working conditions for Black employees can be improved by managers. For example, managers can ensure that all employees believe that their opinions count at work by carefully fostering an inclusive environment in which all team members feel that their perspectives are heard and valued both by the manager and by the team collectively. Facilitating a team where everyone feels included and valued can also help employees develop a more positive view about their coworkers' commitment to doing quality work. One easy way that managers can achieve this is by encouraging team members to have conversations about non-work-related topics in which members engage in mutual self-disclosure, the reciprocal sharing of personal information, including information about background and experiences as well as thoughts and feelings (Phillips, Dumas, & Rothbard, 2018). Research demonstrates that even a ten-minute feedback conversation has lasting benefits for team functioning for months (Polzer, Milton, & Swarm, 2002).

Further, managers can help employees feel a sense of connection to their organization's mission and purpose by helping them see how their daily work connects to a larger goal that has personal and interpersonal value. This will require that managers take the time to have deep conversations with their employees to discover what is important to them and how they can make their jobs feel meaningful. One way managers can connect work to what employees value is to leverage their strengths. Strengths highlight what employees naturally do best; moreover, having conversations about individual strengths demonstrates to employees that their organization celebrates and values their uniqueness and diverse ways of thinking. For example, Gallup conducted a study to determine the extent to which strength-development efforts affected employees' perceptions of inclusion in a *Fortune* 100 corporation. When evaluated as a single group, teams who took an assessment to learn about their strengths reported significantly higher levels of inclusion. In this study, the process of learning about and communicating individual strengths helped employees satisfy the needs of belonging and uniqueness. Although employees can take some initiative in finding ways to learn and grow at work, it is also managers' responsibility to help support this sort of development by identifying and encouraging new learning and development opportunities for their employees. Importantly, managers need to develop an awareness of how to execute their responsibilities with respect to their Black employees, whose needs and expectations may differ in regard to each of these facets of engagement.

Indeed, two of the primary predictors of employee engagement are job characteristics, such as making employees feel their jobs are important and giving them autonomy in their roles, and feelings of procedural justice (Saks, 2006). Additionally, given the myriad positive outcomes associated with workers who are engaged, differential treatment across demographic groups can not only influence their engagement but also affect their performance. Therefore, one of the most common practical recommendations to improve employee engagement across groups is manager or team leader training. Managers should be aware of their biases and any differential treatment that they might demonstrate as team leaders. Managers need development and support through internal and external learning resources, mentorship systems, leader support, and consistent feedback from their team members and peers. Team leaders need to develop the skills necessary to have critical conversations with their team about workplace processes and expectations. At the same time, workers need to feel that their opinions and ideas count and that there is some procedural justice in how work and recognition are distributed throughout the team.

Team leaders who are effective at individualizing their feedback and coaching to each member of their team will create the most inclusive and engaging environment. This means being skilled at facilitating conversations about diversity that have the potential to be tense. There is often a misconception among leaders that in order to be effective at talking about diversity and inclusion, one has to have a high level of expertise. Though cultural competence should be the goal of all leaders, at the core, inclusive conversations are about fostering environments where employees can express themselves in what they perceive to be a "safe" place (Shao, Feng, & Wang, 2017). For leaders, sometimes this simply means acknowledging that one does not know everything about inclusion. When managers are open to learning about employees' differences and are reflective about how personal and social identities can influence these interactions, they are able to build an environment of conversational excellence around inclusion. Simply taking the time to have conversations about employees' life circumstances can go a long way; research consistently shows that feeling accepted and valued by leaders in and of itself is critical to employees' perceptions of inclusion (Brimhall, Lizano, & Mor Barak, 2014; Brimhall et al., 2017; Shore et al., 2011).

This includes establishing clear expectations, coaching the employee on a continuous basis, and creating accountability around that employee's performance. However, it is also critical for the manager to take into consideration the employee's life situation. For instance, if the employee is a single mother who also takes night classes, the manager should be flexible enough to shift expectations of the hours the employee is at work. Managers must balance their expectations of high performance with team member needs for individualized work conditions and assignments.

This process can only work if managers listen to their team members and act on that feedback.

Organizations can also create policies that enable managers to better support the needs of Black employees—for example, introducing formal mentoring and sponsorship programs that provide institutional support for managers to take responsibility for the career development of another employee, such as by offering advice and experiences that can help an employee learn and grow or by advocating for promotions and other opportunities on the employee's behalf (Cocchiara, Connerley, & Bell, 2010; Kalev et al., 2006). Mentoring and sponsorship relationships help to provide a clear career path to success for those who typically lack one due to institutional barriers (Kalev et al., 2006; Society for Human Resource Management, 2009). Such mentoring relationships within organizations have been shown to be effective for increasing diversity among management through the promotion of diverse employees (Kalev et al., 2006).

Importantly, the latest Gallup research emphasizes that after taking into consideration their employees' feedback and life circumstances, managers must consider the unique ways in which they can make their Black employees feel that they are heard on a continual basis, that their work is meaningful, that they have a sense of belonging and team commitment, and that they are encouraged to learn and grow in their roles. Managers' ability to bridge these gaps in engagement will make the difference for their organizations in leveraging the benefits of workforce diversity, which is a critical competitive advantage in the ever-changing marketplace. Black professionals have a lot to offer to their organizations, but they will only do so when they are engaged.

Conclusion

Achieving high employee engagement is a goal for most organizations today as a way to demonstrate care and investment in their workforce, as well as reap the performance and productivity benefits of an engaged workplace. This chapter illuminates disparities in engagement for Black professionals in the workplace. The findings of this work provide an area of opportunity for managers and leaders to analyze their own organizational dynamics that may lead to lower engagement for some populations. Though there are likely many factors, including historical, cultural, structural, and individual ones, that are likely to influence engagement for Black professionals, it is clear that managers can have a profound impact on engagement by proactively creating more inclusive teams for all.

NOTES

1. In all analyses, the sample was weighted to be demographically representative of the US adult population based on the Current Population Survey, and relevant factors, including gender, age, industry, income, and position, were controlled for as covariates. Comparisons are only made between White, Black, and Hispanic groups based on adequate sample size (more than 2 percent of total sample).

2. Managers are defined as those who selected "I am a manager/supervisor whose main responsibilities are the work output of other people" in response to the following question: Which of the following best describes your role or job responsibilities within your organization?

1. I am a leader who manages other managers.
2. I am a manager/supervisor whose main responsibilities are the work output of other people.
3. I am a project manager who is responsible for other people's work.
4. I am an individual contributor responsible for my own work or output.

REFERENCES

BoardSource. (2017). *Leading with intent: 2017 national index of nonprofit board practices.* Retrieved from https://boardsource.org/research-critical-issues/nonprofit-sector-research/

Brimhall, K. C., Lizano, E. L., & Mor Barak, M. E. (2014). The mediating role of inclusion: A longitudinal study of the effects of leader–member exchange and diversity climate on job satisfaction and intention to leave among child welfare workers. *Children and Youth Services Review, 40,* 79–88.

Brimhall, K. C., Mor Barak, M. E., Hurlburt, M., McArdle, J. J., Palinkas, L., & Henwood, B. (2017). Increasing workplace inclusion: The promise of leader-member exchange. *Human Service Organizations: Management, Leadership & Governance, 41*(3), 222–239.

Bureau of Labor Statistics. (2017). Household data, annual averages: 11. Employed persons by detailed occupation, sex, race, and Hispanic or Latino ethnicity. Retrieved from https://www.bls.gov/cps/cpsaat11.pdf

Campbell, A., & Yeung, S. (1991). Creating a sense of mission. *Long Range Planning, 24*(4), 10–20.

Cavounidis, C., & Lang, K. (2015). *Discrimination and worker evaluation* (NBER Working Paper w21612). Cambridge, MA: National Bureau of Economic Research.

Cocchiara, F. K., Connerley, M. L., & Bell, M. P. (2010). "A GEM" for increasing the effectiveness of diversity training. *Human Resource Management, 49*(6), 1089–1106.

Downey, S. N., van der Werff, L., Thomas, K. M., & Plaut, V. C. (2015). The role of diversity practices and inclusion in promoting trust and employee engagement. *Journal of Applied Psychology, 45*(1), 35–44.

Gallup. (2015). *State of the American manager: Analytics and advice for leaders* (Report). Omaha, NE: Gallup.

Gallup. (2016a). *State of the American workplace* (Report). Omaha, NE: Gallup.

Gallup. (2016b). *Women in America: Work and life well-lived* (Report). Omaha, NE: Gallup.

Gallup. (2017a). *American workforce panel survey* [Data file]. Omaha, NE: Gallup.

Gallup. (2017b). *Gallup daily well-being poll* [Data file]. Omaha, NE: Gallup.

Gallup. (2017c). *State of the global workplace* (Report). Omaha, NE: Gallup.

Greenhaus, J. H., Parasuraman, S., & Wormley, W. M. (1990). Effects of race on organizational experiences, job performance evaluations, and career outcomes. *Academy of Management Journal, 33*(1), 64–86.

Harber, K. D. (2004). The positive feedback bias as a response to out-group unfriendliness. *Journal of Applied Social Psychology, 34*(11), 2272–2297.

Harter, J. K., Schmidt, F. L., Agrawal, S., Plowman, S. K., & Blue, A. (2016). *The relationship between engagement at work and organizational outcomes: 2016 Q12 meta-analysis* (9th ed.). Omaha, NE: Gallup.

Harter, J. K., Schmidt, F. L., & Hayes, T. L. (2002). Business-unit-level relationship between employee satisfaction, employee engagement, and business outcomes: A meta-analysis. *Journal of Applied Psychology, 87*(2), 268–279.

James, E. H. (2000). Race-related differences in promotions and support: Underlying effects of human and social capital. *Organization Science, 11*(5), 493–508.

Jones, S. (2017, June 9). White men account for 72% of corporate leadership at 16 of the Fortune 500 companies. *Fortune*. Retrieved from http://fortune.com/2017/06/09/white-men-senior-executives-fortune-500-companies-diversity-data

Judge, T. A., Thoresen, C. J., Bono, J. E., & Patton, G. K. (2001). The job satisfaction–job performance relationship: A qualitative and quantitative review. *Psychological Bulletin, 127*(3), 376–407.

Kahn, W. A. (1990). Psychological conditions of personal engagement and disengagement at work. *Academy of Management Journal, 33*(4), 692–724.

Kalev, A., Dobbin, F., & Kelly, E. (2006). Best practices or best guesses? Assessing the efficacy of corporate affirmative action and diversity policies. *American Sociological Review, 71*(4), 589–617.

Knight, J. L., Hebl, M. R., Foster, J. B., & Mannix, L. M. (2003). Out of role? Out of luck: The influence of race and leadership status on performance appraisals. *Journal of Leadership & Organizational Studies, 9*(3), 85–93.

Macey, W. H., Schneider, B., Barbera, K. M., & Young, S. A. (2011). *Employee engagement: Tools for analysis, practice, and competitive advantage* (Vol. 31). Hoboken, NJ: John Wiley & Sons.

Mathieu, J. E., & Zajac, D. M. (1990). A review and meta-analysis of the antecedents, correlates, and consequences of organizational commitment. *Psychological Bulletin, 108*(2), 171–194.

Nink, M. (2013). Low employee well-being and engagement hurt German companies. *Gallup Business Journal.* Retrieved from http://news.gallup.com/businessjournal/162053/low-employee-wellbeing-engagement-hurt-german-companies.aspx

Phillips, K. W., Dumas, T. L., & Rothbard, N. P. (2018, March–April). Diversity and authenticity. *Harvard Business Review, 132–136.*

Polzer, J. T., Milton, L. P., & Swarm, W. B., Jr. (2002). Capitalizing on diversity: Interpersonal congruence in small work groups. *Administrative Science Quarterly, 47*(2), 296–324.

Robinson, D., Perryman, S., & Hayday, S. (2004). *The drivers of employee engagement* (Report 408). Brighton, England: Institute for Employment Studies.

Roethlisberger, F. J., & Dickson, W. J. (1939). *Management and the worker: An account of a research program conducted by the Western Electric Company, Hawthorne Works, Chicago.* Cambridge, MA: Harvard University Press.

Rothbard, N. P. (2001). Enriching or depleting? The dynamics of engagement in work and family roles. *Administrative Science Quarterly, 46*(4), 655–684.

Saks, A. M. (2006). Antecedents and consequences of employee engagement. *Journal of Managerial Psychology, 21*(7), 600–619.

Schmitt, M. T., Branscombe, N. R., Postmes, T., & Garcia, A. (2014). The consequences of perceived discrimination for psychological well-being: A meta-analytic review. *Psychological Bulletin, 140*(4), 921–948.

Shao, Z., Feng, Y., & Wang, T. (2017). Charismatic leadership and tacit knowledge sharing in the context of enterprise systems learning: The mediating effect of psychological safety climate and intrinsic motivation. *Behaviour & Information Technology, 36*(2), 194–208.

Shelton, C., & Thomas, D. A. (2013). The study on White men leading through diversity & inclusion. Retrieved from http://www.whitemensleadershipstudy.com/

Shore, L. M., Randel, A. E., Chung, B. G., Dean, M. A., Holcombe Ehrhart, K., & Singh, G. (2011). Inclusion and diversity in work groups: A review and model for future research. *Journal of Management, 37*(4), 1262–1289.

Society for Human Resource Management. (2009). *Global diversity and inclusion: Perceptions, practices, and attitudes* (Report). Retrieved from https://www.shrm.org/hr-today/trends-and-forecasting/research-and-surveys/Documents/09-Diversity_and_Inclusion_Report.pdf

Thomas, D. A. (2001). The truth about mentoring minorities: Race matters. *Harvard Business Review, 79*(4), 98–107.

Weisenfeld, L. W., & Robinson-Backmon, I. B. (2007). Upward mobility and the African American accountant: An analysis of perceived discrimination, perceived career advancement curtailment, and intent to remain. *Accounting and the Public Interest, 7*(1), 26–49.

Wigert, B., & Harter, J. (2017). *Re-engineering performance management* (Report). Omaha, NE: Gallup.

6

Authenticity in the Workplace

An African American Perspective

PATRICIA FAISON HEWLIN *and* ANNA-MARIA BROOMES

The people I wanted to work with left, and those who stayed are not minority friendly. As a minority, I feel that they don't want me there. It is so obvious. The head partner doesn't even speak to me. I try to downplay my cultural differences and laugh at their stupid jokes. I play the game and let them think I believe in the firm's goals.

—*Hewlin, 2009, p. 732*

The foregoing quote is from an African American male lawyer who is sharing his experience of working in a firm that does not value diversity. He "plays the game" by suppressing personal views and conveying alignment with the goals of the firm, a behavior termed "creating facades of conformity" (Hewlin, 2003). Facades of conformity are false representations that individuals in organizations create to convey that they embrace the organization's values (Hewlin, 2003, 2009). In essence, creating a facade is a strategy people use to survive and succeed when they do not feel free to express their true selves at work. Research on facades of conformity resides within scholarly discussions of authenticity, particularly on how authentic self-expression is constrained when one's personal perspectives (e.g., those related to one's cultural background) are different or not valued in one's workplace (Roberts, Cha,

Hewlin, & Settles, 2009). Existing findings on facades of conformity highlight the experience of holding a minority status across a combination of personal characteristics, such as gender, race, culture, work experience, and values. In particular, a core finding is that the number of personal characteristics in which one identifies himself or herself as a minority is positively associated with the degree to which one creates facades of conformity, suppressing personal values and pretending to embrace organization values. The theoretical basis of this finding is that a high level of distinctiveness can leave one vulnerable to isolation and stigmatization from majority group members (Brewer, 1981; Kanter, 1977). Moreover, distinctive social categories can lead to feelings of self-consciousness whereby those in the minority feel that they are different or stand out. Such feelings might even lead minorities to overestimate the degree that they are under scrutiny by others (Kramer, 1998). As a result, research suggests that individuals who perceive that they are minorities in their organizations sometimes find it important to manage carefully the extent to which they express divergent points of view to avoid any negative publicity that may be associated with expressing unacceptable values (Dryburgh, 1999; Meyerson, 2001).

Although the research on facades of conformity has shown that minority status can influence inauthentic behavior, this line of research has not addressed nuanced dynamics associated with being a minority in a specific characteristic such as race. Furthermore, there is limited systematic attention to the relative experiences of authentic expression among different racial groups and ethnicities. These omissions limit the degree to which scholars and organizational leaders can comprehensively address factors that hinder authentic self-expression among diverse members. In this chapter, we consider the experience of African Americans in the context of authenticity and personal well-being, with a particular emphasis on the historical roots underpinning this experience. Indeed, the historical foundation of race dynamics in the United States has caused race to be a highly salient factor in social, political, and organizational settings (see Fiske, 2010, for a review), often shaping disparities with respect to promotions, salary, and general treatment (Goldman, Gutek, Stein, & Lewis, 2006), as well as individuals' sense of belongingness in the workplace (e.g., Dumas, Phillips, & Rothbard, 2013).

In this chapter, we discuss findings from two samples representing a wide set of industries among the general US population. The samples include 2,226 workers and 243 professionals. Our findings show that

African Americans engage in inauthentic behavior (i.e., creating facades) more often than those of different racial backgrounds and ethnicities, and that the highest level of facade creation occurs among individuals working in the legal sector. We offer insight on these findings from interviews with African American lawyers who spoke to us about their experiences of juggling authenticity and creating facades of conformity, and the associated consequences. We seek to stimulate future research in this arena while simultaneously challenging the way scholars and business leaders think about leveraging diversity, and promoting authenticity that benefits organizational learning and the personal well-being of employees. Furthermore, our exploratory research on the legal sector offers initial insight on unique industry-related factors that are critical to address when considering organizational practices and tools for building safe environments for authentic self-expression.

Relevant Theory and Empirical Findings

In workplace contexts, authentic self-expression, which is the outward expression of inward experiences such as beliefs and values (e.g., Roberts et al., 2009), is positively associated with employee well-being, satisfaction, positive affect, the perception of meaningful work (Ménard & Brunet, 2011), and work engagement (Hewlin, Kim, & Song, 2016; Van den Bosch & Taris, 2014). However, authenticity can feel restricted when employees perceive that their personal values conflict with organizational values and the values of those in the majority (e.g., Hewlin, 2003). Hewlin (2003) coined the term *facades of conformity* to illustrate how employees pretend to embrace organizational values that are incongruent with their personal values. Broadly, the term *organizational values* encompasses espoused organizational values and personal values held by the majority of organization members (Stormer & Devine, 2008). Thus, facades may result from incongruence on organizational values and norms, such as competitiveness versus cooperation and inclusion versus exclusion (e.g., employees of a given racial background are exceeding in their careers at the exclusion of others). In some environments, certain political, cultural, and religious perspectives, as well as values related to sexual orientation and lifestyle choices, may be more favored than others, which can create strong pressures to "blend in" and give the impression of conformity when one does not hold values that are considered most acceptable at work. Accordingly, research has found that facade creation is influenced by work environments that are intolerant to diverse perspectives and values (Hewlin, 2009; Stormer & Devine, 2008).

When employees perceive that they are unable to express themselves authentically at work, there are significantly heightened risks for both the employees and the organizations that they work for. Stormer and Devine (2008) found that facade creation, in the form of pretending to conform in appearance but not in action (e.g., publicly agreeing to a new initiative yet privately refusing to participate), can express itself through veiled sabotage, a concept also known as symbolic covert conflict (Morrill, Zald, & Rao, 2003). Veiled sabotage signifies the subtle acts of noncooperation and resistance toward organizational policies and rules (e.g., daydreaming, taking extended breaks, and malicious gossip) and could partially explain why organizations struggle to implement changes despite apparent employee support.

In light of our focus on the African American experience, we center attention on the finding that minority status is positively related to creating facades of conformity as an initial step to understanding the experience of individuals who bring diverse values to the organization. We argue that the unique, nuanced experiences of African Americans in the workplace will cause them to feel pressured to create facades at higher levels than members of other racial groups. We base our assertion on the historical, deeply ingrained, negative stereotypes about blackness that have been upheld by dominant narratives and have created distinct challenges and consequences for African Americans who dare to express themselves authentically in today's workplace (Durr & Wingfield, 2011; Hall, Everett, & Hamilton-Mason, 2011; Harlow, 2003; Jackson & Wingfield, 2013; McDowell & Carter-Francique, 2017; Opie & Phillips, 2015; Wingfield, 2007). Notably, pressures to conform to the dominant value system can be traced to the severe punishment of African American slaves for expressing themselves authentically. Epperson (1990) describes how White plantation owners in Virginia imposed European American names on slaves, erasing a significant connection to their African roots and enforcing a permanent reminder of their subservience.

In today's workplace, African Americans still contend with negative images that shape how they are viewed in the workplace and society at large. For example, Collins (1986) and Wingfield (2007) describe images of Black women as treacherous, hypersexual, aggressive, and ideal for service, and of Black men as dangerous, criminal, and threatening. The burden of discriminatory practices in the workplace may result in African

American workers who experience internal and external pressures to present themselves in ways that minimize visible traits connecting them to African American culture (Hall et al., 2011; Jackson & Wingfield, 2013; Opie & Phillips, 2015). This may include chemically relaxing one's hair to appear more Eurocentric (Opie & Phillips, 2015), assimilating to coworkers' behaviors (McDowell & Carter-Francique, 2017; Whitfield-Harris & Lockhart, 2016), whitewashing résumés, hiding minority beliefs (Hewlin, 2009), and managing and suppressing emotions related to racism in the workplace (Wingfield, 2007, 2010).

Additionally, research suggests that African American men and women engage in different strategies to minimize and suppress their feelings (Hall et al., 2011; Wingfield, 2007). African American men may try to portray themselves as nonthreatening, cordial, genial, humble, and agreeable, concealing traditionally masculine traits such as arrogance (Jackson & Wingfield, 2013; Wingfield, 2007). Black men studied by Wingfield (2007) discussed experiencing more exclusion and social isolation than Black women and finding fewer outlets to express their feelings. Black women must learn to navigate a professional world in which they are heavily penalized by racism, sexism, and the intersection of the two. Refusals to conform to particular stereotypes may result in Black women being further stereotyped as cold, stuck-up, and humorless (Wingfield, 2007). Black women interviewed by Hall and coauthors (2011) spoke candidly about the emotional and psychological distress of having to deal with scrutiny and the fear of being "branded" if they behaved in any way that might confirm the stereotypical beliefs of their coworkers.

The dual processes of actively not conforming to negative stereotypes about Black people while at the same time trying to conform to organizational values can be emotionally, psychologically, and physically exhausting (Durr & Wingfield, 2011; Hall et al., 2011; Harlow, 2003; Jackson & Wingfield, 2013; McDowell & Carter-Francique, 2017; Wingfield, 2007, 2010). These findings are consistent with outcomes associated with creating facades of conformity, which include emotional exhaustion and reduced work engagement (Hewlin, 2009; Hewlin, Dumas, & Burnett, 2017). In the inaugural study of facades of conformity, emotional exhaustion mediated the relationship between facades of conformity and intention to leave the organization (Hewlin, 2009), suggesting that organizations are at risk of losing talented workers when African Americans do not feel free to express their authentic selves at work.

These historical and contemporary pressures to conform led us to predict that we would see the highest level of facade creation among African American employees. We tested our predictions using cross-sectional, self-report survey data from a larger study on facades of conformity. We also evaluated interview data to shed more insight on our findings.

The Research

The participants were part of a US-based survey response panel run by QualtricsTM. Panel members were working adults paid by QualtricsTM with points they can redeem for merchandise from online merchants. The number of participants who opened the survey invitation were 5,497, and 2,587 of them completed it, representing a 47 percent response rate. A quality review of the completions resulted in a total of 2,226 final respondents. Fifty-six percent were female, and the average age was 39.5 years ($SD = 11.1$). Twenty industries (including finance, health care, education, and legal services) were represented. The breakdown of race/ethnicity is as follows: Asian (non-Indian) (3.2 percent), Black or African American (22.3 percent), Indian (1 percent), Latin American or Hispanic (5.4 percent), and White (45 percent).

Results

We used the facades of conformity six-item, seven-point scale (1 = never, 7 = all of the time) that evaluates employees' comfort levels with expressing themselves authentically in the workplace (Hewlin, 2009). Sample items include the following: "I behave in a manner that reflects the organization's value system even though it is inconsistent with my personal values," and "I say things I don't believe at work." The internal consistency for this scale was .92. To evaluate our prediction that African Americans will engage in the highest level of facade creation, we performed a one-way analysis of variance, which allowed us to compare the means of creating facades among African Americans with the means of participants in other racial groups. Results showed that there was a significant difference of means [$F(1, 2201) = 187.68, p = .00$] between African American participants ($M = 4.90, SD = 1.71$) and the means across the participants of other racial groups ($M = 3.82, SD = 1.49$). Figure 6-1 provides an illustration of the means associated with each race or ethnicity.

FIGURE 6-1

Facades of conformity by race and ethnicity

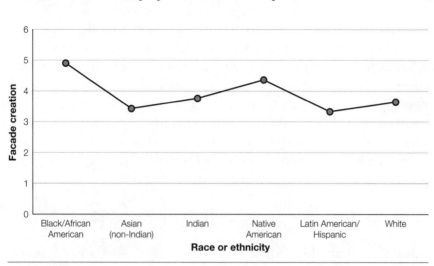

In addition to this finding, the research team explored the possibility of industry effects as they related to facade creation, using a sample of similarly situated participants with respect to education (MBA alumni in two northeastern business schools). Using alumni lists provided by the schools, 500 students were contacted by email and invited to partake in an online survey, and 243 (48 percent) completed the survey. Participants worked in fifteen different industries, with the largest composition in financial services, law, consulting, advertising, and health care. The average age of respondents was thirty-four years ($SD = 8.0$), and the average organizational tenure was five years ($SD = 5.0$). The majority of participants were in middle-management positions (76.5 percent). Of the total number of participants, 28 percent identified as non-White, which included 9 percent identifying as African American.

In this second sample, we found that there was a statistically significant difference between industries, as determined by a one-way analysis of variance [$F(14, 225) = 1.97, p = .021$]. In comparing levels of facade creation across the industries, the legal sector had the highest degree of facade creation ($M = 3.04, SD = .67$) among respondents of all races, compared with the fourteen other industries, and thus higher than the total mean of participants across all industries ($M = 2.60, SD = .70$). In light of the wide range of industries in which the respondents were employed, we found it particularly interesting to see this result, which prompted us to explore the lived experience of African Americans and their authentic self-expression in the legal profession, which is part of a larger interview study that aims to understand factors that cause individuals to create facades of conformity in the workplace.[1] This data collection was initiated with the MBA alumni participants and continued with referrals to colleagues and other professional contacts in a "snowball" fashion (Robinson, 2014). Out of this set of fifteen respondents, seven were African American lawyers. Although this interview sample is small and exploratory in nature, our initial findings suggest that managing the degree to which one can be authentic at work is a salient and often challenging experience for African Americans in the legal profession.

African Americans in the Legal Sector

In 1868, Macon Bolling Allen became the first licensed African American attorney and the first African American to legally practice law in the United States (Smith, 2000). It was not until 1950 that the Supreme Court of the United States declared it unconstitutional to deny African Americans admission to law schools previously reserved for White students only (*Sweatt v. Painter*, 1950). Institutional barriers continue to hinder African Americans in their attempts to enter the legal profession (Nussbaumer, 2012; Weatherspoon, 2010). In its 2017 report, the National Association for Law Placement (2017) reported that African Americans represent only 4.28 percent of associates in the United States, a figure that has decreased from 4.66 percent since 2009. Women are 2.42 percent of associates. African Americans account for just 1.8 percent of partners in American law firms.

This considerable underrepresentation in the legal profession is mirrored in other prestigious professions, such as medicine and dentistry, which Nance and Madsen (2014) purport is a reflection of greater societal, educational, and institutional barriers that prevent African Americans from attaining advanced degrees in law. Scholars propose a number of theories to explain African Americans' restricted entry into the legal profession, such as the mass incarceration of Black males in the United States and the resulting distrust and hostility toward the legal system, unjust law school admission procedures, racial isolation in law school, and a lack of African American role models working in the field (Nussbaumer, 2012; Weatherspoon, 2010). Conley (2006) concluded that outside of progressive, boutique law firms (e.g., Black law firms, Jewish law firms), large firms do not seem to value diversity beyond what is deemed socially acceptable, noting a collective "metaphorical shrug" from elite firms (p. 843). In acknowledgment of this prevailing indifference to diversity issues in the legal sector, we interviewed African Americans who had beaten the odds and completed the long, arduous journey to become lawyers.

Method

We conducted semistructured interviews to generate discussion about our research and provide a platform for African Africans to reflect on their legal careers and express their voices as experts of their own experiences as racial minorities. Rooted in Hewlin's (2003, 2009) theoretical framework of facades of conformity and drawing from pilot studies on the concept (see Hewlin, 2009; Stormer & Devine, 2008), we constructed an interview protocol to assess the organizational and personal factors that contribute to experiences of both authentic and inauthentic behaviors for Black lawyers working in US law firms in which the partners and associates were predominantly White males. Our interviews lasted approximately forty-five to sixty minutes each, were done over the phone, were tape-recorded, and then were transcribed.

Findings: Relationships, Facades, and the Resolve to Be Authentic

Consistent with research that addresses the difficulty that Black professionals have in developing close professional relationships as a result of different experiences, interests, and cultural values (Dumas et al., 2013; Garth & Sterling, 2009), our respondents discussed this as a core issue in the law firm context. Developing close professional relationships is particularly critical in a law firm environment because relationships create opportunities to join work teams that can lead to visibility and, importantly, billable hours, which generate revenues for the law firm. The following quotes from two of our respondents reflect this issue.

> Certain relationships are developed almost seamlessly or innately amongst White attorneys. I see myself almost on the outside or having to work harder just to get into the circle.

When there is a lot of work and everyone is busy, there is not a problem. But it is when there are slow periods when you begin to see how the network works. There are people who are always busy and are kept fed with work. People within my own background, we have a harder time with that, so when it was slow, people within the network get the best deals, and that compounds with time. It is a challenge for us because we have to make an extra effort. . . . [S]ome connections are just natural, and when you don't have partners who have the same background as yours, then it is difficult to form those connections. . . . [Y]ou have to work double time to find common ground . . . or you are sunk.

In light of the importance of relationships, the pressure to conform and create facades of conformity is salient.

I don't believe that a Black person can ever truly be authentic in corporate America. I just don't believe that.

I have certain behaviors that are literally me, but you won't ever see them in the workplace because I am afraid of being judged. I have adopted the culture and sort of reflect back to them what they reflect as opposed to me projecting my own image. . . . I think it is kind of a shame because companies are starving for authenticity because that is how they can innovate.

As well, one respondent indicated that he cannot fully be authentic as a result of cultural insensitivity and unawareness: "If you never went to school with Black people, if you've never practiced law with Black people, if there's a dearth of Black attorneys at the law firms you've worked at and you've never had to report to a Black attorney, there are cultural nuances that you're so oblivious to. . . . [Y]ou've never ever had to confront your own racial ignorance because it seems perfectly normal. And if I say it the way I want to and need to, . . . [i]t's going to make for a very uncomfortable situation . . . for the rest of the year."

Is there ever a place for authenticity? We had mixed responses with respect to when participants felt authentic. Authenticity can come from a place of comfort *after* establishing credibility as an exceptional performer, as one respondent observed: "I had set a foundation of excellence . . . so that was clear. There was never a question about my ability. . . . Once you see that, all of your feedback is the same. . . . I have a proven [track record], . . . so now they can begin to see parts of me they haven't seen. I don't think any of us have that sigh of relief until you get to that point, but it is hard because some of us never fully get to that point [of establishing one's credibility] to be authentic . . . then you never get to be authentic."

We also found that authenticity, when displayed, might hinder one's career progress. This respondent sought and obtained a position more suitable to her desire to exude authenticity in the workplace: "I try to be true to myself the best I can, but maybe that was the problem. I did not do a good job at playing the game, and in fact, it cost me. I believe that is why I did not progress at [the firm] . . . which was very clubish. . . . It is different in my new job. . . . I still say that it is better to be your authentic self because it is already hard enough . . . and you are probably not in the right environment. Black culture is not a secret. . . . I believe people will gravitate to you more if you are authentic."

Finally, the choice to be authentic can come from a place of "having enough" of feeling scrutinized and singled out as a Black person.

> Being Black is a moving target. When I was somewhat younger . . . I was acutely aware of no matter where I went, no matter what I did, what were my achievements, I always knew that everyone was looking at me as the Black guy. Obviously, I always knew I was Black, but I knew that other people were looking at me that way. . . . I think through my life . . . probably early on . . . I got to the point where that's your problem, not mine so you can, whatever your reaction to me is, knock yourself out. I'm not going to let that bother me anymore and it's going to be your problem, not my problem. And that being, if blackness was going to be a problem, it was going to be someone else's problem, not my problem. So, I would spend a lot of time saying, well thinking, and pursuing that I am a very skilled trial lawyer, and it doesn't matter who you are on the other end, you're going to get hell.

Discussion and Recommendations

Our findings among a general population of workers in the United States show that African Americans engage in inauthentic behavior (i.e., creating facades) more often than workers of different racial backgrounds. This finding confirms and highlights the ongoing sense of duality or "double consciousness" that African Americans have experienced in and outside the workplace for decades (e.g., Du Bois, 1903). Whereas some have been successful to find professions and work contexts that promote and appreciate diverse perspectives and values, as a community, being Black in the workplace comes with unique and salient pressures to conform to dominant norms and values. Our qualitative findings from an initial sample of professionals illustrate that this is particularly the case in the legal profession, in which building relationships with partners and clients is critical to one's success, as is noted by our interview respondents. Continued qualitative and quantitative research in this arena will help to identify specific trends in how African Americans manage their sense of authenticity in the legal profession.

Given that emotional and psychological strain, along with reduced levels of work engagement and organizational commitment, is associated with suppressing one's true self in the workplace (e.g., Hewlin, 2009; Hewlin et al., 2016; Hewlin et al., 2017), it is critical that future research focuses on ways that organizations can employ practices that not only promote authenticity but also integrate sensitivity to historical, entrenched barriers to authenticity for African Americans and members of other underrepresented groups. This should be done by paying particular attention to certain industries, such as the legal profession and other client-driven professions, in which conformity and professional relationships are particularly crucial to one's career success. Specifically, we recommend that organizational practices for promoting authenticity and diversity be a part of a holistic effort to create a learning environment (Argyris & Schön, 1996). A core component of an organizational learning environment is psychological safety, which encourages a shared belief that a team or the organization is safe for interpersonal risk-taking such as expressing divergent values and points of view (Edmondson, 1999). Psychological safety begins with top-down leadership communications and actions, such as formal and informal open discussions where all members are free to share ideas and address issues without fear of recourse. This will likely require leadership training and long-term coaching partnerships with professionals who can help guide the organization to a place of psychological safety and well-being. We emphasize again that sensitivity to the unique experiences of underrepresented groups must be integrated into such efforts. As well noted by Opie and Freeman (2017), encouraging authenticity in the context of organizational norms that are infused with bias will not render authentic self-expression among those who are traditionally the recipients of that bias in their daily interactions at work. Thus, efforts to promote authenticity will necessitate a reevaluation of organizational values that systemically promote bias, and the establishment of new ones that liberate diverse, authentic self-expression among all employees.

NOTES

1. The research team is conducting ongoing research that explores the dynamics of authenticity and creating facades of conformity in multiple industries and cultures.

REFERENCES

Argyris, C., & Schön, D. (1996). *Organizational learning II: Theory, methods, and practice*. Reading, MA: Addison-Wesley.

Brewer, M. B. (1981). Ethnocentrism and its role in interpersonal trust. In M. Brewer & B. Collins (Eds.), *Scientific inquiry and the social sciences* (pp. 345–360). San Francisco, CA: Jossey-Bass.

Collins, P. H. (1986). Learning from the outsider within: The sociological significance of Black feminist thought. *Social Problems, 33*(6), S14–S32.

Conley, J. M. (2006). Tales of diversity: Lawyers' narratives of racial equity in private firms. *Law & Social Inquiry, 31*(4), 831–853.

Dryburgh, H. (1999). Work hard, play hard: Women and professionalization in engineering: Adapting to the culture. *Gender and Society, 5*, 664–682.

Du Bois, W. E. B. (1903). *The souls of Black folk*. Chicago, IL: A. C. McClurg.

Dumas, T. L., Phillips, K. W., & Rothbard, N. P. (2013). Getting closer at the company party: Integration experiences, racial dissimilarity, and workplace relationships. *Organization Science, 24*(5), 1377–1401.

Durr, M., & Wingfield, A. H. (2011). Keep your "N" in check: African American women and the interactive effects of etiquette and emotional labor. *Critical Sociology, 37*(5), 557–571.

Edmondson, A. (1999). Psychological safety and learning behavior in work teams. *Administrative Science Quarterly, 44*(2), 350–383.

Epperson, T. (1990). Race and the disciplines of the plantation. *Historical Archaeology, 24*(4), 29–36. Retrieved from http://www.jstor.org/stable/25616047

Fiske, S. T. (2010). Interpersonal stratification: Status, power, and subordination. In S. T. Fiske, D. T. Gilbert, & G. Lindzey (Eds.), *Handbook of social psychology* (5th ed.) (pp. 941–982). New York, NY: Wiley.

Garth, B. G., & Sterling, J. (2009). Exploring inequality in the corporate law firm apprenticeship: Doing the time, finding the love. *Georgetown Journal of Legal Ethics, 22*, 1361–1394.

Goldman, B. M., Gutek, B. A., Stein, J. H., & Lewis, K. (2006). Employment discrimination in organizations: Antecedents and consequences. *Journal of Management, 32*(6), 786–830.

Hall, J. C., Everett, J. E., & Hamilton-Mason, J. (2011). Black women talk about workplace stress and how they cope. *Journal of Black Studies, 43*(2), 207–226.

Harlow, R. (2003). "Race doesn't matter, but . . .": The effect of race on professors' experiences and emotion management in the undergraduate college classroom. *Social Psychology Quarterly, 66*(4), 348–363.

Hewlin, P. F. (2003). And the award for best actor goes to . . . : Facades of conformity in organizational settings. *Academy of Management Review, 28*, 633–642.

Hewlin, P. F. (2009). Wearing the cloak: Antecedents and consequences of creating facades of conformity. *Journal of Applied Psychology, 94*(3), 727–741.

Hewlin, P. F., Dumas, T. L., & Burnett, M. F. (2017). To thine own self be true? Facades of conformity, values incongruence, and the moderating impact of leader integrity. *Academy of Management Journal, 60*(1), 178–199.

Hewlin, P. F., Kim, S. S., & Song, Y. H. (2016). Creating facades of conformity in the face of job insecurity: A study of consequences and conditions. *Journal of Occupational and Organizational Psychology, 89*(3), 539–567.

Jackson, B. A., & Wingfield, A. H. (2013). Getting angry to get ahead: Black college men, emotional performance, and encouraging respectable masculinity. *Symbolic Interaction, 36*(3), 275–292.

Kanter, R. M. (1977). *Men and women of the corporation.* New York, NY: Basic Books.

Kramer, R. M. (1998). Paranoid cognition in social systems: Thinking and acting in the shadow of doubt. *Personality and Social Psychology Review, 4*, 251–275.

McDowell, J., & Carter-Francique, A. (2017). An intersectional analysis of the workplace experiences of African American female athletic directors. *Sex Roles, 77*(5), 393–408.

Ménard, J., & Brunet, L. (2011). Authenticity and well-being in the workplace: A mediation model. *Journal of Managerial Psychology, 26*(4), 331–346.

Meyerson, D. E. (2001). *Tempered radicals: How people use difference to inspire change at work.* Cambridge, MA: Harvard Business School Press.

Morrill, C., Zald, M. N., & Rao, H. (2003). Covert political conflict in organizations: Challenges from below. *Annual Review of Sociology, 29*(1), 391–415.

Nance, J. P., & Madsen, P. E. (2014). An empirical analysis of diversity in the legal profession. *Connecticut Law Review, 47*(2), 271–320.

National Association for Law Placement. (2017, December). *NALP 2017 report on diversity in U.S. law firms.* Retrieved from https://www.nalp.org/uploads/2017N ALPReportonDiversityinUSLawFirms.pdf

Nussbaumer, J. (2012). Misuse of the Law School Admissions Test, racial discrimination, and the de facto quota system for restricting African-American access to the legal profession. *St. John's Law Review, 80*(1), 167–182.

Opie, T. R., & Freeman, R. E. (2017, 5 July). Our biases undermine our colleagues' attempts to be authentic. Retrieved from https://hbr.org/2017/07/our-biases -undermine-our-colleagues-attempts-to-be-authentic

Opie, T. R., & Phillips, K. W. (2015). Hair penalties: The negative influence of Afrocentric hair on ratings of Black women's dominance and professionalism. *Frontiers in Psychology, 6*, article 1311.

Roberts, L. M., Cha, S., Hewlin, P. F., & Settles, I. H. (2009). Bringing the inside out: Enhancing authenticity and positive identity in organizations. In L. M.

Roberts & J. Dutton (Eds.), *Exploring positive identities and organizations: Building a theoretical and research foundation* (pp. 149–169). Philadelphia, PA: Lawrence Erlbaum Associates.

Robinson, O. C. (2014). Sampling in interview-based qualitative research: A theoretical and practical guide. *Qualitative Research in Psychology, 11*(1), 25–41.

Smith, J. D. (2000). Allen, Macon Bolling (1816–1894). In *American National Biography Online.* Retrieved from https://dx.doi.org/10.1093/anb/9780198606697.article .1100009

Stormer, F., & Devine, K. (2008). Acting at work: Facades of conformity in academia. *Journal of Management Inquiry, 17*(2), 112–134.

Sweatt v. Painter, 339 U.S. 629, 70 S. Ct. 848, 94 L. Ed. 1114 (1950).

Van den Bosch, R., & Taris, T. W. (2014). The authentic worker's well-being and performance: The relationship between authenticity at work, well-being, and work outcomes. *Journal of Psychology, 148*(6), 659–681.

Weatherspoon, F. D. (2010). The status of African American males in the legal profession: A pipeline of institutional roadblocks and barriers. *Mississippi Law Journal, 80*(1), 259–298.

Whitfield-Harris, L., & Lockhart, J. S. (2016). The workplace environment for African-American faculty employed in predominately White institutions. *ABNF Journal: Official Journal of the Association of Black Nursing Faculty in Higher Education, 27*(2), 28–38.

Wingfield, A. H. (2007). The modern mammy and the angry Black man: African American professionals' experiences with gendered racism in the workplace. *Race, Gender & Class, 14*(1/2), 196–212.

Wingfield, A. H. (2010). Are some emotions marked "Whites only"? Racialized feeling rules in professional workplaces. *Social Problems, 57*(2), 251–268.

7

Feeling Connected

The Importance of Engagement,
Authenticity, and Relationships
in the Careers of Diverse Professionals

STACY BLAKE-BEARD, LAURA MORGAN ROBERTS,
BEVERLY EDGEHILL, *and* ELLA F. WASHINGTON

As projected, ethnic diversity in the US workforce continues to increase in the twenty-first century (M. P. Bell, 2006; Blancero, Mouriño-Ruiz, & Padilla, 2018; Cox & Blake, 1991; Thomas & Ely, 1996). Given these trends, organizations must ensure that they are creating the conditions that will enable all members to thrive at work. Organizational leaders are charged with building capacity for effectively hiring, developing, and advancing diverse talent (Hunt, Layton, & Prince, 2015; Mazur, 2010; Naff, 2018; Ortlieb & Sieben, 2013).

This charge is no small feat as we look at the impact of context on the experiences of diverse talent. Women and people of color are often in institutional milieus where they are one of few; this tokenism is accompanied by isolation, increased scrutiny, and presumptions about their competence. Firms must address how to support and enable relationships among people who come from diverse cultures, backgrounds, and perspectives. Further, organizations need to consider ways to enable underrepresented groups to break through the barriers keeping women and people of color from attaining leadership positions in organizations (Barnes, 2017; Nugent, Pollack, & Travis, 2016; Tomlinson, 2001; Travis & Thorpe-Moscon, 2018; Wyatt & Silvester, 2015).

In the face of challenging organizational contexts, how are the careers of diverse professionals sustained? How do organizations provide spaces where diverse employees can bring their best and most authentic selves to work? The current study focused on factors that have traditionally contributed to the career experiences of diverse talent—the importance of feeling connected to work (engagement), to self (authenticity), and to others (managers, coworkers, and mentors)—and their relationship to well-being outcomes. Our data set of diverse professionals also allowed us the rare opportunity to statistically compare the experiences of Black professionals with those of White, Hispanic, and Asian American professionals.

Feeling Connected

Relationships across organizational levels are important to effective retention and engagement of diverse talent. Interactions with managers, coworkers, and mentors can all be positive contributors to the career experiences of diverse employees (Ashikali & Groeneveld, 2015; Jones & George, 2014; Offermann & Basford, 2014; Ugorji, 1997). Supportive managers have been linked to enhanced employee performance, as well as a more committed and effective workforce. Peer support has been positively related to a sense of empowerment. Mentors have also been linked to a number of outcomes for protégés; those who are mentored are more satisfied with their careers, receive more promotions, feel a stronger commitment to the organization, and are less likely to leave. Research clearly shows the power of mentoring in helping people of color break through to senior levels within the organization (Blake-Beard, 2003; Creary & Roberts, 2017; Thomas & Gabarro, 1999; Wang, 2016).

Not only are relationships surrounding diverse professionals important, but a growing body of work points to the need for diverse professionals to bring their whole selves to work (E. L. Bell & Nkomo, 2001; Dumas, Phillips, & Rothbard, 2013; Hewlett, Luce, & West, 2005; Kahn, 1990, 1992; Phillips, Dumas, & Rothbard, 2018; Roberts, 2005; Roberts, Mayo, Ely, & Thomas, 2018). For example, Phillips, Dumas, and Rothbard (2018) discussed the costs to diverse professionals when they leave important parts of their lives and identities at the organizational door. As importantly, they noted the negative implications that also accrue to organizations as a result of this compartmentalized approach.

The goal of our research was to explore these factors related to employee engagement, with a particular focus on the experiences of professionals from diverse cultural backgrounds. Specifically, we aimed to answer the following questions regarding engagement, authenticity, and relationships in the careers of racially diverse professionals:

1) Which professionals report the highest levels of engagement, authenticity, and satisfaction with their careers and their employers?

2) How do key constituents (managers, coworkers, mentors) support diverse professionals to make frequent, valuable contributions to their employing organizations?

3) What are the benefits of providing work contexts where diverse professionals are able to bring their whole selves to their work?

Methodology

Sample

The population for this study consisted of participants who attended the Partnership's[1] Annual Workforce Retention Conference.[2] Of the approximately 400 participants attending the conference, 201 respondents completed the study questionnaire, for a response rate of 50 percent. The survey sample was largely female (70 percent), close to forty years of age on average, married (53 percent), and highly educated (53 percent of the sample had a professional degree). The average income was greater than US$100,000 a year (table 7-1).

Regarding race, more than half of the sample was Black/African American (53 percent), one-quarter of the sample was White, and the remaining quarter was almost evenly distributed among Hispanic, Asian, or other (figure 7-1).

The Survey

The first section of the survey asked for information about relationships at work. Respondents were asked to indicate whether they currently have an informal mentor. A mentor was defined as "an influential individual

TABLE 7-1

Descriptive statistics of demographic variables

Variable	Survey data
Gender (N = 201)	
Men	0.30
Women	0.70
Race (N = 201)	
White	0.25
Black/African American	0.53
Hispanic	0.07
Asian or Pacific Islander	0.06
Other	0.08
Age (N = 201)	39.7
	(9.6)
Education (N = 201)	
Some college	0.06
Bachelor degree	0.32
Some graduate school	0.08
Professional degree	0.53
Income (N = 197)	108,249
	(75,731)
Marital status (N = 201)	
Married	0.53
Partnered or committed	0.08
Single/never married	0.27
Single/previously married	0.11

Note: Standard deviations are in parentheses.

who takes an active interest in developing your career." The survey stated, "We are particularly interested in your experience with informal mentoring relationships. An informal mentor is an individual with whom you have built a relationship on your own, without assistance or intervention from an organizational initiative." Respondents were also asked to report how many informal mentors they have had in their careers and how many intraorganizational informal mentors they have had. Respondents rated the perceived level of support that they received from their informal mentors, as well as their managers and coworkers. Items were rated on a five-point Likert scale, with 1 being "not at all" and 5 being "to a very large extent."

The second section of the survey solicited information about several variables related to attitudes at work. Variables measured included work engagement, perceived job fit, career satisfaction, authenticity, organizational commitment, and intention to leave. The same five-

FIGURE 7-1

Ethnic composition of respondents

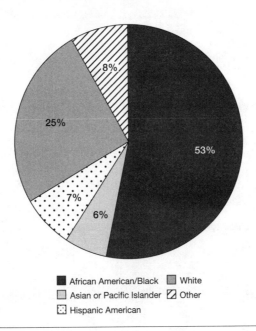

African American/Black ■ White
Asian or Pacific Islander ▨ Other
Hispanic American

point Likert scale just described was used to rate these attitudinal measures.[3]

The final section of the survey was devoted to demographic variables. Respondents were asked to provide information about number of promotions, annual compensation, size of current employer, sex, ethnicity, sexual orientation, marital status, educational level, US citizenship, age, number of children, current employment status, current job title, and industry of current employing organizations.

Key Findings

Relationships Matter

The influence of relationships on the careers of our study respondents is clearly evident. Mentoring is a process to which many of the respondents have access; 81 percent of study respondents indicated that they currently have a mentor (table 7-2). And these respondents have a history

TABLE 7-2

Descriptive statistics of mentorship and selected scales

Variable	Summary
Mentorship	
Ever had a mentor (N = 201)	0.81
Average number if had (N = 162)	3.79
	(0.68)
Scales	
Relationship with mentor (N = 162)	3.79
	(0.68)
Relationship with manager (N = 194)	3.43
	(0.90)
Relationship with coworker (N = 195)	3.54
	(0.73)
Work engagement (N = 201)	3.85
	(0.52)
Perceived job fit (N = 201)	3.49
	(1.02)
Career satisfaction (N = 201)	3.50
	(0.81)
Inauthenticity (N = 201)	2.39
	(0.70)
Commitment (N = 201)	3.20
	(0.85)
Intent to leave (N = 201)	2.56
	(1.35)

Note: Scale scores are an average of responses to the scale items, ranging from 1 ("not at all") to 5 ("to a very large extent"). Standard deviations are in parentheses.

of building mentoring relationships; they have, on average, had three mentors over the course of their careers. In light of the extant literature acknowledging the importance of mentoring to diverse professionals, it is encouraging to see the high percentage of study participants who have access to this developmental process. In fact, in this study, people of color were more likely to have a mentor than Whites. Notably, 81 percent of African American respondents indicated that they currently have a mentor, in comparison with 76 percent of White respondents. Surprisingly, mentoring was not significantly related to any of the attitudinal variables in the study.

In terms of manager and coworker support, study respondents reported moderate levels of perceived support from each of these sources; on a scale of 1 to 5, respondents gave managers an average score of 3.43 and coworkers an average score of 3.54 (see table 7-2).

FIGURE 7-2

Manager effects on career outcomes

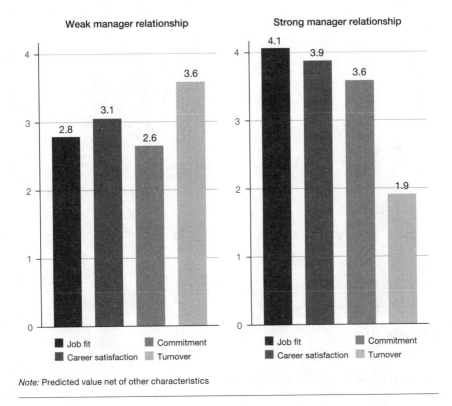

Note: Predicted value net of other characteristics

There were several significant findings regarding the relationship be-tween having strong connections (i.e., above-average connections) with managers and coworkers and selected attitudinal measures. People who had strong relationships with managers (above 3.8 on a five-point scale) and coworkers (above 3.4 on a five-point scale) reported higher levels of career satisfaction, organizational commitment, and perceived job fit. They were also less likely to consider leaving their job—their intent to leave was lower than it was for those whose relationships with managers and coworkers were not as strong (figures 7-2 and 7-3). Note that these relationships held even when controlling for age, gender, income, and education.

FIGURE 7-3

Coworker effects on career outcomes

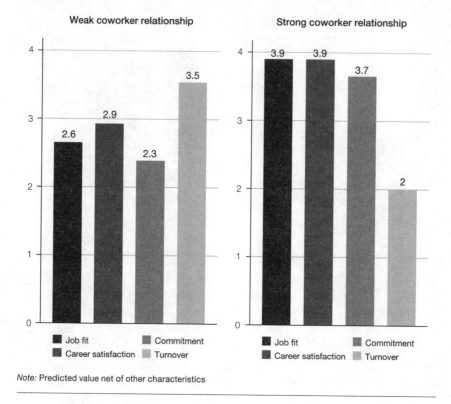

Note: Predicted value net of other characteristics

Respondents with a strong manager relationship had an average score of 4.1 for job fit, in contrast with the 2.8 average score reported by respondents whose managerial relationship was weak. And those respondents with strong perceived support from their managers had an average score of 1.9 on intention to leave, which was significantly less than the 2.8 reported by those with a weak managerial relationship. We found similar statistically significant results for coworker support. Respondents who had strong coworker relationships reported an average score of 3.9 on career satisfaction. In contrast, their colleagues with weak coworker relationships reported an average score of 2.9 for career satisfaction. And the impact on intention to leave is striking; those with strong coworker relationships reported an average score of 2.0 on intent to leave, compared with respondents with weak coworker relationships, whose average score was 3.5. In other words, stronger relationships with managers and co-workers indicated less likelihood of turnover and higher levels of satisfaction.

Attitudes Matter

We also found strong results indicating the importance of respondents' perceptions and attitudes regarding their workplaces. Respondents who feel highly inauthentic at work also reported lower feelings of job fit, career satisfaction, and commitment, and they were more likely to have plans to leave their employment (figure 7-4). One of the most striking findings is the relationship between inauthenticity and intention to leave;

FIGURE 7-4

Inauthenticity effects on career outcomes

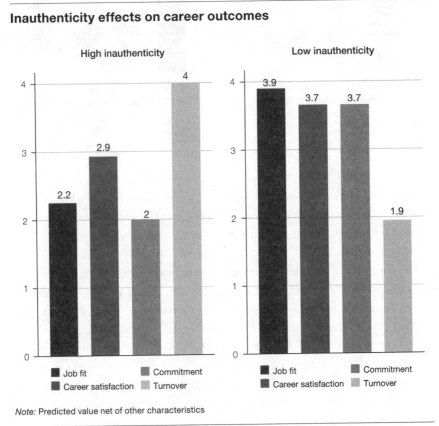

Note: Predicted value net of other characteristics

FIGURE 7-5

Engagement effects on career outcomes

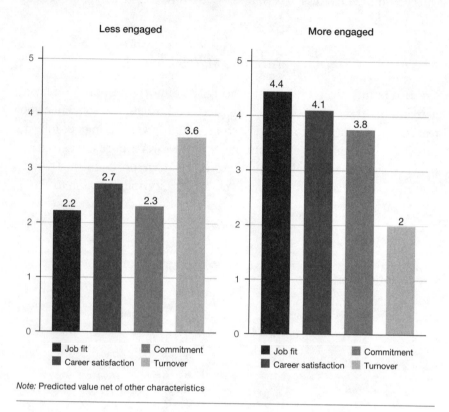

Note: Predicted value net of other characteristics

respondents who felt that they were not able to bring their whole selves to work reported an average score of 4.0 for intention to leave, in comparison with the 1.9 average score for respondents who reported low levels of inauthenticity.

We found similar effects with engagement (figure 7-5). Respondents who reported high levels of engagement with their jobs also reported higher levels of job fit (4.4 average score) and career satisfaction (4.1 average score) than those who had low levels of engagement (with an average job fit score of 2.2 and an average career satisfaction score of 2.7). Respondents who were more engaged were also less likely to leave, as evidenced by their average score of 2.0 on intent to leave, in comparison with respondents who were less engaged (and their average score on intent to leave at 3.6).

FIGURE 7-6

Racial differences in relationships, engagement, and authenticity

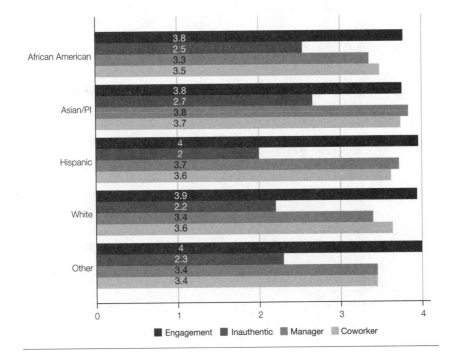

Race/Ethnicity Matters

We found that race/ethnicity also matters in explaining work attitudes for diverse talent (figures 7-6 and 7-7). An examination of racial/ethnic trends in manager and coworker relationships, engagement, and authenticity reveals some variation among the different ethnic groups. Interestingly enough, each racial/ethnic group reported moderately high levels of engagement, with African Americans and Asians indicating an average score of 3.8 and Whites and Hispanics indicating an average score of 4.0. African Americans reported the lowest levels of both manager support and coworker support. While most groups feel a sense of authenticity, African Americans and Asian Americans reported lower levels of felt authenticity than their counterparts. Hispanics, with an average score of 2.0 for inauthenticity, were the most positive in terms of their ability to be authentic at work.

FIGURE 7-7

Racial differences in career outcomes

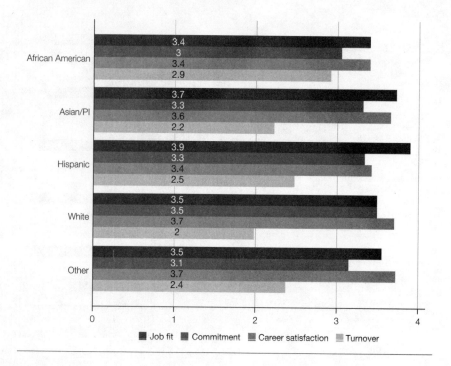

There were similar trends in the career outcomes for each racial group. African American respondents in particular reported the lowest levels in several of the career outcome variables. African Americans had the lowest level of commitment (average score of 3.0), the lowest job fit (average score of 3.4), and the highest intention to leave (average score of 2.9). Hispanics had the highest level of job fit (average score of 3.9). And after Whites, Asian and other respondents reported the next-highest level of career satisfaction (average score of 3.7 for others and 3.6 for Asians).

Implications

Taken in sum, findings from this study on the career experiences of diverse professionals have several important implications. Before discussing these, two points bear mentioning. First, this research effort supports the findings of Thomas and Ely's (1996) classic work on diversity in organizations. Simply having diversity present in organizations is not enough. Without a strategic plan to encourage supportive relationships or to shape a more inclusive culture, recruiting diverse talent will likely result in a revolving door of high turnover.

A second point worth mentioning is that one of the benefits of this study is the diverse sample. Much of the research that considers race tends to focus on African Americans and Whites. And while there is still certainly a story evoked by that particular dynamic, it is not the only story. Now, more than ever, it is time for other stories to start being told and for other career experiences to be explored. Organizations need this information, as it is a source of guidance on how to support and assist employees across dimensions of diversity in building effective career narratives.

This study confirms that professionals of diverse backgrounds benefit tremendously from a cadre of supportive relationships. The impact of respondents' supportive relationships with their managers and coworkers can be seen in their strong scores for job fit, career satisfaction, and organizational commitment, as well as in their reduced intention to leave. The relationship with one's manager is particularly important. There is a popular adage, "People don't leave their organizations; they leave their managers." If we see managers as the front line in dealing with increasing workforce diversity, it is important that they are equipped and trained to effectively leverage the opportunities provided by the new workforce. Organizations will need to be proactive in honing managers' cultural competence and other skills that will aid them in managing diversity. The Partnership provides an instructive example of supporting managers to help them support their diverse talent. The Partnership's comprehensive leadership development programs for diverse talent have interactive and support opportunities built into the one-year curriculum for program participants' managers. These opportunities include welcoming managers to the orientation at the start of the program, encouraging managers to attend a showcase workshop with their direct reports, and inviting managers to conclude the program at a celebratory dinner. In addition, the Partnership's program arms participants with several developmental tools and inventories, as well as practical frameworks and best practices, that can be used with managers back in sponsoring organizations.

The importance of peers is also critical; coworker support emerged as a substantive contributor to the career effectiveness of diverse professionals. A growing dependence on peer support should come as no surprise. Work in organizations is increasingly dependent on an ability to join across disparate communication styles, dissimilar cultural backgrounds, dispersed geographic locations, and varied leadership styles. The increases in work teams and virtual projects are two trends that contribute to the need for strong peer support.

Although mentoring did not emerge as a significant contributor in this study, there is ample research that supports the importance of these developmental relationships (Murrell & Blake-Beard, 2017). While the value of supportive relationships and mentoring has been reinforced and often linked with better outcomes for diversity, there still exists a gap in implementing robust mentoring programs or initiatives (McDonald & Westphal, 2013; Gandhi & Johnson, 2016; McAlearney, 2005; Poulsen 2013; Ragins, 2017). Ragins (2017) identified the need to move our mentoring relationships from ordinary to extraordinary by adopting a relational approach. Hence, organizations must nurture high-quality mentoring relationships to help minority professionals achieve accelerated growth. McAlearney (2005) also discovered that the integration of leadership development with mentoring, talent management, and human resource activities will ensure the maximum impact on organizational effectiveness. Yet how do we build and sustain the commitment of senior management to invest in such leadership development practices?

Larry (2003) advocated for establishing specific practices within "diversity-driven" mentoring programs. The author affirmed that cross-cultural and cross-gender mentoring programs improve senior-leadership appreciation of diversity principles, enhancing the integration of these practices within health-care organizations. Larry additionally specified several principles for diversity-driven mentoring programs, including communication skill development and diversity-awareness training, to augment understanding of difference, generate support from top management, and solicit input from all parties involved.

Murrell, Blake-Beard, Porter, and Perkins-Williamson (2008) also provided support for the benefits of formal mentoring programs, even those reaching across organizational boundaries. They defined interorganizational formal mentoring (IOFM) as formal mentoring activities, programs, or experiences that cut across traditional organizational boundaries and target the unique developmental needs of a specific stakeholder or identity group. In their study of such mentoring practices, they found that participants gained valuable access to mentoring relations that engendered trust and psychosocial support, access to legitimate organizational power, and the sharing of social capital across traditional organizational boundaries.

There may be some unique characteristics of this group of respondents that could help us understand why mentoring was not significantly related to the study outcomes. It could be that these respondents, who, interestingly enough, reported a high level of access to a current mentor, are such a high-achieving group that mentoring is only one of the tools that they use to advance their careers and maintain satisfaction. Given that these respondents were of a relatively high income level (over $100,000) and education level (college degree or above, several with graduate degrees), we imagine that their access to informal mentoring has facilitated their career success. We also suspect that this group might use their mentors to serve certain developmental and networking functions that we did not capture in our assessment.

The theme of this study is "feeling connected." Our findings indicate that relationships are but one component of feeling connected at work. This study also affirms the importance of authenticity and engagement as psychological measures with real implications for the experiences of diverse professionals. Employees who are more engaged in their jobs and experience a deeper sense of authenticity at work are more likely to make valuable, unique contributions to their employing organizations. Authenticity and work engagement can also reinforce the formation of strong relationships with managers, coworkers, and mentors. Yet when employees don't feel connected to their work or able to be authentic at their jobs, they suffer a personal cost. These findings reinforce that the workplace climate toward diversity plays a critical role in fostering engagement, welcoming authenticity, and strengthening interpersonal connections among employees from diverse backgrounds.

However, our survey population is drawn from a group of individuals who are highly motivated to engage in career development experiences. Many survey respondents were nominated and sponsored by their employers to participate in these career development experiences to promote their ability to feel connected and advance in their workplaces. As such, our findings may likely present a more positive portrayal of the career experiences of diverse talent than would be found in a general population. On the other hand, these respondents may be more sensitized to diversity dynamics, given their participation in the Partnership's annual conference, and this may have tempered their reported career attitudes. Additional research among the broader population, such as that reported in this edited volume by Ella F. Washington and colleagues, helps to lend additional insight on diversity and engagement.

For example, our nuanced examination of racial dynamics reveals both similarities and differences among diverse professionals' experiences of feeling connected. There are some similarities that cross ethnicity; the level of engagement is moderately high across all of the groups. These respondents are also effectively drawing on support from relationships at work—their managers and coworkers are helping them to be successful in their jobs. It is affirming to learn that these highly educated, well-paid, diverse professionals are, by and large, engaged in their work and leveraging their relationships effectively. But then there are also some noticeable differences among the groups. African Americans fare worse on several aspects—they are less committed, less satisfied with their careers, lower in job fit, and more likely to consider leaving their organizations. The experience of African Americans feels familiar; the data echoes intergroup dynamics, firmly grounded in a sociohistorical context, that still challenge organizations today. Then there are results that are more novel, calling for further investigation. Why did Asians report the highest level of inauthenticity? And what allowed Hispanics to report the lowest level of inauthenticity? Hispanics also reported the highest average score for job fit. These findings speak to the need for future research efforts that focus on the career experiences of other ethnically diverse professionals.

In conclusion, this research illuminates a very complex set of factors that influence career satisfaction and organizational commitment among diverse professionals. The critical takeaway from this study is that the experience of feeling connected is a powerful force in shaping overall attitudes toward one's job and one's employing organizations. Ironically, this multidimensional experience of connection is often ignored or discounted as less critical to job performance than knowledge, skills, abilities, and personality. Though not conclusive, our findings at least raise the question of whether feeling connected—to one's work, one's self, and one's significant others—provides a needed anchor for deep-level commitment and genuine contribution from diverse talent. In revealing that certain employees feel less connected than others, we also charge leaders with taking the initiative to create a climate that fully engages the best of their diverse talent base.

Acknowledgments

This study was designed by a research team commissioned by the Partnership. We thank the following individuals for their assistance with designing the study: Nancy Brodsky, Alesia Latson, and Annica White MacDonald. We thank Steven Shafer for his assistance with data collection and analyses. We also thank the following individuals for their assistance with data collection for this study at the Workforce Retention Conference: Eleanor Chin, Gloria Cotton, Laurie Hunt, and Anna Kerr. The authors of this report acknowledge the support of the Simmons School of Management and Harvard Business School.

NOTES

1. The Partnership is a not-for-profit organization dedicated to providing talent management solutions for professionals of color.

2. The Partnership hosts an annual leadership conference for program participants and their managers to learn effective talent-management strategies. The participants in this study were among the attendees at the December 2006 conference.

3. Please contact the first author for additional information regarding the scales or permission for use in future research.

REFERENCES

Ashikali, T., & Groeneveld, S. (2015). Diversity management in public organizations and its effect on employees' affective commitment: The role of transformational leadership and the inclusiveness of the organizational culture. *Review of Public Personnel Administration, 35*(2), 146–168.

Barnes, J. (2017). Climbing the stairs to leadership: Reflections on moving beyond the stained-glass ceiling. *Journal of Leadership Studies, 10*(4), 47–53.

Bell, E. L. & Nkomo, S. (2001). *Our separate ways: Black and White women and the struggle for professional identity.* Boston, MA: Harvard Business School Press.

Bell, M. P. (2006). *Diversity in organizations.* Mason, OH: Thomson South-Western.

Blake-Beard, S. D. (2003). Critical trends and shifts in the mentoring experiences of professional women. *CGO Insights* (Briefing Note No. 15). Boston, MA: CGO, Simmons School of Management.

Blancero, D. M., Mouriño-Ruiz, E., & Padilla, A. M. (2018). Latino millennials— The new diverse workforce: Challenges and opportunities. *Hispanic Journal of Behavioral Sciences, 40*(1), 3–21.

Cox, T. H., & Blake, S. (1991). Managing cultural diversity: Implications for organizational competitiveness. *Academy of Management Executive, 5*(3), 45–56.

Creary, S. J., & Roberts, L. M. (2017). GIVE-based mentoring in diverse organizations: Cultivating positive identities in diverse leaders. In A. J. Murrell & S. Blake-Beard (Eds.), *Mentoring Diverse Leaders* (pp. 3–24). New York, NY: Routledge.

Dumas, T., Phillips, K., & Rothbard, N. (2013). Getting closer at the company party: Integration experiences, racial dissimilarity, and workplace relationships. *Organization Science, 24*(5), 1377–1401.

Gandhi, M., & Johnson, M. (2016). Creating more effective mentors: Mentoring the mentor. *AIDS and Behavior, 20*(2), 294–303.

Hewlett, S. A., Luce, C. B., & West, C. (2005). Leadership in your midst. *Harvard Business Review, 83*(11), 74–82.

Hunt, V., Layton, D., & Prince, S. (2015, February 2). *Diversity matters.* McKinsey&Company. Retrieved from https://assets.mckinsey.com/~/media/857 F440109AA4D13A54D9C496D86ED58.ashx.

Jones, G. R., & George, J. M. (2014). *Contemporary management* (8th ed.). New York, NY: McGraw-Hill.

Kahn, W. A. (1990). Psychological conditions of personal engagement and disengagement at work. *Academy of Management Journal, 33*(4), 692–724.

Kahn, W. A. (1992). To be fully there: Psychological presence at work. *Human Relations, 45*(4), 321–349.

Larry, A. (2003). Mentoring diversity. *Healthcare Executive.* 18(5), 60.

Mazur, B. (2010). Cultural diversity in organisational theory and practice. *Journal of Intercultural Management, 2*(2), 5–15.

McAlearney, A. (2005). Exploring mentoring and leadership development in healthcare organizations. *Career Development International, 10*(617), 493–511.

McDonald, M. L., & Westphal, J. D. (2013). Access denied: Low mentoring of women and minority first-time directors and its negative effects on appointments to additional boards. *Academy of Management Journal, 56*(4), 1169–1198.

Murrell, A. J. & Blake-Beard, S.D. (2017). Mentoring diverse leaders: Creating change for people, processes, and paradigms. New York, NY: Routledge.

Murrell, A. J., Blake-Beard, S., Porter, D. M., & Perkins-Williamson, A. (2008). Interorganizational formal mentoring: Breaking the concrete ceiling sometimes requires support from the outside. *Human Resource Management, 47*(2), 275–294.

Naff, K. C. (2018). *To look like America: Dismantling barriers for women and minorities in government.* New York, NY: Routledge.

Nugent, J. S., Pollack, A., & Travis, D. J. (2016). *The day-to-day experiences of workplace inclusion and exclusion* (Report). New York, NY: Catalyst.

Offermann, L. R., & Basford, T. E. (2014). Inclusive human resource management: Best practices and the changing role of human resources. In B. M. Ferdman & Barbara R. Deane (Eds.), *Diversity at work: The practice of inclusion* (pp. 229–259). San Francisco, CA: Jossey-Bass.

Ortlieb, R., & Sieben, B. (2013). Diversity strategies and business logic: Why do companies employ ethnic minorities? *Group & Organization Management, 38*(4), 480–511.

Phillips, K. W., Dumas, T. L., & Rothbard, N. P. (2018, March–April). Diversity and authenticity. *Harvard Business Review,* 132–136.

Poulsen, K. M. (2013). Mentoring programmes: Learning opportunities for mentees, for mentors, for organisations and for society. *Industrial and Commercial Training, 45*(5), 255–263.

Ragins, B. R. (2017). From the ordinary to the extraordinary: High-quality mentoring relationships at work. *Organizational Dynamics, 45,* 228–244.

Roberts, L. (2005). Changing faces: Professional image construction in diverse organizational settings. *Academy of Management Review, 30,* 685–711.

Roberts, L., Mayo, A., Ely, R., & Thomas, D. (2018, March–April). Beating the odds. *Harvard Business Review,* 126–131.

Thomas, D. A., & Ely, R. J. (1996, September–October). Making differences matter: A new paradigm for managing diversity. *Harvard Business Review,* 79–90.

Thomas, D. A., & Gabarro, J. J. (1999). *Breaking through: The making of minority executives in corporate America.* Boston, MA: Harvard Business School Press.

Tomlinson, A. (2001, December 17). Concrete ceiling harder than glass to break for women of color. *Canadian HR Reporter,* pp. 7, 13.

Travis, D. J., & Thorpe-Moscon, J. (2018). *Day-to-day experiences of emotional tax among women and men of color in the workplace* (Report). New York, NY: Catalyst.

Ugorji, U. O. (1997). Career-impending supervisory behaviors: Perceptions of African American and European American professionals. *Public Administration Review, 57*(3), 250–255.

Wang, M. L. (2016). *Positive corporate mentoring: Evidence-based positive mentoring for immigrant achievement in corporate settings* (Unpublished master's thesis). University of Pennsylvania, Philadelphia.

Wyatt, M., & Silvester, J. (2015). Reflections on the labyrinth: Investigating Black and minority ethnic leaders' career experiences. *Human Relations, 68*(8), 1243–1269.

PHENOMENOLOGICAL STUDIES

The Lived Experience

8

Views from the Other Side

Black Professionals' Perceptions of Diversity Management

ADIA HARVEY WINGFIELD

M ost organizations today will state that they value and welcome diversity, and that it is important to them to have an inclusive work-force. In particular, organizations claim that they support more diversity at their top levels and that they want to cultivate environments where people of color are well represented in and have access to leadership roles. Yet sociologists have pointed out that this rhetoric usually fails to match the reality. The top levels of many organizations and influen-tial occupations remain predominantly white and male. Researchers conclude that these statements do not necessarily indicate a commit-ment to change, and generally suggest that such initiatives have not succeeded in creating more racial or gender diversity in formal lead-ership roles within organizations or occupations (Berrey, 2015; Edelman, 2015).

This chapter focuses on the ways black professionals view diversity initiatives, programs, and outreach efforts that claim to create or improve leadership opportunities for workers of color. Black workers are under-represented in a variety of high-status occupations and thus are uniquely situated to offer a perspective on how these programs are received by those purported to be most affected by them. In this chapter, I examine how black health-care workers view diversity initiatives in their respec-tive occupations. Based on in-depth interviews with black doctors, nurses, and technicians, I show that occupational status matters in shaping not only how health-care workers see diversity efforts but also their assessments of how these programs affect their own work and pathways to leadership in organizational settings.

Gaps in Knowledge

Race and Diversity Management

Since the civil rights era, many industries and organizations have begun to address the need to recruit and retain more workers of color in high-status professions. Having previously been composed mostly of white male workers, occupations in legal, medical, and financial fields (among others) now wrestle with becoming more racially and gender inclusive in order to reflect changing demographics. More diversity means that organizations can benefit from a broad slate of workers in leadership and management roles.

In the immediate aftermath of the civil rights reforms, many private-sector companies began to hire black professionals in high-ranking managerial roles. These positions provided black workers with opportunities for organizational leadership, as well as comfortable incomes that allowed a middle-class lifestyle. However, these jobs came with some caveats too. For one thing, they frequently involved managing newly created community relations or urban affairs departments, which meant that black managers in these jobs became the go-to people when organizations needed someone to address internal or external racial issues. Second, they rarely offered clear-cut paths to upper-level management positions or any other sort of upward mobility. Ultimately, black professionals operated on a parallel track wherein their leadership roles were relegated to managing racial issues rather than being effectively integrated into the organizational structure (Collins, 1988).

In time, changes in the political economy and the rise of anti–affirmative action discourse weakened social and organizational support for race-conscious policies designed to draw in workers of color. Whereas organizations once prioritized affirmative action and devoted specific attention to rectifying racial and gender inequality, today they emphasize a diversity discourse. In this context, rather than dwelling on structural or institutionalized processes that restrict opportunities for groups who have been systemically disadvantaged (women of all races, racial minority men), managers today frame diversity in bland terms that are divorced from cultural and institutional biases, emphasizing factors such as regional diversity, diversity of opinions, and diversity of thought (Dobbin, 1997). Following this logic, Apple vice president for diversity and inclusion Denise Young Smith stated to an audience at the One Young World Summit in 2017, "There can be twelve white, blue-eyed, blonde men in a room and they're going to be diverse too because they're going to bring a different life experience and life perspective to the conversation." This perspective allows companies to ignore the ways systemic and structural processes continue to exclude black workers in particular from high-status occupations that would allow them to take a decisive role in leading organizations (Collins, 2011; Dobbin, 1997; Moore & Bell, 2011).

It is perhaps not surprising that with this popular framework and the persistent underrepresentation of workers of color, many researchers have concluded that diversity initiatives as currently implemented have failed to bring racial minorities into leadership roles in the top ranks of organizations. As Williams, Mueller, and Kilanski (2012) have noted, most studies assess these programs by examining the success (or lack thereof) of widely used policies or through interviews with (mostly white) managers themselves. In a study of corporate managers, Embrick (2011) found that most were unaware or dismissive of company policies that focused on issues of diversity. Kalev, Dobbin, and Kelly (2006) found that most of the commonly used policies for increasing diversity—trainings, mentoring programs, and so on—do not actually generate results, and that the most effective measure, which involves tying diversity outcomes to managerial responsibilities, was underused. Ely and Thomas (2001) also note that when organizations explicitly highlight the importance of racial and cultural change, they can achieve greater minority representation. Yet despite this evidence from research studies, many organizations do not follow this path. Edelman, Fuller, and Mara-Drita (2001) conclude that diversity measures are designed more to shield organizations from liability and litigation than to create real systemic change or to restructure organizational leadership.

These are important methods for addressing whether and how diversity initiatives are able to achieve concrete changes, but they do not offer insights into how workers who are affected by these programs perceive them and their ability to shape organizational outcomes. We know that diversity trainings often engender resentment and pushback from white professionals who see them as unnecessary efforts that waste valuable company time and resources (Berrey, 2015; Kalev et al., 2006). But there is very little study of how the presence of these sorts of programs affects blacks who work in predominantly white professions or organizations. Do they find that diversity initiatives seem to serve as valuable resources? Do diversity programs provide or cultivate effective leadership? What other categories engender differences in black professionals' responses?

Black Professionals in Predominantly White Environments

For black employees, working in professional settings can pose certain challenges. Only 34 percent of employed black women work in professional or managerial jobs, and just 26 percent of black men are in this occupational category (Bureau of Labor Statistics, 2013). In many cases, this underrepresentation can lead to stereotyping, marginalization, and isolation. Black workers encounter difficulties tapping into and leveraging the social networks that are critical for advancement and leadership roles in professional work (Kaplan, 2006). They may also lack familiarity with the sort of cultural practices and hobbies that managers value in elite professional service workers (Rivera, 2014). For black women, race and gender may render them doubly excluded, exacerbating difficulties in finding mentors and being taken seriously, particularly if they work in male-dominated professions (Bell & Nkomo, 2001; Evans, 2013; St. Jean & Feagin, 1998). Black men have more opportunities to form gender-based bonds with their white male colleagues, but they, too, are often stereotyped as incompetent, unintelligent, or unsuited for high-status work (Wingfield, 2012). All these factors can make it difficult for black workers to access the sort of leadership roles that allow for organizational change and transformation.

This positionality uniquely situates black professionals to evaluate modern-day diversity initiatives in the occupations in which they are employed. In many professions, they are acutely aware of their minority status and the way it informs aspects of their work ranging from their available emotional responses to their ability to expect respect (Harlow, 2003; Harris & Sellers, 2017; Wingfield, 2010). Thus, their perspectives on the current successes and failures of diversity work are informed by their firsthand experiences with the challenges present for those who are underrepresented in these environments. Given this vantage point, what assessments of diversity initiatives do they offer? Do they agree that diversity programs are failing to position underrepresented minorities for leadership roles, or do they see some value in the organizational efforts that exist?

Contextually Relevant Methodology

In order to answer these questions, I conducted a study of black professionals in the health-care industry. Health care is a useful site in which to study how black workers perceive diversity initiatives because it is composed of multiple interrelated professions, and members of several of these (medicine and nursing, for example) have publicly acknowledged the need to bring more racial and gender diversity into their ranks. Blacks represent only 5 percent of those employed in medicine and 9 percent of nurses. When these numbers are broken down by gender, further disparities emerge. Only 3.4 percent of doctors and 8.5 percent of nurses are black women, while 2.8 percent of doctors and a meager 1.2 percent of nurses are black men. At the same time, US demographics are changing so that the population has an increasing number of members of racial minority groups, and these are more likely to respond favorably to medical care and treatment when coming from a practitioner of the same racial background (Sewell, 2015). Consequently, professional organizations such as the American Medical Association and the American Nursing Association now publicly acknowledge the important role that a more multiracial work force will play in treating patients who are increasingly people of color.

To assess how black health-care workers perceive the utility of diversity initiatives, I interviewed seventy-five health-care workers, sixty of whom were black and fifteen of whom were white. Respondents were employed across a broad swath of the health-care industry as doctors, nurses, physician assistants, and technicians. Furthermore, they represented a variety of specialty areas in health care (e.g., emergency medicine, patient care technicians, nurses on mother and baby floors) and worked in both public and private facilities. By focusing on health-care workers in a variety of occupations, I was able to identify how black professionals view the successes and failures of diversity initiatives at the occupational level. Thus, this study does not seek to offer information about how well (or how poorly) various institutions fare at increasing diversity. Instead, it gives a much broader viewpoint of the degree to which black professionals believe the industries in which they work are successfully solving these issues.

I located respondents through several methods. One involved using snowball sampling, where I reached out to personal and professional contacts and requested that they refer me to potential interviewees who fit the criteria for my study. Though snowball sampling can replicate existing social networks, it is a useful methodological approach for studying black professionals and other populations that can be underrepresented or difficult to locate. I also contacted professional associations in order to locate black doctors and nurses who might be interested in participating. Finally, I relied on social media sites such as LinkedIn to point me toward black health-care workers who might not be in any of the aforementioned social networks.

Once respondents agreed to be interviewed, we met in a mutually convenient location where they could speak comfortably. Some interviews also took place via telephone. All interviews were audio recorded with respondents' permission, and I took detailed notes in the few cases in which respondents did not agree to be recorded. Interviews were generally approximately ninety minutes and were later transcribed. Questions addressed respondents' initial interest in health care, whether and how racial issues emerged in their work, their perspectives on recent changes in the health-care industry, and their relationships with colleagues, supervisors, and patients. I coded data according to themes that emerged inductively. All respondents' names have been changed to protect their anonymity.

In addition to interviews, I also spent a few weeks shadowing three doctors in different facilities. One doctor, a black woman, worked in a university hospital in a major city on a labor and delivery floor. She primarily treated poor minority patients, many of whom were uninsured, but the hospital sought to attract wealthier (usually white) patients as well. I also shadowed a black male emergency medicine doctor who worked in a publicly funded city hospital whose patients were usually people of color. Finally, I shadowed a black woman pediatrician who had a partnership stake in a private practice in a midsize city. Most of her colleagues and patients were white and middle or upper class.

Relevant Theory and Empirical Findings

Diversity initiatives can vary widely between institutions and even between professions, but in the health-care industry, a few strategies emerge as the most popular. However, this is not to say that programs were

TABLE 8-1

Diversity initiatives and responses

Occupation	Diversity initiative	Response
Doctor	Cultural competence training	Annoyance, indifference
Nurse	Statement in support	Skepticism, doubting organizational sincerity
Technician	None	Support for initiatives overall

consistent across occupations. Occupational status informed the sorts of diversity initiatives to which black workers were exposed. Black doctors noted that when they encountered diversity initiatives in the workplace, they typically took the form of cultural competence training that consisted of online modules they had to complete. A smaller number of nurses indicated that they had undergone some cultural competence training, but by far the majority noted that the limits of their organizations' diversity work included legal statements on their facilities' websites that the companies were in fact committed to creating diverse and inclusive spaces. Notably, in keeping with Berrey's (2015) assertion that lower-status workers are often excluded from diversity initiatives, technicians reported that they were rarely, if ever, directly subjected to diversity efforts but believed that higher-status workers such as nurses and doctors underwent extensive training in this area (table 8-1). None of the professionals in my sample reported knowing about or being involved in programs specifically tailored to create more diversity among the leadership ranks of the organizations where they worked. Thus, these programs formed their basis for assessing institutional commitment to diversifying.

Given the occupational differences in how diversity programs are enacted (or overlooked), I found that perceptions of these efforts vary by occupational status. Doctors largely had some experience with cultural competence training but expressed serious concerns as to whether and how these initiatives could create real change in the medical profession. These concerns about the efficacy of cultural competence training programs in supporting leadership opportunities for black physicians often resulted in doctors feeling annoyed or indifferent. Nurses noted that many programs' efforts to improve diversity consisted of organizational statements indicating general support for this issue, but doubted that these statements signified serious institutional efforts to recruit and retain more underrepresented minorities. Technicians, who were not directly subjected to any efforts designed to improve diversity in their professions, were most hopeful about these initiatives, but even they expected that diversity programs would create change for nurses and doctors rather than for themselves. Ironically, the professions that were subject to the most attention from diversity managers had respondents who were the least enthusiastic about the prospects of success.

Black Doctors: "Another Box to Check"

It might seem that black doctors would strongly support diversity initiatives. Recent research indicates that white doctors continue to adhere to racial stereotypes in their treatment of black patients, erroneously believing that blacks are biologically different from whites in ways that include skin thickness and susceptibility to pain (Hoberman, 2012; Hoffman, Trawalter, Axt, & Oliver, 2016). The results of studies like these, as well as others showing that patients of color respond more favorably when their practitioners are of the same race, help explain why professional medical associations now publicly acknowledge that it is critical to attract more doctors of color in order to treat a rapidly diversifying patient population more effectively (Alsan, Garrick, & Graziani 2018; Greenwood, Carnahan, & Huang 2018; Skrentny, 2014).

Perhaps as a consequence of these studies, some organizations now attempt to replicate black practitioners' successes treating diverse patient populations. In practice, this has meant that doctors in some facilities are required to undergo cultural competence training, which usually consists of periodically administered online modules. These modules emphasize the importance of understanding that patients' cultural views and backgrounds can have an effect on their medical decisions and treatment preferences. But how do black doctors perceive the efficacy of these sorts of diversity efforts, particularly when it comes to increasing access to leadership roles?

The physicians interviewed for this study were largely indifferent. Though they expressed appreciation for the idea behind cultural competence training, it did not offer a vehicle or a pathway through which they felt they could improve their access to organizational leadership. In fact, more than a few doctors interviewed expressed annoyance at these sorts of measures. In these cases, doctors generally regarded these initiatives as cumbersome bureaucratic intrusions that cut into their other priorities—namely, practicing medicine. Esther, an obstetrician-gynecologist, told me, "It's kind of a pain, to be honest with you. It is just another box to check. I already have a million things to do and this just becomes one more kind of bureaucratic hassle." Esther did not consider diversity initiatives useful or helpful in her work as a physician. Rather, she found them irritating and somewhat intrusive. They interrupted what she thought of as her real work of treating patients.

Ricky, an emergency medicine doctor, offered a similar assessment. In response to a question about what diversity measures he saw in medicine and whether they helped to attract more people of color, he scoffed: "It's the right idea, but that stuff doesn't mean anything. Nobody takes it seriously! The way they do it, the trainings and modules, it's just one more box to check. They just want quick fixes. Doing the hard work, really changing the profession to get more black and brown people in here—that's not sexy." Like Esther, Ricky was not enthusiastic about the diversity initiatives at the hospital where he worked. He even uses the same metaphor of "checking a box" to describe the routinized, bureaucratic feelings that this process evokes.

For doctors like Esther and Ricky, diversity initiatives fell flat because they were limited to training modules that did not go far enough to create real change. Not only were they perceived to be ineffective in opening doors to leadership roles, but black doctors saw these diversity outreach efforts as unable to do the basic work of bringing more people of color into the profession. As a consequence, these initiatives actually created more work for black doctors, who resented the intrusion into their time practicing medicine, especially when the trainings did not produce the desired result. When doctors, who are already notoriously stretched thin and bombarded with paperwork, had to complete these cultural competence modules without seeing organizations also do more to attract minority physicians, they grew to resent them and regard them as a waste of valuable time. This sort of diversity initiative offers a nod to black physicians' awareness of how cultural and social factors matter in health care but does little to reform institutional pathways that make it more difficult for black physicians to access leadership roles. The emphasis is not in a place that would create more avenues for their mobility.

Black Nurses: Being "Diverse on Paper"

A few nurses stated that they had undergone cultural competence training, but by far the most stated that the diversity efforts at their workplaces consisted of official statements in support of this principle. As a result, nurses, like doctors, expressed skepticism about their workplaces' commitment to diversity initiatives in place. They, too, noted the juxtaposition between organizational rhetoric and practices. As a result, black nurses did not evince confidence that statements in support of diversity were enough to engender leadership opportunities, particularly because they believed little other action was forthcoming. Janice, a geriatric nurse and a faculty member at a university, told me, "One of the things that I know that a lot of nursing schools are pushing towards, and a lot of schools in general, is diversifying their faculty. That said, I think if that actually does happen, in more of a real way as opposed to kind of on paper as it is happening now, I think that that will really benefit black nursing students."

Janice was clear to emphasize the distinction between the tepid written statements in support of more diversity and the practices that universities like hers could take if they truly wanted to create an infrastructure that supported faculty and students of color. This discrepancy left her doubtful that the nursing school with which she was affiliated would really attract or retain more minority nurses.

Sean was even more explicit in expressing his suspicions that organizations do not genuinely want to diversify: "When you look at schools, the more people say that they're diverse, the more that they are not diverse. They're diverse on paper because you have to be. But if you're diverse on paper, you ought to be diverse in practice. One cannot go without the other." Again, from Sean's perspective, it was fairly easy for organizations to profess their commitment to and belief in diversity. However, they seemed to be less proactive when it came to doing the work necessary for creating a multiracial faculty and student body.

Janice and Sean were also dismissive of diversity initiatives, but for different reasons from Esther's and Ricky's. While doctors completed cultural competence trainings that they believed were insufficient without broader systemic action, the facilities where Janice and Sean worked did not take even those ceremonial steps. Their organizations produced statements saying that they valued diversity but did nothing more. Consequently, these respondents did not believe that the institutions in which they worked were genuinely serious about wanting to see an influx of workers of color. They certainly were not convinced that diversity initiatives in these forms could enhance leadership opportunities for black nurses. Instead, to nurses, diversity appeared to be window dressing and a superficial organizational attempt to appear to be doing the right thing. Incidentally, many researchers agree with this assessment, describing private-sector organizations as more concerned with evading antidiscrimination lawsuits than truly committed to creating systemic and institutional change (Collins, 2011; Edelman et al., 2001; Moore & Bell, 2011).

Technicians: Looking for Change from the Top

Unlike doctors and nurses, black technicians reported that they rarely, if ever, were subject to organizational policies related to improving diversity. They were not required to undergo the cultural competence training that doctors completed, and did not know whether the schools or institutions where they worked professed a commitment to diversity at large. Thus, when they evaluated diversity initiatives, they offered beliefs regarding whether diversity initiatives, broadly speaking, seemed to be effective.

Ironically, however, of the three groups of health-care workers interviewed for this study, black technicians expressed the least ambivalence and the most hope about diversity initiatives. Unlike black doctors and nurses, they were less likely to regard these efforts as well intentioned but toothless or, less charitably, empty promises designed to appease critics. Black technicians spoke favorably about how the organizations where they worked made efforts to acknowledge and endorse the need for a diverse workforce. Catie, one technician, stated, "I just want to say that I think most hospitals are really on board with the diversity training, and I think that's such a wonderful thing that these companies are doing. I think that is helping out a lot in the workplace. I think it stands for what we're not tolerating. You've got to respect one another and people's cultures and backgrounds. And I really think that it's a good start. It's a start in the right direction." Catie's comments contrast sharply with those of doctors like Esther and nurses like Sean who are much more lukewarm about the diversity efforts in their workplaces. Unlike them, she is proud that these initiatives are offered and believes they are having a favorable result.

Jared, another technician, believed that these initiatives would be helpful in assisting white health-care workers with understanding cultural nuances that could potentially inform how patients of color behaved and responded to treatment. In observing the high numbers of immigrant women patients in his hospital who had undergone female genital mutilation, he noted that some of his white women coworkers could benefit from more familiarity with this issue: "Usually, I catch it when they, usually when they come back into the staff area and they're talking about it, and some of the Caucasian nurses say, 'Well, I never heard of that,' or 'I never saw that.' It's out there. And these are nurses that have been around for ten or fifteen years, you know? I go, 'No, it's out there, it exists. You just got to expand your horizons.'" From Jared's viewpoint, additional diversity training and education could only help, as it would serve to bridge some of the racial gaps that exist between mostly white practitioners and the patients of color they serve, particularly when those patients have unfamiliar social or cultural practices that could affect their health care.

It is important to note that while technicians were the most optimistic about diversity efforts, they also were the group least likely to experience them directly. Indeed, diversity initiatives are much more likely to focus on bringing workers of color into high-ranking, high-status occupations that have the potential for institutional leadership than they are to address the small numbers of white workers in lower-status jobs (Berrey, 2011, 2015). This certainly was the case for technicians, who were not required to complete any sort of diversity modules or trainings in order to be certified for their work.

What, then, explains their support for these programs? Technicians professed the most appreciation for diversity initiatives because they believed they would help doctors and nurses avoid missteps when treating minority patients. Note that in Jared's earlier quote, he expressed hope that this sort of training would make white *nurses* more familiar with various cultural practices that affect patients of color. Ayana, another technician, expressed a similar viewpoint: "I don't think that it'll impact the work that I do just because of my minimal patient contact that I have. But as far as everyone else, I do believe that it'll impact them. I'm thinking of the nurses and doctors that are being trained. It might make them go a little bit more of the extra mile to make sure everyone is comforted and kind of on the same level. Of course they always go the extra mile, but now it's just adding another key role." Note that like Jared, Ayana is optimistic that diversity efforts will help the white doctors and nurses with whom she works to be a bit more sensitive. Hence, black technicians are the most supportive of diversity efforts though, paradoxically, they have the least direct involvement with them. Technicians like Jared do not categorize diversity management as an organizational effort that will open doors for black leadership. Instead, they limit its potential to helping improve patient outcomes and creating more racial equity in care.

Contemporary Interventions

The research here shows that black professionals have complicated relationships with how diversity initiatives are enacted at work. While we might expect that they would support efforts to attract more workers of color to the institutions and settings where they are employed, there are structural and occupational realities that inform both their exposure and their responses to diversity programs. For doctors, diversity initiatives take the form of cultural competence training; for nurses, they consist of organizational statements in support of diversity; and technicians observe that higher-status workers are the focus of general efforts in this direction. As a result, these occupational differences yield divergent perceptions of diversity work. Black doctors are skeptical of programs' ability to create change, black nurses are doubtful of their organizations' sincerity, and black technicians are hopeful that those positioned above them on the occupational spectrum will see some benefits. Overall, however, none of the members of the professions represented here expected that diversity programs would improve black workers' access to leadership roles.

There are a few interventions that could potentially offset the complicated relationships black professionals have with diversity work. One would be for organizations to implement strategies and programs that are shown to be effective in increasing the representation of white women and people of color in the workplace. For instance, Kalev, Dobbin, and Kelly (2006) find that when organizations task managers with this specific focus, this practice is more effective than mentoring programs or diversity training in changing organizational demographics. For doctors in particular, who primarily referenced training modules, implementing this sort of concrete, specific change could be more effective in winning their support for and buy-in to diversity programs.

A similar intervention could be useful for offsetting nurses' skepticism and doubts. Recall that black nurses believed the organizations for which they worked put the right rhetoric down on paper but were much less committed to achieving actual results. Introducing proven strategies that can create organizational change might ameliorate some of their misgivings.

Finally, technicians were the one group that expressed support for diversity efforts, yet they did so because they hoped that initiatives directed at their colleagues in nursing and medicine would have a positive effect on how patients of color were treated. Yet occupational hierarchies meant technicians rarely had a window into the frustrations that black nurses and doctors had with diversity efforts. In this case, implementing the sort of efforts that actually yield successes would likely further enhance black technicians' support for diversity work, particularly once concrete results become evident.

Another intervention would be for organizations to value, recognize, and reward the leadership work that black professionals take on in the absence of formally acknowledged roles. Across professions, blacks regularly complete the informal, invisible work of mentoring junior colleagues of color, serving on committees that focus on diversity and inclusion, and performing other labor that legal scholars Carbado and Gulati (2013) refer to as "lumpy citizenship tasks." This work can be critical to the success of people of color in predominantly white organizations, but it usually goes unnoticed. Thus, organizations might consider creating procedures in which this sort of labor is valued and compensated rather than taken for granted and ignored.

Overall, it is essential for organizations to adopt measures designed to integrate workers of color more fully into their ranks. As the US population demographics change, minority workers will become an even more integral part of the labor force and will become increasingly critical to how organizations operate. Diversity initiatives have, thus far, failed to improve the numbers of workers of color and white women in measurable numbers, particularly in high-status occupations. Other interventions are necessary to make this change.

REFERENCES

Alsan, M., Garrick, O., & Graziani, G. (2018). *Does diversity matter for health? Experimental evidence from Oakland* (Working paper). National Bureau of Economic Research.

Bell, E., & Nkomo, S. (2001). *Our separate ways: Black and white women and the struggle for professional identity.* Cambridge, MA: Harvard Business Review Press.

Berrey, E. (2011). Why diversity became orthodox in higher education, and how it changed the meaning of race on campus. *Critical Sociology, 37,* 573–596.

Berrey, E. (2015). *The enigma of diversity: The language of race and the limits of racial justice.* Chicago, IL: University of Chicago Press.

Bureau of Labor Statistics. (2013). *Labor force characteristics by race and ethnicity, 2012: Report 1044.* Washington, DC.

Carbado, D., & Gulati, M. (2013). *Acting white? Rethinking race in post-racial America.* New York, NY: Oxford University Press.

Collins, S. (1988). *Black corporate executives.* Philadelphia, PA: Temple University Press.

Collins, S. (2011). Diversity in the post affirmative action labor market: A proxy for racial progress? *Critical Sociology, 37,* 521–540.

Dobbin, F. (1997). *Inventing equal opportunity.* Princeton, NJ: Princeton University Press.

Edelman, L. (2015). *Working law: Courts, corporations, and symbolic civil rights.* Chicago: University of Chicago Press.

Edelman, L. B., Fuller, S. R. & Mara-Drita, I. (2001). Diversity rhetoric and the managerialization of law. *American Journal of Sociology, 106,* 1589–1641.

Ely, R., & Thomas, D. (2001). Cultural diversity at work: The effects of diversity perspectives on work group processes and outcomes. *Administrative Science Quarterly, 46,* 229–273.

Embrick, D. (2011). The diversity ideology in the business world: A new oppression for a new age. *Critical Sociology, 37,* 541–556.

Evans, L. (2013). *Cabin pressure: African American pilots, flight attendants, and emotional labor.* Lanham, MD: Rowman and Littlefield.

Greenwood, B., Carnahan, S., & Huang, L. (2018). Patient-physician gender concordance and increased mortality among female heart attack patients. *Proceedings of the National Academy of Sciences of the United States of America, 115,* 8569–8574.

Harlow, R. (2003). "Race doesn't matter, but . . .": The effect of race on professors' experiences and emotion management in the undergraduate college classroom. *Social Psychology Quarterly, 66,* 348–363.

Harris, M., & Sellers, S. (2017). *Stories from the front of the room.* Lanham, MD: Rowman and Littlefield.

Hoberman, J. (2012). *Black and blue.* Berkeley: University of California Press.

Hoffman, K., Trawalter, S., Axt, J., & Oliver, N. (2016). Racial bias in pain assessment and treatment recommendations, and false beliefs about biological differences between blacks and whites. *Proceedings of the National Academy of Sciences of the United States of America, 113,* 4296–5301.

Kalev, A., Dobbin, F., & Kelly, E. (2006). Best practices or best guesses? Assessing the efficacy of corporate affirmative action and diversity policies. *American Sociological Review, 71,* 589–617.

Kaplan, Victoria. (2006). *Structural inequality.* Lanham, MD: Rowman and Littlefield.

Moore, W. L., & Bell, J. (2011). Maneuvers of whiteness: Diversity as a mechanism of retrenchment in the affirmative action discourse. *Critical Sociology, 37,* 597–613.

Rivera, L. (2014). *Pedigree.* Princeton, NJ: Princeton University Press.

Sewell, A. (2015). Desegregating ethnoracial disparities in physician trust. *Social Science Research, 54*, 1–20.

Skrentny, J. (2014). *After civil rights: Racial realism in the new American workplace.* Princeton, NJ: Princeton University Press.

St. Jean, Y., & Feagin, J. R. (1998). *Double burden: Black women and everyday racism.* Lanham, MD: Rowman and Littlefield.

Williams, C., Mueller, C., & Kilanski, K. (2012). Gendered organizations in the new economy. *Gender & Society, 26*, 549–573.

Wingfield, A. H. (2010). Are some emotions marked "whites only"? Racialized feeling rules in professional workplaces. *Social Problems, 57*, 251–268.

Wingfield, A. H. (2012). *No more invisible man: Race and gender in men's work.* Philadelphia, PA: Temple University Press.

9

Overcoming Barriers to Developing and Retaining Diverse Talent in Health-Care Professions

LAURA MORGAN ROBERTS, STACY BLAKE-BEARD, STEPHANIE CREARY, BEVERLY EDGEHILL, *and* SAKSHI GHAI

Health-care organizations face a number of challenges with respect to the effective development and retention of diverse talent. In the United States, they continue to face rising labor shortages and increased cost of operations, and in response, these organizations seek innovative ways to develop competitive advantage. Yet few organizations have developed practices for successfully attracting and advancing underrepresented minorities in health care.

In this chapter, we present the findings of an empirical study of Black and Hispanic American health-care professionals' perceptions of personal and organizational factors that enable and constrain their career advancement and leadership development. We first highlight the findings of previous research on the recruitment and retention of diverse health-care professionals. Second, we outline the goals, participants, and procedures of our focus-group study of health-care professionals of color. Third, we reveal the comprehensive insights gleaned from the eight focus groups regarding facilitators of and challenges to participants' career advancement and leadership development. We then offer several recommendations for both senior-level executives in decision-making roles and minorities who seek to advance to senior levels in health care. Our recommendations are based on focus-group participants' comments, our interpretation of underlying patterns in the data, and empirically based best practices for diversity, leadership development, and talent management.

Background Research on Diversity and Health-Care Professionals

Though much has been written about challenges to career advancement and methods for attracting and advancing underrepresented minorities, diverse talent continues to be underdeveloped and underrepresented in leadership positions in the health-care industry. To begin, much of the research to date that focuses on the careers of minority health-care professionals is concerned with the challenges that health-care organizations face in recruiting these professionals into patient care roles (Bleich, Mac-Williams, & Schmidt, 2015; Brooks-Carthon, Nguyen, Chittams, Park, & Guevara, 2014; Colville, Cottom, Robinette, Wald, & Waters, 2015; Murray, Pole, Ciarlo, & Holmes, 2016; Phillips and Malone, 2014; Villarruel, Washington, Lecher, & Carver, 2015) and the challenges these professionals experience in these roles once recruited (Black, 2016; Carter, Powell, Derouin, & Cusatis, 2015; Gates, 2018; Hubber, 2018; Jeffreys, 2016). The limited insights we currently have on their leadership suggest that they struggle to advance beyond middle management and experience a "middle-management plateau" (Larson, 2006; Silver, 2017; Voges, 2006)—that is, in spite of having considerable experience in middle-management roles, they tend to lack mentoring and visibility in the organization, become frustrated with their lack of career progress, and decide to leave health care altogether (Voges, 2006).

This middle-management plateau highlights the importance of mentoring for diverse health-care professionals. Mentoring, which is described as the provision of career and psychosocial functions, has received considerable attention in discussions of diversity and talent management, particularly in health-care organizations (see Ambrose, 2003; Barney, 2002; Bowen, 1994; Chyna, 2001; Dolan, 1993; Dreachslin, Jimpson, Sprainer, & Evans, 2001; Dufault, 2007; Gathers, 2003; Henault, 2004; Jessamy, 1997; Kahn, 1994; King, 2005; Larson, 2006; Moore, 1999; Romano, 2005a, 2005b; Sloane, 2006; Voges, 2006). For example, Dolan (1993) suggested several benefits to establishing a "climate for mentoring" among senior-level executives and minorities, in light of the many pressures that senior-level executives experience with respect to cost containment and time management. Dolan argued that mentoring would provide protégés with critical guidance and direction from senior-level mentors and allow protégés to usher innovative ideas into organizations, draw on more recent interactions with academic institutions, and present perspectives from their diverse set of experiences. Dolan further proposed that cross-gender, cross-cultural, and cross-generational mentoring was pivotal in creating value for diversity within health-care organizations. As a result of effective mentoring, Dolan proposed that organizations may realize increased satisfaction and retention of underrepresented minorities.

Lack of access to mentoring is only one factor that may be affecting the careers of diverse professionals. Other research suggests that the diversity climate of health-care organizations (with the undercurrent of implicit and explicit racism) may also play a role in the limited advancement of minority health-care professionals (Dotson, Bonam, & Jagers, 2017; Selvam, 2012; Valantine and Collins, 2015). Further, the lack of commitment from top management and health-care boards may also explain the lack of diversity in health-care leadership (Witt/Kieffer, 2015). While some majority group members argue that health-care organizations lack access to diverse candidates to promote from within, minority group members (i.e., African American, Hispanic, and Asian respondents) argue that there is a lack of commitment among senior leadership to increasing the representation of underrepresented minorities in health-care leadership positions.

From the standpoint of practice, it is clear that some health-care organizations are beginning to design and implement interventions focused on advancing underrepresented minority midcareer professionals to leadership roles (Day et al., 2016; Dolan, 2013; Winkfield et al., 2017). For example, executive leadership initiatives such as the Thomas C. Dolan Executive Diversity Program (2013) focus on preparing midcareer minorities to advance to more-senior management roles. Professional medical organizations such as the American Society of Clinical Oncology and the American Society for Gastrointestinal Endoscopy have also launched strategic plans to increase the diversity of health-care leadership (Day et al., 2016; Winkfield et al., 2017). Less understood is how minority professionals access developmental opportunities such as these given the obstacles just outlined.

The Current Study

We sought to broaden our understanding of the engagement, retention, and advancement of underrepresented minorities in health-care organizations. In particular, we sought to more fully characterize obstacles to career advancement for underrepresented minorities in health-care and identify methods of increasing maximal engagement of both minority and majority group members in health-care leadership positions. Our research questions were as follows:

1) What are the challenges that professionals of color face in advancing to more-senior leadership within health care?

2) What recommendations can be offered to underrepresented minorities and senior executives for increasing diversity among senior health-care leadership?

Methods

To answer these questions, we conducted eight focus-group discussions in Boston, Massachusetts. We chose to conduct focus groups rather than individual in-depth interviews or surveys because we believed participants would have some shared experiences and that unexpected themes would arise from the group discussion, allowing for further deliberation (Odom, Roberts, Johnson, & Cooper, 2007). Additionally, focus groups, as a method of conducting qualitative research, capitalize on the group process, which can stimulate conversation and help participants to clarify their views (Kitzinger, 1995). We elected to conduct this study in the Boston area due to the dense concentration of top-ranked academic teaching hospitals there. Focus-group sessions were held at the headquarters of the Partnership.[1] Four of the focus groups were formed with members of the same professions (two groups of physicians and two groups of administrators); the other groups were randomized by profession. All groups were randomized by ethnicity and gender. Three of the authors facilitated the groups; the fourth author was the CEO of the Partnership at the time of data collection, and helped to design the study, but did not attend or facilitate any focus groups, nor did she have access to any identifying information of the participants.

Participants

Twenty-five Boston-area health-care professionals self-identifying as members of underrepresented minority groups participated in the eight focus groups. Eight participants were male and seventeen were female. The vast majority self-identified as African American ($n = 18$), three identified as African American and White, one identified as African American and Hispanic, and three identified as Hispanic. Participants represented the following range of professional experience: eleven non-physician administrators, eight physicians with some administrative or faculty responsibility, three psychologists, two registered nurses, and one pharmacist. Notably, all of the participants held college degrees and graduate degrees, several from elite academic institutions in the Boston area.

Procedure

Each focus group discussion lasted ninety minutes and was facilitated by two researchers. Participants were informed that the purpose of the focus group was to (1) gain insight into the most relevant questions and topics that should be pursued for future research and (2) offer preliminary advice to health-care executives about how to maximally engage and develop underrepresented minorities within their organizations. Participants provided written consent for participating in the confidential sessions and having them audiotaped. Refreshments were provided to participants in exchange for their time, but no other form of compensation was given. The facilitators asked participants several open-ended questions about their experiences as health-care professionals, definitions of success, enablers and obstacles to success, and recommendations for increasing diversity among senior health-care leadership. At the end of the discussion, participants were told that they could contact the facilitator should any questions or comments about the study arise.[2]

Data Analysis

Audiotapes of the focus-group discussions were transcribed verbatim. Each researcher individually reviewed the transcripts and their notes in their entirety, qualitatively compiling themes derived from the sessions. The researchers then discussed the themes as a group and found that the deduced themes were consistently strong in each of the focus groups and across reviewers. The researchers represented expertise in health-care, qualitative research, health and social behavior, diversity management, and organizational behavior.

Findings: Facilitators of Success

In this section, we summarize the major themes that emerged from participants' discussions of the factors that facilitated and inhibited their success as health-care professionals. Table 9-1 details each theme and provides illustrative quotes of facilitators and inhibitors. It is important to mention that participants' personal definitions of success framed the conversation about facilitators and inhibitors. In this study, participants viewed *success* as *having recognizable and progressive achievements at different levels and stages within one's career.* Success additionally involved *having a certain degree of control over one's career path and the ability to balance personal and professional goals.* Yet nearly all health-care professionals of color believed that there were significant inhibitors to their career success; some were related to organizational-level practices, while many others were related to individual and group-level practices.

Three facilitators of success were mentioned frequently: *supportive relationships, training and education,* and *personal characteristics.* The most prominent theme in this discussion of facilitators was supportive relationships. Many participants recounted how role models and mentors inspired, motivated, and developed them. Role models were generally noted as family or community members who held prominent professional positions and inspired participants to achieve but were not necessarily guides in the participants' careers. Mentors, also holding distinguished appointments within their organizations, were those individuals who proffered both psychosocial and career support. Participants reported that mentors were generally responsible for introducing them to health care, encouraged them to seek out opportunities, wrote recommendation letters, or taught them how to politically navigate the health-care organization. Additionally, mentors empowered participants to not get discouraged by obstacles and to balance personal and professional commitments.

One participant described how her college mentor enabled her success: "Someone . . . was encouraging me to just take your biggest dream and do it. And I'd said, well I don't want to go to medical school unless

TABLE 9-1

Themes and illustrative quotes

Theme	Facilitator	Obstacle	Personal strategy
Supportive relationships *Inspire and motivate*	Role models, mentors, social networks	Inaccessibility and active discouragement	Proactivity
	"I think that I've been very lucky to have formal networks of support, whether it's mentors or peers. And typically [my support comes from] women of color and typically African American women, who have really supported me in having my vision and being very determined and seeking out opportunities that will help me fulfill that." (Group 3)	"I always hear, like 'you're so articulate,' but I don't hear anybody else being told that. So, I almost find that a little bit patronizing. 'Don't worry about moving forward. You're still very young. You're too ambitious.' Yeah, those are the same traits I see in my [white] colleagues, but they're never called ambition." (Group 8)	"You have to resist the urge to stay at the computer from nine o'clock to five o'clock and just do your work. . . . You have to build alliances with people throughout the organization and outside the organization. I think it's definitely helpful to have a variety of people to give you feedback, and also bounce ideas off of." (Group 5)
		"Stop using the big words. You don't have to use the big words around us to show that you're smart." (Group 8)	
Training and education *Knowledge of business and management*	Administrative graduate degrees, administrative fellowship programs, leadership development programs	Lack of "pedigree" or exposure	Persistence
	"The Partnership has opened the doors for many different avenues of my career personally and professionally. I've built a lot of relationships with a lot of people that I probably wouldn't have been able to meet outside of the Partnership." (Group 5)	"I felt like there definitely was this kind of [Ivy League] undergrad group that was recognized differently than those who came from state schools or historically black colleges and universities." (Group 8)	"There were no people of color in regards to management at all. There was no one to mentor me. So it would have to be resiliency on my behalf that pushed me to try to attain higher education [MBA]." (Group 8)
		"We can come up with a million ideas that are probably well connected to the needs of the patient, but have no sense of how to assess it, measure it, follow it, create a scope, create a budget. Not because we can't think that way, because we never thought about it and because in medicine you are not trained to think about it." (Group 1)	"You're making yourself a marketable asset, and you want to continue to increase your value. And how do you increase your value? Well, you don't just sit there and depreciate by saying, 'OK, I've done all my schooling, now I'm done, I'm just here.' No, you continually learn new skills. You find out what's needed, not just in your organization, but in other organizations, so you have more options in front of you." (Group 5)

(continued)

TABLE 9-1 (continued)

Theme	Facilitator	Obstacle	Personal strategy
Organizational diversity	**Strategic, comprehensive approaches** *"I think that when the institution, in some important ways, lets the employees know that this is a key initiative ('We're going to make a cultural change in this direction'), that creates buy-in. [When the institution] rolls out a whole program, the way they would for anything else (you know, like patient safety or quality improvement), then, I think it becomes a part of the fabric of the institution. . . . Unfortunately, what happens when we have a seminar here and a consultant there ('This department had a crisis, so we're going to have somebody go to that department'), it's just not holistic."* (Group 5) *"Acknowledge that racism exists . . . [a]nd that it's morphed into a very covert, culturally embedded, make nice, ignoring the systemic oppression and racism. I honestly feel like if institutions could even acknowledge that, that would be a tremendous first step."* (Group 3)	**Stereotyping and unwelcoming climate** *"Institutions have history, they have their own identities, and they have a strong sense of pride in being very, very selective. . . . So there's an assumption that the people who come in are going to be so glad to be there. And so then you come in, and you start making suggestions about how things might be different, and it's hard to do that in an organization that feels they're great, and the world tells them that they're great."* (Group 5) **Pigeonholing** *"I'm interested in minority health, and I'm interested in disparities in health . . . and I hate to say this in the wrong way, but it's almost like they've pigeonholed me into being the minority that's going to do the minority stuff, and thus I can't do work on anything else or talk about all the other things intelligently."* (Group 8)	**Strategic self-presentation** *"Because I was a woman of color, [I] recognize[d] that I was probably pegged with a certain reputation or type of image if I came off in a certain way. And I think it just made me much more strategic about how I present myself initially, so that I could develop relationships with people. So that later on I could say whatever the hell I wanted to say, but have it be attributed to me rather than women of color. . . . Rarely am I angry or heated in public with other professionals because of certain stereotypes."* (Group 3) **Prioritizing** *"I think that race, if anything, is a challenge because of all the things that come with it. . . . I am the only black female physician. I am the only black researcher. . . . There have been a lot of calls or requests that my contemporaries who are white males don't have to deal with, so they can just focus on research. And it's something I've enjoyed doing, but I have to tell you, I came to a point where I realized that since I'm primarily a researcher, if I'm not hitting those goals as a researcher, then it doesn't matter."* (Group 3).

I go to School X, and she said, well, apply. And it was the only school I applied to, and I luckily got in. It was one of those situations where if she hadn't told me that, I probably would have never gone. So, it was a huge enabler" (group 8).

The vice president of human resources facilitated another person's career placement: "Early on, when I said, 'I know what I want to do, [but] I don't know if the job is here at the hospital for me,' he said, 'We'll create the job.' And it's been like carte blanche, and incredibly supportive" (group 5).

Other participants described how their social networks provided an extra boost for their career opportunities in health care. Many benefited from their status as alumni of elite educational institutions and noted that alumni networks were significant in their career advancement by "opening doors" and providing connections to people in key decision-making roles. One participant indicated that every employment position she had held involved a connection with her undergraduate institution.

Training and Education

The majority of participants commented on how their higher education and developmental experiences facilitated their success. Some participants who held administrative graduate degrees stated that their knowledge of business and management in organizations enabled them to advance their health-care careers. Those who participated in administrative fellowship programs following graduate degree programs in health administration believed these fellowships were critical to their success, because they provided greater access to management, career advancement planning, and a structured learning environment.

One participant spoke highly of her fellowship experience: "The fellowship really helped me to get an institutional perspective that I don't think the vast majority of the people get. . . . At a fairly young age, [I] jumped into a job that I don't think I probably would have gotten had I not had the history at the organization, and had they not known me as a somewhat proven entity" (group 2).

Other participants reported that the opportunity to engage in leadership training programs external to the work setting assisted their career advancement. For example, alumni of the Partnership's leadership development programs indicated that these programs provided a forum for important career discussion, facilitated social interaction, and enhanced their social networks among professionals of color with shared experiences.

Personal Characteristics

Several participants ascribed their success in part to personal attributes by acknowledging the importance of internal motivation and drive. Participants indicated that in the presence or absence of a support system, the ability to take initiative, actively earn trust, and persevere despite adversity was key to minorities' career advancement in health care.

Findings: Inhibitors of Success

On balance, discussion of inhibitors to success far outweighed dialogue regarding facilitators of success in both breadth and depth. Inhibitors to success were categorized according to the following three themes: *lack of leadership development training and industry-specific expertise, lack of support for career advancement*, and *organizational diversity climate and stereotyping*. Several inhibitors reflected a lack of access to the aforementioned facilitators—namely, formal training or education and career support. Further, while participants attributed their success to personal attributes (e.g., internal drive and persistence), they identified structural and systemic factors (e.g., organizational diversity climate and stereotyping) as inhibitors of success.

Lack of Leadership Development Training and Industry-Specific Expertise

Many participants proposed that minorities were not readily advancing within health care on account of insufficient business training and health-care experience. Among those participants with administrative graduate degrees, one implied that an inadequate supply of administrative fellowships prohibited many minority candidates from effectively bridging theoretical and practical knowledge, making them less competitive for administrative roles. In addition, some participants without health-care experience believed that they were recruited because of their transferable skills; yet, once in health care, their lack of industry experience inhibited them from being recognized as knowledgeable.

Participants also voiced concerns about the lack of transparency, objectivity, or accessibility of systems for selection and promotion in their organizations and perceived that their organizations were only providing resources to "check the box" on diversity management. Participants reported that while some opportunities were available, they did not support a path to senior administrative leadership. Many opportunities were bound to clinical leadership and middle-management positions. Consequently, our participants experienced the pathways to leadership as hidden from their purview. Many participants argued that providing minority professionals with leadership and management training would benefit health-care organizations. But they also reported that most health-care organizations have restricted financial scholarships to those employees seeking clinical roles.

Lack of Support for Career Advancement

Lack of opportunity and support systems was a major theme in the discussion of career advancement inhibitors. Focus-group participants stated that their career advancement opportunities were not challenging enough, inaccessible, or nonexistent. Though most participants reported pursuing advanced degrees as a means of introducing opportunity, they concurred that the inaccessibility of role models, mentors, and networks inhibited promotion. Participants discussed how they had become discouraged due to the absence of career guidance from senior-level executives, the lack of access to mentoring programs or networks, and the lack of minority representation in top management positions.

Moreover, participants stated that their desire to advance to leadership roles was not supported by their colleagues or managers, who advised them to be patient and downplay their intelligence. In general, participants were unclear about how one could obtain more leadership responsibility or advance their careers in health-care organizations. Some struggled with whom to enlist in the process of identifying career opportunities, while others felt that the right opportunities had not been created for them because they did not have the necessary mentorship. Still others felt that their attempts to attain additional credentials and responsibilities were shunned by managers and peers.

Organizational Diversity Climate and Stereotyping

Describing this process as "the quiet fight," several participants reported feeling a void or loneliness given the relatively low numbers of health-care professionals of color in their employing organizations. In addition, they experienced the workplace diversity climate as unwelcoming or sending mixed messages about opportunities for professionals of color. Many participants, especially Black males, commented on the necessity of tempering their emotional expressions in order to advance in their careers. Specifically, several participants believed that despite their attempts to exhibit friendly and nonthreatening demeanors, White colleagues continued to respond with surprising levels of apprehension. Participants also felt that their passion and enthusiasm for work was often misperceived as threatening, and that advocacy for diversity causes may be confused with overemotional behavior. Others worried that their interests in minority health would constrain their future leadership opportunities.

One focus group participant stated, "I felt like I was dying. They were appreciating me as I was dying. All the stuff about me, all the stuff that made me special, the Black side of me, it was all just dying. And they were happy. It made them comfortable. And I felt like I was wilting" (group 3).

Implications of Career Inhibitors:
The Leaky Pipeline

Most studies of diversity in health care refer to the underrepresentation of certain ethnic groups in leadership roles. Our data helped to explain why many professionals of color plateau in or exit their health-care careers. Participants identified a number of individual limitations to career advancement associated with health-care organizations' diversity climate. Frustrated by the lack of opportunity and stagnant careers, participants noted that many of their underrepresented minority counterparts had left the organization, industry, or region altogether. In their roles as caretakers for biological children and extended families, some participants cited the personal sacrifices they made for their profession (e.g., financial challenges of undergraduate and graduate student loan debt, moving away from family) and wondered whether these sacrifices had been worthwhile. This tension leads to a "leaky pipeline" phenome-non, in which underrepresented talent enters the system (e.g., science, technology, engineering, and mathematics or health-care pipeline) at early career stages but stagnates or leaves altogether when opportunities for advancement are not apparent and the benefits of remaining do not outweigh the financial and psychological costs of remaining in a disaf-firming or constraining environment. In sum, many professionals of color find it too great a sacrifice to remain in the organizations where they (perceive they) are receiving fewer rewards and having little impact.

In the words of one clinician,

> I didn't come to Harvard with the idea of ending up in an under-served area, just tossed into the trenches, do your work, get your visa, and leave. . . . I think once you are sent to an underserved area within the system, there's no support to grow. You're supposed to take care of "them" and that's it. . . . All of these quiet fights in the racist environment. For me, it has been draining, really draining. I'm ready to leave. I'm waiting for this year to end and then I'm leaving. It has been so draining for me that I really feel that I'm almost going to change careers. . . . And I suddenly feel that I have become a mediocre person, a mediocre professional. And it's not what I came here for. (Group 3)

Findings: Participants' Suggestions

In light of the aforementioned challenges, participants provided sugges-tions both to minority health-care professionals seeking to advance within health care and to senior executives seeking to maximally engage minorities. We summarize these suggestions in this section.

Advice for Minority Health-Care Professionals Seeking to Advance within Health Care

- Gain skills and industry knowledge for successful leadership.

  - Pursue advanced degrees.

  - Pursue activities that distinguish minority professionals as leaders, including serving on committees and being involved in high-visibility change initiatives.

- Pursue opportunities to become more knowledgeable about the US health-care system, financing, and their difficulties.

- Balance assertiveness, advocacy, and self-promotion to pursue opportunities and navigate interpersonal interactions.

  - Network with senior-level executives and actively seek opportunities that align with one's desires for career advancement.

  - Gauge tone and temper one's responses to situations at work in order to establish credibility as a leader.

  - Refrain from advocating too frequently or intensely for diversity issues, unless one is willing to deal with the possibility of being pigeonholed as the diversity champion for the organization.

  - Use caution to avoid adapting one's style too much, given the deleterious psychological impact of inauthenticity. (See the earlier quote: "I felt like I was wilting." See also chapter 6 in this volume, in which Patricia Faison Hewlin and Anna-Maria Broomes provide a detailed review of the negative outcomes associated with inauthenticity.)

Advice for Senior Health-Care Executives Seeking to Maximally Engage Minorities

- Clarify and expand the rationale for diversity.

  - Extend beyond quota-based diversity practices to understand how to best leverage diversity within one's organization.

  - Cultivate diversity as an organization value.

- Establish support systems.

  - Encourage top-down supported formal and informal mentoring, encouraged by senior leadership.

  - Provide opportunities for minority professionals to network with one another.

- Promote from within.

  - Actively search within one's organization before consulting executive search firms.

- Invest in training and development programs for minority professionals that will equip them to succeed in senior-level positions.

- Conduct exit interviews.

  - Actively consider factors surrounding resignations as a means of uncovering systemic challenges within one's organization.

  - Proactively seek feedback from departing minority professionals about how to increase support, development, and retention of other minority professionals.

Our Recommendations

Our findings are similar to those of past research that suggest that a number of barriers to career advancement exist for underrepresented minorities in health care, yet it extends the discussion by considering the roles of both executives and minorities in improving talent management and leadership development. We have built on these findings in order to offer general recommendations for creating maximal engagement in the management of diverse talent in health care. First, this study proposes that in order to develop and retain diverse talent in health care, senior executives and minority professionals each need to be able to articulate the value of diversity within their organizations in order for diversity management to become more tangible and institutionalized. Second, it infers that a range of contributors facilitate and inhibit the success of underrepresented minorities, including organizational practices and personal actions. Personal attributes, role models and mentors, training and education, and networking were all defined as facilitators of success. Positive individual traits were related to the ability to take initiative in establishing trust with managers, pursuing educational opportunities, and accessing professional networking opportunities. Yet our recommendations extend far beyond minority professionals' personal characteristics. This study shows that by offering strategies to both senior executives and underrepresented minorities, the pathway to senior leadership in health care would be more easily navigated and organizations would better engage the full range of talent in their workforce. Together, these inclusive practices would contribute to more effective health-care delivery.

Diversity Climate

Of particular significance is the diversity climate that leaders create in health-care organizations. Focus-group participants reported receiving mixed messages about the relevance of diversity in their health-care organizations. Regardless of the public commitment to increasing cultural competence and reducing health disparities, professionals of color feel constrained by limited expectations for their roles in health care. In their view, they were hired to contribute to diversity initiatives (e.g., cultural competence and community partnerships), but once hired, they felt their ability to lead deep change within the organization was constrained.

For example, one participant commented, "For me, that's the struggle of being this cultural broker when it's convenient for them. And then when there's other times that I think that there are cultural issues that need to be addressed that they don't want to hear, then they don't want to hear it" (group 3).

Therefore, participants reported feeling unable to contribute fully or to build credibility as thought leaders. As a result, they feel they have a limited leadership impact in health care. This dynamic persists because dialogue about diversity is often inhibited, particularly in discussing the unique challenges that members of various national, ethnic, and socioeconomic groups face.

Minding these challenges, participants in this study proffered several recommendations to increase diversity among senior health-care leadership. An overarching theme was that the ability to *comprehend and articulate the value of diversity within health-care settings* was critical to the success of diversity programs and a valuable skill for all persons concerned. One participant remarked, "If you really want to promote diversity, it needs to be some sort of an organizational value. It needs to be something that's cultivated." Other participants in that focus group agreed with this conclusion and believed that without setting this precedent, an organization's future diversity efforts would be substantially less effective.

We also suggest that leaders *enrich the diversity dialogue to account for the various dimensions of difference* that exist and their accompanying challenges. Participants believed that there has been "inhibited dialogue" within their organizations. Differences in class, ethnicity, and gender were all highlighted as affecting both working relationships and career advancement; yet discussions related to these concepts were not generally viewed as prevalent in diversity conversations. In terms of class, participants indicated that the hierarchical divisions predominant within health-care institutions often separated clinical and administrative staff and further alienated in-group minorities from their cohorts elsewhere in the organization. One physician reported being reprimanded by a White supervisor for speaking to other same-race staff who held lower-level positions. Since levels of educational attainment are often pronounced in health-care settings, class differences may inhibit adequate social networking and may also inhibit more-senior professionals of color from mentoring their lower-status counterparts in their health-care career advancement. Adia Harvey Wingfield offers a more detailed discussion of class dynamics among minority health-care professionals in chapter 8 of this volume.

Conclusion

One of our goals in selecting focus groups as a method of gathering data was to gain insight into the most relevant questions and topics that should be pursued for future research. Through this effort, we have been able to identify a number of underexplored areas in the research whose investigation may further explain why diverse talent continues to be significantly underdeveloped in the health-care industry. Suggested topics for future research include stereotypes, prejudices, and fear as barriers to diversity management; class distinctions in hierarchical health-care organizations; majority group members' attitudes toward diverse talent management as factors affecting institutionalization; and professional and social networking systems used by underrepresented minorities for career advancement in health care. We also recommend empirical research that examines the linkages between effectively leveraged and empowered professionals of color and organizational effectiveness in health care, as measured by well-being and performance indicators. While these suggestions do not represent an exhaustive list of topics that may shed some light on the experiences of diverse professionals in health care, they offer an appropriate starting place to delve into the issues with which organizations are grappling. With the changing face of the American health-care system, organizations' abilities to attract, retain, and advance diverse professionals are critical. The future of health care will depend on our ability to shine a light on the pathways to leadership for diverse talent.

NOTES

1. The Partnership is a not-for-profit organization dedicated to providing talent management solutions for professionals of color. As the region's premier resource dedicated to talent management, the Partnership provides tailored workplace solutions to senior executives and leadership training for professionals of color, conducts research into the latest trends and issues, and convenes thought leaders to identify best practices.

2. Please contact the first author for more information on the study protocol.

REFERENCES

Ambrose, L. (2003, September/October). Mentoring diversity: Serving a diverse patient population calls for diverse leadership. *Healthcare Executive, 18*(5), 60–61.

Barney, S. (2002, November/December). The inclusive, diverse workplace: We are not there yet. *Journal of Healthcare Management 47*(6), 356–359. Retrieved from https://search.proquest.com/openview/9c9f04659e779084e4e75a5c29262e1d/1?pq-origsite=gscholar&cbl=7080

Black, B. P. (2016). *Professional nursing: Concepts & challenges.* Saint Louis, MO: Elsevier.

Bleich, M., MacWilliams, B., & Schmidt, B. (2015, March/April). Advancing diversity through inclusive excellence in nursing education. *Journal of Professional Nursing, 31*(2), 89–94.

Bowen, D. (1994, January/February). Action steps to enhance minority opportunities. *Healthcare Executive, 9*(1), 43.

Brooks-Carthon, J., Nguyen, T., Chittams, J., Park, E., & Guevara, J. (2014, July/August). Measuring success: Results from a national survey of recruitment and retention initiatives in the nursing workforce. *Nursing Outlook, 62*(4), 259–267.

Carter, B. M., Powell, D. L., Derouin, A. L., & Cusatis, J. (2015, March/April). Beginning with the end in mind: Cultivating minority nurse leaders. *Journal of Professional Nursing, 31*(2), 95–103.

Chyna, J. (2001, March/April). Mirroring your community: A good reflection on you. *Healthcare Executive, 16*(2), 18–23.

Colville, J., Cottom, S., Robinette, T., Wald, H., & Waters, T. (2015, February). A community college model to support nursing workforce diversity. *Journal of Nursing Education, 54*(2), 65–71.

Day, L., Gonzalez, S., Mendoza Ladd, A., Bucobo, J., Pickett-Blakely, O., Tilara, A., & Christie, J. (2016, January). Diversity in gastroenterology in the United

States: Where are we now? Where should we go? *Gastrointestinal Endoscopy*, *83*(4), 679–683.

Dolan, T. (1993, November/December). Mentoring in the 1990s. *Healthcare Executive*, *8*(6), 3.

Dolan, T. (2013, March/April). Increasing diversity in governance and management. *Journal of Healthcare Management*, *58*(2), 84–86.

Dotson, E., Bonam, C., & Jagers, J. (2017, Spring). Redefining race as a process: Implications for healthcare leadership. *Journal of Health Administration Education*, *34*(24), 295–318.

Dreachslin, J., Jimpson, G., Sprainer, E., & Evans, R., Sr. (2001, November/December). Race, ethnicity, and careers in healthcare management: Practitioner response. *Journal of Healthcare Management*, *46*(6), 397–410.

Dufault, K. (2007, March). Diversity at the top. *Trustee*, *60*(3), 28–29.

Gates, S. A. (2018, April). What works in promoting and maintaining diversity in nursing programs. *Nursing Forum*, *53*(2), 190–197.

Gathers, D. (2003, Summer). Diversity management: An imperative for healthcare organizations. *Hospital Topics: Research and Perspectives on Healthcare*, *81*(3), 14–20.

Henault, R. (2004, March). Race matters. *Modern Healthcare*. Retrieved from https://www.modernhealthcare.com/article/20040301/NEWS/403010319/race-matters

Hubber, D. (2018). *Leadership and nursing care management* (6th ed.). Saint Louis, MO: Elsevier.

Jeffreys, M. R. (2016). *Teaching cultural competence in nursing and health care: Inquiry, action, and innovation.* (3rd ed.). New York, NY: Springer.

Jessamy, H. (1997, May). Opening up to diversity. *Modern Healthcare*. Retrieved from https://www.modernhealthcare.com/article/19970505/NEWS/705050319/commentary-opening-up-to-diversity-how-your-organization-can-better-recruit-and-retain-minorities-for-executive-posts

Kahn, L. (1994, January/February). Career development strategies for minorities. *Healthcare Executive*, *9*, 40–41.

King, C. (2005, November/December). Conquering health disparities. *Healthcare Executive*, *20*(6): 34–36.

Kitzinger, J. (1995, July 29). Qualitative research: Introducing focus groups. *BMJ*. Retrieved from http://www.bmj.com/cgi/content/full/311/7000/299

Larson, L. (2006, March). Getting to the "C" suite: What will it take to see diversity across health care leadership? *Trustee*, *59*(3), 12–19.

Moore, J. D., Jr. (1999, December). Tapping hidden resources. *Modern Healthcare*, *29*(50), 30–36.

Murray, T. A., Pole, D. C., Ciarlo, E. M., & Holmes, S. (2016, May/June). Nursing workforce diversity project: Strategies for recruitment, retention, graduation, and NCLEX-RN success. *Nursing Education Perspectives*, *37*, 138–143.

Odom, K., Roberts, L. M., Johnson, R., & Cooper, L. (2007). Exploring obstacles to and opportunities for professional success among ethnic minority medical students. *Academic Medicine*, *82*, 146–153.

Phillips, J. M., & Malone, B. (2014, January/February). Increasing racial/ethnic diversity in nursing to reduce health disparities and achieve health equity. *Public Health Reports*, *129*, 45–50.

Romano, M. (2005a, February). Diversifying healthcare. *Modern Healthcare*. Retrieved from https://www.modernhealthcare.com/article/20050214/PREMIUM/502140331/diversifying-healthcare

Romano, M. (2005b, September). Opening doors. *Modern Healthcare.* Retrieved from https://www.modernhealthcare.com/article/20050926/PREMIUM/509260309/opening-doors

Selvam, A. (2012, April). Diverse perspectives: Minority executives and their peers tout the benefits of broader representation in the C-suite, boardrooms. *Modern Healthcare, 42*(15), 6–7.

Silver, R. (2017, February). Healthcare leadership's diversity paradox. *Leadership in Health Services, 30,* 68–75.

Sloane, T. (2006, April). Through the Teflon ceiling. *Modern Healthcare.* Retrieved from https://www.modernhealthcare.com/article/20060410/NEWS/604100316/through-the-teflon-ceiling

Valantine, H. A., & Collins, F. S. (2015, September). National Institutes of Health addresses the science of diversity. *Proceedings of the National Academy of Sciences, 112*(40), 12240–12242.

Villarruel, A., Washington, D., Lecher, W. T., & Carver, N. A. (2015, May). A more diverse nursing workforce. *AJN: The American Journal of Nursing, 115*(5), 57–62.

Voges, N. (2006, April). Diversity in the executive suite. *Modern Healthcare, 36*(15), 24–30.

Winkfield, K., Flowers, C., Patel, J., Rodriguez, G., Robinson, P., Agarwal, A., . . . Hayes, D. F. (2017, August). American Society of Clinical Oncology Strategic Plan for Increasing Racial and Ethnic Diversity in the Oncology Workforce. *Journal of Clinical Oncology, 35*(22), 2576–2579.

Witt/Kieffer. (2015). *Closing the gap in healthcare leadership diversity: A Witt/Kieffer study* (Report). Retrieved from http://wittkieffer.com/file/pdfs/Closing%20the%20Gap%20in%20Healthcare%20Leadership%20Diversity%20Final(1).pdf

10

From C-Suite to Startups

The Illusion of Inclusion

TOIGO FOUNDATION (NANCY SIMS, SUE TOIGO,
MAURA ALLEN, *and* TONI CORNELIUS)

Courage and a willingness to be open and grow are required leadership traits for pushing forward into unknown territory—including the unknown of working with others outside your familiar sphere of experience. To date, there have been only fifteen black CEOs leading a *Fortune* 500 company, according to *Fortune*'s "Why Race and Culture Matter in the C-Suite" (McGirt, 2016). Because so few African Americans have reached senior levels of leadership in global enterprises, few of their peers have a road map for how interactions with these (and upcoming) leaders should unfold. While the leaders within the organization may be working for a common objective—for example, growth, inclusion, profits, brand strength, or innovation—a shared understanding of how to work together and relate to someone different from themselves is often a critical, unspoken missing link.

The lack of presence of African American leaders extends well beyond corporate America, into startups and emerging investment funds. Of the more than $70 trillion in federal dollars that are managed by registered asset-management firms in the United States, less than 1 percent is handled by minority firms, as reported by the United States Government Accountability Office (2017) in its *Key Practices Could Provide More Options for Federal Entities and Opportunities for Minority- and Women-Owned Asset Managers*. Within the alternative investment arena, which includes nontraditional asset classes from private equity and venture capital to hedge funds and real estate, minority firms manage 3.8 percent of the

$67.1 trillion in assets under management, as the Knight Foundation's (2017) *Diversifying Investments* report notes. In findings shared in a 2017 New Financial report of one hundred global asset allocators with a combined $8 trillion in assets under management, some respondents still expressed reluctance driven by a "widely held and deeply entrenched belief that improving diversity compromises returns" (Seddon-Daines & Chinwala, 2017, p. 4). The unintended consequence of this environment is that it stifles the creation of African American–owned finance businesses while deferring growing assets under management to existing majority-owned firms. The big get bigger and the small cannot survive, a case of what economists call correlated novelties, or, in layman's terms, one thing leads to another.

Established, global finance firms face a leadership gap—one that warrants attention if these firms are to leverage the documented advantage that diverse teams deliver, especially when tackling complex challenges. Data from a Money Management Institute (2017) report, published in partnership with the *Financial Times*, provides the breakdown within senior leadership positions:

Executive committee member	88% white	2.4% black
Managing director	86% white	1.4% black
Senior portfolio manager	84% white	1.4% black

That equates to a staggering 51 African American senior professionals out of a reported total senior workforce of 3,086. The representation of African American leaders was lower than any other minority group in the leadership category. Given such a small peer group, the fact that these leaders have a limited voice and feel isolated and marginalized is not surprising.

While the value that diverse talent brings is critical in all areas of business, a lack of a meaningful representation of African Americans at the table where billion-dollar capital allocation decisions are being made has a direct and dramatic impact on our nation's competitiveness. These are decisions that go beyond a product launch; they offer opportunity to infuse capital into underserved communities, improve the retirement savings of millions of public servants, and stimulate business and job growth. This disparity and leadership gap in finance, one of our

Thirty Years on the Front Line of Inclusion

- The Toigo team conducted fifty interviews over the period from November 2017 to February 2018 with African American finance leaders across gender, career roles, and various levels of corporate impact.

- All regions of the country were equally represented. Individuals included those with direct and indirect relationships with the foundation, as well as business association leaders who advocate for inclusion with respect to access to capital, equity participation, and entrepreneurship.

- Working at the intersection of finance and inclusion for three decades has provided the foundation's team with deep relationships and perspectives, a selection of which were also incorporated into summary comments.

The backdrop for the Toigo Foundation's work over the past three decades is centered in the world of finance—including global Wall Street firms, publicly traded investment management businesses, funds in a mix of investment asset classes, public pensions, and more. In this arena, business leaders exercise tremendous control over decisions concerning capital allocation benefiting our nation, but African American leaders are disproportionately absent.

nation's core sectors, has a direct, cascading impact on economic development, housing, jobs, quality of schools and other services, access to education, infrastructure spending, consumer credit, retirement savings, and more. With individuals of African American heritage forming 17.9 percent of the population in the United States today according to the 2017 African American History Month report (United States Census Bureau, 2017), it is incumbent on all to bring that cultural voice and perspective forward. Virtually every part of our everyday life is affected by decisions being made within the finance sector; it's a cornerstone of any economy and one that directly benefits from differing perspectives at every turn.

Understanding the Experiences of African Americans in the Finance Sector

With a thirty-year perspective honed through one-on-one interactions, industry discussions, and thought leadership, the Toigo team has a direct and differentiated view into the individual career aspirations and struggles of thousands of minority individuals with careers in finance, the greatest percentage of whom are African American. With this lens, Toigo presents a deep look into the complexities that surround the inclusion and leadership advancement of African Americans in both established, majority-led firms and emerging organizations today. What we have observed is that whether in an established corporate environment or in a business startup, the expressed desire and appreciation for inclusion may be high, but the mechanics of it are still uncharted territory for many.

Issues surrounding the inclusion and leadership advancement of African Americans in business, whether in structured corporate environments or startups, are rooted in a tangled mix of history, emotions, and human nature. To offer a timely, frontline, and forward-facing perspective, we conducted focused interviews to gather insights into the mindset of current African American business leaders. This includes a look into what today's leaders are experiencing, and the career strategies they've employed to advance and navigate traditional expectations of leadership. We believe these perspectives and experiences are representative of a broader population of African American business professionals.

The African American leaders Toigo interviewed have significant work experience with established, large-scale financial institutions. Having hit a real or perceived ceiling of advancement, a selection of those interviewed decided to leave senior financial positions in global firms to establish their own finance-focused startups. With these entrepreneurs, we explored what prompted them to "opt out" of the global firms where they held increasingly more-senior leadership roles to launch their own business ventures. We investigated issues of credibility, confidence, sponsorship, and other leadership challenges and explored whether those issues persist even in an environment where African Americans have direct control over workplace culture and talent practices.

We know that leading organizations have taken critical steps to create a more comprehensive system for talent to thrive. We've witnessed initiatives that draw specific attention to African American leaders as a way to address the imbalance in the workforce, as well as organizations that partner with Toigo specifically to focus on tapping African American leaders for their own organizations or board positions. Insights shared by African American leaders signal that systemic and systematic change requires even greater and more meaningful dialogue (the tough conversations) and broader education and support for those who have achieved senior-level success. While past efforts and current practices are making a difference, a radical shift in approach is clearly needed if meaningful and sustainable changes are to take hold. A candid, direct lens into the experiences of those directly affected provides a valuable and often overlooked perspective. This lens reveals a widening gap between the way organizations market and promote diversity and the realities of day-to-day work life.

The Quest for Credibility

Many African American leaders possess the credentials and confidence to assume C-suite responsibilities based on requisite skills and experience; yet many we interviewed at this level commented that they still battle with credibility and "right to be there" feelings. We believe this constant feeling of not truly belonging, of doubt, of not having earned their rightful place in leadership amplifies this notion of the illusion of inclusion and may be at the root of why African American leaders must strategically "promote their own credibility markers in fostering meaningful points of connection with majority peers," as one leader we interviewed shared.

Another leader noted that upon his arrival midcareer at his current firm, he was often referred to as "the guy we hired from [prominent firm]," underscoring that the gold-standard brand on his résumé was viewed as the most critical element he brought into his senior role—it was the lens through which others qualified and perceived his value. "I realized it was the credibility marker they needed to welcome me, the only senior African American leader on the line." Sparked by that seemingly (to some) innocuous but nevertheless insulting "from" comment, this savvy executive began reframing how he introduced himself to firm colleagues with clients. Rather than leading with the prior firm's moniker, he purposefully used very different references as a way to begin establishing meaningful connections to his leadership and accomplishments and the new role he was assuming. "Where I worked does not define me or my potential," he decided. We heard consistently that African American leaders felt they needed to be more attuned than their white colleagues to navigating and managing against these "brand qualifiers," which ultimately detract from and devalue the successes the individual has achieved and the value he or she has delivered.

The reality that the credibility marker may not rest in the hands of even the most experienced African American leader was discussed by an entrepreneur Toigo interviewed: "I had proposed a minority spin-out five years prior to my boss and he laughed and said 'no.' Not once, but year after year. Then one unsolicited remark made by a client (who was white) during a meeting gave my boss the confidence to change his thinking. While I had the required pedigree, education, and professional track record, that wasn't enough without someone, a white male, making an endorsement." Even with all the right elements in place, added intervention was needed to validate—and catapult—this African American entrepreneur's rise.

Let's Not Lower the Bar

Ingrained attitudes, many deeply rooted in individual psyches, present very real obstacles to driving greater diversity and ultimately more minority senior leaders. Attribution theory explains, in part, how these obstacles play out: *We believe we're inherently good and talented, yet others are merely lucky, beneficiaries of good fortune. We believe we do bad things because of the situations we are in, not because of who we are. In contrast, we assume others do bad things because they are predisposed to being bad* (Gilbert & Malone, 1995). The "We really do want to be diverse, but we don't want to sacrifice quality in any way" mantra falls squarely into this arena. David Thomas, the H. Naylor Fitzhugh Professor of Business Administration, Emeritus, at Harvard Business School and president of Morehouse College, explains in "Why Race and Culture Matter in the C-Suite" (McGirt, 2016), "If you're not expecting positive performance from a particular group, such as black men, you may attribute their success to external factors, like affirmative action or luck," rather than their own character. Research by Ashleigh Rosette and colleagues supports this pattern of attribution bias in performance evaluations, specifically with respect to African American leaders (Rosette, Leonardelli, & Phillips, 2008).

Not even the highest echelons of leadership are immune. Robert Smith, founder, chairman, and CEO of Vista Equity Partners and the only African American to sign the Giving Pledge, a commitment by the world's wealthiest individuals and families to dedicate the majority of their wealth to giving back, is just one example. In a *Forbes* article, he shared that he "faces constant, if often unwitting, racism" (Vardi, 2018). After completing a deal and being complimented for his success, a white colleague then said, "But you still have your heritage to overcome." "It meant I had to work harder. And that's what I did," Smith reflected. Smith and his team at Vista have produced returns exceeding those of the most prominent private equity funds, dispelling all notions of added risk or of lowering the bar for African Americans in business leadership.

Isolation Grows

While "It's lonely at the top" may sound trite, one female black executive said, "It's true—and it's even more true when you're 'the first and the only.'" That sense of isolation, of solitude, can take a toll. One leader shared, "It's like facing each day with a core of uncertainty. It's wondering each day if the floor you're standing on is concrete or dirt, whether it's solid or not."

African American leaders quickly acknowledge the absence of a deeply rooted internal support network, which is needed to navigate the headwinds they will inevitably encounter. For multiple reasons, key drivers for organizational success must be developed by diverse leaders through creative and self-initiated means—mostly informal or external. As one leader called it, "creating my own 'safe place.'"

The absence of adequate representation of African Americans at the senior level and peer support often fuels an undercurrent of vulnerability and isolation within the workplace, as reported by some of our interviewees. For example, one shared, "When I left a major Wall Street firm, I had no idea what I was in for [by] joining a smaller, but still hugely successful, firm. It was like leaving a country club and going to a Klan rally." The individual further explained that working in finance or the asset management business is like joining a country club, with clear, albeit exclusionary, rules of entry. However, when working within a smaller team, the interviewee found that the environment was unapologetically homogenous (white and male): "Private companies do not operate under the same rules as larger institutions. The 'this is our culture' mindset is much more overt and the message is loud and clear. If you want access, there is unapologetic harshness. That one needs to conform when you are working in an environment like that, you step back and say, 'How can there be a meritocracy here when everybody here looks the same?'"

Even when the overall culture of an organization appears to be inviting, progress in confronting and addressing substantive issues can be difficult; of course, this sluggishness and lack of traction can be frustrating—for all. One interviewee observed, "People will tell you—come on in, the water is fine. The warning instead should be to have a very good wet suit. And floaties, because the water is a lot deeper and colder than you could ever imagine."

The sense of isolation and constantly pushing was a common issue voiced by the African American leaders we interviewed. When we asked one entrepreneur to share the moment when he really felt he and his fund had made it, this leader of a high-performing, fifteen-year fund with allocations from the largest pension plans in the country paused and replied, "I don't know if I feel that way today. I still question if we've made it."

One executive we interviewed is trying to change the narrative by presenting himself as a culture resource within his organization, intentionally positioning himself as a "source of expertise" and leveraging his broad, diverse network to educate his corporate stakeholders on the value of inclusive practices. He proactively pursued opportunities and initiated discussions, both personal and professional, that could make a measurable impact in closing the cultural gap that often exists between leaders from underrepresented groups and their majority colleagues.

We probed to determine whether this "cultural ambassador" model led to greater understanding about the necessity for inclusion by the firm and whether the blind spots no longer exist. Sadly, he said no. While these efforts may have an impact at the individual level, the translation of this effort to the broader, institutional level is much less visible. The raw truth is that on a corporate level this highly regarded African American leader is viewed as an outlier or an exception instead of an example of many, which is disheartening. "They are a long way from seeing me as a multiplier," he stated. "I am still an anomaly, which I do not own." Classifying African American or other diverse leaders as "exceptional" only fuels the organization's cultural complacency and can serve to further isolate the leader of color and slow any efforts for change.

"I have the opportunity and the obligation to change the narrative around complex conversations like race that help us work together toward common objectives," Bernard J. Tyson, the CEO of the $60 billion Kaiser Permanente health-care organization, recently stated. "[T]o do that, we have to tell the truth," he noted in "Why Race and Culture Matter in the C-Suite" (McGirt, 2016). To drive these needed conversations, leaders will need to change the script.

Unspoken Expectations

The burden of being "the only" is often compounded by both external and internal forces unique to African Americans more than any other group, as there is an unspoken expectation that the leader should address the needs of other black employees. While this is natural given the limited number of those with a leadership voice, this expectation may sometimes be unrealistic or complex. "People need to recalibrate their expectations of African American leaders," one executive said. "This would go a long way in improving the relationship we have with each other."

A few of our leaders shared that their history within their firms has often been tethered to elements directly connected to their "minority status," most often their presence in diversity recruitment activities. "There are responsibilities that come with your role as a diverse leader that you can rarely talk about—if you did, peers would view it as complaining, even those in your own community, which is disheartening. But trying to fulfill these expectations of helping 'my own' can come with a cost; this responsibility can require a lot of extra time and emotional energy and often gets relegated to 'personal' time, which, of no surprise, is a scarce commodity for senior leaders with obligations for family or others," commented one senior African American executive.

Another executive stated, "Diversity recruiting activities can be the kiss of death." As a result of being professionals of color, many diverse leaders are asked to assist. "The natural instinct is to be with people like you. But then you realize, there's a big conflict. Those events aren't on your boss's radar and you have work to be done. I almost lost my job because my time and attention kept getting diverted—and I was a party to it." As one executive noted, efforts to assist minorities that appear too visible and aligned with inclusive efforts may backfire on the individual, even if the organizational goal is achieved and the individual is qualified.

Some have dubbed this implied requirement "two jobs"—the official one the individual was hired to do and a second one as a champion for members of the individual's own minority group.

Efforts by leaders to assist rising African American professionals within their organizations often require a more measured or softened approach compared with the more overt way in which other talent is championed. "The academic pedigree of my team is the same if not better than the majority," one leader noted. "I can do a lot, but it's got to be stealth. I can't do it in a way that shoves 'I'm black' in everybody's face."

Center for Talent Innovation research presented in the report *Vaulting the Color Bar: How Sponsorship Levers Multicultural Professionals into Leadership* (Hewlett, Jackson, & Cose, 2012) shows that 26 percent of senior-level African Americans felt obligated to sponsor employees of the same gender or ethnicity as themselves; in contrast, 7 percent of their white counterparts felt the same and hesitated to act. "To sponsors of color who often feel insecure in their positions of power, backing a protégé of color who doesn't fit the prototypical model of success seems like an extra high-risk gamble" the report noted. Assistance must be subtle, one leader asserted.

That may be why just 21 percent of African Americans step up to sponsorship, versus 25 percent of Hispanics and 27 percent of Caucasians, the Center for Talent Innovation report noted. Sadly, the lower percentage suggests that African Americans perceive much greater risk in using their position and influence to aid sponsorship and advocacy for those rising up the ranks, even though they feel a sense of obligation to do so. What may on the surface appear to be disinterest or a lack of commitment by those who come behind the leader is, in fact, often the diverse leader attempting to calibrate the best way forward. There is a lack of understanding and appreciation in general of the careful balance between "public and private activity" necessary to position and promote others.

When asked about the experience our interviewees had of mentoring and sponsorship, none of the leaders reported a traditional mentor or sponsor history. For one executive, the process was "transient and contextual," occurring only when interactions would provide critical insights. She reflected on that fact when she set out to build her team, working to ensure that mentoring and sponsorship were part of the mix for her diverse hires.

In that process, she experienced heightened scrutiny about the diverse staffing in her area; she likened the process of building a diverse team to "making moves in a chess game." She observed that many minorities underestimate what it takes, even from the C-suite, to effect significant change in organizational structure and practice. And while she agreed that leaders should do all they can to open doors, "these efforts may not manifest themselves as people anticipate, especially when it comes to the method and speed these interactions require. That's when negativity kicks in," she explained.

Paving the Path through Shared Experiences

The traditions of African American culture are rooted in the power of storytelling—the passage of experience, struggles, and wisdom from the days of slavery to the dining rooms of many homes. One executive summed it up in this way: "I've committed twenty-five years to my career. It is a journey for me and others, not a ride. The emotions that surround African American business leaders' ascent in their careers could provide a deeper road map into the direction others might consider to ensure the momentum and legacy of African American leadership is not lost at the C-suite level and beyond."

The wisdom and knowledge passed from one African American leader to another can provide invaluable guidance and profound inspiration; yet too few engage in this way. The impact of a more open leadership narrative within the African American community is immeasurable. And, unlike diversity programs, these efforts would not require millions of dollars of investments and corporate underwriting. It's a human-powered movement, leader to leader. What is needed is a shift in openness and in the value assigned to what the narrative offers to both the teller and the listener.

Organizations must create a safe environment to foster a richer, more substantive narrative by encouraging their own diverse leaders to be candid and open about their leadership paths. The media, too, must play a critical part by promoting successes and providing more details about how challenges were addressed. In fact, it's the twists and turns of a leader's career—the obstacles and how they were navigated—that can be the most telling. We've seen the narrative about failure take off in Silicon Valley among technology entrepreneurs; no surprise, many venture capitalists are now using those shared moments of failure as a leadership metric for grit, determination, and resiliency, all the sought-after qualities in a startup CEO.

Above all, a concerted individual effort by African American leaders to be more open to sharing their stories will serve as the foundation for much deeper emotional connections among other black men and women seeking leadership. Deeper bonds are forged and needed inspiration stoked when honest stories of success and challenges overcome are shared; it's a needed and missing foundation for keeping future African American leaders focused on what's possible. In interview after interview—and in feedback from rising MBAs and leaders of color—the dearth of stories and insights shared by one African American professional with another was pronounced. Those who have the insights and road map to help fuel the dreams of contemporary leaders exist, but sadly, few have yet to share.

What is at the root of this reluctance among senior African American professionals to share their complete stories—to speak their truth? Some stated that they had worked hard to build a personal brand that echoed strength, and worried that showing any sign of weakness or setback would undermine that persona. If hardship and socioeconomic challenges were part of their upbringing, feelings of shame, weakness, and vulnerability could create a reluctance to be forthcoming. With today's rising leaders increasingly seeking more personal connection and authenticity, sharing these stories is imperative. An open exchange of stories of both success and failure by African American leaders could be one of the most powerful and profound ways to support emerging senior leaders as they navigate their way forward. "We must be more open—and trusting," one shared.

Reaching Beyond

Inclusion, as evidenced through our interviews and many of our real-world interactions and experiences, can be an illusion. The "like likes like" element of our nature—the comfort in the familiar, in surrounding ourselves with others who think and look like us—can overwhelm even the best of intentions and business practices. Corporate practices engineered to meet the basic level of diversity recruitment and retention must reach for a more systemic and systematic way of working—and leading. Toigo often draws parallels between implementing a true culture of inclusiveness and the total quality management movement of the 1980s, which became a pervasive way of working and thinking that permeated every corner of an organization. The push for quality became a mindset infused in the culture of the organization, not a side initiative or program or the domain of a small group within the institution. It penetrated every area of the business, at every level of leadership. It was also measurable, which made its impact and meaning even greater—and more sustainable.

Focused efforts to help African Americans deepen their professional networks to match those their majority peers enjoy are an area that could net tremendous results. Creating a vibrant network is fundamental for leaders at the senior level—the needed antidote for addressing the isolation and vulnerability that interviewees expressed.

As Toigo has shared, several leaders voiced their opinion that too few senior, influential African American executives are leveraging their influence on behalf of the next wave of senior leaders. This cautious approach has a compound effect for future leaders. "It may be generational," one leader said. "But it creates a critical missing link—the transfer of connectivity and endorsement from generation to generation." This affects opportunities for further corporate leadership success, greater visibility, growth in income for families, and presence on corporate boards or in entrepreneurship.

What is clear is that efforts and investments by organizations to address diversity and a culture of inclusion cannot be made in isolation or as "add-on" initiatives. They must be authentic, thoughtful, and sustained. They must be supported by more organic efforts built on the perspectives of African American leaders; without this combined force to drive change, we will forever be in the cycle of illusion, not inclusion. As one leader stated, "For those who have achieved executive status, it is incumbent on them to consider not just how they arrived but what they experienced. Sharing these treasures of wisdom is part of the building blocks of the African American leadership legacy."

REFERENCES

Gilbert, D. T., & Malone, P. S. (1995). The correspondence bias. *Psychological Bulletin, 17*(1), 21–38. Retrieved from http://www.danielgilbert.com/Gilbert%20 &%20Malone%20%28CORRESPONDENCE%20BIAS%29.pdf

Hewlett, S. A., Jackson, M., & Cose, E. (2012, October 16). *Vaulting the color bar: How sponsorship levers multicultural professionals into leadership* (Report). Retrieved from https://www.talentinnovation.org/_private/assets/VaultingTheColorBar-KeyFindings-CTI.pdf

Knight Foundation. (2017). *Diversifying investments* (Report). Retrieved from https://knightfoundation.org/reports/diversifying-investments

McGirt, E. (2016, January 22). Why race and culture matter in the C-suite. *Fortune*. Retrieved from http://fortune.com/black-executives-men-c-suite/

Money Management Institute. (2017, November 8). MMI/FundFire survey highlights racial diversity gaps across asset management industry. Retrieved from https://www.mminst.org/press-releases/mmifundfire-survey-highlights-racial-diversity-gaps-across-asset-management-industry

Rosette, A. S., Leonardelli, G. J., & Phillips, K. W. (2008). The white standard: Racial bias in leader categorization. *Journal of Applied Psychology, 93*(4), 758–777.

Seddon-Daines, O., & Chinwala, Y. (2017, November). *Diversity from an investor's perspective: Why and how the most forward-looking asset owners are addressing diversity and inclusion* (Report). London: New Financial.

United States Census Bureau. (2017). *National African-American History Month: February 2017* (Release No. CB17-FF.01). Retrieved from https://www.census.gov/newsroom/facts-for-features/2017/cb17-ff01.html

United States Government Accountability Office. (2017, September). *Key practices could provide more options for federal entities and opportunities for minority- and women-owned asset managers* (Report No. GAO-17-726). Washington, DC: GAO. Retrieved from https://www.gao.gov/products/GAO-17-726

Vardi, N. (2018, March 6). Richer than Oprah: How the nation's wealthiest African American conquered tech and Wall Street. *Forbes*.

11

Rough Waters of Resistance

Black Instructional Coaches Affected by Implicit Bias

MICHELLE SMITH MACCHIA *and* KISHA PORCHER

Testing the Waters: Am I in the Right Place?

Tiffany showed up on the first day of an assignment, ready to launch a new project with each grade-level team of teachers at a school in a large, urban school district. A White teacher entered the room as she was setting up for the workshop and asked in a friendly voice, "Are you setting up for the presenter?"

Tiffany shuddered inside but answered with a big smile, "Hi! My name is Dr. Watson and I am the presenter."

The teacher responded with a puzzled look, "Am I in the right place? Is this the room for today's team meetings?"

Tiffany said, "Yes."

Feeling the Waves: What Did You Study?

Leah observed two veteran teachers at the request of the school's assistant principal. The administrator was alarmed by the teachers' consistently weak instruction when working with small groups of kindergarten and first-grade students in the beginning stages of learning English. Leah's observations were aligned with the administrator's concerns. After school, Leah met with each teacher to provide feedback on what she had observed. The teachers agreed to work on instructional strategies, then meet in two weeks to discuss their progress.

When Leah returned to the school two weeks later, both teachers were cordial, but not chummy and jovial as they had been in all of her previous encounters with them. During their follow-up meeting, one teacher casually asked, "So, what did you study in grad school? I mean . . . what's your doctorate in?"

Introduction

To the casual observer, the questions posed by the teachers in the foregoing scenarios are harmless. However, we posit that when viewed in the broader context, including the consultants' and teachers' races, the schools' demographic makeup, and the organizational culture of the schools, these teachers' questions are emblematic of a phenomenon that commonly affects one's ability to be effective in the workplace: implicit racial bias.

The narratives shared in this chapter are true accounts of events experienced by the authors and their Black instructional coach colleagues, five Black female educational consultants who work with K–12 educators in schools located in large metropolitan areas of the United States. These narratives illustrate how Black instructional coaches often experience implicit racial bias in their client schools and internalize it. Our aim in sharing them is threefold: we want first to illuminate the struggles faced by Black instructional coaches hired to provide effective professional development; second, we endeavor to help the reader understand how existing research on the sociocultural foundations of teaching and learning informs the narratives of the consultants we meet in this chapter; and third, we seek to make the case for greater research into understanding how implicit racial bias affects Black instructional coaches' ability to help educators improve student achievement.

Using critical race theory (CRT), as conceptualized by Bell (2004) and Crenshaw (1995), as the lens through which we view these coaches' experiences, we explore the notion of cultural mismatch driven by implicit racial bias, which is pervasive within the K–12 community (Delpit, 2006; Ladson-Billings, 1995). We propose that the implicit racial biases educators hold against their students may transfer to their behaviors during teacher-coach interactions with Black instructional coaches, negatively affecting a coach's ability to be effective.

Understanding the effects of implicit racial bias on the work of Black instructional coaches is critical to helping Black coaches and those who organize professional learning for educators ensure that professional learning leads to improved learning outcomes for children, regardless of who delivers that professional learning. We end this chapter with recommendations for future research and practice aimed at understanding (1) how educators perceive Black coaches and how these perceptions impact their professional learning, and (2) how Black instructional coaches use self-care to improve their effectiveness.

Background

Today, Blacks form an estimated 13.4 percent of the total US population (US Census Bureau, n.d.), with Black women representing a little over half of that population (US Census Bureau, 2017). Yet during the 2015–2016 school year, Black women—approximately 6.5 percent of the total US population—earned 11.8 percent of all bachelor's degrees, 15.2 percent of all master's degrees, and 10.3 percent of all doctorates conferred by US postsecondary institutions (National Center for Education Statistics, 2017a, 2017b, 2017c). Over the past nearly four decades, Black women have consistently pursued and earned an increasing share of all college degrees conferred and in numbers that surpass their representation. Despite these facts, they are often not shown appropriate professional respect by their White colleagues and are generally not respected in their careers as being highly qualified or knowledgeable enough to serve in leadership roles. In their study of women in leadership conducted for the American Association of University Women, Hill, Miller, Benson, and Handley (2016) found that Black women make up only 8 percent of people who hold private-sector jobs and less than 2 percent of those who serve in leadership roles. There is clearly a misalignment between Black women's educational attainment and their representation in the private sector and in leadership roles.

We and the Black instructional coaches with whom we network provide strategic planning and professional development support to school leaders and instructional coaching to teachers for the purpose of improving literacy learning outcomes for students. Our effectiveness is evaluated annually through a variety of measures, including standardized state and benchmark reading assessment scores, client school and satisfaction survey data, and superintendent evaluations. We know we have been successful when teachers and school leaders have improved their practice in the areas in which we coached them and student achievement increases as a result. Therefore, our success hinges on teachers' ability to improve their practice by working with us.

Rising Tide: Humanize Them

As Shonta stood in the hallway, a nearby classroom door quickly swung open. Two students of color skipped out of the classroom and down the hall, chattering loudly. Their teacher dashed into the hallway, fussing, "Walk quietly! I'm gonna make you both come back here and try that again if you don't slow down!!!" The exasperated teacher, a White veteran teacher near retirement, glanced at Shonta and shook her head in frustrated disbelief. "It's hard to get anything done with these kids. We have to humanize them before we can get anything done." The words hurt, but Shonta tried not to show her pain as she stared at the teacher with a neutral expression.

High Tide: Eyes Forward, Hands at Your Sides

Renee sat in the assistant principal's office, located three doors down from an experienced first-grade teacher. Suddenly, she and the administrator heard this teacher yelling irately at the same two Black male students the teacher regularly admonished.

When Renee raised her concern about these instances of repeated verbal abuse, the administrator acknowledged that she knew about the teacher's chronic, aggressive behavior. She added that there was nothing she or the principal could do. Based on the administrator's response, Renee doubted the teacher would ever receive the help she needed.

Cultural Mismatch in Schools

The students in the schools in which we and our colleagues work come from a wide variety of cultural, linguistic, and socioeconomic backgrounds. The demographic breakdown of students in this school system during the 2017–2018 school year was 16 percent Asian, 26 percent

Black, 40.5 percent Hispanic, 2.5 percent multirace not specified, and 15 percent White. Approximately 20 percent of students had disabilities, 13.5 percent were English-language learners, and 74 percent lived in poverty. Despite the profound diversity of this school system's student body, approximately 76 percent of all teachers in this system were female, and approximately 58.6 percent of all teachers were White (Anonymous Metropolitan School System, 2018).

A vast body of literature on the sociocultural foundations of education (Anyon, 1980; Carter, 2007; Delpit, 1988, 2006; Gay & Howard, 2000; Ladson-Billings, 1995, 2001, 2009; Noguera, 2009) points to this overrepresentation in chronically underperforming schools and identifies cultural mismatch between students and teachers as a major cause of inequitable education. Gay and Howard (2000) describe cultural mismatch as a "demographic divide" between White teachers and the students they teach, resulting in unequal and inadequate education for students of color. Similarly, Delpit (1988) describes how the culture of power plays out in the classroom, leading to tensions between teachers and those students who possess cultural and linguistic backgrounds different from their own. This power dynamic almost always leads to disappointing outcomes for children of color and students in poverty, including high disciplinary referral rates, anemic academic performance, and underrepresentation in gifted education programs among children of color, Black and Latinx male students in particular (Bonner, 2000; Delpit, 1988; Lewis, Butler, Bonner, & Joubert, 2010; Noguera, 2009; Schott Foundation for Public Education, 2015). We suggest that mindset and implicit racial bias are at the heart of these issues and use CRT to support why and how they work.

Critical Race Theory, Implicit Bias, and Teacher Mindset

It is difficult to say that the resistance exhibited by many of the teachers with whom we work is purely coincidental when we consider the research on CRT (Bell, 2004; Crenshaw, 1995), implicit bias (Desai, 2016; Kang, 2005), and teacher mindset (Dweck & Legget, 1988; Plaks, Levy, & Dweck, 2009). CRT posits that mainstream American society systematically uses the socially constructed notion of race to maintain power over "minority" groups in ways that are pervasive, often unrecognizable, and normalized (Taylor, Gillborn, & Ladson-Billings, 2009). As a result of this normalization, most oppression does not appear as oppression to the perpetrating group. For instance, the White teacher's comment about humanizing students may appear on the surface to be a demonstration of that teacher's frustration, but it is rooted in racism—yet another example of the historical stereotype that people of color are animals, inhumane, and therefore unable to be taught.

Implicit biases, which are underlying, subconscious thoughts and beliefs about other people's "goodness" or "badness," influence the way we see the world and move through life. Kang (2005) argues that most of us have implicit biases that have real-world consequences for our social interactions (Desai, 2016). Well-respected scholars (Anyon, 1980; Carter, 2007; Delpit, 1988, 2006; Dweck, 2006; Gay & Howard, 2000; Ladson-Billings, 1995, 2001, 2009; Noguera, 2009) argue that many educators act in ways that produce inequitable outcomes for their students. Even well-intentioned educators who profess egalitarian intentions and attempt to treat all individuals fairly still unknowingly act in ways that reflect their implicit—rather than explicit—biases (Staats, 2016).

Based on our coaching experiences with a variety of teachers, we can conclude that many of the teachers in our client schools engage in thinking about students based on alleged genetic, cultural, cognitive, and motivational deficits (Howard, 2010; Nieto, 2000). Johnson (1994) defines deficit thinking as the labeling of poor students of color and their families as disadvantaged, at risk, and uninvolved—a mindset that causes educators to fault students and their families when students do not perform well academically, citing a student's lack of readiness to learn in the classroom, parents' lack of interest in their child's education, and a family's overall lifestyle as reasons for academic underperformance (Walker, 2011). If a teacher does not believe in his or her students, then he or she is highly likely to either dumb down instruction to make it easier for students or hold off on teaching a particular skill or concept because he or she believes the students are not ready to receive that instruction. For some educators, this may even mean holding off on teaching of any kind until they can teach the students how to behave, as Shonta learned.

Low Expectations for Other People's Children

We see firsthand in our daily work how cultural mismatches driven by implicit racial bias contribute to low expectations of students of color and students in low-performing schools, affecting children in profound and lasting ways (Ladson-Billings, 1995, 2001, 2009; Nieto & Bode, 2008; Noguera, 2009). We and our colleagues have collectively worked in approximately fifty different schools within this K–12 school system and nearly one hundred schools in other districts across the nation. We have all heard countless educators openly express a deficit mindset about their students of color and set low expectations for them, a phenomenon referred to by Noguera (2009) as the "normalization of failure." In addition, we have all witnessed teachers freely yelling at young children out of frustration when they do not walk in a straight line or sit with their hands folded during storytime. Sadly, we have all seen school leaders turn a blind eye to these oppressive teacher behaviors toward children from historically marginalized groups. As Delpit (2006) suggests, these teachers treat their students like "other people's children," rather than protecting and cultivating them as they would protect and cultivate their own.

We hypothesize that these same poor perceptions of historically underserved students drive aggressive behaviors rooted in historical racism and influence the way educators interact with instructional coaches of the same race, culture, and heritage as the students they subconsciously hold in low regard. In other words, this same deficit mindset driven by implicit racial bias transfers over to educators' interactions with Black instructional coaches, causing them to question our ability to coach them effectively, as Vera experienced.

Undercurrent and Crashing Waves: Make This Project Work

Vera worked in an elementary school in an affluent district where the teachers and the vast majority of the students were White. During her first meeting with teachers, Vera knew that she was not welcome in the school. One teacher angrily expressed the belief that Vera had nothing to bring to their school, then proceeded to yell expletives at her throughout the rest of the session.

By the time Vera met with the principal at the end of the day, the teacher had already spoken to the principal. When Vera described the teacher's unprofessional behavior, the principal told her that she did not feel comfortable addressing the teacher because she was her friend and, "quite frankly, one of the best teachers in the school."

Knowing she would have to proceed without the principal's full support, Vera emailed her supervisor to express her extreme discomfort working in this school. Her supervisor replied that her colleague, a White male, would support her during her next visit to the school. When he arrived, Vera told him why she was uncomfortable working in the school. He responded, "You—not the school—are the problem. Get over yourself. Just figure out what we need to do to make this project work." A week later, the principal requested that Vera be replaced by her White male colleague.

Teacher Mindset Affecting Instructional Coaching

Instructional coaching is teacher-centered and inquiry-based learning aimed at helping teachers find ways to address gaps in teacher practice and student learning. It is one high-leverage professional development practice that can yield excellent results (Knight, 2007, 2017; Lytle & Cochran-Smith, 1992). It is multifaceted and requires a responsive touch due to the nuances and complex challenges surrounding it.

Desimone and Pak (2017) found that effective coaches provide coaching that (1) is content focused, (2) involves active learning, (3) takes place consistently over a period of time, (4) involves collective participation, and (5) provides coherence to teachers. Further, the first principles of adult learning hold that the process of building professional knowledge is deeply rooted in trust and relationship building, both of which are influenced by mindset. For teachers to learn with and from an instructional coach, not only must they believe in the validity of professional learning, they must also view the instructional coach as a trustworthy, more knowledgeable professional who is capable of teaching them something that will help them improve their practice.

Sadly, some Black instructional coaches never get the opportunity to affect teacher practice in a positive way because educators resist our efforts before we can even get started. In some cases, teachers openly express disbelief that a Black coach is the one leading their team's professional learning efforts, as Tiffany experienced. Staff also sometimes question their coach's qualifications to make observation- and data-based recommendations about how to improve their instructional practice, as we saw with Leah. In Vera's case, her attempts to develop a relationship with teachers were thwarted by one teacher who prevented her from sharing her ideas with the team. When implicit racial bias prevents teachers and coaches from learning together, it is exceptionally difficult to attain goals of improved teacher-student relationships and improved student learning. This difficulty is exacerbated when Black instructional coaches stretch themselves mentally—and sometimes physically—in an effort to overcome such obstacles.

Internal Struggles

As each of us encountered resistance in different forms in our client schools, we experienced a persistent, nagging feeling in our gut when preparing to return to a school where educators resisted our support in both overt and covert, but clearly oppositional, ways. Educator resistance driven by implicit bias tends to wear on us, causing us to engage in an internal struggle that manifests itself in many ways. In the face of challenge, one's natural inclination may be to hunker down and brace for the storm ahead, as Vera did. Such resistance also caused us to internalize aspects of imposter syndrome (Dancy & Brown, 2011), ranging from experiencing negative emotions about the people with whom we were trying to connect and the work we were trying to accomplish, to doubting ourselves.

Negative emotions and self-doubt caused us to engage in hyperperfectionism, which is particularly ironic because we possess the experience and education required for the position, including track records for influencing teacher development and student achievement. Yet we felt an overwhelming need to prove to resistant educators that we are not just qualified for the job but *highly* qualified to lead them in improving their practice and, in turn, student achievement. We dreaded the thought of facing these and other specific, observable behaviors that sent a clear message to us that the professional learning we were offering was of little or no value to them.

Survey Data Revelations

One question we asked ourselves as we wrote this chapter was, What do we know about the interactions between Black instructional coaches and Black and Latinx educators? We thought it was important to examine Black educators' satisfaction with their Black instructional coach. To explore this question, we looked at evaluation survey data submitted by a range of educators over a three-year period for one of

TABLE 11-1

Survey results regarding coach satisfaction

Total number of respondents	32
Total number of responses	42
Racial demographics of respondents	Black: 5 White: 19 Latinx: 7 Asian: 1

Respondents' evaluations of coach by racial identity	Black:
	    Excellent: 86%
	    Good: 14%
	    Fair: N/A
	
	Latinx:
	    Excellent: 43%
	    Good: 57%
	    Fair: N/A
	
	White:
	    Excellent: 54%
	    Good: 27%
	    Fair: 19%

the coaches featured in this chapter. Table 11-1 summarizes the survey responses.

In an interview with the coach who received these ratings, we learned more about the context surrounding the poor ratings from four teachers, all of whom were White. Two were novice teachers who worked with thoughtful, detail-oriented, highly effective colleagues who carried the bulk of the responsibilities for their teams. Both openly exhibited a fixed mindset about teaching and learning through their interactions with students and their planning for instruction. The other two were seasoned teachers who, although smart, organized, and knowledgeable, exhibited oppositional behaviors toward the coach on numerous occasions, including by galvanizing their colleagues in a silent protest against the program the coach was trying to implement in their schools. Interestingly, one of these teachers worked with a Black coteacher who was equally organized and experienced but far more adept at delivering clear, culturally responsive instruction. This teacher was consistently rated "highly effective" by her administrators. She also implemented the feedback offered by the Black coach into her teaching and participated fully in the professional learning sessions with this coach.

We could not help but wonder whether race played a role in these educators' responses to us. After all, we were all in positions of power as experts hired to help struggling teachers improve their practice, which takes us back to Bell's (2004) and Crenshaw's (1995) work on CRT and Delpit's (1988, 2006) work regarding power in K–12 school settings. Additionally, our Black colleagues reported that they had tried to work silently through these feelings because the culture of the schools in which they worked was not collegial toward them. We all deliberate whether to let the offensive events slide or share them with school leaders and other colleagues.

Implications for Research and Practice

As subject-matter experts hired to help school leaders and teacher teams design and implement strategic plans for school improvement, we have an obligation to break down barriers that prevent educators from effectively teaching children. Fortunately for us practitioners, there is a robust body of research on and recommendations for using instructional coaching as a form of teacher professional development to improve student achievement (Calo, Sturtevant, & Kopfman, 2015; Desimone & Pak, 2017; Knight, 2007, 2017; Kowal & Steiner, 2007; L'Allier, Elish-Piper, & Bean, 2010). However, insights from Black instructional coaches are sorely absent from the literature.

In conducting our own literature review for this chapter, we searched for empirical studies examining the experiences and effectiveness of Black instructional coaches working with K–12 educators who were, by simple demographics, predominantly White. We looked for such studies in an effort to help ourselves better understand the challenges and nuances of "coaching while Black." While the studies we found identified teacher perception and building relationships as core competencies of effective instructional coaches, the literature did not explore how educators respond to Black instructional coaches and how Blackness affects an instructional coach's effectiveness in schools. The literature also did not treat the impact of implicit racial bias on a coach's ability to be effective.

Without a research base for Black instructional coaches, we could only look to existing research-based theoretical frameworks on two topics:

literacy coaching and CRT as it relates to the sociocultural foundations of K–12 education. We urge social scientists to examine how Blackness influences educational consultants' effectiveness in schools. Research efforts in this area will help practitioners—organizations and school leaders responsible for organizing the work of Black instructional coaches in K–12 schools and Black instructional coaches themselves—better understand how implicit racial bias affects their ability to effectively engage teachers in professional learning.

Possible research questions include the following: What are the similarities and differences between the experiences of Black and non-Black instructional coaches? How do school leaders and teachers perceive Black coaches, and how do their perceptions impact their interactions with these coaches? We make the following specific recommendations for future research aimed at filling this gap:

- Compile statistics on Black instructional coaches.

- Conduct a national survey of Black instructional coaches.

- Conduct a national survey of educators receiving support from a Black instructional coach.

- Perform a double-blind randomized study of educators' perceptions of highly qualified Black instructional coaches and how these perceptions may affect educator growth and coach effectiveness.

Findings from empirical studies can be used to develop frameworks for engaging educators and coaches in cross-cultural professional learning. These same findings can also inform the design of models for enhancing perceptions and relationships between Black instructional coaches and the educators they guide.

Our recommendations for practice include two regarding self-care and scholarship. First, we encourage Black instructional coaches to find, create, and engage in self-care opportunities (widely defined). This means creating safe communities where we can openly share our narratives, unpack our professional experiences, and learn how to change the narrative from one of oppression and resistance to one of collegial professional learning. Second, we encourage Black instructional coaches to conduct research on themselves and others in their field as a part of the self-care we recommend.

Conclusion

Each story we heard from our colleagues reminded us that systemic, institutional racism is an oppressive tool wielded by educators who feel protective of their territory and vulnerable in the presence of an outsider offering guidance. As we continue to think about the most salient aspects of how our Blackness has influenced our own effectiveness, we realize that there is much to uncover about the lived experiences of Black instructional coaches. Data on what it means to "coach while Black" will help future Black instructional coaches in their work. This data will also help non-Black education practitioners begin to reconcile their feelings about taking direction from Black coaches and learn how to create conditions that foster an environment in which they can work *with* Black coaches instead of against them. Until then, we and other Black coaches will continue to navigate the rough waters of resistance from educators on our own.

REFERENCES

Anyon, J. (1980). Social class and the hidden curriculum of work. *Journal of Education, 162*(2), 67–92.

Bell, D. A. (2004). *Race, racism, and American law.* New York, NY: Aspen.

Bonner, F. A. (2000). African American giftedness: Our nation's deferred dream. *Journal of Black Studies, 30*(5), 643–663.

Calo, K. M., Sturtevant, E. G., & Kopfman, K. M. (2015). Literacy coaches' perspectives of themselves as literacy leaders: Results from a national study on K–12 literacy coaching and leadership. *Literacy Research and Instruction, 54*, 1–18.

Carter, P. L. (2007). *Keepin' it real: School success beyond Black and White.* Oxford, England: Oxford University Press.

Crenshaw, K. (1995). *Critical race theory: The key writings that formed the movement.* New York, NY: New Press.

Dancy, T. E., & Brown, M. C. (2011). The mentoring and induction of educators of color: Addressing the imposter syndrome in academe. *Journal of School Leadership, 21*, 607–634.

Delpit, L. (1988). The silenced dialogue: Power and pedagogy in educating other people's children. *Harvard Educational Review, 58*(3), 280–299.

Delpit, L. (2006). *Other people's children: Cultural conflict in the classroom.* New York, NY: New Press.

Desai, S. R. (2016). Humanizing Trayvon Martin: Racial profiling, implicit biases, and teacher education. *Urban Education*, 1–27. First published online. doi:10.1177/0042085916646609

Desimone, L. M., & Pak, K. (2017). Instructional coaching as high-quality professional development. *Theory into Practice, 56*(1), 3–12.

Dweck, C. S. (2006). *Mindset: The new psychology of success.* New York, NY: Random House.

Dweck, C. S., & Leggett, E. L. (1988). A social-cognitive approach to motivation and personality. *Psychological Review, 95*(2), 256–273.

Gay, G., & Howard, T. C. (2000). Multicultural teacher education for the 21st century. *The Teacher Educator, 36*(1), 1–16.

Hill, C., Miller, K., Benson, K., & Handley, G. (2016). *Barriers and bias: The status of women in leadership.* American Association of University Women. Retrieved from https://www.aauw.org/resource/barriers-and-bias/

Howard, T.C. (2010). *Why race and culture matter in schools: Closing the achievement gap in America's classrooms.* New York, NY: Teachers College Press.

Johnson, G. M. (1994). An ecological framework for conceptualizing educational risk. *Urban Education, 29*(1), 34–49.

Kang, J. (2005). Trojan horses of race. *Harvard Law Review, 118*, 1490–2005.

Knight, J. (2007). *Instructional coaching: A partnership approach to improving instruction.* Thousand Oaks, CA: Corwin.

Knight, J. (2017). *The impact cycle: What instructional coaches should do to foster powerful improvements in teaching.* Thousand Oaks, CA: Corwin.

Kowal, J., & Steiner, L. (2007). *Instructional coaching* (Issue brief). Washington, DC: Center for Comprehensive School Reform and Improvement.

Ladson-Billings, G. (1995). But that's just good teaching! The case for culturally relevant pedagogy. *Theory into Practice, 34*(3), 159–165.

Ladson-Billings, G. (2001). *Crossing over to Canaan: The journey of new teachers in diverse classrooms. Jossey-Bass Education Series.* San Francisco, CA: Jossey-Bass.

Ladson-Billings, G. (2009). *The dreamkeepers: Successful teachers of African American children.* San Francisco, CA: John Wiley & Sons.

L'Allier, S., Elish-Piper, L., & Bean, R. M. (2010). What matters for elementary literacy coaching? Guiding principles for instructional improvement and student achievement. *The Reading Teacher, 63*(7), 544–554.

Lewis, C. W., Butler, B. R., Bonner, F. A., III, & Joubert, M. (2010). African American male discipline patterns and school district responses resulting impact on academic achievement: Implications for urban educators and policy makers. *Journal of African American Males in Education, 1*(1), 7–25.

Lytle, S., & Cochran-Smith, M. (1992). Teacher research as a way of knowing. *Harvard Educational Review, 62*(4), 447–475.

National Center for Education Statistics. (2017a). *Bachelor's degrees conferred by postsecondary institutions, by race/ethnicity and sex of student: Selected years, 1976–77 through 2015–16.* Washington, DC: National Center for Education Statistics. Retrieved from https://nces.ed.gov/programs/digest/d17/tables/dt17_322.20.asp

National Center for Education Statistics. (2017b). *Doctor's degrees conferred by postsecondary institutions, by race/ethnicity and sex of student: Selected years, 1976–77 through 2015–16.* Washington, DC: National Center for Education Statistics. Retrieved from https://nces.ed.gov/programs/digest/d17/tables/dt17_324.20.asp

National Center for Education Statistics. (2017c). *Master's degrees conferred by postsecondary institutions, by race/ethnicity and sex of student: Selected years, 1976–77 through 2015–16.* Washington, DC: National Center for Education Statistics. Retrieved from https://nces.ed.gov/programs/digest/d17/tables/dt17_323.20.asp

Nieto, S. (2000). Placing equity front and center: Thoughts on transforming teacher education for a new century. *Journal of Teacher Education, 51*(3), 180–187.

Nieto, S., & Bode, P. (2008). *Affirming diversity: The sociopolitical context of multicultural education.* New York, NY: Pearson.

Noguera, P. A. (2009). *The trouble with Black boys: And other reflections on race, equity, and the future of public education.* Hoboken, NJ: John Wiley & Sons.

Plaks, J. E., Levy, S. R., & Dweck, C. S. (2009). Lay theories of personality: Cornerstones of meaning in social cognition. *Social and Personality Psychology Compass, 3*(6), 1069–1081.

Schott Foundation for Public Education. (2015). *Black lives matter: The Schott 50 state report on public education and Black males.* Cambridge, MA: Schott Foundation for Public Education.

Staats, C. (2016). Understanding implicit bias: What educators should know. *Education Digest, 82*(1), 29–38.

Taylor, E., Gillborn, D., & Ladson-Billings, G. (2009). *Foundations of critical race theory in education.* New York, NY: Routledge.

US Census Bureau. (n.d.). *Quick Facts United States: Black or African American alone, percent.* Washington, DC: US Census Bureau. Retrieved from https://www.census.gov/quickfacts/fact/table/US/RHI225217

US Census Bureau. (2017). *American Community Survey 1-Year Estimates.* Washington, DC: US Census Bureau. Retrieved from https://factfinder.census.gov/faces/tableservices/jsf/pages/productview.xhtml?src=bkmk#

Walker, K. L. (2011). Deficit thinking and the effective teacher. *Education and Urban Society, 43*(5), 576–597.

12

A Million Gray Areas

*How Two Friends Crossed Paths Professionally
and Personally and Mutually Enhanced Their
Understanding of Relationships of Race,
Gender, Class, and Power*

KATHRYN FRASER *and* KAREN SAMUELS

> I lay back on my bunk and thought about people I love, and how
> lucky I was to be white and not poor and just passing briefly
> through a system which is a permanent hell for so many.
>
> —*Zinn (2002)*

The journey of Black professionals these days is often a series of peaks and valleys. When you are first recognized in your new role as the authority and the expert, it is priceless . . . and at the same time can be hard to enjoy. When you are confronted with praise and simultaneously see a look of "I really didn't expect you to be that smart," you feel like a balloon that has a tiny hole, allowing the life-sustaining air inside to seep out and leave nothingness. In majority-White settings, this is often hidden and suffered silently, until you find allies who are willing to walk this journey with you. It can be a painful experience for both as you work out your relationship and confront and also dissipate the barriers between you.

This chapter explores the gaps in the knowledge of relational experience that is necessary to the development of Black leadership in the field of psychology and health. It focuses on our relationship as two female psychologists, discussing the intersectionality of our lives: one as a Black woman in the predominantly White medical profession and the other, her White female colleague and friend. Navigating power, authority, and authenticity are central to understanding why naming White privilege was crucial to this partnership. In our relationship as women from different geographic and racial backgrounds, we have grown more curious about investigating what helps people work together across difference. The points of disconnection are numerous, whether caused by race, gender, class, power, or privilege. Does forging relationships that overtly name these differences foster more productive connections?

We use relational cultural theory (RCT) to examine relationships that support authentic growth in connection. Our relationship began as one between supervisor and supervisee. As Kathryn's clinical supervisor, Karen introduced RCT and the writings of Wellesley College's Stone Center. The theory challenges the traditional medical model of a "separate self" identity-development process. Human beings grow through their experiences in relationships and in the cultural context of their identity formation (Jordan, 2004; Miller, 1986; Walker, 2002). RCT's emphasis is on growth-fostering relationships for healthy development and emotional healing (Jordan, 2010; Walker, 2017). From the beginning of her clinical supervision, Karen attended to Kathryn's experiences as the only person of color, and one of few women, in the Family Medicine Residency Program faculty, where she served as the behavioral medicine coordinator and mental health professional. From the start of our relationship, we focused on the parallel process—a phenomenon between therapist and supervisor, whereby the therapist recreates or parallels the client's problems by way of relating to the supervisor. In our training relationship, Karen's role as a White supervisor mirrored the majority-White medical setting where Kathryn worked as a Black psychologist.

Does the recognition of contrasting identities prepare for enhanced relational possibilities and facilitate intergroup dynamics across differences? We find that the gaps in knowledge and understanding remain problematic in the fields of psychology, health-care delivery, and medical education. Thus, the Black leadership experience is unique and painful. Our individual stories, our "racialized biographies" and cultural histories (Walker & Rosen, 2004) melded together to help us understand the complex dynamics of racism, marginalization, the minimization of the human experience of difference, and the oppressive nature of human disconnection. We embraced our contrasting identities, which strengthened our work together.

Kathryn's Story: Developing My Roots as an American of African Heritage

"Black people don't need to tan!" my White friend said as we sat at the pool shortly after I emigrated from Jamaica. This was the start of my journey toward discovering my Blackness. No matter how I tried to ignore it—moving along with my idea that everyone is the same and race didn't matter—it kept resurfacing. Junior high and high school were a painful time of reckoning for me. I was mainly teased and ostracized for my accent, but certainly my skin color became a factor. The move to Miami when I was thirteen tested my sense of myself and my place in the world. I truly lost my voice because I was afraid to speak and be ridiculed. I regained some confidence in my undergraduate years at the University of Miami when I joined the Jamaican organization and took on some leadership roles. When I began to work with Carolyn Tucker, an African American woman who was the most successful grant writer and prolific researcher in my counseling psychology doctoral program at the University of Florida, I began to experience a shift in my conception of how African Americans and minorities live in America. My experience on her research project helped me learn how racism, microaggressions, and economic oppression reduce Black children's ability to experience growth like their more privileged counterparts. I realized at that time that there was definitely an uneven playing field.

It was a painful time for me to admit that I was living in a racist country. By taking up this fight, it meant that I was acknowledging that I might not be able to succeed because of the color of my skin. I decided to become a champion for racial and social equity, educational achievement, and antioppression forces. That started my journey toward being a cultural competency trainer as part of my role as a health psychologist and behavioral science faculty member in a family medicine residency. It was here that I crossed paths with Karen for the first time.

Ironically, although she is White and Jewish, learning about anti-Semitism and sexism from her viewpoint allowed me to more fully understand and work through my experience of being Black in America. She was in fact the first person to discuss with me that she "acknowledged her White privilege," and she did it shortly after we met. Frankly, I was taken aback and not quite ready to have that conversation. It would eventually become apparent to me that she was bringing attention to the "power over" aspect of our relationship in order to avoid abuse of power or shaming, salient tenets of RCT.

Karen's Story: Acknowledging My White Privilege in Community, Profession, and Relationships

My grandfather settled in Daytona Beach, Florida, in 1910, one of the first Jewish settlers in this community. Fifty-five years later, I was taunted in my elementary school cafeteria by classmates demanding to see the horns hidden in my thick, curly, brown hair. Threats that I was destined to burn in hell for eternity terrified me. My parents owned a roofing business; indeed, everyone in my family worked in the family business. We learned early in life of the responsibility that came with White privilege and to manage anti-Semitism. The history of close alliances between the Jewish community and African American community was evident in my home. I won't attempt to sugarcoat it, though: in the roofing business, the men toiling in the Florida sun were primarily African American. We worked inside, in the air conditioning.

My junior high school was integrated in 1969, when I was in seventh grade. In civics class, my best friend was Martin, an African American young man who sat in front of me. Surprisingly, we talked about racism. Our school was beachside. Only a few years earlier, Blacks were not allowed on the beachside without a permit. We shared our memories on the segregated buses, bathrooms, and water fountains as our school was struggling with civil rights. We found a way to bridge our very different perspectives during this tumultuous time.

When I returned to live in this community and practice as a psychologist in 1990, my office was down the street from the site of my former junior high school. The school had been demolished; the site was now a parking lot. The destruction of the building seemed a powerful metaphor. The places we sought to change may be gone, but the invisible boundaries of segregation have taken decades to erase.

When we began our work together in clinical supervision, Kathryn's experience as a Black woman in a predominantly White and male traditional medical workplace brought my White privilege front and center. The traditional supervisory position of authority and power could not be the status quo. It was painful to recognize the microaggressions happening both in her workplace and by my actions. Our relationship became central to every discussion. It was important to name our racial and cultural differences and to examine how my perspective was naive regarding her reality, especially within the dominant health-care system. Adopting the language of RCT, the focus became how we could embody the change we seek while working together with honesty and candor.

Relational Cultural Theory

Our theoretical foundation lies in RCT. Jean Baker Miller's text *Toward a New Psychology of Women* (1986) posits the fundamental notion that humans are relational beings who develop in a cultural context, seeking growth in interpersonal connection. Acknowledgment of racial or cultural dissimilarities is critical to meaningful relationships. Humans beings are hardwired for connection, not isolation, in the face of forces that convey, "You are not enough or don't belong." Chronic disconnections are viewed as the primary source of suffering, exacerbated by abuses of power from the culture. Strategies of disconnection become lifesaving and mind-saving survival tactics, as humans both long for and are terrified of connection. The quality of healing connections is evidenced by an increased sense of worth, clarity, zest, and desire for more (Miller & Stiver, 1997).

In psychology supervision, the internalized messages often are critical and subordinating. Moving away from "thou shalt not" shaming to "how we learn together" collaboration embodies a relational model. Thus our relationship evolved from "mentorship" to collaboration within the first three to four years as we worked together in community social justice activities and presentations at national medical education meetings. The shift from "I" and "you" to "we" required us to work toward something mutually empowering.

People feel shut out of relational possibilities when their "differences" thwart the opportunity to be seen and heard, to know "beloved community." "Beloved community is formed not by the eradication of difference but by its affirmation, by each of us claiming the identities and cultural legacies that shape who we are and how we live in the world" (hooks, 1995, p. 265). The goal is to shield vulnerability, to maintain a safe space so that connections can happen, and to create relational possibilities. When there is authentic communication, the magic happens: we are both seen and heard. The "relational anchors that enable healing and healthy development are empathy, authenticity, and mutuality" (Walker, 2017). We relied on RCT to cocreate a multifaceted alliance over nearly twenty-five years.

The Story of Two Friends, Colleagues, and Allies

We recognized early that our cultural differences bound us together. As xenophiles, we share a curiosity about and attraction to foreign cultures, customs, and people. It seemed inevitable that we would collaborate in social justice action regarding race, gender, and sexual orientation. Kathryn was up against the wave of White male dominance in the medical world. Karen morphed into a "white ally" (Sue, 2017), not only to support Kathryn but also to support our clients, our causes, and our community. We shared a passion to listen and be heard on what matters to us: social justice, health-care disparities, and a "power over" world that continues to crush efforts to empower marginalized "others."

We began antiracism work together in the mid-1990s. We were the two psychologists in Mission United (MU), a group of young professionals that was 50 percent African American and 50 percent White. The group initially formed to address local racial tensions following the Rodney King riots. Our seminal task was to monitor and patrol the activities of Black College Reunion, a weekend during spring break celebrating historically Black colleges and universities. We went to the community events and neighborhoods in pairs, one Black and one White MU member, wearing shirts identifying our organization. The Black College Reunion events ignited a firestorm of local controversy. MU sought to mitigate outcomes with our presence and communication with both visitors and residents. The White residents were suspicious of the convergence of thousands of Black youths along their beachside neighborhoods. The Black visitors and residents, in turn, were outraged at this overt prejudice. The MU pairs served as local ambassadors seeking to promote coexistence. Thankfully, these weekends did not escalate racial conflicts, although arrests skyrocketed compared with the remainder of the spring break week.

MU members recognized the enormity of our goal: assuaging the reactivity across the community sparked by Black College Reunion. RCT reminds us that growth occurs as a yearning for connection in the face of repeated and chronic disconnections. Our efforts in MU emphasized our need for empathic attunement (Walker, 2004) to our group, to the disenfranchised community, and to the dominant cultures' efforts to silence and eradicate these events.

MU continued to address racial concerns in the community for several years. The topic "Why can't we talk about race?" was the subject of numerous MU meetings and community workshops. Group members had backgrounds in business, law, finance, law enforcement, education, health care, hospitality, housing, entertainment, and sports. Kathryn and Karen united to encourage others to bring their professional and personal expertise to the group so we could dismantle misconceptions and create cooperative opportunities. We were frequently tasked with communication skills training when discussions went sideways, and sometimes we were simply asked to intercede.

Despite good intentions, we recognized the group's discomfort with addressing the issues of racial hostility and implicit bias. Membership in the group did not mean we could openly admit our racial bias and stereotypes. As psychologists schooled in RCT, we realized that our unique positions in the group enabled us to steer the conversation in ways that fostered connection rather than division. The group's members needed skills and guidance to work side by side, Black and White, to dispel racial tensions.

As psychologists, we were granted permission to steer discussion of uncomfortable topics toward understanding and compassion. We provided diversity education and additional trainings to promote friendships and professional alliances that likely would not have evolved without this group. This method of developing relationships was not "power over" but "power with," and it explicitly addressed racial disparities among young professional leaders.

We have persevered through anguished conversations, exchanging memories about racial slurs, being ostracized, and "having difficult hair." Our misunderstandings and hurt feelings moved us from disconnection to connection as we shared suffering.

Confronting Race and Culture in Medical Education

Education becomes most rich and alive when it confronts
the reality of moral conflict in the world.

—Zinn (2002)

Family medicine is undoubtedly one of the noblest professions. No other profession concerns itself with the well-being of the entire human being—mind, body, and spirit. Most family medicine residency train-ing programs hire mental health faculty to address the psychosocial as-pects of medicine, and residents are trained in the biopsychosocial model of health care (Sternlieb, 2014). The social, racial, and spiritual complex-ity of our nation, which is only increasing, requires that these emerging physicians understand their patients' backgrounds (American Psycholog-ical Association Working Group on Stress and Health Disparities, 2017; Edgoose et al., 2017; Ring, Nyquist, & Mitchell, 2008). The behavioral science coordinator position was Kathryn's first job out of graduate school, and it involved steep learning curves about the culture and at-mosphere of graduate medical education. Despite being seen as an out-sider as a petite woman of color who couldn't possibly understand the issues of teaching medical residents, she forged on as the driving force in the initiative to recruit more minorities to the program. Being able to talk openly and depend on her alliance with Karen was of major benefit in this cause. There were numerous challenging but ultimately reward-ing experiences when dealing with racial identification and its inter-section with medical education.

In 1997, we had the opportunity to make exponential progress toward our goals. The residency program received two consecutive three-year federal grants, nearly $1,000,000 in funding, to promote cultural com-petence as well as technological advances in health-care education. The curriculum was dedicated to teaching medical residents techniques to improve care of ethnically diverse and medically underserved popula-tions, with Karen playing major roles in developing lectures and pro-viding consultation in topics regarding diversity and women's health.

When we began to develop the lectures and seminars, the cultural competency curriculum in medical education was in its infancy. We focused mostly on trying to teach about the health beliefs of the major cultural groups in the United States. As the White ally and an outsider to the program, Karen would often raise the more provocative challenges to status quo health care. We quickly learned that Kathryn's role as a Black female spearheading these conversations was a crucial part of the process. Though we did not specifically intend it to be the catalyst of a movement, it became clear from some of the residents' reactions that this presence was unsettling, disturbing, and in fact a target to rebel against. This prompted difficult discussions. It also laid the foundations for fur-ther attention to how diversity in providers, as well as patients, could pre-sent barriers to communication and ultimately result in inequitable health care if not addressed (Bahls, 2011; Edgoose et al., 2017; Rodgers, Wending, Saba, Mahoney, & Brown Speights, 2017; Smedley, Stith, & Nelson, 2003).

Evolution of the Curriculum: Teaching about Culture, Racism, and Socially Responsible Medicine

Reni Eddo-Lodge (2017) wrote, "White privilege is an absence of the consequences of racism. An absence of structural discrimination, an absence of your race being viewed as a problem first and foremost" (p. 60).

So what could we do about the negative feedback, the attempts to marginalize us and this work, and the personal hurt felt as we started this journey? We raised some provocative questions about racism and its effects on health care and professional relationships. When participating in discussions about moving minority candidates on a rank list as part of resident recruitment meetings (at the behest of her White male program director, interestingly enough), Kathryn was often confronted by some of the White males. Once, one of the White females came and offered supportive statements—this kindness encouraged Kathryn to "press on." In those days, it didn't take much to feel like a fool in front of this tough audience of medical trainees.

That's where Karen's support and can-do spirit were instrumental. Her empathy, energy, and respect were zestful. We found that instead of backing off, we needed to take the conversations deeper and further. When asking the residents questions about what they learned in their families and communities regarding those who are different, we were often met with chagrined looks, defensiveness, and more silence than we had hoped for. Karen was able to use her experience as a White person to make it OK for the group to talk about our nation's complex history with racism. The residents didn't necessarily expect to be talking about racism during a lecture like this. They were used to being given formulas, algorithms, and decision trees to make their choices about patient care. This was a much deeper and more emotional process than they usually experienced in a lecture. Our partnership became a model for them of how differences can be bridged and how lessons can be learned by having challenging conversations in a supportive and nurturing atmosphere. Our rapport and obvious camaraderie fostered the belief that awareness and transformation were possible.

Over the years, medical education about culture and diversity has grown from simply trying to make sure our students understand different cultures to in fact teaching them about the complexity of living in a multicultural, democratic society. Camara Jones (2000) describes the tripartite approach to racisms at three levels: *institutionalized*—propagated and accepted by institutions; *personally mediated*—differential actions toward others; and *internalized*—instilled in persons of color by racist attitudes around them. All of these feed implicit bias, which exists in all of us. Those of us in medical education should help our learners unearth destructive racist attitudes and promote healing approaches in equitable, relationally based care. These are challenging tasks, and we have learned that White allies like Karen are instrumental in advancing these causes.

Professional Development as a Black Female Educator

There is somewhat of a paradox in the fact that as a Black female educator, you may be highly sought after to fill a position to satisfy your organization's desire for diversification. However, once you get there, they often don't know what to do with you. Black females remain underrepresented in this field, and it is important to be well versed in the medical facts of health-care education, as well as the social issues that affect and are affected by the topic of health care for minorities. Having forged a firm alliance around principles of RCT, Karen and I have used methods of mutual empowerment and goals of authentic actualization to strengthen our work and our friendship. Our partnership has been instrumental over the years, and many elements of this have been captured in a recent issue of *Counseling Psychology* entitled "White Allies: Current Perspectives." These articles detailed the joys and challenges of being White and doing this kind of work, voicing strong encouragement to take on an antiracist identity that "walks the talk" (Sue, 2017).

As a minority, it is easy to become the target of anger and resentment, to experience feelings of shame when doing this work. White allies can help bridge the gap between the learning experience and changes in actual practice. We must help our learners unearth the deeper factors that feed implicit bias (Cooper et al. 2012). This blocks providers from accessing skills for equitable health care. Kathryn's dedication to these practices undoubtedly contributed to her rise to leadership in behavioral medicine education; she was appointed to direct a national training fellowship for early career faculty. Karen has also received a national award for community activism and advocacy. Clearly, our collaborative work with diverse groups has created advantages in being able to reach greater numbers.

Future Directions and Collaborations

Bell hooks (1988) wrote, "Even in the face of powerful structures of domination, it remains possible for each of us, especially those of us who are members of oppressed and/or exploited groups as well as those radical visionaries who may have race, class and sex privilege, to define and determine alternative standards, to decide on the nature and extent of compromise" (p. 81).

Multicultural relationships and social inequity seem to be more pronounced and glaring today than ever before. The question remains: What factors have emerged that are crucial to propel effective Black leadership? If we are empowering difference in the face of inequity, what are the gray areas of power, race, gender, and class that remain the roadblocks to change? The advances, triumphs, and travails of our partnership have all led to a deeper mutual understanding. The exciting discovery of relational possibilities fuels our work, and we continue to strive to embrace the challenges that accompany growth.

We encourage others to move toward and work through conflicts that arise due to difference, and we feel that effectively doing so will allow Black leaders to emerge more powerful and skillful. In their work *Toolkit for Teaching about Racism in the Context of Persistent Health and Healthcare Disparities*, Edgoose and colleagues (2017, pp. 4–5) offer guidelines for conducting provocative discussions on race, racism, disparities, and privilege:

Before the Discussion:

- Take some time to self-reflect.

  - What are comments, situations, and feelings that trigger you? How will you handle it if they come up during the session that you are leading?

  - Consider the impact of your own identity. What might White facilitators need to be sensitive of? What might facilitators of color need to be sensitive of?

During the Discussion:

General Do's and Don'ts of Facilitating

- **Do** practice empathy
- **Do** be prepared that everyone will not agree with your points
- **Do** explore emotions in addition to content
- **Don't** make anyone a spokesperson
- **Don't** rescue or reassure White people
- **Don't** turn to people of color (POC) as experts

Ways that Privilege Presents Itself and Common Defense Mechanisms

- Invalidating/reframing experiences of POC
- People of privilege distancing themselves from their group (e.g., a White person talking about the way other White people behave in an attempt to separate themselves as exceptional)
- Focusing on ways in which one has been oppressed other than race (e.g., bringing up class or a White woman focusing on her identity as a woman rather than her White privilege)

We have presented at national conferences, published articles, and provided trainings on health care with diverse, minority, and under-served populations. We also cofounded a local not-for-profit in 2001 dedicated to raising awareness about eating disorders and body image concerns across the life span that affect all ethnicities and populations of all socioeconomic statuses. Our partnership has been the common thread that has elevated us to better understand the dynamics of the populations we serve. It has not always been easy for us as women from such varied backgrounds, but we have learned from our own differences how to bridge the gaps of race, culture, ethnicity, and spiritual beliefs.

Ultimately, our friendship has deepened as our lives unfolded, losing loved ones, enduring health crises, getting married, having children, experiencing rites of passages, and evolving into seasoned psychologists in our respective specialties. We are constantly reminded that Kathryn's Black identity and Karen's White identity are central to our deep connection. Meeting at the points of connection across difference reinforces the idea that "getting along is not enough," as Maureen Walker (2017) reminds us. We must do more to confront White racial privilege and Black oppression. Complacency is not an option.

A Final Note: Our Lessons for Black Leaders

1. Start where you are, do what you can, and speak your truth, even if it is spoken quietly at first.

2. Find small causes, assess local needs, and gather support, even if it is a small but loyal following. Find your allies and start some conversations about your experience.

3. Question the status quo. Ask why or why not. Why shouldn't I get involved with this cause?

4. Allow yourself your down days, where you question yourself and your efforts. Be sad, feel deflated, but keep going even if you have to slow down a bit.

5. Find bigger causes, speak your truth even louder, and gather your tribe.

6. Find more allies, those who are different from you, who want to learn about your experience. Continue those conversations, even bigger and louder as you go along.

7. Teach about your experience and reach out to those who are just starting. Encourage them through the process.

REFERENCES

American Psychological Association Working Group on Stress and Health Disparities. (2017). *Stress and health disparities: Contexts, mechanisms, and interventions among racial/ethnic minorities and low socioeconomic status populations* (Report). Retrieved from http://www.apa.org/pi/health-disparities/resources/stress-report.aspx

Bahls, C. (2011). *Health policy brief: Achieving equity in health* (Health Affairs Brief). Retrieved from https://www.healthaffairs.org/do/10.1377/hpb20111006.957918/full/

Cooper, L. A., Roter, D. L., Carson, K. A., Beach, M. C., Sabin, J. A., Greenwald, A.G., & Inui, T. S. (2012). The associations of clinicians' implicit attitudes about race with medical visit communication and patient ratings of interpersonal care. *American Journal of Public Health, 102*(5), 979–987.

Eddo-Lodge, R. (2017). *Why I'm no longer talking to White people about race*. London, England: Bloomsbury.

Edgoose, J., Anderson, A., Brown-Speights J. S., Bullock, K., Ferguson, W., Fraser, K., . . . & Wu, D. (2017). *Toolkit for teaching about racism in the context of persistent health and healthcare disparities*. Retrieved from https://resourcelibrary.stfm.org /viewdocument/toolkit-for-teaching-about-racism-i

hooks, b. (1988). *Talking back: Thinking feminist, thinking Black*. Toronto, ON: Between the Lines.

hooks, b. (1995). *Killing rage: Ending racism*. New York, NY: Henry Holt.

Jones, C. P. (2000). Levels of racism: A theoretic framework and gardener's tale. *American Journal of Public Health, 90*(8), 1212–1215.

Jordan, J. V. (2004). Restoring empathic possibility. In J. V. Jordan, M. Walker, & L. Hartling (Eds.), *The complexity of connection: Writings from the Stone Center's Jean Baker Miller Training Institute* (pp. 122–127). New York, NY: Guilford Press.

Jordan, J. V. (2010). *Relational-cultural therapy*. Washington, DC: American Psychological Association.

Miller, J. B. (1986). *Toward a new psychology of women*. Boston, MA: Beacon Press.

Miller, J. B., & Stiver, I. P. (1997). *The healing connection: How women form relationships in therapy and life*. Boston, MA: Beacon Press.

Ring, J., Nyquist, J., & Mitchell, J. (2008). Curriculum for culturally responsible healthcare: The step-by-step guide for cultural competence training. Oxford, England: Radcliffe.

Rodgers, D. V., Wending, A. L., Saba, G. W., Mahoney, M. R., & Brown Speights, J. S. (2017). Preparing family physicians to care for underserved populations. *Family Medicine, 49*(4), 304–310.

Smedley, B. D., Stith, A. Y., & Nelson, A. R. (2003). *Unequal treatment: Confronting racial and ethnic disparities in health care*. Washington, DC: National Academy Press.

Sternlieb, J. (2014). The unique contribution of behavioral scientists to medical education: The top ten competencies. *International Journal of Psychiatry in Medicine, 47*(4), 317–326.

Sue, D. W. (2017). The challenges of becoming a White ally. *Counseling Psychologist, 45*(5), 706–716.

Walker, M. (2002). How therapy helps when the culture hurts (Work in Progress No. 95). Stone Center Working Paper Series, Wellesley, MA.

Walker, M. (2017). What to do when getting along is not enough. Retrieved from https://gallery.mailchimp.com/1dec0578fdd7038e74c09f816/files/6ec93cbc-995d -4693-bcca-13b93eb1c260/What_to_Do_When_Just_Getting_Along_Is_Not _Enough_FINAL.pdf

Walker, M., & Rosen, W. B. Eds. (2004) *How Connections Heal: Stories from Relational-Cultural Therapy*. New York: Guilford Press.

Zinn, H. (2002). *You can't be neutral on a moving train: A personal history of our times*. Boston, MA: Beacon Press.

13

African American Women as Change Agents in the White Academy

Pivoting the Margin via Grounded Theory

―――――

MURIEL E. SHOCKLEY *and* ELIZABETH L. HOLLOWAY

In this chapter, we discuss African American women scholar-activists and the ways in which they act as catalysts for transformational societal, institutional, and individual change. Through the use of grounded theory methodology (GTM), we have uncovered the institutional conditions of the white academy under which African American women establish their presence as change agents, a process that leads to personal strength, resilience, and institutional change. Through our research findings, we describe a holistic model of their lived experiences with their voices and perspectives at the center. The model has implications for African American women as change agents actively engaging and strategizing within white institutional and organizational contexts.

Existing Scholarship

Only 4 percent of faculty in higher education are African American women (Snyder & Dillow, 2012), but they have a long history of contribution to the academy. The intersectional identities of African American women often produce conditions that devalue "both their sex and their race" (Myers, 2002, p. 5). This results in the experience of gendered racism in the context of everyday life experiences or, as Essed (1990) describes, "the integration of racism into everyday situations through practices that activate underlying power relations" (p. 50). It is particularly important in this historical moment that we illuminate the subaltern leadership knowledge possessed by African American women, as these experiences may have broad applicability across a variety of organizational settings.

Existing scholarship on African American women's experiences in the academy locates these academicians in predominantly white research universities and liberal arts colleges, as well as historically black colleges and universities, and focuses on the tenure process, recruitment and retention, evaluation, student relationships, career satisfaction, mentoring, survival strategies, and administrative leadership.[1] Overwhelmingly, the foci of the research are the challenges African American women scholars face and the concomitant strategies employed to mitigate the consequences. Less apparent are the ways African American women scholar-activists in the white academy act as catalysts for transformational societal, institutional, and individual change (hooks, 1994).

Studies of race and ethnicity in the professoriate have discovered that faculty of color were significantly more likely to see their position as an opportunity and responsibility to create social change (Antonio, 2002; Astin, Antonio, Cress & Astin, 1997; G. D. Thomas, 2001; Tyson, 2001). Davis (1999), drawing a parallel between the plantation kitchen and the academy as contested spaces for African American women, advanced the notion of the power of the "kitchen legacy" as a transformative metaphorical space for African American women. She asserts, "The kitchen provided a space within which black women during and after slavery transformed their oppression into resistance and transformed an institution of white dominance" (p. 370). This kitchen-table space is similar to the space hooks (1990) invites us to as she distinguishes between being marginalized and recognizing the power that conscious location at the margin can bring. She names the margin a "space of radical openness . . . a profound edge . . . [a] site of radical possibility, a space of resistance" (p. 149). She suggests an embodied location here "nourishes one's capacity to resist. It offers to one the possibility of radical perspectives from which to see and create, to imagine alternative, new worlds" (p. 150). Davis (1999) suggested that the legacy of the kitchen can be used to "redefine [our] importance in the domain of whiteness . . . transform students and faculty . . . and . . . define and inform experience through provocative scholarship" (p. 372). In spite of and because of our outsider/within status (Collins, 2000) in the white academy, Hoke (1997) recognized the "potential for social change" as African American women initiate "individual and collective acts of resistance" in the academy (p. 299). It is here, in this interstitial space at the margins of the academy, that a postmodern grounded theory approach is adept at uncovering the lived power of African American women in academe.

We chose to study the ways in which African American women faculty have navigated and influenced the institutions in which they have worked. More specifically, our study is centered on black feminist thought (Collins, 2000) and intersectionality (Crenshaw, 1991) as defining frameworks in the professional and personal lives of the women interviewed. Through this process, we sought to uncover the ways these women embody and understand leadership and change in the academy. Specifically, we articulate the processes by which African American women initiate and participate in the decolonization of the academy. The landscape of methodological approaches to African American women in the academy has been dominated by descriptive quantitative and qualitative approaches—for example, survey (A. J. Thomas, Witherspoon, & Speight, 2008), case study (Carter-Frye, 2015), autoethnography (Perlow, 2018), and narrative (Nash, 2004). Thus, our methodological approach to this study of lived experience claims a framework that positions African American women as agents of knowledge, rejects additive notions of oppression, and validates an alternative epistemological system. It is our contention that the unique capability of an approach to GTM that takes a postmodern, feminist stance (Olesen, 2007) both honors the voices of those marginalized and builds conceptual understanding of silencing in complex social situations (O'Neil, Green, Creswell, Shope, & Plano Clark, 2010).

A Feminist and Constructivist Stance

Constructivist GTM (Charmaz, 2006; Morse, 2009) is a rigorous qualitative approach that honors the voices of those individuals who are embedded in the situation of interest. GTM supports inquiry into the conceptual and theoretical understanding of "what all is happening" (Schatzman, 1991) in a given situation, thus going beyond mere description of actions. A feminist stance to this methodological approach allowed us to "not merely describe women's situations, but consider how race, class, gender, sexual orientation, age, and material circumstances in multiple contexts render the taken for granted problematic in ways that move toward social justice (Olesen, 2005; Roman, 1992)" (Olesen, 2007, p. 421). For the interested reader, a detailed examination of the GTM approach to studies of equality, diversity, and inclusion can be found in Holloway & Schwartz (2018).

As researchers immersed in the discovery of these processes and the meaning they hold for African American women, we were acutely aware of our own positionality in relation to the work and in relation to each other. At this time, we are colleagues and professors in different progressive universities; however, our relationship has embraced a multitude of roles, beginning with those of student and professor and extending to those of friends, colleagues, and coauthors. Although we have much in common as psychologists, professors, and women close in age, we have very different origins and cultural sensitivities. Muriel is African American and is the third generation in her family to have obtained college and advanced degrees. She has spent a lifetime immersed in the culture of the white academy. Elizabeth is an Anglo-Canadian, first-generation college student who came to the United States in the social upheaval of 1968–1969 to pursue her education. Her graduate education and career were in major public institutions in the United States until joining Antioch University in 2001.

In the remainder of this discussion, we highlight the findings from this study that related to the central concept that emerged: African American women's *Robust Sense of Self.* This sense of self undergirded a presence of being and becoming that allowed these women to think and strategize as activists in their places of work. Using quotes from the interviews completed for this study, we illustrate the emergent themes that characterize their perception of the conditions in the academy and their engagement as they traverse the topography.[2] First, we provide a brief outline of the sample and data-collection procedures to situate our discussion of findings.

The Research Approach

A purposive sample of African American scholar-activists in predominantly white institutions of higher education was sought for participation in the study. A total of eighteen women participated in the study, with an age range of thirty to seventy years. The participants were faculty at the early, mid-, and senior career levels in tenured and nontenured positions in the social sciences and the humanities across eighteen different institutions. Although five of the participants taught in the same institution, they also taught in a second, predominantly white university and spoke about their experiences in both, thus bringing the total count of institutions represented to nineteen. The types of institutions represented were public and private Research I universities, state and city colleges and universities, and private liberal arts colleges. The institutions are geographically located in urban, suburban, and rural communities.

The women were interviewed from the fall of 2011 through late spring 2012. Two broad, open-ended prompts began each interview: "Talk to me about your experience as an African American woman in a predominantly white institution," and "What impact, if any, do you believe your presence has on the environment in which you work?" The interviews were an average of sixty minutes in length.

All elements of the GTM approach were exercised in the implementation of the study, including line-by-line coding, axial coding, memoing, dimensional analysis, and theorizing.[3] Three coders of different cultural backgrounds worked with the interviews to gain rich and varied perspectives in the interpretation of the stories told. Once this coding process was completed, the most robust concepts representing social processes in the context of organizational life were labeled primary dimensions.

Naming Social Processes

Our sample of African American women scholar-activists ably and vividly told the story of everyday life in the white academy. Their stories as a whole created a rich avenue of microprocesses that were transacted with students, colleagues, administrators, and friends. In the interviews, the participants revealed the intricate dynamics they face on a daily basis; they shared the stress, frustration, discouragement, and rage felt, as well as the energy, zest, and determination. The thematic analysis of the women's stories led to the conceptualization of a central concept, core dimension, and four primary dimensions. The primary dimensions (see table 13-1 later in this chapter) represent the kinds of interactional situations that were deemed critical from the women's perspective. With further analysis and conceptualization, we explored the context in which the social interactions or processes took place, the conditions under which they occurred, and the impact they had on the women, others, or the institution. Throughout this analysis, we became very aware of the power inherent in these interactions and their role in promoting the women's understanding of self. We ultimately named this understanding a *Robust Sense of Self*, a central construct in African American women's engagements at work.

A Robust Sense of Self

Unlike other narrative approaches, GTM takes a systematic view of participant action by contextualizing the conditions and consequences of specific actions. The context is created from the stories told and reflects the constantly changing conditions that emerge from social interaction. An explanatory or theoretical matrix is formed around each of the primary processes (dimensions) identified in the analysis, ultimately leading to a heuristic model that ties all elements of the analysis to answer the fundamental inquiry, "What all is happening here?" For example, a dimension might become a social condition that facilitates or obstructs certain terms of engagement and ultimately results in consequences and impact on self, others, and the social conditions of the situation (Kools, McCarthy, Durham, & Robrecht, 1996).

At the heart of figure 13-1 is the core dimension *Robust Sense of Self*, a condition of living in the white academy; it is the sturdiest dimension. When an architect designs a building, a primary consideration is the load, the force that acts on structures. Buildings must withstand loads, or they will fail. In this study, the loads experienced by African American women scholars are many, and the fulcrum that supports their ability to withstand and negotiate the pressure is this core dimension. This dimension is a social and psychological condition or attribute that the African American woman scholar brings to the context of the white academy. It is the self-knowledge and self-definition reflected by Lorde's (1984) assertion, "If I didn't define myself for myself, I would be crunched into other people's fantasies for me and eaten alive" (p. 137); it is "a belief in self far greater than anyone's disbelief" (Robinson & Ward, 1991, p. 87).

After years of scholarship and preparation, some African American women begin an academic career trajectory in white academic institutions. They bring not only their academic backgrounds but also a strong

FIGURE 13-1

Core dimension: *Robust Sense of Self*

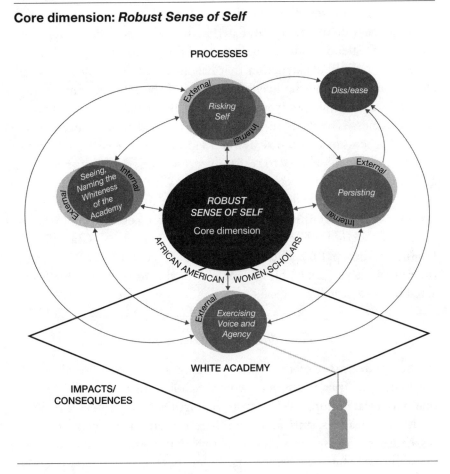

sense of self and an embodied female blackness. They come to the academy with a strong desire to pursue their own intellectual interests, and many of those (though not all) pertain to brown-on-brown research, scholarly inquiry focused on issues relevant to communities of color, as well as a strong commitment to rigor and excellence in the classroom and an expressed commitment to students. Possessing a robust sense of self ensures a protective layer, an armoring of resilience. To survive in the white academy demands certain emotional competencies and the possession of clearly articulated beliefs, values, and a sense of purpose, as one participant noted: "I'm guided by Fanny Lou Hammer. I'm guided by the legacies of Harriet Tubman. This ain't nothing. We ain't picking cotton, not yet." For the participants, their sense of self is inextricably tied to their understanding of self as black women.

Robustness should not be conflated with the myth of the strong black woman who silently endures the weight of the world, an imposed and at times internalized construction that has been used to pathologize and stereotypically define the lived experience of the intersectional identities of African American women (Howard-Baptiste, 2014). Conversely, the robustness articulated in this conceptual visualization represents an internal process of self-knowledge and self-definition that feeds African American women's ability to resist objectification, confront injustices, and guide conscious and critical interactions with the environment. Robustness supports an individual's ability to give voice to lived realities; it is the process of becoming as opposed to "becoming everything to everyone, [and becoming] less of someone to themselves" (Beauboeuf-Lafontant, 2005, p. 107). This construct is about recovering and nurturing the self and developing a black female critical consciousness that is enacted in the external world.

The Context of the Academy

In the environment of the white academy, the mortar board of figure 13-1, the African American woman scholar engages in interactions that have certain impacts. Her work requires her daily interaction with students, colleagues, staff, and administrators, and these encounters necessitate use of the self in a myriad of ways that require her to draw from the well that robustness represents. Robustness operates on two levels, micro and macro; it is an internal process that operates to sustain her, and it also has an external feature that emerges as she navigates the terrain. Notice that the properties *Risking Self, Exercising Voice and Agency, Persisting,* and *Seeing and Naming the Whiteness of the Academy,* which interact with the *Robust Sense of Self* and each other in figure 13-1, contain internal and external processes. We now turn to a discussion of these four social processes and their role in supporting the *Robust Sense of Self.*

The processes of *Risking Self, Seeing and Naming the Whiteness of the Academy, Persisting,* and *Exercising Voice and Agency* all contribute to and challenge a *Robust Sense of Self* (table 13-1). The primary dimensions suggest a dynamic and fluid experience, while the properties named in

TABLE 13-1

Primary dimensions and their properties

Perspective: African American women scholars
Robust Sense of Self

Context: The white academy

Dimensions	Properties (ways in which dimensions are enacted)				
Robust Sense of Self (core dimension)	Embodied female blackness	Aliveness of received values			
Risking Self	*Diss/ease, Impact on Body/Spirit*	*Challenges to Authority*	*Uneven Burden*	*Feeling the Need to be Perfect*	*Inimical Environment*
Seeing and Naming the Whiteness of the Academy	*Critiquing the Topography*	*Under/Over Exposed: Visibility, Invisibility, and Hypervisibility*	*Outsiderness*	*Intraracial Complexities*	
Persisting	*Connectivity*	*Cultivating Reciprocity*	*Actively Learning*		
Exercising Voice and Agency	*Responsibility to Students*	*Acting*	*Valuing Rigor*	*Having an Impact*	*Asserting Personhood*

table 13-1 form and elevate understanding of these experiences by naming related actions and conditions of their occurrence. Properties might be further understood as agentic qualities and inner processes that, as a whole, build the strength of self-awareness and action. These findings dispel any notion of African American women as static recipients of action and instead identify them as engaged, emotionally present agents of action. Their narratives were not reductive accounts of internalized victimization but rather multifaceted tales of redemption through resoluteness, understanding the promise for the future, feeling a sense of responsibility to support the uplift of others, and articulating emancipatory purpose.

Although these were stories of pain and struggle, the metastory shouts a clear declaration of spirit that cannot be denied, a counternarrative of salvation of leading despite the environment found in the white academy, not because of it.

Risking Self

The dimension *Risking Self* illuminates the process that occurs when our participants chose to pursue an academic career in white institutions. There is a difference between being *at risk* and the process of *risking self*. While *at risk* has come to connote some deficit characteristic, such as low socioeconomic status, that puts a particular demographic group at risk in a particular environment, *Risking Self* places the agency, the act of risking, in the hands of the individual who experiences the consequences. The African American women scholars we interviewed chose to engage in the act of risking self in spite of the numerous situational and interpersonal attempts to undermine their sense of worth and value. Women reported being faced with a range of situations in which risking self is evident. Among other things, they reported attempts by colleagues to sabotage their success, feelings of being disposable, being at greater risk of being fired or laid off, and the devaluation of their scholarship when its focus is race, class, gender, or another such topic. They described feeling unsafe and used, experiencing the loss of voice, and being accused of not being collegial. At times they were pitted against each other and penalized for not embracing the projective roles imagined for and assigned to them, all of which can be experienced as attempts to deny personhood. These experiences are articulated in the properties *Diss/ease, Impact on Body/Spirit, Challenges to Authority, Uneven Burden, Feeling the Need to be Perfect*, and *Inimical Environment*, described as follows:

- *Diss/ease, Impact on Body/Spirit.* This property reveals the ways the white academy has affected the physical, emotional, and spiritual selves of interviewees. Participants made a direct connection between their identity as African American women and the strain and taxing weight on their spirit that they experience.

- *Challenges to Authority.* Participants reported experiences in which their authority and intellectual ability were challenged by students. Challenges come in the form of outright disrespect, lack of boundaries, being tested in the classroom, and confrontation.

- *Uneven Burden.* This property reveals the ways in which African American women in the academy are vulnerable to an "invisible" workload that includes the material work as well as the psychological burden that results from the stress they endure.

- *Feeling the Need to be Perfect.* Participants reported feeling the need to be perfect, to be "better than." This need to work harder is based not on deficit ability or the need to "catch up" but rather on the knowledge that ability, appearance, and command of Standard English are judged and scrutinized, no matter our qualifications or achievements.

- *Inimical Environment.* Participants found the white academy a hostile and unwelcoming environment. Some spoke of outright hostility, others the subtle hostility that comes with the lack of support from colleagues and administrators.

Participants make a direct connection between their identity as African American women and the strain and taxing weight on their spirit that they experience: "Our emotions and spirits are always at stake, if we don't respond properly. If you respond positively, then you're rewarded; and if you don't respond positively, then you're not rewarded. And so, either you're the kind of *go-to* happy Negro, or you're the person to avoid. Either you're the angry black woman or the nurturing nanny figure . . . so I can't really think about the impact because I feel disposable and replaceable. You know that if it's not me, it's someone else who is performing those functions." Being present physically, intellectually, and emotionally in the academy requires an enormous amount of energy and internal processing. The reflections revealed in this dimension allow a glimpse into the participants' deep understanding of the dear price that commitment to the white academy can have and the significance of risking self to maintain a presence and space for their agency.

Seeing and Naming the Whiteness of the Academy

This dimension represents the whiteness of the academy as experienced by the respondents. The respondents' experiences occurred in a specific environment, a white academic environment that is not benign. The respondents have keen observational and analytic skills. *Seeing and Naming the Whiteness of the Academy* represents the respondents' ability to reflect on and make meaning about the environment in which they work in terms of the sociopolitical landscape, historically and in the present.

This ability to unpack and understand the environment supports their continued sense of agency and ability to proceed and be impactful despite the significant challenges they face. These insights include the impact of class differences of African American women in the academy and how this may affect how they are seen by others, as well as their comfort level and ability to navigate the academy. This dimension also recognizes the embedded nature and often covert insidiousness of racism in the academy and the difficult nature of changing the system. As one participant observed, "It's a plantation. Yep, it's a plantation," a theme that surfaced in the review of the literature (Davis, 1999; Harley, 2008; John, 1997). These experiences are named *Critiquing the Topography*; *Under/Over Exposed: Visibility, Invisibility, and Hypervisibility*; *Outsiderness*; and *Intraracial Complexity*. These properties expand understanding of participants' experiences in the white academy.

- *Critiquing the Topography.* Participants offered insights about and displayed awareness of the realities of the sociopolitical landscape of the white academy. They demonstrated an ability to see and analyze the context in which they work while making personal meaning as they are confronted with the external environment.

- *Under/Over Exposed: Visibility, Invisibility, and Hypervisibility.* This property reveals the common paradoxical experience of being invisible in the white academy while simultaneously being hypervisible.

- *Outsiderness.* This property describes how the lack of a critical mass of African American scholars magnifies the alienation and isolation of African American women's experience in academia. The unwritten institutional codes are not shared with them but serve to perpetuate their outsider status.

- *Intraracial Complexity.* This property reveals the impact of white normativity in the academy on relationships between African American scholars. Participants described colleagues being co-opted by the system, accommodated to white interests, and subjected to competition based on scarcity of positions and resources, as well as a replication of power over relationships and the feeling that the actions of other black faculty reflect on them.

These properties are illustrated in the following quote from a study participant: "The invisibility that I feel as an African American woman in institutions, and the hypervisibility that I feel also sometimes simultaneously in institutions because I'm outspoken. So I'm one of those people that has spoken back when I see an inequality. And when I see people acting out in ways that to me say this is more about my race and what your stereotype about me than it is about you really listening to me." Outsider status can ultimately result in dismissal or an individual making the choice to leave the institution and ultimately the academy, as one respondent described: "My experience as an African American woman in a white—predominantly white—academic institution, it's been a kind of mixed bag of great intellectual growth, community, and culture stymied by just a kind of lack of sense of belonging. . . . I've taught at three universities now that are in these kind of rural spaces, . . . so, those are the kind of isolating factors in addition to kind of the institutional ways in which, I guess, systemic racism functions in the academy at these various levels."

Persisting

This dimension represents the tenacious and steadfast resolve demonstrated by African American women scholars in the white academy. Despite the ongoing challenges to their very presence in the academy, participants recounted bringing the full force of their lifelong experiences as women of color and concomitant skill at border crossing, their intellect, and their emotional intelligence to bear by utilizing strategies that ease the impact of outsiderness. These features are demonstrated in the properties *Connectivity*, *Cultivating Reciprocity*, and *Actively Learning*. These persisting properties are described as follows:

- *Connectivity.* This property represents participants' yearning for community as a way to support their presence in the academy. It has the power to mitigate the impact of isolation and outsider status experienced by many.

- *Cultivating Reciprocity.* Participants observed the importance of having white allies in the academy. White allies are individuals who are doing their personal work on issues of power and privilege, as well as the microaggressions aimed at people of color in the academy.

- *Actively Learning.* This property reveals the ways in which participants found ways to carve out space to do the work necessary to develop agentic strategies that transform the challenges that they face.

Participants reported a yearning for and appreciation of community as a way to support their presence in the academy. This persistence through connectivity and reciprocity with colleagues is particularly important; it has the potential to mitigate the impact of isolation and outsider status experienced by many. Some participants rely on being a part of or building community outside the academy, while others attempt to create nurturing spaces for contact and engagement within it. One participant stated communities provide spaces for African American women scholars to "kind of drop the masks" and breathe deeply into their true selves. Although it is not unusual for workplaces to support lasting friendships and a social life for employees, several of the participants revealed the expectation that community for them is to be found outside the white academy: "I don't rely on where I work to have friends and colleagues. . . . [I]t does make you feel vulnerable sometimes when you're dealing with issues of race, gender, those kinds of things. But in terms of community, I get my community from so many places, that didn't matter."

Exercising Voice and Agency

The dimension *Exercising Voice and Agency* represents the assertions and demonstrations of personhood by women in the white academy. This dimension illuminates the ways in which African American women's presence through action affects the environment of the academy. Many respondents directly tied their call to exercise voice and claim agency to familial and cultural value systems that they named as an impetus for their action. These are revealed in the properties *Responsibility to Students, Acting, Valuing Rigor, Impacting,* and *Asserting Personhood,* which are described as follows:

- *Responsibility to Students.* This property reveals a deeply felt responsibility to students. Participants recognized the embodiment of that responsibility as central to their ability to affect their environment. Acting for students in some ways means acting on behalf of themselves.

- *Acting.* Participants feel responsible for speaking up and out because there are so few African American women. The women, on the whole, understood that their engaged presence is necessary for change to occur in the academy.

- *Valuing Rigor.* Participants spoke about their love of and dedication to rigorous inquiry in their own research and in the classroom. Participants described creating containers for rigorous inquiry for students and themselves.

- *Impacting.* This property reveals the multitude of ways that African American women scholars understand their impact on the academy.

- *Asserting Personhood.* This property illuminates the ways that participants, when faced with multiple challenges to their personhood, intellect, and presence in the academy, control their environments to mitigate the assaults and assert their personhood.

The need to take action by speaking out against the embedded nature of the injustices noted in the academy was a strong theme in all of the interviews. It was clear that for these women, this was not just a choice but in fact an imperative. As one observed, "The people who were most invested and like showed up for those meetings and have those conversations were almost all faculty of color. And so, that's what is like this unequal burden." Although committed to all students they teach, participants understood the potential impact their presence has on African American students in particular: "I care about all my students equally, or I shouldn't be teaching. But I realize that students who are in a minority and have to negotiate different types of subjectivity have a story that I can understand. . . . I have to be available because I might be one of the few people who intimately understand that story. And so, if I don't talk to them about it, if I don't help them, they will not be helped because there is no other support system for them."

Robust Sense of Self, to which all other dimensions and their properties are related, reflects the interconnectedness and significance of these elements and becomes a heuristic model of African American women's perception of life in the academy (see figure 13-1).

Theoretical Propositions

The theoretical matrix describes the potential explanation of the women's experience in the academy. In figure 13-1, the matrix is visually represented to illustrate the relationships between the social processes, both internal and external, in which the women participated and their contribution to the women's strength, presence, and awareness of the conditions of the academy and their impact on building a *Robust Sense of Self.* The final step in GTM, posing theoretical propositions, seeks to articulate the underlying human processes that govern the dynamic interplay of processes described in the theoretical matrix. Theoretical propositions offer both the practitioner and the researcher an opportunity to place the findings of this study in the broader scholarly discourse on African American women in the academy and to suggest ways of acting as change agents in institutionalized "whiteness." Three theoretical propositions emerge from this study to explain how African American women in the academy are change agents of the academy: *Seeking Full Range of Motion, Creating and Claiming Free Space,* and *Living Truth to Power.*

Proposition One: Seeking Full Range of Motion

African American women scholars have a desire to live productive lives in the academy and experience satisfaction through engagement in their communities and relationships. This yearning is represented in the first theoretical proposition, *Seeking Full Range of Motion*. African American women scholars choose careers in the academy for a variety of reasons: to stretch themselves intellectually and make significant contributions through new scholarship that many times troubles the status quo, to support their communities, and to inspire and engage students to be critical thinkers and engaged members in a global society. The data surfaced not only the myriad of ways that African American women's range of motion is systemically limited but also the ways in which they resist and fight to lead full intellectual and personal lives, as reflected in the primary dimension *Persisting*.

Used in this context, *full range of motion* refers to the African American woman scholar's ability to contribute abundantly and freely while bringing the fullness and complexity of her personhood to bear on the environment. These women "take up space"—physical space, intellectual space, and emotional space; by virtue of their being, they cannot be ignored, even when being rendered invisible.

As reflected in the property *Diss/ease*, there are casualties, for how can individuals continue to live under constant stress without real consequences—the physical, emotional, social, and psychic impact of the everyday assaults they described? Being mistaken for service staff or students, having their authority challenged in the classroom, and being accused of a lack of collegiality all create racial battle fatigue. Taken at face value, what is known about the lived experiences of African American women in the white academy is disheartening and demoralizing. The attempts to restrict the movement of African American women take many forms, and these women's acts of positive resistance contribute to the robustness of their personhood.

Proposition Two: Creating and Claiming Free Spaces

The white academy remains contested ground, yet participants found "sites of resistance" (hooks, 1990). These interstitial spaces, as described by the women in this study, take various forms: physical (e.g., the classroom), psychological (e.g., a robust sense of self), relational (e.g., creating generative connections via community, affinity groups, and allies), and intellectual (e.g., scholarship and research). The women in our study claimed psychological and intellectual space in the academy that thereby nurtured their *Robust Sense of Self*. One participant reflected on how much healthier she has been since refusing to be silenced and embracing her whole self: "I'm not leaving who I am at home anymore, because that's what I was doing. I was leaving myself at home, close that door, go to work, take on that persona, do well, leave work, close that door, come home, and embrace who I am. And I decided I wasn't going to do that anymore, that I was going to bring who I was to the table."

This participant acknowledged that the embrace and articulation of self in the context of external interactions in the academy was not a foregone conclusion; it didn't just occur but was part of her process of "becoming" whole. Crucial for the psychological health of African American women is the dimension of exercising voice and agency, which is liberatory when one is faced with the convergence of multiple oppressions. The relational space serves the psychological space and vice versa. The creation of intentional space to cultivate supportive relationships with other African American women, foster connections with white allies, and, in some cases, work with students of color is essential in the white academy (Pitt, Vaughn, Shamburger-Rousseau, & Harris, 2015). The connectivity afforded in relational space provides a counterspace that militates against the onslaught of discouraging messages, explicit and subtle, that emanate from the academy.

Proposition Three: Living Truth to Power: Leaving Footprints

The women in this study struggle to live truth to power, a theoretical proposition that illuminates the impact and import of critical resistance and the need to birth and nurture a radical black female subjectivity. *Living Truth to Power* speaks directly to the embodiment of critical resistance. The participants in this study inhabit the white academy with courage, authenticity, and purpose. They honor the multiplicity of their identities and recognize the ways in which intersectional aspects of self converge in social and political spaces—in this case, the white academy—resulting in differing impacts and outcomes. They fight back from silence even when faced with seemingly insurmountable odds. This is the knowing, being, and expression of the *Robust Sense of Self.*

Some of the ways African American women leave footprints is documented; their presence in the academy has a positive impact on the retention of students of color (Myers, 2002), and they have changed the topography of disciplinary study with the advent of black studies departments and scholarship (McKay, 1997). These material ways are significant. What are less obvious, but no less significant, are the ways in which African American women have reordered relationships in the white academy—or, if not reordered them, then at least exerted tangible pressure on the norm. As one participant stated, "I've talked about the challenges of being in that environment, the alienation, the isolation, the being viewed with suspicion, my scholarship questioned, feeling like the mammy; in some ways I have to compromise my standards [yet] I really believe that if I wasn't there, and other women like myself were not there, that these institutions would be poorer for the fact."

Final Remarks

This study holds significance for African American women in the white academy, as well as having potential contributions to the larger discourse on the nature of leading and leadership. A feminist stance to GTM enhanced the discovery of microprocesses in the academy that became the center and foreground of making meaning of the African American woman's experience. The propositions embody the "we-ness" of African American women. The African American women in this study do not seek full range of motion solely for themselves; their desire for free expression and healthy, whole lives is an aim extended to their sisters in the academy, their students, their communities, their institutions, and the global community. When a participant made the potent assertion, "I'll choose which hill to die on," she spoke directly of her intent to take control of her own destiny and exercise discretion, informed by received knowledge. The context was not only about her survival but also about her strategic assessment of ways to bring about change in the institutional environment—choosing which battles to fight—to benefit the whole.

NOTES

Portions of this manuscript are from the first author's dissertation (Shockley, 2013) at Graduate School of Leadership and Change, Antioch University. The dissertation was supervised by the second author.

1. A comprehensive review of related studies may be found in Shockley (2013).

2. A full description of the method of the study and findings is available in Shockley (2013).

3. The emergent coding protocol builds theoretical understanding by first identifying in the transcripts key phrases and language, named *properties*; clustering these properties into categories, named *focused coding*; establishing the relationship among codes, named *axial coding*; and, finally, moving from codes to broader concepts, named *dimensions*, that cluster categories together (Holloway & Schwartz, 2018).

REFERENCES

Antonio, A. L. (2002). Faculty of color reconsidered: Reassessing contributions to scholarship. *Journal of Higher Education, 73*, 582–602.

Astin, H. S., Antonio, A. L., Cress, C. M., & Astin, A. W. (1997). *Race and ethnicity in the American professoriate, 1995–96.* Los Angeles: Higher Education Research Institute, UCLA.

Beauboeuf-Lafontant, T. (2005). Keeping up appearance, getting fed up. *Meridians: Feminism, Race, Transnationalism, 5*(2), 104–123.

Carter-Frye, M. (2015). *An association case study that explores African-American female representation in higher education administrative leadership and executive roles* (Doctoral dissertation). Available from ProQuest. (10153739)

Charmaz, K. (2006). *Constructing grounded theory.* Thousand Oaks, CA: Sage.

Collins, P. H. (2000). *Black feminist thought: Knowledge, consciousness, and the politics of empowerment.* New York, NY: Routledge.

Crenshaw, K. W. (1991). Mapping the margins: Intersectionality, identity politics, and violence against women of color. *Stanford Law Review, 43*(6), 1243–1299.

Davis, O. I. (1999). In the kitchen: Transforming the academy through safe spaces of resistance. *Western Journal of Communication, 63*(3), 364–381.

Essed, P. (1990). *Everyday racism: Reports from women of two cultures.* Claremont, CA: Hunter House.

Harley, D. A. (2008). Maids of academe: African American women faculty at predominately white institutions. *Journal of African American Studies, 12*(1), 19–36.

Holloway, E. L., & Schwartz, H. L. (2018). Drawing from the margins: Grounded theory research design and EDI studies. In R. Bendl, L. A. Booysen, & J. Pringle (Eds.), *Handbook of research methods on diversity management, equality and inclusion at work* (pp. 660–681). Northampton, MA: Edward Elgar.

Hoke, B. (1997). Women's colleges: The intersection of race, class and gender. In L. Benjamin (Ed.), *Black women in the academy: Promises and perils* (pp. 291–302). Gainesville: University Press of Florida.

hooks, b. (1990). *Yearning: Race, gender, and cultural politics.* Boston, MA: South End Press.

hooks, b. (1994). *Outlaw culture: Resisting representations.* New York, NY: Routledge.

Howard-Baptiste, S. (2014). Arctic space, lonely place: "Mammy moments" in higher education. *Urban Review, 46*(4), 764–782.

John, B. M. (1997). The African American female ontology. In L. Benjamin (Ed.), *Black women in the academy: Promises and perils* (pp. 53–63). Gainesville: University Press of Florida.

Kools, S., McCarthy, M., Durham, R., & Robrecht, L. (1996). Dimensional analysis: Broadening the conception of grounded theory. *Qualitative Health Research, 6*(3), 312–330.

Lorde, A. (1984). *Sister outsider: Essays and speeches.* Trumansburg, NY: Crossing Press.

McKay, N. Y. (1997). A troubled peace: Black women in the halls of the white academy. In L. Benjamin (Ed.), *Black women in the academy: Promises and perils* (pp. 11–22). Gainesville: University Press of Florida.

Morse, J. M. (2009). Tussles, tensions, and resolutions. In J. M. Morse, P. N. Stern, & J. Corbin (Eds.), *Developing grounded theory: The second generation* (pp. 13–21). Walnut Creek, CA: Left Coast Press.

Myers, L. W. (2002). *A broken silence: Voices of African American women in the academy.* Westport, CT: Bergin & Garvey.

Nash, R. J. (2004). *Liberating scholarly writing: The power of personal narrative.* New York, NY: Teachers College Press.

Olesen, V. (2005). Early millennial feminist qualitative research: Challenges and contours. In N. K. Denzin & Y. S. Lincoln (Eds.), *The Sage handbook of qualitative research* (3rd ed., pp. 235–279). Thousand Oaks, CA: Sage.

Olesen, V. (2007). Feminist qualitative research and grounded theory: Complexities, criticisms, and opportunities. In A. Bryant & K. Charmaz (Eds.), *The Sage handbook of grounded theory* (pp. 417–435). Thousand Oaks, CA: Sage.

O'Neil, D., Green, D., Creswell, J. W., Shope, R. J., & Plano Clark, V. L. (2010). Grounded theory and racial/ethnic diversity. In A. Bryant & K. Charmaz (Eds.), *The Sage handbook of grounded theory* (paperback ed., pp. 472–492). Thousand Oaks, CA: Sage.

Perlow, O. N. (2018). Gettin' free: Anger as resistance to white supremacy within and beyond the academy. In O. N. Perlow, D. Wheeler, S. L. Bethea, & B. M. Scott (Eds.), *Black women's liberatory pedagogies: Resistance, transformation, and healing within and beyond the academy* (pp. 1–18). London, England: Palgrave Macmillan.

Pitt, J. S., Vaughn, M., Shamburger-Rousseau, A., & Harris, L. L. (2015). Black women in academia: The invisible life. In J. L. Martin (Ed.), *Racial battle fatigue: Insights from the front lines of social justice advocacy* (pp. 209–223). Santa Barbara, CA: Praeger.

Robinson, T., & Ward, J. V. (1991). A belief in self far greater than anyone's disbelief: Cultivating resistance among African American female adolescents. In C. Gilligan, A. G. Rogers, & D. L. Tolman (Eds.), *Women, girls and psychotherapy: Reframing resistance* (pp. 87–103). Binghamton, NY: Haworth Press.

Roman, L. G. (1992). The political significance of other ways of narrating ethnography. In M. D. LeCompte, W. L. Millroy, & J. Preissle (Eds.), *The handbook of qualitative research in education* (pp. 555–594). San Diego, CA: Academic Press.

Schatzman, L. (1991). Dimensional analysis: Notes on an alternative approach to the grounding of theory in qualitative research. In D. R. Maines (Ed.), *Social organization and social process* (pp. 303–314). New York, NY: Aldine de Gruyter.

Shockley, M. (2013). *I'll choose which hill I'm going to die on: African American women scholar-activists in the white academy* (Electronic dissertation). Retrieved from http://rave.ohiolink.edu/etdc/view?acc_num=antioch1370378305

Snyder, T. D., & Dillow, S. A. (2012). *Digest of education statistics 2011*. Washington, DC: National Center for Education Statistics, Institute of Education Sciences.

Thomas, A. J., Witherspoon, K. M., & Speight, S. L. (2008). Gendered racism, psychological distress, and coping styles of African American women. *Cultural Diversity and Ethnic Minority Psychology, 14*(4), 307–314.

Thomas, G. D. (2001). The dual role of scholar and social change agent: Reflections from tenured African American and Latina faculty. In R. O. Mabokela & A. L. Green (Eds.), *Sisters of the academy: Emergent black women scholars in higher education* (pp. 81–92). Sterling, VA: Stylus.

Tyson, C. (2001). From the classroom to the field. In R. Mabokela & A. L. Green (Eds.), *Sisters of the academy* (pp. 139–149). Sterling, VA: Stylus.

14

The Transformational Impact of Black Women/ Womanist Theologians Leading Intergroup Dialogue in Liberation Work of the Oppressed and the Oppressor

TAWANA DAVIS

Intellect is the critical, creative and contemplative side of mind. Whereas intelligence seeks to grasp, manipulate, re-order, adjust; intellect examines, ponders, wonders, theorizes, criticizes, imagines. Intellect will seize the immediate meaning [of a] situation and evaluate it. Intellect evaluates evaluations, and looks for the meanings of situations as a whole.

—*Pierce (1966)*

A BLACKWOMAN HOLLA
Tawana Davis and Dawn Riley Duval

As a Blackwoman
     Mother Grandmother Daughter
Blackwoman
     Sister Friend Minister

Blackwoman
Student   Activist   Imago   Dei
As a Blackwoman
In this history-in-the-making
Black Lives Matter moment
Religion Faith Knowing
Is saving me
Saving us
In the midst of injustice
In the midst of inequity
Is keeping me
Keeping us
In joy and triumph
In love and life
Our Religion   Faith   Knowing
Is holding us
In the midst
Of
Our
Holla.

Yes
I want to holla   want to scream and holla
With love and joy
When I see my son and daughter
who are 12 and 10
See them laugh and run with their hands in the air
Just beautiful, big, black, shiny
And free.
I want to holla . . .
Throw up both my hands
In honor of Michael Brown
In praise for my 23-year-old son for still being
alive
Living a life Michael Brown and others were
not afforded
In praise for G-d's protection of my 31-year-old
daughter
Same age as the late Sandra Bland

And in intercessory prayer for my 8-year-old
grandson
Praying for protection from the racist ills of
this world

And I want to holla
Just ecstatic full
When I complete a task
With flash and flair
After folk told me to just
Stop
Try something else
Or recommended that I
Seek assistance from
Brother so-in-so

I want to holla . . .
Love me!
As I love you
See me!
As I see you
Dignity works both ways and I am somebody

And there are sometimes and some things
Some places and some spaces
some people and some powers
that just make
me wanna holla
and throw up both my hands

When people assume that
Because of my Black skin
I am expecting a handout.
When people assume that
Because I am a Black woman
I need their pity or platitudes

What we need is opportunity
Opportunity to live

Live life more abundantly

Live with human rights and human dignity

Live unafraid for our Black lives

Live unafraid for our Black children and grandchildren

What we need is to
Live and flourish and prosper
After all that's what we're promised
In the Declaration of Independence
Which says
                "We hold these truths to be sacred
                And undeniable:
                That all men
And women
                Are created equal and independent;
                That from the equal creation
                They derive rights
                Inherent and inalienable
                Among which are the preservation of life
                And liberty
                And the pursuit of happiness"
So today
And everyday
Until our lives and liberties
are protected

                for our children
                our future
                our faith
                for G-d
we must holla.

We are living in a world in which women are emerging from the shadows, from behind the veil, from the engine that drives this country's, this world's, survival. Out from the shadows as ghost writers, silent organizers; reclaiming voice, agency, capacity, and power. This is a journey of Black girl magic and Black woman mysticism as the driving force for liberation for all through a Black lens of fem divine, spirituality, intellect, resilience, intersectionality, hope, courage, self-love, self-care, and Power divine. This chapter heralds the ubiquitous, holistic, antibinary leadership of Black women and womanist theologians leading in opposition to the invisibility, silence, gender roles, and marginalization they faced in the past.

This chapter features ongoing research and documentation of Black women[1] who, desiring to do the work necessary to address personal and systemic white supremacy and privilege, lead intergroup dialogue in white institutions. As a retired itinerant elder in the African Methodist Episcopal Church, my lens and approach to this racial justice work are rooted in spirituality and interfaith work. Attending seminary at a historically black school, the Interdenominational Theological Center, set my roots in womanist theology and womanism. Womanism is revolutionary. Womanism is a paradigm shift wherein Black women no longer look to others for their liberation but instead look to themselves. Womanism centers the lives and experiences of Black women. Just as critical thinking requires objectivity but does not diminish or ignore one's own experiences, womanism supports offering critical feeling and spirituality as ways to counteract fractionalization and judgment. As intellectual revolutionaries, womanist scholars undertake praxis that liberates theory from its captivity to the intellectual frames and cultural values that cause and perpetuate the marginalization of Black women in the first place (Floyd-Thomas, 2006, p. 2). We must begin to ask how people learn, hear, respond, and inculcate new behavioral patterns. The intellect is one way, but it must be complemented by the imaginative faculties (Hoyt, 1991).

Countering the inculcation of heteropatriarchy and white-dominant culture requires a praxis of transformation and liberation for the oppressed and the oppressor. It is only when the oppressed "find the oppressor out" and become involved in the organized struggle for their liberation that they begin to believe in themselves. This discovery cannot be purely intellectual but rather must involve action; nor can it be limited to mere activism but rather must include serious reflection—only then will it be a praxis (Freire, 2009, p. 65). This is the foundational premise of the importance of Black women leading liberating work in the twenty-first century. For years Black women have been erased from sacred texts, leadership in the history of the movement for Black lives, and current leadership positions in religious, secular, and communal organizations. Our voices have been silenced. Our presence has been marginalized. Our impactful, transforming, and liberating work has been co-opted by others. It is time to document the transformational impact of Black women leaders as we are in this history-in-the-making movement for Black lives.

By no means am I suggesting that Black women be solely responsible for this work. Black women have collectively identified and called out oppression and have become involved in the struggle for liberation as leaders by passing the baton, tools, spiritual prowess, and resilient exemplars to those who are accountable for fixing this conundrum they created—namely, white supremacy, white privilege, and white-dominant culture. This work is not exclusively intellectual but rather holistic: intelligent, divine, mystical, reflective, shared, dignified, prophetic, and Black centered (Pierce, 1966). Therefore, I am suggesting that when we move to praxis, the oppressor does the much-needed work and the Black women rest. This is not a linear movement but rather a cyclical, nascent movement for Black lives with aspirations of liberation for all as Black women conspicuously lead the way. Soul 2 Soul exemplifies this work, as it is headed by two womanist theologians who are leading antiracism work in predominantly white spaces, planting seeds of holistic work that includes feeling and soul work beyond the intellect while centering Black lives and experiences that are often invisible in mainstream media, conversations, and white supremacy culture. We refute and reject mammying. The mammy is known as a nurturing, loyal, self-sacrificing woman (Reynolds-Dobbs, Thomas, & Harrison, 2008) who does the oppressive work the oppressors must and demand to have to maintain white supremacy and white-dominant culture. Although we embrace the Strong Black Womxn, we also include in that motif a model of rest, respite, and doing the work our (own) souls must have (Johnson, 2018). Therefore, we reject the notion of white-dominant thought and culture that includes power hoarding and individualism and refuses to open the door to other cultures and cultural norms (Okun, n.d.). We raise a level of consciousness that names racism and offers a language for white people and white-dominant culture to address and dismantle and with which to build egalitarian norms, relationships, and communities. We then send them forth to do the work in themselves, with their families, on the job, and in communities. Freire (2009) says, "This, then, is the great humanistic and historical task of the oppressed: to liberate themselves and their oppressors as well. The oppressors, who oppress, exploit, and rape by virtue of their power, cannot find in this power the strength to liberate either the oppressed or themselves. Only power that springs from the weakness of the oppressed will be sufficiently strong to free both" (p. 44).

Soul 2 Soul: Black Women/Womanist Theologians Leading Intergroup Dialogue for Liberation

For years I have led antiracist work in predominantly white congregations, organizations, and educational institutions as a cofounder and coconsultant of Soul 2 Soul. Soul 2 Soul is a Black-women-led, faith-based racial justice organization that centers Black lives for the liberation of all. The intergroup, dialogical model used raises consciousness of Black struggle and resilience in the midst of oppression; offers language to address white supremacy and white privilege in personal, professional, political, communal, and congregational settings; and offers tools to do the work required of white people. The power of dialogue as it relates to race talk is what is referred to as intergroup dialogue.

Black women/womanist theologians are called to liberate the oppressed and the oppressor through the soul work of love. As Black women faith leaders, we, the leaders of Soul 2 Soul, speak Truth to power and create a space to engage, reflect, experience, and identify behaviors, thoughts, and norms that have plagued Black and Brown people, often resulting in death, incarceration, poverty, marginalization, and hate. Although we often face moments during which we are inclined toward reminding members of the dominant culture of their barbaric history and current inhumane culture of behavior and walk away, instead, Soul 2 Soul accepts the call to educate, reveal, and share experiences of the Black (and Brown and Indigenous) diaspora that are not told in mainstream media or by the 1 percent of dominant capitalistic thought and culture. Black women faith-based leaders, with all of their dynamic mysticism and power, take on the charge to lead white people to do the lifelong work required to dismantle the racist structures white-dominant culture has created while setting boundaries. These boundaries include avoidance of an unhealthy dependency of Black women leaders, Black women bearing the brunt of the work, and a lack of rest, respite, and recuperation. Our philosophy is that the antiracist work must be done by the very people who continue to institute racism: members of the white-dominant culture. Black women of faith, leading from the margins, offer a powerful approach to dismantling racism by meeting the dominant culture at the level of its members' ignorance and journeying toward removing the veil of racism and oppression through emotional intelligence, spiritual prowess, and healing practices.

To set the tone for this intergroup dialogue as womanist theologians, in the first two sessions, we cleanse the space in African and Indigenous tradition with the use of sage. Inviting white people into this ritual has been described by one of our participants as "an exorcism and a blessing." Since we are centering Black lives, we start by immersing participants in spiritual prowess. We do this not only to provide them with a learning experience but also to create a sacred space that is not always deemed as safe. The sacred setting also calls on our resilient ancestors and those who have gone before us for strength and protection while engaging in emotional, vulnerable work.

In order to establish a system of trust in which we can move from intelligence to intellect, we insert our personal narratives. We do this work in order to save and protect our beautiful Black children from systemic ills that perceive our skin color as a threat. In addition to sharing our personal narratives and experiences, we journey through the lived experiences of Black people through various mediums, including storytelling, listening to music such as "Black Rage" by Lauryn Hill, watching music videos such as "This Is America" by Childish Gambino, and reflecting on articles, blogs, and books centering Black lives and racial justice work. Soul 2 Soul's curriculum focuses on the intersection of economic justice, reproductive justice, disparity in health care, misogyny, systemic racism in law enforcement, food deserts, voter engagement, gentrification, and how they affect healthy outcomes for sustainable, just communities.

By sessions 3 and 4, participants are ready to begin a plan of action for racial justice work. We encourage participants to dream and visualize aspirations of just communities in both individual and collective settings. In facilitating a plan of action for participants to lead racial justice work, we have now actualized our praxis. The oppressor is now doing the much-needed work, and the Black women rest. Here, Black women conspicuously lead the way while creating a cyclical, emerging movement.

A system of support has been established. The participants go on to create a community of like-mindedness and face racism with a new, transforming, and liberating lens and heightened awareness of injustice. From here, the participants go forth and lead racial justice work to dismantle the individual, collective, systemic racism in their homes, jobs, communities, and selves.

Soul 2 Soul's pre- and poststudies show that out of 160 participants,

- 95 percent report that the information learned during the study sessions helps them more deeply analyze racial justice issues concerning Black people;

- 95 percent report that since participating in the Facing Racism training sessions, they have a better picture of how we can both center Black people and Black liberation, and connect that work with the liberation of all people;

- 92 percent report confidence that they will take action toward raising awareness and educating beloveds, colleagues, and congregants about racial justice issues concerning Black people; and

- 77 percent report confidence that their congregation or religious group will take action toward raising awareness and educating congregants about racial justice issues concerning Black people.

Transformational outcomes include the following:

- Cohort attendees have created grassroots programming, racial justice curriculum, ministries, advocacy groups, plays, sermons, and interfaith and community-wide forums.

- An alumni group meets monthly as an open forum to build community and share ideas and experiences, including mistakes and areas of improvement.

- Several congregations have developed or enhanced social justice efforts in the following areas:

  - Preaching sermon series

  - Developing social justice ministries

  - Participating in movements such as Showing Up for Racial Justice, Black Lives Matter, and Change the Name of Stapleton (a neighborhood in Denver named after a former Ku Klux Klan politician); taking political and legislative action; and working toward individual transformation within racial/racist family dynamics.

Intergroup dialogue and race talk is a diverse exchange between white people who subscribe to the dominant narrative and Black people or people of color who have been oppressed and marginalized by the dominant group. The dialogue is not a haphazard exchange of information and life stories. It is what scholars call counterstorytelling or counternarratives. Counternarrative stories "tell on" or bear witness to social relations that the dominant culture tends to deny or minimize. The dialogical discourse requires authority but is not authoritarian, and it requires freedom but not licentiousness (Freire, 2009). It is the personal stories that challenge the dominant narrative and bring to light the harrowing impact of racism and racist behavior, one voice in a dialogue among people who have been silenced (Collins, 2009, p. x).

Conceptual Underpinnings of Soul 2 Soul: Why Black Women?

We have pursued the shadow, they have obtained the substance; we have performed the labor, they have received the profits; we have planted the vines, they have eaten the fruits of them.

—*Maria W. Stewart, address at the African Masonic Hall, 1833*

Affirming the fullness of Black women of the African diaspora is salient and imperative, particularly as Black women's voices have been silenced and Black women's leading presence has been erased, marginalized, or moved to the background. In an American context, Black women embody the intersectionality of race, gender, and class. Forms of oppression appear in these three areas, coalescing to form the moment in which one identity is not disconnected from the others but all emerge to our disadvantage. Intersectionality illustrates " . . . that many of the experiences Black women face are not subsumed within the traditional boundaries of race or gender discrimination these boundaries are currently understood, and that the intersection of racism and sexism factors into Black women's lives in ways that cannot captured wholly by looking at the race or gender dimensions of those experiences separately" (Crenshaw, 1991, p. 1244).

Black women who have been and continue to be the driving force in family, community, politics, religious institutions, and corporations are emerging from hidden intellectualism, excavating Black women's intellectual history, history-in-the-making movements, and epistemic erasure (Cooper, 2017). Discussions of scholarly work have consisted of predominantly male discourse, with Black women informing the discussion but not telling our own stories (Cooper, 2017, p. 130). This chapter, and the praxis it features, aligns with the call for Black women to rise up to tell our own stories, document these stories as intellectual and scholarly property, and rise as leaders at the forefront of movements. This country has thrived on the backs, blood, sweat, tears, and lives of Black women since its inception. Through resilience, strength, communal prowess, emotional capacity, intellectual proficiency, and power born of the intersectionality of race, gender, and class, Black women are inserting ourselves into a narrative that has ignored, erased, silence, co-opted, used, abused, marginalized, and oppressed Black women in mind, body, and spirit. This emergence is nothing new, nor is it something that we just discovered. It is Black women who have understood and continue to understand the double consciousness and often triple consciousness (Townes, 2011, p. 38) of survival; hence, we must be the disruption of heteropatriarchy, misogyny, and bigotry while caring for ourselves and empowering others—the oppressors, colonizers, and dominant culture—to do the necessary work of transformation and liberation.

It is important to note the avoidance of meritocracy, especially with Black women having a leading position in liberation. It is a white, capitalistic tendency to measure leadership based solely on merit: education, access, opportunity, and economic wealth. Black women must place the Black experience at the center of the narrative with our existence as mere resistance; with our cultural prowess, which builds community from individualism; with the power to make something out of nothing. "Educated elites typically claim that only they are qualified. . . ." It is this belief that upholds their own privilege and dominant culture. (Collins, 2009, p. viii). "However, care must be taken to neither idealize nor romanticize African American women" (Townes, 2011, p. 39). It is very easy to become enamored with Black women's mysticism and power. White fragility may cause one to depend on leadership and guidance from Black women. White guilt may lead one to rely continuously on Black women for leadership and for absolution of one's own guilt.

It is imperative for Black women to define and drive the narrative of liberation. It is not our responsibility to do the physical, emotional, and spiritual labor required to liberate white people from oppressive behaviors. Rather, this work is about our survival, the survival of Black women, Black men, Black children, Black communities, Black educational institutions, Black churches, and Black life. Black women should not kill ourselves for the sake of the movement, nor will we be crunched into a paradigm that continues to nurse this country economically, spiritually, and physically. Black women are galvanizing, redefining leadership roles, commanding intellectual property, and defining how we show up in this country for our survival with community in mind.

Why Black women? Black women are in crisis. A crisis may be defined as a dangerous opportunity. We are at the crucible of change, shaping a movement born of strength in the midst of misogyny, racism, bigotry, and classism, in the midst of the Black Lives Matter movement and the Me Too movement created and organized by Black women. We are co-creating opportunities to offer a space of possibility and place in which to cathect our best thinking about how to get free (Cooper, 2017, p. 142). It is time to take seriously the work of Black women thinkers, doers, creators, believers, sustainers, maintainers, nurturers, and leaders and demonstrate Black women's long history of knowledge and powerful transformational and liberative prowess (Cooper, 2017). "[N]ot all Black women are womanist, but the womanist potential is embedded in all Black women's experiences" (Gilkes, 2011, p. 87). Womanist theology is intersectional and religious and centers Black women (Townes, 2003). Black feminism, which must be acknowledged and named, as previously mentioned, doesn't offer the salient centering of Black women as an independent methodology and thought.

It is Black women who must mobilize for collective power to oppose the power vested in existing male-dominant, white supremacist cultures (Townes, 1993). Presently, and historically, Black women are at the bottom of the economic ladder when ranked with white men, white women, and Black men; Black women compose nearly 75 percent of the traditional Black church, and this is not reflected in its leadership (Townes, 1993). Since the mid-1800s, before the abolishment of slavery, Black women have served as leaders in the oppressor's home; have served as leaders for social justice, abolitionist, women's rights activism (Horsford, 2012); and have been, oftentimes, the engine behind major organizations such as the Southern Christian Leadership Conference (Barnett, 1993) and the

Black Panther Party (Seifert, 2009). It is absolutely essential that Black women who have been oppressed, marginalized, sexualized, and dehumanized participate in the revolutionary process with a critical awareness of their role as subjects of the transformation toward liberation for all (Freire, 2009).

Conceptual Underpinnings of Soul 2 Soul: Why Womanist Ontology?

A womanist ontology of wholeness is, finally, radically relational.

—Townes (2011)

In its simplest form, theology is the study of the nature, existence, manifestation, and being of G-d. Theology is not necessarily associated with a particular religious sect and leans toward a universalist thought about G-d. "Theology can never be neutral or fail to take sides on issues related to the plight of the oppressed. For this reason, it can never engage in conversation about the nature of G-d without confronting those elements of human existence which threaten anyone's existence as a person. Whatever theology says about G-d and the world must arise out of its sole reason for existence as a discipline: to assist the oppressed in their liberation. Its language is always language about human liberation, proclaiming the end of bondage and interpreting the religious dimensions of revolutionary struggle" (Cone, 1990, p. 4).

Womanist theology is a lens, study, reflection, stance, and affirmation that places Black women and the perspectives of Black women at the center while identifying racism, classism, and sexism as theological issues (Townes, 2003). A womanist theologian is one who engages in the study of G-d at a level of contextual analysis and scholarly research while centering Black women. Womanist theology moves Black women beyond traditional parameters of formal education, refutes patriarchy and dominant cultural values, exemplifies intersectionality while creating spaces for dynamic consciousness in anti-Black-racism work, and encourages others to look to the margins for liberative justice work (Williams, 2013). Womanist ontology brings Black women, Black people of the diaspora, from the margins to the center of liberative justice work. Through intergroup dialogue, womanist ontology creates a space for Black women to be, give voice, and use their agency to speak Truth that is antithetical to the oppressive audiences we engage. This is rooted in a concern for being centered in wholeness and liberation, not white-dominant culture, white supremacy, or dehumanizing racist structures (Townes, 1993). At the heart of a womanist ontology is the self-other relation grounded in concrete existence and succor in the flawed transcendent powers of our spirituality (Townes, 1993, p. 113) while being mindful of the miasma of a white supremacy that will call for Black women to do the work for the dominant culture. Black women leading racial justice activism works because it is antithetical to the dominant structures, which were not created for the Black diaspora to begin with. We have an opportunity to create a model of justice that brings those on the margins to the center of the narrative that illuminates, questions, challenges, and begins the eradication of radical oppression (Townes, 1993).

It is important to note the developed paradigm of Black women leading this work without doing all of the work physically, emotionally, and spiritually. Black women/womanist theologians are liberators whose stories and lived experiences of resilience are examples for all to embody. It is absolutely essential to the revolutionary process to develop an increasingly critical awareness of their role as subjects of the transformation (Freire, 2009, p. 127). It is a revolutionary praxis for all to emulate and inculcate. The revolutionary praxis for liberation must include dialogue—specifically, intergroup dialogue that charges, implores, and invokes transformation by dismantling white supremacist culture through the very people who created it.

Conclusion

Black women know what it is to live, survive, thrive, suffer, get free, and live free in the system of oppression and beyond the system. Given Black women's expertise in flourishing in the United States, the centering of Black women's leadership is essential when engaging in Black-centered racial justice work. It is important to note that this mode of racial justice centers Black lives and Black experiences, honors the Black woman, creates a space of rest and respite for Black women and the Black diaspora, and creates a model for Brown and Indigenous people to center their experiences in order to bring about liberation for all. This model increases awareness of white privilege and white supremacy; invokes compassion and empathy toward the oppressed; invites critical feeling that is attentive to emotional intelligence versus intellectual prowess; creates a sacred space for confession, repentance, forgiveness, and atonement; and builds a community of justice seekers that includes those liberated from oppression as the oppressed and the oppressor.

NOTES

1. I will use the terms *Black* and *Black women* to refer to a sociopolitical, revolutionary identity centering the Afro-diasporic race and culture of women exclusive of the dominant culture and narrative. *African American*, for the purpose of this chapter, centers America as white and African as a part of a white culture we are actively and intentionally dismantling.

REFERENCES

Barnett, B. (1993). Invisible southern Black women leaders in the civil rights movement: The triple constraints of gender, race, and class. *Gender and Society, 7*(2), 162–182.

Collins, P. H. (2009). *Black feminist thought*. New York: Routledge.

Cone, J. H. (1990). *A Black theology of liberation*. New York: Orbis.

Cooper, B. C. (2017). *Beyond respectability: The intellectual thought of race women*. Urbana: University of Illinois Press.

Crenshaw, K. (1991). Mapping the margins: Intersectionality, identity politics, and violence against women of color. *Stanford Law Review, 43*(6), 1241–1299.

Floyd-Thomas, S. M. (2006). Writing for our lives: Womanism as an epistemological revolution. In S. M. Floyd-Thomas (Ed.), *Deeper shades of purple: Womanism in religion and society* (pp. 1–14). New York, NY: New York University Press. Retrieved from https://nyupress.org/webchapters/0814727522intro.pdf

Freire, P. (2009). *Pedagogy of the oppressed*. New York, NY: Continuum.

Gilkes, C. T. (2011). The "loves" and "troubles" of African-American women's bodies: The womanist challenge to cultural humiliation and community ambivalence (pp. 81–97). In K. G. Cannon, E. M. Townes, & A. D. Sims (Eds.), *Womanist theological ethics*. Louisville, KY: Westminster John Knox Press.

Horsford, S. D. (2012). This bridge called my leadership: An essay on Black women as bridge leaders in education. *International Journal of Qualitative Studies in Education, 24*(1), 11–22.

Hoyt, T. (1991). Interpreting biblical scholarship for the Black tradition. In C. H. Felder (Ed.), *Stony the road we trod* (pp.17–39). Minneapolis, MN: Fortress Press.

Johnson, A. G. (2018). Dancing redemption's song, across generations: An interview with Katie G. Cannon. *Journal of Feminist Studies in Religion, 34*(2), 75–88.

Maria W. Stewart. (2018, December 17). In *Wikipedia*. Retrieved from https://en.wikipedia.org/wiki/Maria_W._Stewart

Okun, T. (n.d.). White supremacy culture. Retrieved from http://www
.dismantlingracism.org/uploads/4/3/5/7/43579015/whitesupcul13.pdf

Pierce, P. (1966). Problems of the negro woman intellectual. *Ebony Magazine*,
144–149.

Reynolds-Dobbs, W., Thomas, K. M., & Harrison, M. S. (2008). From mammy to
superwoman: Images that hinder Black women's career development. *Journal of
Career Development, 35*(2), 129–150.

Seifert, M. (2009). Political art of the Black Panther Party: Cultural contrasts in the
nineteen sixties countermovement. *Journal of Undergraduate Research at Minne-
sota State University, Mankato, 9*(15), 1–10.

Townes, E. (1993). To be called beloved: Womanist ontology in postmodern refrac-
tion. *Annual of the Society of Christian Ethics, 13,* 93–115.

Townes, E. (2003). Womanist theology. *Union Seminary Quarterly Review, 57* (3–4):
159–176. Retrieved from http://discoverarchive.vanderbilt.edu/bitstream/handle
/1803/8226/Townes-WomanistTheology.pdf?sequence=1

Townes, E. (2011). Ethics as an art of doing the work our souls must have. In K. G.
Cannon, E. M. Townes, & A. D. Sims (Eds.), *Womanist theological ethics* (pp.35–
50). Louisville, KY: Westminster John Knox Press.

Williams, D. (2013). *Sisters in the wilderness: The challenge of womanist God-talk.*
New York, NY: Orbis Books.

15

Psychodynamics of Black Authority—Sentience and Sellouts

Ol' Skool Civil Rights and Woke Black Lives Matter

DIANE FORBES BERTHOUD, FLORA TAYLOR,
and ZACHARY GREEN

The state of Black authority relations is fraught, at the conscious and unconscious levels of examination, with attacks from across race and from within. For the second time in twenty years, a group relations conference focused on the study of Black authority in a multicultural context was offered in the United States. The experience proved to be challenging and enriching and brought to light how the dynamics between leadership, authority, and roles remain complex in the American psyche. "On the Matter of Black Lives," an intense, experiential conference, was both resistive and revolutionary. At its core, the conference stood as a challenge to a Eurocentric model of learning, a creative design and deliberation that centered Black lives. As members of the conference management team, we served in roles of director (Green), associate director (Forbes), and large study group team leader (Taylor). In this chapter, we discuss our perspectives on critical events from the conference to elucidate the complexities of our experiences studying Black authority and to offer a framework to understand the psychodynamics of Black authority. Finally, we discuss implications for the study of leadership and authority.

Theoretical Framework

Group relations theory is the central framework that guides our work in group relations conferences—temporary organizations created to study conscious and unconscious group and organizational dynamics as they occur. In group relations contexts, this study occurs in the here and now, and it provides members with opportunities to collectively experience and study group dynamics: leadership, followership, roles, task, boundaries, collusion, and, most importantly, *authority*.

Key contributors to this theory include Bion (1961), Klein (1946), and Wells (1985). Collectively, their work forms the basis for a systems and psychoanalytic approach to groups that is focused on the interrelatedness of and influence between individuals and groups and groups as systems. Complexities such as tensions around authority relations, belonging, anxiety, roles, and leadership abound.

Bion (1961) contributed to the development of group relations theory by arguing that groups function in two contrasting ways: engaging in behaviors and activities focused on rational work tasks and those that are associated with emotions, such as anxiety and fear. At once, the group consciously engages in its task (work group behavior) and unconsciously avoids its task (basic assumption behavior) in order to manage its anxiety. Klein (1946) focuses on infant life, the experience with the mother, and the connectedness of the two in the development of the infant. Using as its model an infant's positive and negative instinctive responses when he or she receives comfort or has unmet needs (food, warmth, etc.), Klein's work connects the push-pull of group membership with negative and positive experiences of group life, with our quest for belonging, comfort, and identity from groups.

Another central component of group relations theory is Wells's group-as-a-whole theoretical perspective (1985, 1995), which conceptualizes groups as having a *different life* from, but related to, the dynamics of the individual co-actors; group behavior is understood as a social system. The group emerges from an open systems framework (group-level phenomena) and makes available the study of the *group gestalt*—unconscious systemic dynamics that provide information about what the group's "voice" or "identity" may be in a given moment. The gestalt has also been framed as the group or unconscious mind, wherein the collective mind shapes individual activities and meaning emerges from a socially structured or constructed field (Weick & Roberts, 1993).

Bion, the father of British group relations, and A. Kenneth Rice and Margaret Rioch, its American parents, developed the conference model in the mid-twentieth century. These two white men and one white woman led the way for this work through the Tavistock Institute (London) and the A. K. Rice Institute (Washington, DC). This background has both historical and racial implications for the development and evaluation of the model. Conferences uphold particular critical principles:

1. The study of authority and the unconscious is paramount.

2. The staff endeavors at all times to operate within strict boundaries when consulting with a group. Being on time, staying on task, and scrupulously adhering to one's role supports a clear focus on studying the group's behavior.

3. The staff takes a neutral stance intended to invite members to reflect on their experience, which might reflect projections of their internalized experience of authority.

4. Staff members carefully examine their own unconscious dynamics.

5. The staff endeavors to make meaning of whatever occurs because, in group relations, *everything* is available for study.

Identity Gains a Foothold

Initially, the conferences did not explicitly attend to racial, cultural, gender, or other identity dynamics. More recent scholarship expanded the systems approach to group relations to consider demographic variables in the study of authority. For example, membership in cultural, ethnic, age, racial, sexual identity, and orientation groups may be complicated when negative stereotypes, societal scripts, identities, and group dynamics intersect. These stereotypes may serve as catalysts for conflict around group inclusion and exclusion. Group members' perceptions of their own and other groups' power and privilege often affect their attitudes and behaviors in the group, their perceptions of self, and the group as a whole. A systems analysis contributes to a more complex and nuanced understanding of these dynamics as they intersect with racial-cultural factors and systemic factors such as authority, roles, leadership, power, and interpersonal relations (McRae & Short, 2005, 2009; Green & Molenkamp,

2005, 2015). The BART framework specifically advances group and organizational systems study through the lenses of boundaries, authority, roles, and tasks. Focusing on learning from group relations conferences, the authors point to the intersections among the elements of BART, group dynamics, and the influence of identity and demographic factors (Green & Molenkamp, 2005, 2015).

Group Relations, Black Authority, and Leadership

Early group relations theory and practice focused primarily on authority relations and hierarchies that were identity neutral and somewhat limited. In this section, we discuss and build on the theoretical foundations of group relations and the complexity of Black authority through an analysis of our experiences in the "On the Matter of Black Lives" conference.

Figure 15-1 illustrates the complex, multilayered, and simultaneous analyses that inform and constitute organizations. The work of Wells holds important theoretical, intellectual, and experiential implications for group relations tradition and practice, in part, because of its keen focus on systems-level analyses and their application in multicultural contexts, particularly in the study of Black authority. Wells's scholarship also centered the socio- and psychodynamics of predominantly Black organizations and race relations in complex organizational systems. The group-as-a-whole concept deepened our understanding of the complex and nuanced dynamics of projection, scapegoating, and role suction that are uniquely experienced by those "othered" in organizations.

The existing Black authority frameworks did not, however, attend explicitly to gendered discourses, intersectionality, and leadership dynamics with Black women in authority. Forbes (2002, 2017) and Moffitt, Harris, and Forbes (2012) offered an intersectional approach to leadership that integrates gender, class, nationality, culture, and other social identities. Race and gender are approached not as separate systems but as mutually constituted systems of relationships that affect Black women's organizational experiences in and of leadership and authority. This intersectional framework aptly informs the conference experience, as demonstrated by the complex interplay of gender, race, age, and other identities that we encountered there. In sum, the study of Black authority has extended beyond a Black, male, middle-class, and middle-aged perspective.

FIGURE 15-1

Levels of organizational analysis

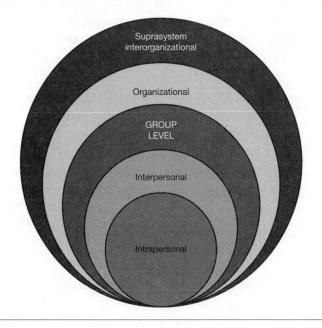

The Conference

For years, elders in group relations work spoke of offering an all-Black staff conference. This became a reality in 1995 when "Authority and Identity: An African American Perspective" was held at the American University in Washington, DC. It became one of the largest group relations conferences in a decade, signaling a deeper need to understand the unconscious processes influencing the exercise of Black authority. In 1995, some playfully touted Bill Clinton as the "first Black president," and to many, Barack Obama's and Donald J. Trump's presidencies seemed unimaginable. This first conference, like the United States, was far more "Black and white" in membership, that is, with members who identified as African American or White; whereas, the 2017 "On the Matter of Black Lives" conference was more a part of a larger global, multiethnic network of group relations study with an all-Black staff and a more diverse membership.

In March 2017, we were authorized by Group Relations International and RISE San Diego to design and hold a conference where we studied the authority of Black people and how members both authorized and de-authorized us in that enterprise. "On the Matter of Black Lives" was a three-day, nonresidential conference with the task of exploring the unconscious elements of leadership, authority, and identity in human systems with a particular focus on the matter of Black lives. Whereas the previous conference was held during the O. J. Simpson trial, the Clinton presidency, and a period of economic prosperity, the "On the Matter of Black Lives" conference was conceived during a contentious election season and conducted during the post-Obama, early Trump era in the heat of the Black Lives Matter movement.

The racially and ethnically mixed membership was predominantly composed of women and people of color, and unlike at the previous conference, gender fluidity and a wide range of sexual orientations were evident. Relatedly, generational dynamics were evidenced, with members and staff ranging in age from twenty to eighty-plus years old. Both experienced and first-time members attended.

Generational Complexity

The conference reflected critical voices on race, powerful themes in contemporary discourse, and distinct generational approaches to the study of Black authority. A very public debate between Ta-Nehisi Coates, whom some have touted as the Baldwin of this age, and Cornel West, a leading voice on race matters, took place at the conference. Coates represented those voices most aligned with the Black Lives Matter movement, and his writings directly critique a politic in which Black bodies are subject to routine annihilation through white supremacist practices.

West, in contrast, lamented that Coates "fetishizes" white supremacy and promotes the diminution rather than advancement of Black political power. He called for a broader coalition of identity groups, consistent with intersectionality (Crenshaw, 1991). This Coates-West tension was also present in the conference among the staff—some of whom subscribed to a post–civil rights era ethos in which Black identity and nationalist sentiments dominate—and members of the younger generation who rejected "one drop" notions of racial identity and placed other social identities, such as sexual orientation, on par with race. This split appeared in "On the Matter of Black Lives" in the Community Event, soon to be described in detail.

We learned more about millennials' (born between 1985 and 2004) approaches to Black authority and activism. Millennial activism has been more fluid, with Black authority viewed as more nuanced and intersectional than, for example, during the civil rights era. Research shows that most Americans in their fifties and sixties are removed from the concerns and interests of millennials and Generation Xers. They tend to favor lower taxes and a smaller government that provides resources for health, education, and social mobility, and the generational divide persists across racial groups in their core values and approaches to activism (Frey, 2015). The data reveals a lack of investment in the future of younger generations, and in the absence of economic and academic investments, leadership, and mentorship, millennials have emerged with a more independent approach to life.

Civil rights leaders recall a more nuanced, organized, and nonviolent movement, while millennials, with a more direct and confrontational approach, see them as having joined an establishment they had intended to fight. They see the civil rights movement as having little relevance and having achieved few concrete developments that currently benefit their generation. Black Lives Matter activists stated that civil rights activists interacted with and advised them as parents, not as partners and peers. A strong resistance to being told how to "do" activism emerged. They perceive figures such as John Lewis, Andrew Young, and Coretta Scott King not only as removed from their current reality (Friedersdorf, 2016; Jarvie, 2016) but as having failed them, dropped the baton along the way, and chosen not to partner with millennials because they disapproved of the younger generation's approach to activism and social justice (Friedersdorf, 2016). This dynamic was evident in the conference.

The conference included an activity called the Community Event. Unlike in other conference events, where the group members, topics, and approach are predetermined, the Community Event offers members the option to choose who and what to work with—typically organized around identity membership (e.g., all people interested in studying race) or a topic (e.g., exploring boundaries). Once settled into groups, members are tasked with studying the groups, including the group they formed and those that others formed. The staff group constitutes one of these and is available to be observed and interacted with to explore hypotheses of what dynamics exist in the system. At the end of four sessions, everyone meets for a plenary session to share their learning. This event stands out as the most emotional and challenging of any of the conference events for the staff. We felt to differing degrees admiring, envious, disrespected, embarrassed, anxious, disillusioned, frustrated, and bewildered. What happened to evoke these powerful emotional responses? We frame the discussion through the lens of generations and generativity, boomer and millennial, Coates and West. We felt pushed and provoked in very uncomfortable ways by those who were our juniors, an age group that most of the members are in, and while we were proud to provide an educational forum with participants ranging from twenty to more than eighty years old, we felt the sting of fending off a coup even as we felt love for the deposers.

In the Community Event, one group leader (a young Black male), whose group explored the role of education in Black communities and whom a Black female member described as a "king," partly because of his stately African garb, experienced the staff as betraying his group. He asserted that staff denigrated their efforts, excluded them from an initial hypothesis, and sought to silence their contributions, which echoes millennials' lament about the boomer generation. To let us know their hurt and anger, they had enacted a piece of performance art in the staff room earlier. We felt chastened but also admired their agency and creativity. In the plenary session, that enactment was followed by a few powerful and revealing moments led by the same group. This young Black male member addressed the conference staff as "my staff," which received support from the same female member who had earlier ascribed to him the royal label; and the young man, who knows Dr. Green outside the conference, offered his own framework (drawn on the whiteboard and accompanied by a lecturette) about Black authority. The member then took the director to task for raising the elder of his sons without a decent "fade" or the "right jeans," which he had very generously corrected by taking the child out and getting him a "proper" (Black) barber and jeans. In the moment, we felt protective of both Dr. Green and the enterprise. Were these young Black folks staging a coup? We felt trapped between wanting to support this young man's leadership potential and guarding against his possible effort to tear down Dr. Green in the process. At once, the member seemed to authorize himself and deauthorize Dr. Green. We felt disoriented and somewhat puzzled. From the perch of advanced degrees and a methodology we wanted desperately to share with this generation for their use and benefit, we felt annoyed and embarrassed that the markers of a fade and proper jeans appeared to be most significant to this young man. (Sit down, boy. What are you doing?) We felt put on the spot to maintain and even protect our authority, *and* we felt admiration that he, with no college degree or previous staff experience, would speak up so publicly. We felt afraid that this perceived rejection of a model to which each of us is devoted signaled a potential ending of the model's usefulness in teaching generally, and perhaps to Black people in particular, as we worried that our "offspring" might be the ones to dismiss it.

On yet another level, we also considered that perhaps this member did what the staff would not do. Many of us disagreed with decisions Dr. Green made to guide this enterprise, including hiring many inexperienced staff and at times failing to address indiscipline among the staff. Culturally, it is interesting that no members of the staff humiliated or publicly disowned Dr. Green. Warts and all, he was one of us and we would stand with him, especially in the face of challenge. Here, the African diasporic cultural value of respecting our elders and never publicly challenging them prevailed. Our joint staff work concerning our individual formulations of and insecurities about Blackness and the admission and revocation of "Black cards"—dancing the wobble and sharing actual gifts from our African and African American ancestors in the work—built a foundation of love among the staff and across the staff-member boundary. This bond seemed to come under assault with the various generational struggles, and we felt as if we had been told to take our "gifts" back to where we came from.

We entertain the hypothesis that both the younger people on staff and in the membership and the older ones on staff wished to be seen, respected, and loved; suffered the injury of having felt overlooked and the discomfort of operating in an unfamiliar methodology or generational space; and suffered a deep sense of hurt and disappointment, even if they grew wiser as a result. What we could not see was that generational dynamics were unconsciously operating on a more powerful level than we could consciously grasp. The envy, longing, contempt ("I guess we'll just have to wait for you to die," as one member stated to Dr. Mack), and competition were not broached, but they were felt and recognized.

Black Archetypes of Authority

We also learned about the complex representations of and longing for the familiar archetypes of Black authority in the conference. The staff held diverse understandings of Blackness, which caused some consternation when familiar tropes of Blackness were unavailable. So, what do we know about Black authority in American history and culture?

Associations of Black authority evoke images and expectations of militant, outspoken men—civil rights activists and scholars such as Dr. Martin Luther King Jr., Malcolm X, and Stokely Carmichael, whom many viewed as strong, uncompromising, and bold. Others include "barbershop" community members such as Jesse Jackson and Johnnie Cochran, models that some have critiqued as reductionist and regressive. These activist archetypes have pervaded our consciousness and informed our ideas about leadership. Black male representations are nuanced and diverse—Barack Obama, Colin Powell, Clarence Thomas, Ben Carson, Cornel West, and Jay-Z. Also differentiated and complex are representations of Black females—for example, Michelle Obama, Condoleezza Rice, Kamala Harris, Oprah Winfrey, Maxine Waters, and Angela Davis—all leaders in their own right, with none occupying the category "Black woman leader."

Research has addressed barriers to Black women's leadership and controlling images that perpetuate oppressive discourses (Collins, 1990, 2002, 2004; Dumas, 1980). The Mammy, a strong yet subservient figure who is expected to be nurturing and supportive of white family and social structures, possesses little authority and understands and knows "her place." This figure captures society's perception of the ideal Black female relationship to elite white male power—an asexual and loyal figure who denies herself and meets the need of those more powerful. The Sapphire, hypersexual, hot-tempered, and devoid of intellectual and psychological prowess, promotes the sexual exploitation of Black women in service of (white) patriarchal structures. In such images, Black women are cast as asexual mothers or hypersexual whores. Jezebel represents a Black woman who serves or seduces white male structures and is sexually aggressive or deviant. This controlling image has been central to the (unconscious) discursive justification of sexual harassment and violence, which Black women experience at higher rates than any other group (Harris-Perry, 2011; Petrosky et al., 2017).

Forbes (2009) addressed dialectical tensions of commodification and sexualized discourses about Black women who had varied responses to hypersexuality through co-modification: "Black women's bodies are a contested terrain of organizing, which gives rise to complex dynamics of (con)scription (others' joint definitions), resistance, (re)definition, and accommodation" (p. 580).

Her study reveals that Black women respond in nuanced and complex ways to shift and engage these images, which in more recent studies are conceptualized as dynamic and fluid. Taken together, these stereotypes operate as a system of controlling discourses that seek to subordinate Black women. Opportunities for leadership are greatly reduced because of the active, (un)conscious resistance to Black female authority necessary to reproduce white male structures. In the conference, no one management team member wholly represented any of these images. In the absence of familiar scripts of Black authority, rage and confusion emerged: What kind of conference is this? What kind of Black man/woman are you? One instance that we thought represented some of this skepticism and doubt was when a white male with a position of authority in the A. K. Rice Institute for the Study of Social Systems, stated that he attended the conference to make sure that the staff did not "mess up" the group relations tradition.

In the large study group led by Dr. Taylor with Dr. Mack and Dr. Forbes as consultants—an all-Black and mostly female authority team—consultations were, for the most part, met with resistance and violence. In one instance, a member who was an attorney described in detail a case in which a rapist stated during his trial that the woman whom he assaulted pleaded with him, "Please. Why are you doing this? I'm a mother," and mentioned other aspects of her life, hoping it might stir some compassion in him. He, however, responded, "I f— hate my mother!" and continued the assault. As this member recounted the incident, the group gasped and members wept. We consulted with one another about this story and wondered among ourselves what connections might exist between the discursive trends of violence and assault, while studying and learning about Black authority with a mostly female team. We found the (ab)use of power to maim and injure in a way that would have a lasting impact striking, in both word and deed. The members of the large group consulting team expressed in staff debriefs how difficult it had been at times to find their voices. In group relations study and practice, *every* action represents a cohesive whole of the story of the unconscious, and, as consultants, we offer possible interpretations to guide this study. The team persevered to consult regarding this dynamic, pointing out the potential resistance to Black female authority and the level of aggression being expressed, which could be related to the experience and study of Black authority. In this instance, we also felt some helplessness, sadness, and pain as this narrative was recounted. We empathized with the trauma that others had experienced sexually and felt that it might have been similar to our difficult and complex experience of Black leadership.

The "Other" in the Midst of Blackness

As we learned about generational complexity and the relationship of archetypes to Black authority, we also wondered, Where did the white and Brown people fit in a conference with open membership that focused on the authority of Black people? The data suggests that the Latino and mixed Asian conference members were perhaps unduly burdened in this context. The two Latinas left the conference for a whole day because of a sense of not belonging, experiencing the historically American racial dynamic of Black or white, but not Brown. Later, one of the women shared with the large group that while she was absent, Immigration and Customs Enforcement came to her community, a real-life example of many immigrants' experiences of the current American political landscape. Who is a legitimate member of America and, by extrapolation, the conference?

An older, experienced, multiethnic member, noticing the absence of the two Latinas on day two, spoke to the large group as if on their behalf, but without their permission, claiming that they left because they did not feel as though they belonged. She formed a group without their authorization, claiming they were members. The women returned and spoke to their feelings of displacement and expressed rage about this member co-opting their voices. Outside, life's pressures became a cauldron. Inside, they felt obliterated or used; the Brown people ended up fighting with and wiping out each other. For us as an administrative team consisting of all Black members—one immigrant and two based in San Diego (a border city)—we felt torn in our respective roles and somewhat protective of the women who left. Half of us had concrete ties to them, as they were part of an urban leader's fellowship program that we led for a year. We were concerned and anxious. Would their departure represent our inability to hold the system? Were we leading an enterprise that colluded in an expulsion of that which was not Black as we sought to center Blackness? The immigration tensions are very present to us, as authors, because in our institutions, communities, and social circles there are people whom these crises (in)directly affect. As we studied Black authority, we experienced the interconnectedness of displacement, belonging, and trauma that also characterizes the experiences of Blacks in multiple contexts. We learned more about the intersections among marginalized populations at both the organizational and the larger systems levels.

The white members took up a number of roles, all of which seemed to share an aspect of either taking cover or claiming traditional hierarchical roles: Some white members said nothing throughout the three days. Some focused on the experience of Black people as if it weren't OK for them to talk about their own experience. Some tried to explain to other white people how to be empathic across the racial divide. One left early and later explained that without an identity with currency (e.g., Jewishness or being gay), the "cost" was too great. And finally, some came with historical white authority, "I came to see if 'they' [the Black staff] would mess it up." As staff, we felt the razor's edge of being Black authorities in a mixed-race context and scrutinized by both the Black and the white people for missteps.

The theme of white surveillance emerged along with the traditional questioning and challenging of Black competence. We felt on display and tested to some degree, given the comments that were made about reporting on what we did and learning from us, which we read suspiciously as "extract to reuse," that is, take our ideas and organizational and structural innovations and reuse in another context. We also felt nervous: How well could we accomplish this task of studying and centering Blackness, particularly in this tenuous political moment in the United States?

This experience was made both powerful and excruciating by the emotional connections to one another, the pressure on us, and the (ambivalent) longing for the approval and love of Black authority. Figure 15-2 summarizes our learning from the experience.

Discussion and Implications

The study and experience of Black authority brought with it complex dynamics that were almost uncontainable, including the following:

- *Generations/generativity*—Born out of great pain and injustice, multigenerational groups and movements converge around common missions, yet across generations, ideas about process, authority structures, and norms sometimes differ. Also evident are the ways in which diverse family, regional, and faith backgrounds intersect with the experience across generations and must be negotiated anew with *each* effort.

FIGURE 15-2

Cycle of containment: responses to Black authority

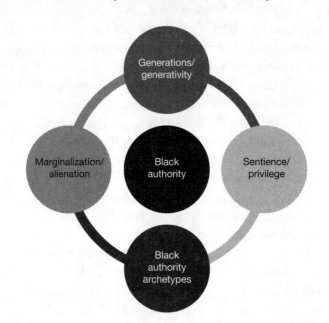

- *Sentience/privilege*—Complications of connections, love, desire, and important and formative relationships produce tensions with the requirements of the tasks. Through sentience, love and desire either prevail or become the basis from which a sense of deep betrayal can emanate. There are also cultural aspects of connection, respect, age, and values integrated in these dynamics.

- *Marginalization/alienation*—There are complex dynamics at work in negotiating how to be both authorized and deauthorized or challenged in and out of authority roles as Black, leaders, followers, and participants. For Blacks in positions of authority, the culturally embedded experience of personal and historical oppression is a part of the currency, as are the differentiated experiences of being or feeling marginalized.

- *Black authority archetypes*—Pervasive stereotypes and images are evoked in and through the unconscious that intersect with the learning and processual experiences of a group relations conference focused on the study of Black authority.

In many respects, the conference represented ongoing adaptive challenges much as posited by Heifetz (1994) and Thomas (1990), who researched Blacks in corporations.

Our work also has implications for the generativity and leadership of (Black) political and social movements: Black Lives Matter; the Women's March and the reemergence of the women's movement; the Me Too movement; the Time's Up movement; the Never Again movement; Concerned Black Men, a group based in Washington, DC; and 2BU (Black and Brown Union), RISE San Diego Leadership Fellows. These movements experience generational tensions and leadership challenges as well. In order to survive and thrive, they must understand and negotiate processes, structures, and norms to achieve their common goals as the multiple intersections of gender, race, age, and other factors complicate these efforts.

The group relations model provides a framework to deconstruct and better understand systemic structures, authority, and their relatedness to historical, sociopolitical, and organizational oppression. Study and exploration of conscious and unconscious dynamics increase our ability to work effectively within and across diverse group and organizational contexts.

Our study and experience of Black authority revealed complicated and nuanced dynamics in "On the Matter of Black Lives." Our intersectional approach to the group relations model enriched systems theory and practice and offered opportunities to study and learn about political and organizational systems. Our work also informs research about contemporary political movements and invites a deeper exploration of Black leadership and authority.

REFERENCES

Bion, W. R. (1961). *Experiences in groups and other papers*. London, England: Tavistock.
Collins, P. H. (1990). *Black feminist thought*. New York, NY: Routledge.
Collins, P. H. (2002). *Black feminist thought: Knowledge, consciousness, and the politics of empowerment* (2nd ed.). New York, NY: Routledge.
Collins, P. H. (2004). *Black sexual politics: African Americans, gender, and the new racism*. New York, NY: Routledge.
Crenshaw, K. (1991). Mapping the margins: Intersectionality, identity politics, and violence against women of color. *Stanford Law Review, 43*(6), 1241–1299.

Dumas, R. G. (1980). Dilemmas of black females in leadership. *Journal of Personality and Social Systems, 2,* 1, 3–14.

Forbes, D. A. (2002). Internalized masculinity and women's discourse: A critical analysis of the (re)production of masculinity in organizations. *Communication Quarterly, 50*(3–4), 269–291.

Forbes, D. A. (2009). Commodification and co-modification: Explicating Black female sexuality in organizations. *Management Communication Quarterly, 22*(4), 577–613.

Forbes, D. A. (2017). An integrative analysis of diversity and discourse in women's leadership. In C. Cunningham, H. Crandall, & A. M. Dare (Eds.), *Gender, communication, and the leadership gap* (pp. 201–222). Charlotte, NC: Information Age.

Frey, W. (2015, December 29). The new racial generation gap. *Los Angeles Times.* Retrieved from http://www.latimes.com/opinion/op-ed/la-oe-1229-frey-racial-generation-gap-20151229-story.html

Friedersdorf, C. (2016, June 30). Generational differences in Black activism. *Atlantic.* Retrieved from https://www.theatlantic.com/politics/archive/2016/06/generational-differences-in-Black-activism/489398/

Green, Z., & Molenkamp, R. (2005). The BART system of group and organizational analysis: Boundary, authority, role and task. Retrieved from https://www.it.uu.se/edu/course/homepage/projektDV/ht09/BART_Green_Molenkamp.pdf

Green, Z., & Molenkamp, R. (2015). Beyond BART: At the level of the field. The BART system of group and organizational analysis: Boundary, authority, role and task. Retrieved from https://www.grouprelations.org/ssg-readings

Harris-Perry, M. V. (2011). *Sister citizen: Shame, stereotypes, and Black women in America.* New Haven, CT: Yale University Press.

Heifetz, R. A. (1994). *Leadership without easy answers.* Cambridge, MA: Belknap Press of Harvard University Press.

Jarvie, J. (2016, July 28). Why the gap between old and new Black civil rights activists is widening. *Los Angeles Times.* Retrieved from http://www.latimes.com/nation/la-na-civil-rights-generation-gap-20160713-snap-story.html

Klein, M. (1946). Notes on some schizoid mechanisms. *International Journal of Psychoanalysis, 27,* 99–110.

McRae, M. B., & Short, E. L. (2005). Racial-cultural training for group counseling and psychotherapy. *Handbook of Racial–Cultural Psychology and Counseling. Training and Practice, 2,* 135–147.

McRae, M. B., & Short, E. L. (2009). *Racial and cultural dynamics in group and organizational life: Crossing boundaries.* Sage.

Moffitt, K., Harris, H., & Forbes, D. (2012). Present and unequal: A third-wave approach to voice parallel experiences in managing oppression and bias in the academy. In G. Gutierrez y Muhs, Y. F. Niemann, C. González, & A. Harris (Eds.), *Presumed incompetent: The intersections of race and class for women in academia* (pp. 78–92). Boulder: University Press of Colorado.

Petrosky, E., Blair, J. M., Betz, C. J., Fowler, K. A., Jack, S. P. D., & Lyons, B. H. (2017). Racial and ethnic differences in homicides of adult women and the role of intimate partner violence—United States, 2003–2014. *Morbidity and Mortality Weekly Report, 66*(28), 741–746.

Thomas, D. A. (1990). The impact of race on managers' experiences of developmental relationships (mentoring and sponsorship): An intra-organizational study. *Journal of Organizational Behavior, 11*(6), 479–492.

Weick, K. E., & Roberts, K. H. (1993). Collective mind in organizations: Heedful interrelating on flight decks. *Administrative Science Quarterly, 38*(3), 357–381.

Wells, L., Jr. (1985). The group-as-whole perspective and its theoretical roots. In A. D. Colman & M. H. Geller (Eds.), *Group relations reader 2* (pp. 109–126). Jupiter, FL: A. K Rice Institute.

Wells, L., Jr. (1995). The group-as-a-whole: A systemic socioanalytic perspective on interpersonal and group relations. In J. Gillette & M. McCollom (Eds.), *Groups in context: A new perspective on group dynamics* (pp. 49–85). Lanham, MD: University Press of America.

THEORIZING BLACK LEADERSHIP

16

Is D&I about Us?

*How Inclusion Practices Undermine
Black Advancement and How to Design
for Real Inclusion*

VALERIE PURDIE-GREENAWAY
and MARTIN N. DAVIDSON

> That inclusion . . . [the company] knows that that has nothing to
> do with African Americans.
>
> —*Alicia Harris, African American manager (personal
> communication, February 27, 2018)*

One way to interpret Harris's statement is that she is a stagnant black manager willing to gripe about her company. A deeper look suggests that she may be tapping into a powerful insight: many black professionals have little evidence that diversity and inclusion (D&I) initiatives actually help them advance in their organizations and careers. D&I initiatives are ubiquitous (Dobbin & Kalev, 2017; Nishii, Khattab, Shemla, & Paluch, 2018), and while they are meant to enhance career trajectories and foster inclusive climates for all groups, people tend to believe that D&I practices primarily benefit blacks (Plaut, 2014). Yet while blacks have been entering the professional and managerial ranks of US corporations for decades, they remain dramatically underrepresented at senior levels. In 2018, only three *Fortune* 500 companies were led by black CEOs (Donnelly, 2018). In three major financial services firms—Goldman Sachs, JP Morgan Chase, and Citigroup—only

2.6 percent of top executives were black, a decline in black leadership in these firms between 2013 and 2018 (Abelson & Holman, 2017). Even when black professionals are moving up the ranks, they frequently feel underutilized and perceive there to be a racial "glass ceiling" limiting their future opportunities (McKay et al., 2007).

We suggest that organizations can dramatically increase the impact of their D&I initiatives on the career trajectories of black professionals by "designing for black inclusion." Designing for inclusion more broadly is defined as attending to a variety of criteria for fostering an inclusive climate by reducing bias in access to resources based on identity-group status, creating opportunities to establish generative relationships across difference, and promoting integration of ideas across boundaries to help solve problems (Nishii, 2013). Designing for black inclusion starts with these concepts and then builds parameters that have been shown to uniquely benefit members of underrepresented groups such as blacks. For example, black leaders benefit from (1) opportunities to learn effective racial identity management competencies across the career life span (Thomas & Gabarro, 1999), (2) partnerships that foster cross-racial relationship intimacy (Davidson & James, 2007; Dutton & Heaphy, 2003), and (3) skills in developing growth-based stories in the wake of professional setbacks (Ospina & Foldy, 2009; Vough & Caza, 2017). Here, we suggest a fourth parameter uniquely critical to the development of inclusion programs and practices that support black leaders: *the need to eradicate the perception that race will be a barrier to advancement.* In this chapter, we examine the underlying psychological processes that make this parameter so critical for developing black leaders and suggest a set of practices that foster black inclusion and support the success of these leaders.

The Psychology of Black Inclusion: A Hidden Imperative

Consider the following scenario: A firm initiates a black leadership development program. The program selects elite black managers, offers leadership training in functional areas (e.g., strategy, accounting) and strategies for black leaders to navigate racial terrain, and encourages mentoring relationships with senior black executives. Would this D&I initiative foster inclusion for blacks? One black professional may welcome such a program, perceiving that the firm is attuned to the unique challenges of black leadership and is committed to inclusion. Another black professional may be repelled by it, perceiving that the firm assimilates blackness into a stereotyped set of experiences and is not serious about inclusion. The answer is, *it depends.*

This example illustrates one fundamental challenge with inclusion: the attributions black professionals make fundamentally shape how they experience any given program and ultimately determine whether the program fosters inclusion. We argue that organizations have the capacity to shape how black professionals come to perceive and experience inclusion programs. Differences in how blacks come to experience inclusion reflect not simply the professional's racial background or cultural fit with the company but the nature of the inclusion program itself and the implicit signals it conveys.

Like most human behaviors, inclusion experiences are symbolic acts (Geertz, 1973). Their meaning depends on their interpretation by the perceiver. Is being asked by the managing director, "How is work going?" in the elevator seen as an affirmation that the director cares or an ominous warning that he or she is tracking one's work? If the first, it may kindle a friendship. If the second, it may cause avoidance. What appears to be the same situation can in fact be very different for different actors, or for the same actor at different times.

One's group membership may add another layer through which one perceives a given situation. When a black person receives negative feedback on an essay from a white evaluator in the next room partitioned by a glass window, the black person may see the situation differently depending on incidental changes (Crocker & Major, 1989). Case in point: When the window blinds between rooms are up, the black individual may perceive evidence of potential bias, leading him or her to discount the feedback. When the blinds are down, however, he or she sees the interaction as an opportunity to learn and attends to the feedback (Crocker & Major, 1989). In this case, the critical design feature is the position of the blinds, which dramatically alters how one perceives the feedback. People tend to wonder, What type of person is more likely to perceive feedback as racially biased? We suggest the more critical question one should ask is, What kinds of situations tend to lead people to perceive feedback as racially biased?

Cultural diversity refers to differences among people in race, ethnicity, gender, religion, nationality, or other dimensions of social identity that are marked by a history of intergroup prejudice, discrimination, or oppression (Ely & Roberts, 2008). Fostering inclusion among such groups is, by definition, an inherently ambiguous task. If the invitation to the leadership training described earlier arrived in a cryptic email to a mysteriously chosen subset of black managers without a clear explanation of the program objectives, the manager may perceive the invitation as racially threatening. In contrast, a knock on the door and an assurance that the training is highly selective and developmental leads the same manager to perceive the invitation as affirming. Practitioners tend to underappreciate that leadership training for black executives is, by definition, ambiguous, conveying either the need for blacks to build skills (i.e., deficiency based) or the opportunity to fast-track the black professional's career (i.e., based on potential). The personal and specific statement that the program is highly selective is a design feature that can (if said genuinely and bolstered by a history of fair practices in the company) nudge the black manager to perceive the program in a positive light with potential positive downstream consequences that last over the course of the program.

Decades of research in social psychology and organizational behavior reveal that individuals questioning the value of their group identity in interactions can become vigilant to cues that could signal psychological threat or safety based on one or more of their social identities (e.g., Cheryan, Davies, Plaut, & Steele, 2009; Purdie-Vaughns, Davies, Steele, Ditlmann, & Crosby, 2008; Roberts & Creary, 2013; Roberts & Roberts, 2007). For members of historically marginalized groups such as black professionals, such cues can give rise to social identity threat—worry or concern about the value of one's social identity in the minds of others (Steele, Spencer, & Aronson, 2002).

Research on how historically marginalized groups such as blacks construe diversity messages shows that black professionals can construe them as threatening or affirming, with implications for retention in the company. For example, the more a sample of law firms emphasizes a "value in equality" framing (affirming that differences will not be an obstacle to career opportunities and advancement), in contrast to a "value in difference" framing (advocating for increasing awareness of differences and bias), the lower the turnover rates among racial minorities in the firms (Apfelbaum, Stephens, & Reagans, 2016). Importantly, Apfelbaum and colleagues both measured the degree to which firms conveyed a value-in-difference framing in their diversity messages on web pages and manipulated the value-in-difference frame experimentally (Apfelbaum et al., 2016). The value-in-equality approach was more effective because among the small population of black lawyers assessed in the firms, it made them feel less distinct from others and it affirmed a commitment to fair access to opportunities. Here, the situation cue—relative minority representation—dramatically altered the attributions black employees made about the value-in-equality frame and hence reduced their desire to leave the firm.

In another demonstration of how historically marginalized groups construe diversity messages, black managers viewed a consulting firm brochure that highlighted either a message embracing similarities or a message embracing diversity (Purdie-Vaughns et al., 2008). Those who viewed the similarity message were much more likely to express trust in, and comfort with, the company. They were also less likely to identify race as the cause in a hypothetical situation in which a black employee was fired (Purdie-Vaughns et al., 2008). In both studies, the company's expressed commitment to fair access to opportunities and fair treatment neutralized concerns about racial injustice, findings consistent with research showing that black employees are attuned to messages an organization sends about fairness (Buttner, Lowe, & Billings-Harris, 2010; Davidson & Friedman, 1998).

In light of these studies, we argue that organizations neutralize the deleterious effects described here by institutionalizing programs, policies, and practices that address these psychological dynamics. Outlining a prescription for specific programs is unlikely to be the best approach. Mentoring programs and employee resource groups abound in corporate settings (Dobbin & Kalev, 2017). What distinguishes successful ones from ineffective ones are the design parameters—the principles of design underlying the specific programs, policies, or practices.

The Blueprint for Black Inclusion

If the situation matters and the person's attributions matter, then one important design parameter for blacks requires that designers attend to and develop nudge strategies that *eradicate the perception that race will be a barrier to advancement*. The benefits of investing in such a design strategy are threefold. First, racial inequity and the perception of racial animus are problematic for any organization operating in the United States. They can undermine employee engagement and diminish work performance (e.g., Greenhaus, Parasuraman, & Wormley, 1990). Second, career development is an inherently collaborative task. Certainly, one must be competent and continue to develop expertise in her or his area of responsibility. However, career development also requires a web of relationships that must include connections across difference. Often, race can be an impediment to developing these connections with mentors, sponsors, and peers (Cokley, Dreher, & Stockdale, 2004; Thomas, 1989). Finally, black people are more than the sum of their responses to identity-based trauma. Like any human being, a black person holds both the aspiration to achieve in the world and the need to make sense of who she or he is and could become in a given situation (Ibarra, 1999). Black people want to experience positive aspects of identity, which include growth and flourishing (Dutton, Roberts, & Bednar, 2010).

When racial reactivity exists, stoked both by a larger societal reality in which racism persists and by everyday experiences of bias at work, the detriment of that reactivity is best neutralized by developing "race-intelligent" inclusion. Race-intelligent inclusion is composed of programs, policies, and practices that explicitly address the importance of eliminating explicit racial inequity in the organization and reducing psychological reactivity to racial animus when black professionals encounter it. This type of inclusion acknowledges that organizations must rigorously combat racial inequity in their practices, policies, and culture. In addition, it equips black leaders with competencies that support them to flourish even in the midst of race-based headwinds. Race-intelligent inclusion benefits the black professional as it affords that person tools to advance in the organization. It also benefits the company in its quest to develop more effective leaders and more functional corporate climates. Moreover, it benefits the larger external community and society, helping to foster a citizenry of whole human beings with high integrity.

It may seem contradictory that blacks would prefer value-in-equality approaches that seem to diminish the importance of race (e.g., Apfelbaum et al., 2016), yet we propose developing a culture of inclusion by promoting practices that foreground race. In fact, racial dynamics are omnipresent for blacks in US organizations. What matters for black professionals in their work experience and their professional growth is how race is *engaged* by the organization. It would not be inconsistent for an organization to engage race by affirming the importance of racial equality while simultaneously promoting race-intelligent inclusion practices. Corporate communication that engages race by promoting a value-in-equality vision that performance matters most signals the aspiration that race won't be a barrier to success, which would be consistent with the Apfelbaum et al. (2016) findings. Inclusion practices that engage race explicitly by tactically leveling the playing field may be seen simply as a step in achieving that vision of racial equality.

Three Design Parameters for Black Inclusion

If the cornerstone of black inclusion is the eradication of race as a psychological impediment for blacks, three organizational practices are necessary to encourage this: facilitating explicit communication about race, building knowledge about race, and developing an organizational learning orientation. These practices alone cannot eliminate racial inequity from an organization. However, they can equip emerging black leaders to engage the company, their colleagues, and their careers in generative ways, even when racial animus arises.

Facilitating Explicit Communication

A hallmark of the dysfunction of race in US companies is the unwillingness to talk about it openly (Ely, Meyerson, & Davidson, 2006). This silence has significant costs for black employees. It reinforces the habit of withholding performance feedback from black employees, depriving them of the opportunity to learn and develop (Thomas, 1993; Yeager et al., 2014). It diminishes the capacity to develop relationship resilience with colleagues across race, including the skill of managing conflict related to racial identity (Davidson & James, 2007). It also has costs for nonblack colleagues, as the trust needed to foster authentic interaction is underdeveloped and they lose the benefits, both pragmatic and affective, of creating high-quality connections with black colleagues (Dutton & Heaphy, 2003; Phillips, Dumas, & Rothbard, 2018).

One company altered this script of "race silence" by creating contexts for its senior leaders to develop skill and comfort in talking about race publicly. Leveraging a highly salient community incident involving racial conflict, the predominantly white leadership team sought coaching on how to talk about race, with emphasis on how they entered into cross-race dialogue by discussing their whiteness. Some executives were less conscious of their race experiences; others, more mindful and articulate. All were accountable for engaging in dialogue with their direct reports on the racial climate. The impact of their openness was to begin to legitimize cross-racial dialogue throughout the organization several months after the impact of the precipitating event had lessened. Importantly, these more general experiences in the company need to be tied explicitly to inclusion programs.

If, as Groysberg and Slind (2012) argue, leadership in the modern economy is predicated on the capacity to communicate, thereby promoting operational flexibility, employee engagement, and strategic alignment, black leaders cannot develop this competency absent a culture of communication about race.

Building Knowledge about Race

Frequently, black employees describe "diversity fatigue" that arises from constantly engaging in conversations about race, serving on a task force, or attending diversity training because they bring diversity to the conversation (Cocchiara, Connerley, & Bell, 2010). A design for black inclusion counteracts this phenomenon by creating contexts for nonblack employees to develop their knowledge about race without requiring their black colleagues to participate in every aspect of the learning. Cross-racial interaction and dialogue are central to building a racially inclusive environment; black employees want and need to be engaged in these interactions. However, a key design parameter for black inclusion is for nonblacks to initiate their own program of learning as a first phase.

Organizations can develop a capability for understanding race (e.g., Davidson, 2011) by relying on a critical mass of nonblack employees taking personal action to learn. In one consulting company, nonblack employees started a book club focused on black writers and organized visits to African American museums and historical sites.

But this knowledge development is not only personal. Like many other retail organizations, American Express has developed a market segmentation strategy that emphasizes understanding the communities and customers it serves, including the African American population. It tried to drive business growth by designing appropriate and appealing products and services for those constituents. To provide the necessary knowledge to expand into new markets, American Express developed a patent-pending process called Diverse Marketplace Intelligence. This system drew insights both from the firm's existing talent base and from strategically chosen external partners. The most prominent avenue for learning within the company was provided by the black employee network group, among others.

Organization-wide learning about race is powerful, not only because it increases knowledge but also because it signals to black employees that race is important. That signal is another clue to black employees that the company is trying to engage with their racial experience.

Developing an Organizational Racial Learning Orientation

Building a knowledge base about race is fundamentally a learning task. However, racial learning cannot be a discrete project with an identifiable endpoint. It is unlikely that any member of an organization would credibly state, "Now I am a race expert and know everything about race in the United States!" Rather, racial intelligence requires all organization members—both nonblack and black—to engage in ongoing learning about race. Cultivating this racial learning orientation is essential because racially significant events persist outside and inside the organization. Externally, demographic shifts continue to create more diversity among black communities in the United States as blacks immigrate from Africa, the Caribbean, and elsewhere. These shifts add complexity to our understanding of what drives black advancement (Anderson & López, 2018). In addition, societal events, often traumatic, persist as social media reveals ongoing discriminatory behavior in places of business, police shootings, and social protest (Opie & Roberts, 2017). Internally, developing black talent requires greater understanding of the evolving professional needs of blacks at different career stages (e.g., how a cohort of black junior analysts learn to collaborate as a group of minorities, or what dynamics accrue to someone who becomes the first black CEO of an organization). A design for black inclusion requires the development of a culture of inquiry about race.

One online financial services firm began to cultivate such a learning orientation after deciding to tap into younger, more ethnically diverse customer bases. The company struggled to understand why its widely successful business model was not appealing to black customers who should have been eager to adopt the online platform. The predominantly white male company instituted a program of cross-race dialogues called Know Us, which focused on bringing small groups of employees together to talk candidly about racially relevant topics. The dialogues started in response to police shootings of blacks in the United States in 2015 and 2016. But they persisted as relationships developed, both colocated and virtual. Some of the groups dissipated, but others have continued. The company is now working to encourage more targeted cross-functional diversity in the groups as a way of learning how to solve emerging business challenges related to its black customer base.

Leaders Emerge from the Design for Black Inclusion

Black leaders thrive in part because they are talented. However, far too often, relying on exceptional talent only creates short-term gain. Companies committed to fostering black excellence must be strategic and relentless in creating the conditions for that excellence. Understanding the underlying psychology of the black experience in such companies allows leaders to construct inclusive climates and cultures that create black leaders. A company knows it has done so successfully when its Alicia Harris comes to believe that inclusion and black inclusion have become one and the same.

REFERENCES

Abelson, M., & Holman, J. (2017, July 27). Black executives are losing ground at some big banks. Retrieved from https://www.bloomberg.com/graphics/2017 -black-executives-are-disappearing-from-biggest-wall-street-banks/

Anderson, M., & López, G. (2018, January 24). Key facts about black immigrants in the U.S. Retrieved from http://www.pewresearch.org/fact-tank/2018/01/24/key -facts-about-black-immigrants-in-the-u-s/

Apfelbaum, E. P., Stephens, N. M., & Reagans, R. E. (2016). Beyond one-size-fits-all: Tailoring diversity approaches to the representation of social groups. *Journal of Personality and Social Psychology, 111*(4), 547–566.

Buttner, E., Lowe, K., & Billings-Harris, L. (2010). The impact of diversity promise fulfillment on professionals of color outcomes in the USA. *Journal of Business Ethics, 91*(4), 501–518.

Cheryan, S., Davies, P. G., Plaut, V. C., & Steele, C. M. (2009). Ambient belonging: How stereotypical cues impact gender participation in computer science. *Journal of Personality & Social Psychology, 97*(6), 1045–1060.

Cocchiara, F. K., Connerley, M. L., & Bell, M. P. (2010). "A gem" for increasing the effectiveness of diversity training. *Human Resource Management, 49*(6), 1089–1106.

Cokley, K., Dreher, G. F., & Stockdale, M. S. (2004). Toward the inclusiveness and career success of African Americans. In M. S. Stockdale & F. J. Crosby (Eds.), *The psychology and management of workplace diversity* (pp. 168–190). Malden, MA: Blackwell.

Crocker, J., & Major, B. (1989). Social stigma and self-esteem: The self-protective properties of stigma. *Psychological Review, 96*(4), 608–630.

Davidson, M. N. (2011). *The end of diversity as we know it: Why diversity efforts fail and how leveraging difference can succeed.* San Francisco, CA: Berrett-Koehler.

Davidson, M. N., & Friedman, R. A. (1998). When excuses don't work: The persistent injustice effect among black managers. *Administrative Science Quarterly, 43*(1), 154–183.

Davidson, M. N., & James, E. H. (2007). The engines of positive relationships across difference: Conflict and learning. In J. Dutton & B. R. Ragins (Eds.), *Exploring positive relationships at work: Building a theoretical and research foundation* (pp. 137–158). Hillsdale, NJ: Lawrence Erlbaum.

Dobbin, F., & Kalev, A. (2017). Are diversity programs merely ceremonial? Evidence-free institutionalization. In R. Greenwood, C. Oliver, T. B. Lawrence, and R. E. Meyer (Eds.), *The Sage handbook of organizational institutionalism* (pp. 808–828), London: Sage.

Donnelly, G. (2018, February 28). The number of black CEOs at *Fortune* 500 companies is at its lowest since 2002. Retrieved from http://fortune.com/2018/02/28/black-history-month-black-ceos-fortune-500/

Dutton, J. E., & Heaphy, E. (2003). The power of high-quality connections. In K. Cameron, J. Dutton, & R. Quinn (Eds.), *Positive organizational scholarship* (pp. 263–278). San Francisco, CA: Berrett-Koehler.

Dutton, J. E., Roberts, L. M., & Bednar, J. (2010). Pathways for positive identity construction at work: Four types of positive identity and the building of social resources. *Academy of Management Review, 35*(2), 265–293.

Ely, R., Meyerson, D., & Davidson, M. N. (2006). Rethinking political correctness. *Harvard Business Review, 84*(9), 79–87.

Ely, R., & Roberts, L. M. (2008). Shifting frames in team-diversity research: From difference to relationships. In A. P. Brief (Ed.), *Diversity at work* (pp. 175–201). New York: Cambridge University Press.

Geertz, C. (1973). *Interpretation of cultures: Selected essays.* New York, NY: Basic Books.

Greenhaus, J. H., Parasuraman, S., & Wormley, W. M. (1990). Effects of race on organizational experiences, job performance evaluations, and career outcomes. *Academy of Management Journal, 33*(1), 64–86.

Groysberg, B., & Slind, M. (2012). Leadership is a conversation. *Harvard Business Review, 90*(6), 76–84.

Ibarra, H. (1999). Provisional selves: Experimenting with image and identity in professional adaptation. *Administrative Science Quarterly, 44*(4), 764–791.

McKay, P. F., Avery, D. R., Toniandel, S., Morris, M. A., Hernandez, M., & Hebl, M. R. (2007). Racial differences in employee retention: Are diversity climate perceptions the key? *Personnel Psychology, 60*(1), 35–62.

Nishii, L. H. (2013). The benefits of climate for inclusion for gender-diverse groups. *Academy of Management Journal, 56*(6), 1754–1774.

Nishii, L. H., Khattab, J., Shemla, M., & Paluch, R. M. (2018). A multi-level process model for understanding diversity practice effectiveness. *Academy of Management Annals, 12*(1), 37–82.

Opie, T., & Roberts, L. M. (2017). Do black lives really matter in the workplace? Restorative justice as a means to reclaim humanity. *Equality, Diversity & Inclusion, 36*(8), 707–719.

Ospina, S., & Foldy, E. (2009). A critical review of race and ethnicity in the leadership literature: Surfacing context, power and the collective dimensions of leadership. *Leadership Quarterly, 20*(6), 876–896.

Phillips, K. W., Dumas, T. L., & Rothbard, N. P. (2018). Diversity and authenticity. *Harvard Business Review, 96*(2), 132–136.

Plaut, V. C. (2014). Diversity science and institutional design. *Policy Insights from the Behavioral and Brain Sciences, 1*(1), 72–80.

Purdie-Vaughns, V., Davies, P. G., Steele, C. M., Ditlmann, R., & Crosby, J. R. (2008). Social identity contingencies: How diversity cues signal threat or safety for African Americans in mainstream institutions. *Journal of Personality & Social Psychology, 94*(4), 615–630.

Roberts, L. M., & Creary, S. J. (2013). Navigating the self in diverse work contexts. In Q. M. Roberson (Ed.), *The Oxford handbook of diversity and work* (pp. 73–97). New York: Oxford University Press.

Roberts, L. M., & Roberts, D. D. (2007). Testing the limits of antidiscrimination law: The business, legal, and ethical ramifications of cultural profiling at work. *Duke Journal of Gender Law & Policy, 14*, 369–405.

Steele, C. M., Spencer, S. J., & Aronson, J. (2002). Contending with group image: The psychology of stereotype and social identity threat. In M. P. Zanna (Ed.), *Advances in experimental social psychology* (Vol. 34, pp. 379–440). San Diego, CA: Academic Press.

Thomas, D. A. (1989). Mentoring and irrationality: The role of racial taboos. *Human Resource Management, 28*(2), 279–290.

Thomas, D. A. (1993). Racial dynamics in cross-race developmental relationships. *Administrative Science Quarterly, 38*(2), 169–194.

Thomas, D. A., & Gabarro, J. J. (1999). *Breaking through: The making of minority executives in corporate America.* Boston, MA: Harvard Business School Press.

Vough, H. C., & Caza, B. B. (2017). Where do I go from here? Sensemaking and the construction of growth-based stories in the wake of denied promotions. *Academy of Management Review, 42*(1), 103–128.

Yeager, D. S., Purdie-Vaughns, V., Garcia, J., Apfel, N., Brzustoski, P., Master, A., . . . Cohen, G. L. (2014). Breaking the cycle of mistrust: Wise interventions to provide critical feedback across the racial divide. *Journal of Experimental Psychology. General, 143*(2), 804–824.

17

The Glass Cliff

African American CEOs as Crisis Leaders

LYNN PERRY WOOTEN *and* ERIKA HAYES JAMES

The presence of African American CEOs in *Fortune* 500 corporations has been described as "glacial"—a slow-moving change with limited progress (White, 2017). In 2001, when we began this millennium, Ken Chenault was appointed CEO of American Express, and throughout the next ten years other *Fortune* 500 companies appointed African American CEOs—Don Thompson at McDonald's, Ursula Burns at Xerox, Roger Ferguson at TIAA-CREF, Kenneth Frazier at Merck, and Marvin Ellison at JCPenney. Although African American CEOs held only 2 percent of *Fortune* 500 CEO positions, their appointments were considered an upward trend. By 2018, however, there appeared to be a halt to this slow but positive trajectory, with only three African American CEOs at *Fortune* 500 companies.

There are speculations about the causes of this trend, including entry barriers to the C-suite for minorities, corporate diversity polices shifting away from race, and the next generation of African American leaders opting out of the C-suite track and pursuing careers as entrepreneurs and in the nonprofit, educational, and government sectors. Why is this so? Could it be that the role of an African American CEO is perceived as a glass cliff—a risky or precarious leadership position that involves the management of organizations in crisis? If this is the case, are African Americans who are considering CEO positions deterred? And are corporate boards aware of the glass cliff phenomenon when appointing African American CEOs?

Previous research on the glass cliff has focused on occupational minorities, or women and people of color who are underrepresented in certain professions or job categories. In the case of women, some research has concluded that they are preferentially selected for leadership roles for organizations in crisis because of the perception that women have the attributes to manage these situations—being sympathetic, emotionally intelligent, understanding, and intuitive—and that these same attributes may be associated with ethnic minorities (Cook & Glass, 2013; Kulich, Ryan, & Haslam, 2014; Ryan, Haslam, Hersby, & Bongiorno, 2011). An alternative rationale for the appointment of women or ethnic minorities to lead crisis situations is that the organization wants to signal that it is in change or reinvention mode. For instance, this may be the case if white men have historically led the organization and it is now believed that a change to the demographic makeup of its leadership will signal a potential transformation (Bruckmüller & Branscombe, 2010).

A somewhat different perspective for the appointment of occupational minorities as leaders of crisis situations is the desire to protect white male leaders from extraordinarily difficult leadership positions or from being the scapegoat for a failed turnaround attempt. On the other hand, occupational minorities may be more willing to accept such leadership positions because of a fear that they will not be hired for leadership roles otherwise, as well as a belief that these jobs are an investment in their future career trajectory (Collins, 1997; Ryan & Haslam, 2007). In these situations, occupational minorities are expected to be "saviors," yet often they have limited social capital, significant resource constraints, unrealistic performance expectations, and considerable visibility, and therefore pressure to succeed (Oelbaum, 2016; Staw, Sandelands, & Dutton, 1981). Moreover, key stakeholders (e.g., members of the board of directors) are often impatient with leadership during crisis situations and expect quick results that may not be feasible to achieve in a short-time frame.

In recent years, numerous articles have been written about the glass cliff. Yet we know little about this phenomenon as it relates to African American leaders in the corporate world. Our study addresses this gap in the literature by exploring the experiences of African American CEOs in *Fortune* 1000 corporations. In particular, we sought to understand the extent to which African American CEOs were appointed to positions that involved leading organizations in crises, characterize the leadership strategies employed during their tenure as CEO, and depict how stakeholders responded to the leadership of these executives.

Research Methodology

As in our previous research in crisis leadership, we used a multiple-case-study methodology to understand the experiences of African American CEOs (James & Wooten, 2006; Wooten & James, 2008). As summarized in table 17-1, the sample comprises seventeen African American CEOs of major corporations who have been featured in the press, including *Black Enterprise, Bloomberg Business, Fortune*, and the *Wall Street Journal*. The average tenure of the African American CEOs in our sample is 6.5 years; by contrast, according to an Equilar study (2017), the average tenure for CEOs in Standard & Poor's companies is 7.2 years.

For our database of articles, Clifton Wharton Jr. was noted as the first CEO of a *Fortune* 500 company when his appointment began in 1987 for TIAA-CREF. Surprisingly, the sample only has one woman, Ursula Burns. But other African American women have served as corporate division presidents and CEOs of smaller companies, including Rosalind Brewer, former head of Walmart's Sam's Club and now chief operating officer of Starbucks; Debra Lee, chairman and CEO of Viacom's BET (Black Entertainment Television) unit; Stacy Brown Philpot, CEO of TaskRabbit; and Channing Dungey, president of ABC, a division of Disney (La Monica, 2017; Zarya, 2017).

For each CEO, secondary qualitative data was collected from the business press to create a case study. We acknowledge that the archival data used to create the case studies has inherent biases because it is information that was shared with the media. These narratives do, however, represent the formal documentation, perceptions of stakeholders, and primary source for communicating with external constituents about the CEOs in our sample (Altheide, 1996; Forster, 1994).

To develop the case study for each CEO, we coded the business articles to look at three time periods: (1) the press release for his or her appointment as CEO and the experiences brought to the role; (2) the tenure as CEO and associated leadership actions, especially as they relate to crisis management; and (3) if the CEO was no longer in the role, the rationale for the resignation. In addition to focusing on the CEO's

TABLE 17-1

Sample of African American CEOs

Name of CEO	Company	Hiring status	Tenure as CEO
1. Ursula Burns	Xerox	Internal	2009–2016
2. Kenneth Chenault	American Express	Internal	2001–2018
3. Arnold Donald	Carnival Cruise	External (but served on Carnival Cruise's board of directors)	2013–present
4. Marvin Ellison	JCPenney	External	2014–2018
5. Roger Ferguson	TIAA-CREF	Internal	2008–present
6. Kenneth Frazier	Merck	External	2011–present
7. Aylwin Lewis	Sears/Kmart	External	2004–2008
8. Ernest Stanley O'Neal	Merrill Lynch	Internal	2002–2007
9. Rodney O'Neal	Delphi	Internal	2007–2014
10. Clarence Otis	Darden Restaurants	Internal	2004–2014
11. Richard Parsons	AOL Time Warner	Internal	2002–2007
12. Franklin Raines	Fannie Mae	External (but previously served as vice-chairman)	1999–2004
13. Don Thompson	McDonald's	Internal	2012–2015
14. John Thompson	Symantec	Internal	1999–2009
15. Lloyd Ward	Maytag	External	1999–2000
16. Clifton Wharton Jr.	TIAA-CREF	External	1987–1993
17. Ronald Williams	Aetna	Internal	2006–2011

leadership journey, the case studies took into account the macroenvironment and industry dynamics so that we could understand the firm's ecosystem and how the CEO responded to it. Using a temporal approach for the case studies enabled us to take a long-term view of the glass cliff phenomenon for analyzing leadership behaviors and responses to external pressures (Langley, 1999; Miles & Huberman, 1994). In addition to analyzing case study data for each CEO, we conducted cross-case analysis to synthesize patterns of behaviors across cases. Table 17-2 summarizes this data.

TABLE 17-2

Summary of CEO's glass cliff situation

CEO	Glass cliff situation	Strategic responses	Departure description
1. Ursula Burns, Xerox	Declining revenues; threat of bankruptcy; economic downturn; technological change	Shifted Xerox's focus from products to services and oversaw the acquisition of Affiliated Computer Services	Retirement
2. Kenneth Chenault, American Express	September 11 terrorist attack; 2008 financial crisis; losing Costco as a customer	Engineered a turnaround plan; demonstrated agility and improvisation and oversaw relocation strategy post-9/11; navigated financial crisis through participation in and early repayment of federal government bank bailout program	Retirement
3. Arnold Donald, Carnival Cruise	Viral outbreak on cruise ship; capsizing of cruise ships	Enhanced brand reputation; focused on innovative services and experiences; built consumer trust; managed safety concerns	*Currently serving as CEO*
4. Marvin Ellison, JCPenney	Management turmoil; declining revenues and significant loss of market share	Led turnaround strategy to boost performance, including e-commerce and a focus on private labels	Appointed president and CEO of Lowe's
5. Roger Ferguson, TIAA-CREF	Stock market volatility and its impact on retirement accounts	Diversified customer base; weathered financial crisis without participation in the government-sponsored financial bailout program	*Currently serving as CEO*
6. Kenneth Frazier, Merck	Integration of acquisitions; product withdrawals	Built product pipeline	*Currently serving as CEO*

(continued)

TABLE 17-2 (continued)

CEO	Glass cliff situation	Strategic responses	Departure description
7. Aylwin Lewis, Sears/Kmart	Declining revenues; store closings; merger integration	Completed corporate restructuring; shifted merchandizing and market strategy	Abrupt announcement of departure, then served as Potbelly's CEO
8. Ernest Stanley O'Neal, Merrill Lynch	Market downturn; largest-ever quarterly loss	Reinforced performance-driven strategy that put greater emphasis on riskier bets	Early retirement after the firm reported a $7.9 billion quarterly write-down because of aggressive bets in mortgage-related securities
9. Rodney O'Neal, Delphi	Bankruptcy	Diversified Delphi's client base; led Delphi out of bankruptcy; cut expenses; streamlined and focused product line; invested in emerging markets	Retirement
10. Clarence Otis, Darden Restaurants	Debt; declining sales of restaurants; changing consumer food preferences	Orchestrated divestures to reconfigure and expand restaurant portfolio; invested in product innovation	Resigned after two years of declining profits and investor pressures
11. Richard Parsons, AOL Time Warner	Massive losses and sharply decreasing stock value after Time Warner merged with AOL	Led strategic, financial, and operational initiatives	Retirement
12. Franklin Raines, Fannie Mae	Attacked by both industry rivals and government officials (critics of the foray into home equity financing and subprime mortgage lending) and for Fannie Mae's accounting irregularities	Accounting irregularities were investigated by the Securities and Exchange Commission; Raines paid $24.7 million as a settlement for the civil lawsuit associated with the irregularities	Early retirement

(continued)

TABLE 17-2 (continued)

CEO	Glass cliff situation	Strategic responses	Departure description
13. Don Thompson, McDonald's	Declining performance; movement toward health foods; competition from fast-casual restaurants; charged with "mak[ing] the Golden Arches golden again"	Led McDonald's digital initiatives and efforts to boost menu innovation	Resigned during a cycle of declining revenues
14. John Thompson, Symantec	Challenged to strengthen Symantec's leadership in three key areas: meeting customers' needs, executing a leading digital strategy, and maintaining strong financial health and return on investment for shareholders	Transformed the company from a consumer software publisher to the leader in internet security, data protection, and storage management; diversified Symantec's customer base; grew revenue tenfold	Retirement
15. Lloyd Ward, Maytag	Losing market share	Brought a new set of expectations and a different approach to brand development	Resigned as chairman and CEO, citing a difference of opinion with the board of directors over the company's strategic outlook and direction
16. Clifton Wharton Jr., TIAA-CREF	Competitive and consumer pressures for product diversification, innovation, and restructuring	Formulated and implemented a strategic plan for product diversification and realigned the organization to focus on customer service and accountability centers	President Bill Clinton named Wharton deputy secretary of state
17. Ronald Williams, Aetna	Loss from continuing operation	Turned a struggling organization into an industry leader, transforming the company's strategy, culture, operating performance, and financial results	Retirement

Crisis Leadership as (Un)usual Business for African American CEOs

From our case studies, several patterns emerged that we believe shed light on the glass cliff experiences of African American CEOs. As discussed earlier in this chapter, the core tenet of the glass cliff phenomenon centers on the idea that occupational minorities are more likely to reach positions of power in precarious circumstances associated with crises or periods of instability (Kulich & Ryan, 2017). It should be noted, though, that in the management literature, there are a wide range of definitions for what is considered a crisis. Our previous research has defined a business crisis as "a rare and significant situation that has the potential to become public and bring about highly undesirable outcomes for the firm and its stakeholders" (James & Wooten, 2010, p. 17).

In addition, we have reviewed several typologies for classifying crises, and in our research, we have used language adopted from the Institute of Crisis Management, a crisis consulting and research firm. The institute has identified two types of crisis situations: sudden crises and smoldering crises (Irvine, 1997). Sudden crises are unexpected events over which the organization has virtually no control and for which it is perceived to have limited fault or responsibility. Sudden crises usually disrupt operations of the business for some time. In contrast, smoldering crises are business problems that begin as small, internal problems within an organization and escalate over time because of management inattention.

Interestingly, our analysis revealed that the appointments of African American CEOs were not explicitly related to "traditional" notions of crises, such as sudden natural disasters or catastrophic events, or smoldering crises such as fraud, labor disputes, or lawsuits. Instead, their appointments were linked to what may be considered a need for the management of strategic crisis, organizational change, corporate turnaround, or industry disrupters. Likewise, for some of the CEOs in our sample, leading in a permanent state of crisis appeared to be their assignments (Heifetz, Grashow, & Linksy, 2009). These sustained crises involved cycles of stabilizing the situation and adjusting the firm's strategy so that it had the capacity to thrive in its new reality. This skill set entails the ability to have an open-system perspective that understands both a firm's internal and external environments and develop adaptive strategies that improve the firm's alignment and, ultimately, performance

(Nadler & Tushman, 1989; Preble, 1997). Hence, the involvement of a dynamic CEO is a necessity as the firm devises routines for strategizing for opportunities and threats because of the firm's need for direction, visionary thinking, and balancing the competing demands of stakeholder groups (Wooten & James, 2014).

Preparing for the CEO Role as Crisis Leader

The CEOs in our sample did not appear to be naively taking their appointments as leaders who were expected to manage a crisis. Instead, they engaged in actions to prepare for their role as crisis leader, and press releases acknowledged that their skills and previous experiences were viewed as assets for resolving a crisis situation or turning around a company. For CEOs who were internal appointments, their preparation work was on-the-job training. This was the case for Ursula Burns. Before becoming CEO, Burns served in the role of president of Xerox, and she and her predecessor, Anne Mulcahy, were described as a dynamic duo who "worked together like combat soldiers in the same foxhole" (Morris, 2007). As the dynamic duo, Burns and Mulcahy reduced debt, produced technology disrupters such as a cost-efficient color printer, and negotiated with company unions to reduce thousands of jobs (Morris, 2007; Zarrolli, 2009). Similar to Burns, Richard Parsons, former CEO of AOL Time Warner, was handpicked by his predecessor, Gerald Levin, to make a merger of an old-line company and online media company work during an economic downturn (Dwyer & Schiesel, 2001). In preparing for this role, Parsons not only served as co–chief operating officer but was also a previous director of Time Warner. While serving as co–chief operating officer, Parsons became known as an indispensable problem solver with an unwavering killer instinct and relentless drive for winning (Bianco & Lowry, 2003).

In contrast to internal appointments for the CEO role, for external appointments the crisis management preparation work was rooted in the expertise the executive would bring into the company to improve the situation. For example, when Marvin Ellison was appointed CEO of JCPenney, he was brought in to clean up an unsuccessful overhaul by former CEO Ron Johnson (Wahba, 2016). Johnson came from Apple and attempted to reposition JCPenney as a hipper retailer, but this had negative financial consequences. The board was willing to take a chance with Ellison, who had led the US operations for Home Depot and thus had retail experience, albeit in a very different segment of the industry (Mc-Intyre, 2017). Even so, he had previously addressed a crisis of lagging sales and low morale and, having partnered with Home Depot's CEO, was credited with fixing customer satisfaction ratings and propelling the company into the world of e-commerce. To build on his Home Depot experience and to prepare for the CEO role at JCPenney, Ellison spent nine months serving as president under Myron E. Ullman III, who was JCPenney's CEO at the time of Ellison's appointment. The two conducted town halls and visited vendors and partners so that Ellison could have a crash course in areas that differed from Home Depot's, such as apparel factories and merchandising.

Ellison's tenure at JCPenney's was a brief four years, among the shortest tenures in our sample. It is worth noting that at the time of this writing, Ellison has been appointed CEO of Home Depot's largest competitor, Lowe's, whose stock performance continues to lag significantly behind Home Depot's. This new executive appointment will put Ellison squarely back in an industry for which he had substantial preparation, given his earlier, twelve-year tenure at Home Depot.

Leading under Pressure

Beyond preparing for their roles as crisis leaders, the African American CEOs in our study perceived the work of managing crises and unstable situations as not an unusual assignment but rather their responsibility. For example, when Clifton Wharton Jr. was CEO of TIAA-CREF, he knew that he was perceived as a crisis manager hired to turn around the company after the 1987 stock market crash. The risk of Wharton's glass cliff assignment was portrayed in a *New York Times* cartoon that showed him walking a tightrope across Wall Street and carrying a safe with TIAA-CREF's spilling currency (Davis, 1988). Yet he was able to use the administrative skills he learned from managing universities and serving on corporate boards to redesign the organization, with a focus on developing human capital and customer service, formulate a strategic plan, and restructure TIAA-CREF's pension funds (Useem, 1998).

Analogous to Wharton's experience, other African American CEOs often faced extreme pressures during their tenures to engage in frame-bending behaviors to save or reorient the firm (Nadler & Tushman, 1989). These pressures required organizational agility and the ability to perceive the crisis as an opportunity (James & Wooten, 2010; Wooten & James, 2008). Organizational agility entails having a comprehensive and thorough knowledge of all aspects of the business and the capacity to efficiently mobilize resources and functions to accomplish a goal or solve a problem.

American Express CEO Kenneth Chenault acknowledged that several times during his tenure, he had to demonstrate organizational agility to manage a crisis (Sweet, 2018). For example, early on, Chenault experienced a sudden crisis when the September 11 terrorist attacks occurred in 2001: American Express's corporate headquarters was damaged and the firm lost eleven employees. Without a headquarters, Chenault had to lead the improvisation of relocating operations to various sites in New York, New Jersey, and Connecticut while demonstrating compassion, effectively communicating the context for the firm's actions, and showing concern for stakeholders (Colvin, 2009).

In addition to responding to the terrorist attacks, Chenault led American Express through the 2008 financial crisis, when the company experienced substantial losses in its consumer credit card business, and he managed yet another crisis in 2015 when Costco ended exclusive use of American Express in its stores (Sweet, 2018). As a consequence of the 2008 financial crisis, American Express received $3.4 billion of funds from the US government bank bailout program, but it was able to repay those funds in less than a year. Costco's business with American Express represented 8 percent of spending for American Express cardholders and 20 percent of the firm's loans. Yet by marketing to Costco customers, American Express was able to persuade many of them to switch to a new version of its credit card even though it was not cobranded with Costco.

Rodney O'Neal, former CEO of Delphi, is another example of a CEO in our sample who inherited a crisis and is credited with resolving it and then reinvigorating the organization. Delphi is a spin-off of General Motors' auto parts subsidiary. O'Neal was appointed as CEO of Delphi in 2007, two years after the company filed bankruptcy, and he committed to financial and strategic actions that would transform the organization (Snavely, 2015). Restructuring pension plans and receiving the aid of investor groups enabled Delphi to emerge from bankruptcy. O'Neal asserts that the turnaround required visionary thinking and the ability to see possibilities and seize opportunities relating to sustainability, technological innovations, and the global marketplace.

Personal Resilience and Reinvention

An assumption of the glass cliff theory is that when occupational minorities are placed in the upper echelon of organizations, their assignments are risky and will be detrimental to their professional development and advancement. Furthermore, if they are not successful in the role, it will reinforce the stereotype that minorities lack the competence required to succeed as CEOs (Bruckmüller & Branscombe, 2010; Rudman & Glick, 2001; Tran, 2015). Thus, when examining our data, we sought to understand whether the CEO had a short tenure or a controversial departure from the role and, if so, how it was perceived and how it affected the person's career. We observed that the narrative for exiting glass cliff assignments varied, but the CEOs in this study used their glass cliff experiences as a bridge to another act in their careers. Put simply, they demonstrated resilience—the ability to bounce back from adversity, repair oneself, and, in some cases, thrive by having a growth mindset and going beyond the original level of functioning (Ledesma, 2014).

The retirement of McDonald's former CEO Don Thompson is an example of a contentious departure. He was blamed for an array of the fast-food chain's problems: decline in sales, confusing menus, not responding to health food trends, fast food's role in childhood obesity, and the underpayment of employees (Brown, 2015). Yet industry analysts noted that Thompson was appointed during a challenging time when traditional restaurants were learning how to compete with fast-casual restaurants like Chipotle, Five Guys, and Shake Shack, and McDonald's leadership team was counting on its past successes and was not nimble enough to change (O'Conner, 2015). After retiring from McDonald's, Thompson leveraged his previous experience to start Cleveland Avenue, a food-focused venture fund (Pletz, 2018). This fund has invested in ZeroCater, which features an online portal for providing lunches to businesses, and Beyond Meat, a company that is developing a plant-based substitute for meat.

Conclusion

It is fair to say that in today's environment, chief executives across all industries and of all demographic backgrounds are finding themselves needing to leverage (or acquire) crisis management skills to do their jobs. The economic, political, and competitive landscape means that no executive, and no organization, is immune from challenge and disruption. In this regard, the astute executive knowingly enters into a C-suite appointment aware that his or her tenure will likely not be characterized by stable leadership; rather, he or she will inevitably face challenges that could ultimately threaten their executive legacy and career. Although we cannot know for certain, nor in totality, the motives for CEO appointments, it is noteworthy that women are seemingly tapped for glass cliff appointments disproportionately more than their white male counterparts. Whether they are simply deemed to be more skilled at managing crisis than men, or whether they are tapped to be the scapegoat for challenged organizations, thereby protecting the prototypical CEO, is inconclusive.

In the first decade of the twenty-first century, more African Americans were appointed to CEO roles than in any other time in history. Although the overall numbers are still small, their appointments appear to follow a similar pattern: they are seemingly tapped for glass cliff CEO assignments disproportionately more than are white executives. This chapter provides a preliminary case study examination of the African American CEOs appointed since 1987. We sought to understand the circumstances of their appointment, their preparation for the role, and their leadership approach while serving as CEO. In short, our look at African American CEOs offers an enhanced understanding of the glass cliff—who steps onto it, why, and to what end.

In our research, we observed that the executives who accepted the CEO challenge did so knowing the personal risks they faced: being blamed or scapegoated for failure, losing status, or interrupting a career track with a premature termination before a crisis is resolved. These outcomes for African Americans are often assumed to be more likely than would be the case for their white counterparts because the likelihood of the latter's being tapped for similar appointments is dauntingly small. In one industry typically dominated by white leaders, professional sports, there is evidence to suggest that compared with whites, African American NFL coaches are less likely to be hired as head coaches (Wolfe, 2017) and more likely to be fired, even when they have a winning record (Berri, 2018). There may be reason to believe that the same is true for African American CEOs, but the sample is yet too small to make such suppositions. That said, when tapped to lead, the executives in our sample took up the mantle despite the risks. And most had meaningful tenures in their role.

One conclusion from this initial examination may be that African American executives see not just risk but also opportunity in crisis—opportunity for their companies and, as important, opportunity for themselves. Recognizing that C-suite appointments are, in fact, rare opportunities, they seize them even if the circumstances of the organizations they will lead are far from ideal. Further and comparative exploration of the propensity for personal risk, or perhaps exploration of the psychological characteristics of executives, is warranted. Are African Americans more willing or more comfortable with risk and ambiguity, the features that define glass cliff opportunities, than their white counterparts? Or do they score differently from whites on key personality dimensions such as openness (preference for novelty and variety) and neuroticism (ability to respond to stress or threatening situations) from the Big Five personality traits? Addressing these and related questions is beyond the scope of this chapter, but we believe it would be a worthwhile extension of the research.

Finally, the executives in our sample demonstrated organizational agility—thorough knowledge of the business and an ability to muster the resources required—which they sometimes tried to reinforce before stepping into a crisis leadership role. Resiliency was a common theme, evident both during their tenure and after it ended. Often, they leveraged the results of their turnaround—its success or failure—into a new opportunity. Ellison's recent appointment to lead Lowe's is noteworthy here. All these executives, it seemed, stepped onto the glass cliff of crisis leadership fully aware of how far there was to fall and with the strength to rebound. For those who seek or are pursuing a leadership career in the corporate world, we caution that one must be fully aware of the risks and opportunities such career trajectories can create. These roles are not for the faint of heart. Clearly, the more organizational and leadership experience one has, and the more diverse it is, the more prepared one will be to lead. This is particularly germane counsel given that those new to the middle-management ranks are demonstrating a desire for more authority and autonomy in their roles earlier in their career than has been true of previous generations of leaders. Failure to understand fully the scope of large and complex organizations before assuming significant positions of leadership may make one an undesirable leadership candidate and an unsuccessful CEO.

REFERENCES

Altheide, D. (1996). *Qualitative media analysis.* Thousand Oaks, CA: Sage.

Berri, D. (2018, January 2). Black NFL coaches appear much more likely to be fired with a winning record. *Forbes.* Retrieved from https://www.forbes.com/sites /davidberri/2018/01/02/black-head-coaches-in-the-nfl-are-much-more-likely-to -be-fired-with-a-winning-record/#6e9afcdc1cb8

Bianco, A., & Lowry, T. (2003, May 19). Can Dick Parsons rescue AOL Time Warner? *Business Week,* pp. 87–96.

Brown, E. (2015, February 10). How McDonald's Don Thompson could have saved his job. *Fortune.* Retrieved from http://fortune.com/2015/02/10/how-mcdonalds -don-thompson-could-have-saved-his-job/

Bruckmüller, S., & Branscombe, N. R. (2010). The glass cliff: When and why women are selected as leaders in crisis contexts. *British Journal of Social Psychology, 49,* 433–451.

Collins, S. (1997). Black mobility in white corporations: Up the corporate ladder but out on a limb. *Social Problems, 44*(1): 55–67.

Colvin, G. (2009, October 15). Crisis chief: AmEx's Chenault. Special Report, Fortune C-Suite Strategies. Retrieved from http://archive.fortune.com/2009/10/14 /news/companies/american_express_chenault.fortune/index.htm

Cook, A., & Glass, C. (2013). Glass cliffs and organizational saviors. *Social Problems, 60,* 168–187.

Davis, L. (1988, March 27). Precious cargo: The $60 billion challenge: Clifton Wharton struggles to preserve a pension fund. Business World, *New York Times.* Retrieved from https://www.nytimes.com/1988/03/27/magazine/article-082388 -no-title.html

Dwyer, J., & Schiesel, S. (2001, December 9). New boss for a media giant is an old hand at New York. *New York Times.* Retrieved from https://www.nytimes.com /2001/12/09/nyregion/new-boss-for-a-media-giant-is-an-old-hand-at-new-york .html

Equilar. (2018, January 19). CEO tenure drops to just five years. Retrieved from https://www.equilar.com/blogs/351-ceo-tenure-drops-to-five-years.html

Forster, N. (1994). The analysis of company documentation. In C. Cassell & G. Symon (Eds.), *Qualitative methods in organizational research: A practical guide* (pp. 147–160). London, England: Sage.

Heifetz, R., Grashow, A., & Linsky, M. (2009, July–August). Leadership in a (permanent) crisis. *Harvard Business Review,* 62–69.

Irvine, R. B. (1997, July 15). What's a crisis, anyway? *Communication World.*

James, E., & Wooten, L. (2006). Diversity crises: How firms manage discrimination lawsuits. *Academy of Management Journal, 49*(6), 1103–1118.

James, E., & Wooten, L. (2010). *Leading under pressure: From surviving to thriving before, during, and after a crisis.* New York, NY: Routledge Academic Press.

Kulich, C., & Ryan, M. (2017). The glass cliff. In *Oxford research encyclopedia of business and management.* Retrieved from http://business.oxfordre.com/view/10.1093 /acrefore/9780190224851.001.0001/acrefore-9780190224851-e-42

Kulich, C., Ryan, M. K., & Haslam, A. S. (2014). The political glass cliff: Understanding how seat selection contributes to the under-performance of ethnic minority candidates. *Political Research Quarterly, 67,* 84–95.

La Monica, P. (2017, September 6). Starbuck names Rosalind Brewer new COO. Retrieved from http://money.cnn.com/2017/09/06/investing/starbucks-rosalind-brewer-coo-walmart-sams-club/index.html

Langley, A. (1999). Strategies for theorizing from process data. *Academy of Management Journal, 24*(4), 691–710.

Ledesma, J. (2014, July–September). Conceptual frameworks and research models on resilience in leadership. *SAGE Open, 4*(3), 1–8.

McIntyre, D. (2017, November 5). After 2-year tenure, JC Penny CEO Marvin Ellison needs to leave. *24/7 Wall Street*. Retrieved from https://finance.yahoo.com/news/two-tenure-j-c-penney-121134935.html

Miles, M. B., & Huberman, A. M. (1994). *Qualitative data analysis*. Beverly Hills, CA: Sage.

Morris, B. (2007, November 19). Xerox's dynamic duo. *Fortune*. Retrieved from http://archive.fortune.com/magazines/fortune/fortune_archive/2007/10/15/100536857/index.htm

Nadler, D., & Tushman, M. (1989). Organizational frame bending: Principles for managing reorientation. *Academy of Management Executive (1987–1989), 3*(3), 194–204.

O'Conner, C. (2015, January 30). What McDonald's must fix after CEO Don Thompson ouster. *Forbes*. Retrieved from https://www.forbes.com/sites/clareoconnor/2015/01/30/what-mcdonalds-must-fix-after-ceo-don-thompson-ouster/#22650b84196a

Oelbaum, Y. (2016). *Understanding the glass cliff effect: Why are female leaders being pushed toward the edge?* (Unpublished doctoral dissertation). The Graduate Center, City University of New York.

Pletz, J. (2018, October 12). Why big food is startup shopping in Chicago. *Crain's Chicago Business*. Retrieved from https://www.chicagobusiness.com/john-pletz-technology/why-big-food-startup-shopping-chicago

Preble, J. (1997). Integrating crisis management perspective into the strategic management process. *Journal of Management Studies, 34*(5), 769–791.

Rudman, L. A., & Glick, P. (2001). Prescriptive gender stereotypes and backlash toward agentic women. *Journal of Social Issues, 57*, 732–762.

Ryan, M. K., & Haslam, S. A. (2007). The glass cliff: Exploring the dynamics surrounding women's appointment to precarious leadership positions. *Academy of Management Review, 32*, 549–572.

Ryan, M. K., Haslam, S. A., Hersby, M. D., & Bongiorno, R. (2011). Think crisis–think female: The glass cliff and contextual variation in the think manager–think male stereotype. *Journal of Applied Psychology, 96*(3), 470–484.

Snavely, B. (2015, March 1). Rodney O'Neal transformed Delphi, regrets pension cuts. *Detroit Free Press*. Retrieved from https://www.freep.com/story/money/business/michigan/2015/03/01/rodney-oneal-delphi-turnaround-retire-pensions/24156921/

Staw, B., Sandelands, L., & Dutton, J. (1981). Threat rigidity effects in organizational behavior: A multilevel analysis. *Administrative Science Quarterly, 26*(4), 501–524.

Sweet, K. (2018, February 19). Q&A: Ken Chenault former CEO of American Express. Associated Press. Retrieved from https://www.usatoday.com/story/money/business/2018/02/19/q-ken-chenault-former-ceo-american-express/350582002/

Tran, N. M. (2015). Who's on the executive glass cliff? Using policy capturing to examine race, gender, and leadership in times of crisis. Presented at the Equality, Diversity and Inclusion International Conference, Tel Aviv, Israel. Retrieved from https://getd.libs.uga.edu/pdfs/tran_ny_m_201505_phd.pdf

Useem, M. (1998). *The leadership moment: Nine true stories of triumph and disaster and their lessons for us all.* New York, NY: Random House.

Wahba, P. (2011, August 11). J.C. Penney shares hit all-time low as turnaround fails. *Fortune.* Retrieved from http://fortune.com/2017/08/11/jcpenney-shares-2/.

White, G. (2017, October 26). There are currently 4 black CEOs in the *Fortune* 500. *The Atlantic.* Retrieved from https://www.theatlantic.com/business/archive/2017/10/black-ceos-fortune-500/543960/

Wolfe, C. (2017, September 11). Climbing a slippery mountain: Why NFL's black offensive coaches struggle to become a head coach, coordinator. *Denver Post.* Retrieved from https://www.denverpost.com/2017/09/11/nfl-black-coaches/

Wooten, L., & James, E. (2008). Linking crisis management and leadership competencies: The role of human resource development. *Advances in Human Resource Management Development, 10*(3), 352–379.

Wooten, L., & James, E. (2014). Creating opportunities from crisis. In J. Dutton & G. Spreitzer (Eds.), *How to be a positive leader: Insights from leading thinkers on positive organizations* (pp. 147–156). San Francisco, CA: Berrett-Koehler.

Zarrolli, J. (2009, May 22). Ursula Burns to succeed Mulcahy as Xerox CEO. National Public Radio. Retrieved from https://www.npr.org/templates/story/story.php?storyId=104426582

Zarya, V. (2017, January 16). Why there are no black women running *Fortune* 500 companies. *Fortune.* Retrieved from http://fortune.com/2017/01/16/black-women-fortune-500/

When Black Leaders Leave

Costs and Consequences

KECIA THOMAS, ASPEN J. ROBINSON,
LAURA PROVOLT, *and* B. LINDSAY BROWN

Frequently, diversity research within the management domain emerges out of the "case for diversity" that focuses on its many organizational benefits. In contrast, the current chapter focuses on the individual, organizational, and societal costs of diversity loss—specifically, when Black leaders leave. The chapter begins with a brief review of what we know about Black leaders today. Next, we'll turn to the reasons why Black leaders leave. The majority of the chapter will subsequently focus on the costs and consequences of Black leader loss—namely, for themselves, for minority followers, and for organizations more broadly. We conclude with recommendations for the support of Black leaders and the many benefits they provide to their organizations and communities.

Status of Black Leadership Today

Black leadership has been severely underrepresented across several domains within the United States, including the workplace, education, and government. White and Black employees make up 78 percent and 12 percent of the overall labor force within the United States, respectively. However, Whites make up 84 percent of all management occupations, while only 7.5 percent of these managers are Black (Bureau of Labor Statistics, 2016). The Bureau of Labor Statistics also reported that this disparity becomes even greater at the executive level, where 88 percent of all CEOs are White and 3 percent are Black. As of 2017, less than 1 percent of all *Fortune* 500 CEOs are Black. More specifically, there are only four Black male CEOs and no Black female CEOs in the *Fortune* 500 (McGirt, 2017). In fact, there have only been fifteen Black CEOs during the *Fortune* 500's life-span of sixty-two years, only one of whom was a woman. Black leaders below the top level do not fare much better, as Black men and women form approximately 4.7 percent of executive team members in the *Fortune* 100 and 6.7 percent of the 16.2 million managerial-level jobs (McGirt, 2016). Not surprisingly, only about 10 percent of businesses are owned by Black men and women (McManus, 2016), some of whom may have opted for entrepreneurship rather than navigating a biased leadership pipeline.

Within academia, Black faculty are underrepresented at all levels, where only 7 percent of all postsecondary teachers are Black (Bureau of Labor Statistics, 2016) and only 4 percent of full professors are Black (McFarland et al., 2017). Although the recent 115th Congress had a record number of African Americans, they make up only 9 percent of voting members of the House and Senate (Brudnick & Manning, 2018), and historically Blacks have only served as leaders in the House. Despite our awareness of the disparities and hurdles that characterize Black leadership experiences, significant gaps remain in our understanding and practice with respect to race and leadership in organizations. Examination of the factors contributing to why Black leaders leave, and what organizations can do to prevent this, is important for the development of workplace practices that will better support these employees, as well as for the development of more scholarship that critically examines current organizational theory and literature on race and leadership.

Why Black Leaders Leave

Previous research has shown racial differences in voluntary turnover or turnover intentions suggesting that Black employees and leaders are more likely to leave an organization than their White counterparts. Differences in experienced or perceived racial discrimination, as well as in perceptions of organizational diversity climates, may explain differences in voluntary turnover between White and Black leaders. Chrobot-Mason (2013) found that White employees were less likely to be aware of ambient racial discrimination than Black employees, and these perceptions positively predicted turnover intentions. A cross-sectional study consisting of 529 practicing physicians in the United States found that Black doctors reported the most workplace discrimination compared with other ethnic groups, and these discriminatory experiences significantly predicted voluntary turnover (Nunez-Smith, Pilgrim, Wynia, Desai, & Bright, 2009). Finally, in their large-scale study of race and employee retention, McKay and colleagues (2007) found that organizational commitment mediated the relationship between diversity climate perceptions and turnover intentions. More specifically, positive diversity climate perceptions predicted higher organizational commitment, which in turn predicted lower turnover intentions. The authors also found that a manager's race significantly moderated these relationships; these effects were found to be stronger for Black managers than White or Hispanic managers.

We must admit that like all leaders, some Black leaders leave their organizations out of a desire to do something new and to conquer bigger or different challenges. However, we also recognize the possibility that the expectations, norms, and cultural default of leadership might contribute to an environment that makes it difficult for Black leaders to thrive. This type of environment may serve as a motivating factor for the leader to find greener pastures.

For example, the prototype of leaders as being White males (e.g., Koenig & Eagly, 2014) presents a pervasive barrier to any non-White and nonmale high-potential person attempting to move up the ladder to leadership and executive positions. The career trajectory for high-performing and high-potential Black workers can be suppressed by systematic biases in job assignment (Pager, Western, & Bonikowski, 2009), performance appraisal (Stauffer & Buckley, 2005), and advancement (Baldi & McBrier, 1997). Additionally, some argue that the pipeline to leadership often rewards dominant, narcissistic, aggressive, and manipulative behaviors (Campbell, Hoffman, Campbell, & Marchisio, 2011), which may be perceived as acceptable traits for a White male but threatening and unprofessional if displayed by someone who does not fit the White male leader prototype (e.g., a person of color; Neubert & Taggar, 2004). Scholars support this argument by highlighting some organizations' tendencies to embrace and favor Black male managers who have a disarming quality about them, referred to as the teddy-bear effect (Livingston & Pearce, 2009).

Black women, who are often the least represented in positions of leadership, are also subject to bias and are left to navigate what are called "pet" and "threat" states (K. M. Thomas, Johnson-Bailey, Phelps, Tran, &

Johnson, 2013). Black women in the early stages of their careers, and who may be seen as token Blacks in their workplaces, often experience treatment that undermines their position as competent professionals. They are instead treated as pets, heavily monitored and looked after by higher-status majority-group members in the organization. When Black employees do transition into some managerial role, they are then perceived as less professional (Block, Aumann, & Chelin, 2012) and less effective. They are also perceived to have less potential for leadership opportunities than White managers (Rosette, Leonardelli, & Phillips, 2008). These assumptions, and the pet treatment that follows, may prevent high-performing Black leaders from receiving opportunities for growth that would otherwise be granted to those identified as potential future executives. The absence of such professional development opportunities, and the bias it indicates, could result in the turnover of Black leaders, who opt to either reside in organizations that value their contributions or pursue entrepreneurial endeavors.

Black women who reject or shed this pet identity and make the decision to remain in their organization are then likely to be perceived as threatening. This perception causes the individual to face hostility and distancing behaviors from coworkers, responses to the striking evidence of a Black woman's success and competence in an environment operating under a clear status quo (K. M. Thomas et al., 2013). Thus, traits that are typically revered, such as resilience and perseverance through hardship, can backfire for Black women. In this instance, these characteristics are viewed as a threat and may welcome even greater instances of isolation and resistance from colleagues (K. M. Thomas et al., 2013).

In sum, Blacks in today's workplace toe the line in order to be perceived as leaders, with certain constraints imposed on them due to prescribed characteristics of leadership and restrictions on who is to be a leader. When that line is crossed, the Black leader is left to operate under conditions that stifle success and productivity. He or she must then grapple with the idea of, yet again, moving on.

Consequences for Black Leaders

Temporary unemployment often has a substantial impact on career trajectory and success that lasts decades after the period of unemployment, even for highly credentialed executives who are expected to make continuous career advances (Reitman & Schneer, 2005). This is partially due to the loss in human capital accumulation, particularly when the employment gap takes place early in one's career (Judiesch & Lyness, 1999). Human capital theory, which reflects the overall accumulation of job knowledge, skills, and social networks, indicates that human capital builds with age and experience (Bryant, Jeon-Slaughter, Kang, & Tax, 2003; Wilson & Musick, 1997). Indeed, the longer the gap in employment, and the subsequent erosion of human capital, the greater the resistance one may encounter to reentry. For example, researchers in one study sent out twelve thousand fictitious resumes in response to job openings and compared the rate of callbacks for applicants with varying terms of unemployment ranging from one to thirty-six months. Applicants who had been unemployed for eight months or more received substantially fewer callbacks than those with shorter unemployment duration or who were currently employed (Kroft, Lange, & Notowidigdo, 2013). Given the historic and ongoing trend of higher unemployment rates among Black workers (Bureau of Labor Statistics, 2018), this bias can indicate discrimination with a broader adverse impact (Karren & Sherman, 2012; Maurath, Wright, Wittorp, & Hardtke, 2015).

Since finding a job becomes more difficult the longer the duration of unemployment (Kosanovich & Theodossiou Sherman, 2015), those who do not have the relatively quick pathway to reentry afforded by economically useful networks (Granovetter, 1997; Massey, 2007) face exacerbated challenges. A gap in employment can make reentry particularly difficult for Black workers, who tend to have less personal access to networks that assist in job placement (e.g., Ibarra, 1995; Parks-Yancy, 2006; Tajfel & Turner, 1979). This assistance comes in the form of access to information about job openings, influence within the hiring process, and status afforded by an internal referral (Lin, 2001).

Job opportunities in leadership positions are often shared within informal social networks, and positions that have access to this type of information are largely dominated by White men (Stainback & Tomaskovic-Devey, 2012). Informal networks tend to reflect the ongoing racial segregation in housing, worship, education, and workplaces (DiTomaso, 2015), particularly for White people, who tend to have more homogenous networks (Ibarra, 1995) and more access to resources to share.

It has widely been argued that the use of social connections in hiring serves to perpetuate inequity and undermine efforts toward equal opportunity and greater diversity in organizations (DiTomaso, 2015). In a study of how people in different groups use their network access in the workplace, McDonald (2011) concluded, "Gender and race segregation in social networks help to consolidate the resource advantages of White men, while also limiting female and minority access to these resources" (p. 328). It should be noted that Black female leaders likely face greater barriers in recovering from temporary unemployment, as they tend to have fewer network connections than White men, who confer the most financially lucrative job connections (McDonald, 2011) compared with White women and Black men.

Long-term unemployment can be particularly consequential for Black workers, even leaders. In addition to wage gaps, Black families tend to have disproportionately lower accumulated wealth than White families (Thompson & Suarez, 2015), making them more vulnerable to financial instability. Aside from practical concerns about meeting daily financial needs, this increases the likelihood of financial strain, the psychological stress and worry surrounding financial hardship (Ullah, 1990).

Additionally, the financial strain of long-term unemployment tends to predict diminished mental and physical well-being (McKee-Ryan, Song, Wanberg, & Kinicki, 2005), which can undermine job-seeking efforts. A meta-analysis of 104 studies examining the impact of unemployment on well-being indicated that personal, social, financial, and time-structure-related coping resources helped to protect well-being (McKee-Ryan et al., 2005). Of the variables in this meta-analysis, financial strain was among the strongest negative correlates with mental health and overall life satisfaction. Expectations for future employment opportunities was also found to be a strong correlate with these outcomes, a variable that may be affected by Black leaders' observations and encounters in the workplace. Experiences of racism and discrimination preceding the period of unemployment likely take a substantial toll on well-being (Clark, Anderson, Clark, & Williams, 1999; Deitch et al., 2003). Past encounters with biased performance ratings (Stauffer & Buckley, 2005) and disproportionate standards for promotions (Baldi & McBrier, 1997) can also undermine confidence in future employment opportunities.

The combined factors of financial vulnerability, physical and mental health, and network access thus make it increasingly difficult for Black workers, even those previously identified as leaders, to resume career trajectories that would lead to more influential positions.

Some Black leaders who leave their positions turn to business ownership. Rather than seek employment in another organization where they may encounter a familiar pattern of resistance, hostility, or limitations, some find the freedom of starting their own business to be worthwhile. Though we could not access comprehensive data tracking the career paths following Black leader turnover, broader data sets of the characteristics and motivations of entrepreneurs reveal how high-performing, leadership-oriented Black workers often turn to self-employment. Data from the US Census 2015 Annual Survey of Entrepreneurs reveals differing motivations and priorities among business owners of different races that are consistent with what we know about barriers that high-achieving Black workers often face in organizations. Among this sample, Black business owners had a higher rate of postgraduate education (a master's, doctorate, or professional degree) than any other racial group (United States Census Bureau, 2015). The reasons that Black entrepreneurs provide for starting their businesses reflect the perception that their alternatives for employment would provide less career growth than self-employment. Black business owners were more likely than White business owners to report that having an avenue for their ideas was "very important" in their motivation to become an entrepreneur (United States Census Bureau, 2015).

Additionally, a greater number of Black versus White business owners reported that flexible scheduling and balancing work and family were very important reasons for starting their businesses. Flexibility is often seen as a perk or reward to high-status employees in larger companies. The perception that employment with another company would offer less flexibility mirrors past evidence that Black workers have less access to flexible work arrangements than others (Bureau of Labor Statistics, 2012; Council of Economic Advisers to the President, 2014).

Black business owners were also more likely to cite the potential for greater income and, to a lesser extent, the difficulty of finding a job as motivators (United States Census Bureau, 2015), reflecting financial and employment disparities reported elsewhere in this chapter. Other reasons, such as having a desire to work for themselves or having a friend or family role model, were similar in importance among White and Black entrepreneurs (United States Census Bureau, 2015).

Despite similarity in these motivators, Black business owners are substantially more likely than White owners to have founded their business, rather than purchase or inherit an existing business (United States Census Bureau, 2012). Despite the substantial investment of time and resources involved in starting a business, the combination of the difficulty of reentering the workforce and the detriments of long-term unemployment may contribute to the greater number of highly educated Black entrepreneurs choosing this alternative.

Consequences for Minority Followers

When Black leaders leave organizations, the negative implications of their departure extend beyond the self. While a Black leader's departure can have some adverse effects for that individual, it also exacerbates barriers for people of color still employed by the organization. With one less Black leader in their workplaces, employees of color are left to navigate settings characterized by implicit biases, few mentors like them, and restricted opportunities for advancement.

Research focused on race inside the workplace suggests that race affects the quality and prevalence of developmental relationships (D. A. Thomas, 1990). Developmental relationships are those in which both the mentor and the mentee benefit, and the mentee receives sufficient career-related support. Studies find that when compared with the support available for White males, support for Blacks may be viewed as a risk and therefore takes longer to attain due to the higher level of competence expected of a Black protégé before he or she is mentored (D. A. Thomas, 1990). This may contribute to D. A. Thomas's (1990) finding that Black employees often form their strong developmental relationships with fellow Black workers. The perception that White leaders may lack adequate cultural understanding and be unable to relate to Black mentees further draws potential protégés to leaders of color, who are suspected to be able to provide more beneficial and life-relevant resources. Therefore, as an alternative to waiting for a developmental relationship to form with a White leader, Black workers are more likely to form close ties with fellow Blacks. Along with mutual understanding, these same-race relationships offer greater psychosocial support than those involving a White leader (D. A. Thomas, 1990). Appropriately, when Black leaders exit the organization, these beneficial relationships are either dismantled or strained, resulting in the problems that arise when Black followers rely on White leaders for their career development.

The dependence on same-race relationships brings another challenge. Because of the fluidity of jobs and roles in today's competitive workplace, it is recommended that workers seek out multiple mentors in order to receive varying degrees of expertise and types of resources. This presents a problem because of the limited number of Black leaders capable of filling these mentor roles for Black protégés who may seek same-race guidance. Therefore, employees of color are often left competing and falling short of proper support (McCarty Kilian, Hukai, & McCarty, 2005). This dearth of Black mentors also contributes to the finding that Blacks have a larger portion of their mentor relationships with those other than immediate superiors (D. A. Thomas, 1990), which introduces an additional strain of having to put forth efforts not expected of their White counterparts. Because of the limited number of leaders of color in the pool of possible mentors, Black employees may report low levels of perceived social support, cultural connectedness, and inclusion.

It should now be understood that a Black leader's exit from the workplace can hold great implications for the employees of color who remain, such as ineffective mentoring relationships and less-than-ideal exposure to high-ranking persons to aid in career lateralization, which subsequently lowers career optimism (Friedman & Holtom, 2002). In the field of academia, these consequences are even more evident, as faculty members of color are few in several disciplines. Generally speaking, faculty lack the competence and training to provide effective mentoring to students of color, leaving them to have deficiencies in career guidance, to lack knowledge of the relevant literature, and to experience feelings of discomfort. For these reasons and others, students of color often venture outside their departments or universities to seek adequate guidance from Black professionals and faculty if they don't perceive complementary matches in-house (K. M. Thomas, Willis, & Davis, 2007). All these factors considered, if the few Black faculty scattered within disciplines in academia were to exit, this issue would be exacerbated. On the extreme end, Black students seeking mentorship may opt out of pursuing a career in academia due to a dearth of interactions with like role models or inadequate mentor-protégé relationships with those who are available. Ultimately, the departure of a Black leader could lead to poor guidance and the subsequent departure of other Blacks.

Consequences for Organizations: Missing Out on Unintended Benefits

Effective Black leaders provide support, supervision, guidance, direction, and correction as any good leader does. However, for many organizations, there are also unintended benefits that are lost or never realized when

Black leaders leave their organizations. When organizations are inclusive, Black leaders can enhance organizational effectiveness by using their unique positionalities to offer novel perspectives, ideas, and analyses that enable institutions to better serve and lead diverse stakeholders. Black leaders can do this by using their "otherness" to disrupt and derail decision making based on historical priorities that may no longer serve the needs of the modern organization, as well as to challenge ideas emerging from team-based group-think that too often pass as meritorious rather than simply affirming of the status quo. Therefore, the loss of Black leadership talent lessens the diversity of perspectives required for the institutional competitiveness that is inherent in an increasingly diverse labor and consumer market.

High-status role models, such as Black leaders, may also challenge implicit stereotypes and biases related to who leaders are. Simply put, they challenge a White standard of leadership (Rosette et al., 2008). As leaders, Blacks may also play an unintended role in challenging anti-Black bias. For example, research on the efficacy of an anti-Black-racism intervention demonstrated that contact with high-status Black models reduced racist behaviors of Whites toward Black men, and a combination of contact with a Black mentor and participation in a cultural diversity workshop resulted in reduced racist behavior of Whites toward Black women (Maluso, 1995). This experiment, which illuminated the potential role of Black leaders as high-level role models or mentors, may help dismantle anti-Black prejudice, stereotyping, and discrimination in organizations. Therefore, the opportunity to disrupt anti-Black bias and detail discrimination is eliminated when Black leaders depart.

Black leaders also create a new chapter in an organization's history and provide a more contemporary and perhaps more diverse institutional image. The role of Black leaders in facilitating an organizational image that values diversity and is inclusive cannot be minimized, given the importance of organizational image to job-seeker attraction (Perkins, K. M. Thomas, & Taylor, 2000; K. M. Thomas & Wise, 1999). When organizations have had challenging histories concerning race, a Black leader can provide an alternative, "new and improved" diversity narrative. The presence of a Black leader may suggest that the organization has evolved to be less hostile to marginalized groups. Black leaders also create an image that conveys to potential job seekers and business partners that the organization is friendly to people of color and reflects an inclusive climate.

Black leaders can be bicultural boundary spanners (Bell, 1990; Ernst & Yip, 2009). That is, Black leaders occupy space in multiple groups, both seen and unseen. As leaders, they hold membership in a high-status, powerful group that is influential and controls resources and power. Yet as Black people, these leaders are also tied to a group that has historically lacked access to education, power, influence, and resources, as well as opportunity. Black leaders therefore have an opportunity to convey the realities, concerns, and values of Blacks to other leaders, while sharing the strategies and currency needed to ascend in one's career with other Blacks.

Not only do Blacks in positions of leadership signal potential professional development to other Blacks, but their status as underrepresented is likely also a signal to a variety of individuals who are "Othered" in organizations (Catalyst, 2014). For example, the presence of Black leadership may signal to women or sexual minorities that the organization can also make space for their leadership. Underrepresented leaders, such as Black leaders, likely convey a message of identity safety (Purdie-Vaughns, Steele, Davies, Ditlmann, & Crosby, 2008) to other marginalized groups. Organizational doors are particularly likely to open to other Blacks when a Black leader has been successful in that same role. That is, pioneers change the pattern of who is considered credible and offered an opportunity to perform once the initial entry barrier has been broken (Greer & Virick, 2008).

Summary

Our examination of Black leaders has attempted to reinforce a positive psychology of their presence and value to organizations and the intended and unintended benefits they provide and that are lost when they leave. Black leadership has consequences for the self-image and identities of those in positions of power. However, Black leaders also help to challenge racist images of who leaders are while providing critical role modeling and mentoring for other upwardly mobile Blacks and those who are designated as the Other. In many ways, Black leaders normalize diversity for other individuals, as well as for the organization.

Prior research has identified several factors that contribute to Black leaders' departure from their organizations, and while much is known about Black leadership experiences and how they may contribute to their turnover, there are many avenues for future research that may augment our current understanding. First, the current literature on Black leadership in the workplace would benefit from studies that are designed to quantitatively examine Black leaders' experiences longitudinally and understand how they may ultimately result in turnover. Understanding how Black leaders' attitudes, behaviors, and perceptions change over time may give insight into how and why Black leaders leave and at what stage in their careers certain factors may be especially damaging or supportive. Second, studies that incorporate multilevel designs that examine within- and between-persons effects of different factors involved in Black leadership experiences (e.g., organizational diversity climate, emotional labor, affective events) may illuminate some of the nuances that Black leaders experience that may contribute to or mitigate their desire to leave the organization. Daily diary methods and experience sampling methodology (Fisher & To, 2012; Mehl & Conner, 2012) are well suited to capturing this type of data due to their ability to test hypotheses related to repeated experiences in the workplace using relatively small sample sizes. Due to the low prevalence of Black leaders, which only increases as one ascends the leadership ladder, the statistical power requirements of most quantitative methodologies that require moderate to extremely large sample sizes are unable to serve research questions focused on this population. Finally, more mixed-methods research should be implemented that examines both quantitative and qualitative data regarding Black leadership and turnover. Using mixed methods allows for a more holistic examination of research questions that may not be addressed using just one method (Creswell & Plano Clark, 2011). Future research on Black leader attrition should consider using longitudinal, multilevel, or mixed-method designs to capture the complex nature of Black leadership and experiences that may contribute to or buffer against their turnover.

In addition to recommendations for future research, there are several recommendations for organizations that may help prevent or mitigate the negative experiences Black leaders have in the workplace. Organizational-level diversity management initiatives should occur at multiple areas of employment, including recruitment, selection, development, and promotion. The motivation for recruiting and retaining Black leaders needs to be centered on the increased value that these individuals will bring to the organization, rather than increasing racial quotas (D. A. Thomas & Ely, 1996). It is also crucial that an organization evaluates its current diversity climate to ensure that current and future employees are effectively supported. Administering an anonymous survey to every employee, across all departments and responsibilities, that assesses the availability of support resources, quality of workplace relationships, and value for diversity is one way of getting a pulse on how well or poorly an organization is managing diversity. Not knowing how well one's organization engages in diversity may lead to unintentional or intentional misrepresentation of inclusive diversity climates during recruitment, which can result in higher distrust and costly turnover of Black leaders. Business organizations should consider sponsoring risk-taking leadership programs and executive coaching specifically for Black women, who often miss out on informal mentoring and networking benefits with high-powered organizational members (Taylor & Nivens, 2011) and who may suffer more than others when performance doesn't meet expectations (Rosette & Livingston, 2012). Same-race mentorship is also an impactful method for reducing the negative effects of workplace microaggressions often faced by Black leaders (Holder, Jackson, & Ponterotto, 2015), which further stresses the importance of having Black men and women at all levels of leadership within the organization. In sum, several strategies are available for organizations to support Black leaders and discourage turnover.

REFERENCES

Baldi, S., & McBrier, D. B. (1997). Do the determinants of promotion differ for Blacks and Whites? *Work and Occupations, 24*, 478–497. doi:10.1177/0730888497024004005

Bell, E. L. (1990). The bicultural life experience of career-oriented Black women. *Journal of Organizational Behavior, 11*, 459–477. doi:10.1002/job.4030110607

Block, C. J., Aumann, K., & Chelin, A. (2012). Assessing stereotypes of Black and White managers: A diagnostic ratio approach. *Journal of Applied Social Psychology, 42*, 128–149. doi:10.1111/j.1559-1816.2012.01014.x

Brudnick, I. A., & Manning, J. E. (2018). *African American members of the United States Congress: 1870–2018* (Congressional Research Service Report 7-5700). Retrieved from https://www.senate.gov/CRSpubs/617f17bb-61e9-40bb-b301-50f48fd239fc.pdf

Bryant, W. K., Jeon-Slaughter, H., Kang, H., & Tax, A. (2003). Participation in philanthropic activities: Donating money and time. *Journal of Consumer Policy, 26*, 43–73. doi:10.1023/a:1022626529603

Bureau of Labor Statistics. (2012). *American Time Use Survey—2011 results* [Data files]. Retrieved from https://www.bls.gov/tus/data.htm

Bureau of Labor Statistics. (2016). *Labor force characteristics by race and gender, 2016* (Report No. 1070). Retrieved from https://www.bls.gov/opub/reports/race-and -ethnicity/2016/home.htm

Bureau of Labor Statistics. (2018). *Labor force statistics from the Current Population Survey, 1948–2018*. Retrieved from https://data.bls.gov/timeseries/LNS14000000

Campbell, W. K., Hoffman, B. J., Campbell, S. M., & Marchisio, G. (2011). Narcissism in organizational contexts. *Human Resource Management Review, 21*(4), 268–284. doi:10.1016/j.hrmr.2010.10.007

Catalyst. (2014). *Feeling different: Being the "other" in US workplaces* (Report). New York, NY: Catalyst.

Chrobot-Mason, D. (2013). Secondhand smoke: Ambient racial harassment at work. *Journal of Managerial Psychology, 28*(5), 470–491. doi:10.1108/jmp-02-2012-0064

Clark, R., Anderson, N. B., Clark, V. R., & Williams, D. R. (1999). Racism as a stressor for African Americans: A biopsychosocial model. *American Psychologist, 54*, 805–816. doi:10.1037/0003-066x.54.10.805

Council of Economic Advisers to the President. (2014). *Work-life balance and the economics of workplace flexibility* (Report). Retrieved from https://obamawhite house.archives.gov/sites/default/files/docs/updated_workplace_flex_report _final_0.pdf

Creswell, J. W., & Plano Clark, V. L. (2011). *Designing and conducting mixed methods research*. Los Angeles, CA: SAGE.

Deitch, E. A., Barsky, A., Butz, R. M., Chan, S., Brief, A. P., & Bradley, J. C. (2003). Subtle yet significant: The existence and impact of everyday racial discrimination in the work place. *Human Relations, 56*, 1299–1324. doi:10.1177/00187267035611002

DiTomaso, N. (2015). Racism and discrimination versus advantage and favoritism: Bias for versus bias against. *Research in Organizational Behavior, 35*, 57–77. doi:10.1016/j .riob.2015.10.001

Ernst, C., & Yip, J. (2009). Boundary spanning leadership: Tactics to bridge social identity groups in organizations. In T. Pittinsky (Ed.), *Crossing the divide: Intergroup leadership in a world of difference* (pp 87–100). Boston, MA: Harvard Business School Press.

Fisher, C. D., & To, M. L. (2012). Using experience sampling methodology in organizational behavior. *Journal of Organizational Behavior, 33*, 865–877. doi:10.1002/job.1803

Friedman, R. A., & Holtom, B. (2002). The effects of network groups on minority employee turnover intentions. *Human Resource Management, 41*, 405–421. doi:10.1002/hrm.10051

Granovetter, M. (1997). Economic action and social structure: The problem of embeddedness. *International Library of Critical Writings in Economics, 83*, 142–171. doi:10.1002/9780470755679.ch5

Greer, C. R., & Virick, M. (2008). Diverse succession planning: Lessons from the industry leaders. *Human Resource Management, 47*, 351–367. doi:10.1108/dlo.2009.08123cad.002

Holder, A., Jackson, M. A., & Ponterotto, J. G. (2015). Racial microaggression experiences and coping strategies of Black women in corporate leadership. *Qualitative Psychology, 2*, 164–180. doi:10.1037/qup0000024

Ibarra, H. (1995). Race, opportunity, and diversity of social circles in managerial networks. *Academy of Management Journal, 38*, 673–703. doi:10.2307/256742

Judiesch, M. K., & Lyness, K. S. (1999). Left behind? The impact of leaves of absence on managers' career success. *Academy of Management Journal, 42*, 641–651. doi:10.5465/256985

Karren, R., & Sherman, K. (2012). Layoffs and unemployment discrimination: A new stigma. *Journal of Managerial Psychology, 27*, 848–863. doi:10.1108/02683941211280193

Koenig, A. M., & Eagly, A. H. (2014). Evidence for the social role theory of stereotype content: Observations of groups' roles shape stereotypes. *Journal of Personality and Social Psychology, 107*, 371–392. doi:10.1037/a0037215

Kosanovich, K., & Theodossiou Sherman, E. (2015). Trends in long-term unemployment. Retrieved from https://www.bls.gov/spotlight/2015/long-term -unemployment/

Kroft, K., Lange, F., & Notowidigdo, M. J. (2013). Duration dependence and labor market conditions: Evidence from a field experiment. *Quarterly Journal of Economics, 128*, 1123–1167. doi:10.3386/w18387

Lin, N. (2001). *Social capital: A theory of social structure and action.* Cambridge, England: Cambridge University Press.

Livingston, R. W., & Pearce, N. A. (2009). The teddy-bear effect: Does having a baby face benefit Black chief executive officers? *Psychological Science, 20*, 1229–1236. doi:10.1111/j.1467-9280.2009.02431.x

Maluso, D. E. (1995). Shaking hands with clenched fists: Interpersonal racism. In B. E. Lott & D. E. Maluso (Eds.), *The social psychology of interpersonal discrimination* (pp. 50–79). New York, NY: Guilford Press.

Massey, D. S. (2007). Categorically unequal: The American stratification system. New York, NY: Russell Sage Foundation.

Maurath, D. T., Wright, C. W., Wittorp, D. E., & Hardtke, D. (2015). Volunteer experience may not bridge gaps in employment. *International Journal of Selection and Assessment, 23*, 284–294. doi:10.1111/ijsa.12114

McCarty Kilian, C., Hukai, D., & McCarty, C. E. (2005). Building diversity in the pipeline to corporate leadership. *Journal of Management Development, 24*, 155–168. doi:10.1108/02621710510579518

McDonald, S. (2011). What's in the "old boys" network? Accessing social capital in gendered and racialized networks. *Social Networks, 33*, 317–330. doi:10.1016/j.socnet.2011.10.002

McFarland, J., Hussar, B., de Brey, C., Snyder, T., Wang, X., Wilkinson-Flicker, S., . . . Hinz, S. (2017). *The condition of education 2017* (NCES 2017-144). Washington, DC: National Center for Education Statistics. Retrieved from https://nces.ed.gov/pubsearch/pubsinfo.asp?pubid=2017144

McGirt, E. (2016, January 22). Why race and culture matter in the C-suite. *Fortune.* Retrieved from http://fortune.com/black-executives-men-c-suite/

McGirt, E. (2017, September 27). The Black ceiling: Why African-American women aren't making it to the top in corporate America. *Fortune.* Retrieved from http://fortune.com/2017/09/27/black-female-ceos-fortune-500-companies/

McKay, P. F., Avery, D. R., Tonidandel, S., Morris, M. A., Hernandez, M. A., & Hebl, M. R. (2007). Racial differences in employee retention: Are diversity climate perceptions the key? *Personnel Psychology, 60*, 35–62. doi:10.1111/j.1744-6570.2007.00064.x

McKee-Ryan, F., Song, Z., Wanberg, C. R., & Kinicki, A. J. (2005). Psychological and physical well-being during unemployment: A meta-analytic study. *Journal of Applied Psychology, 90*, 53–76. doi:10.1037/0021-9010.90.1.53

McManus, M. (2016). *Minority business ownership: Data from the 2012 survey of business owners* (U.S. Small Business Administration Office of Advocacy Issue Brief 12). Retrieved from https://www.sba.gov/sites/default/files/advocacy/Minority-Owned-Businesses-in-the-US.pdf

Mehl, M. R., & Conner, T. S. (Eds.). (2012). *Handbook of research methods for studying daily life*. New York, NY: Guilford Press.

Neubert, M. J., & Taggar, S. (2004). Pathways to informal leadership: The moderating role of gender on the relationship of individual differences and team member network centrality to informal leadership emergence. *Leadership Quarterly, 15*, 175–194. doi:10.1016/j.leaqua.2004.02.00

Nunez-Smith, M., Pilgrim, N., Wynia, M., Desai, M., & Bright, C. (2009). Health care workplace discrimination and physician turnover. *Journal of the National Medical Association, 101*(12), 1274–1282. doi:10.1016/s0027-9684(15)31139-1

Pager, D., Western, B., & Bonikowski, B. (2009). Discrimination in a low-wage labor market: A field experiment. *American Sociological Review, 74*, 777–799. doi:10.1177/000312240907400505

Parks-Yancy, R. (2006). The effect of social group membership and social capital resources on careers. *Journal of Black Studies, 36*, 515–545. doi:10.1177/0021934704273501

Perkins, L. A., Thomas, K. M., & Taylor, G. A. (2000). Advertising and recruitment: Marketing to minorities. *Psychology & Marketing, 17*, 235–255. doi:10.1002/(sici)1520-6793(200003)17:3<235::aid-mar3>3.3.co;2-r

Purdie-Vaughns, V., Steele, C. M., Davies, P. G., Ditlmann, R., & Crosby, J. R. (2008). Social identity contingencies: How diversity cues signal threat or safety for African Americans in mainstream institutions. *Journal of Personality and Social Psychology, 94*, 615–630. doi:10.1037/0022-3514.94.4.615

Reitman, F., & Schneer, J. A. (2005). The long-term negative impacts of managerial career interruptions: A longitudinal study of men and women MBAs. *Group & Organization Management, 30*, 243–262. doi:10.1177/1059601104269110

Rosette, A. S., Leonardelli, G. J., & Phillips, K. W. (2008). The White standard: Racial bias in leader categorization. *Journal of Applied Psychology, 93*, 758–777. doi:10.1037/0021-9010.93.4.758

Rosette, A. S., & Livingston, R. W. (2012). Failure is not an option for Black women: Effects of organizational performance on leaders with single versus dual-subordinate identities. *Journal of Experimental Social Psychology, 48*, 1162–1167. doi:10.1016/j.jesp.2012.05.002

Stainback, K., & Tomaskovic-Devey, D. (2012). *Documenting desegregation: Racial and gender segregation in private-sector employment since the Civil Rights Act*. New York, NY: Russell Sage Foundation.

Stauffer, J. M., & Buckley, M. R. (2005). The existence and nature of racial bias in supervisory ratings. *Journal of Applied Psychology, 90*(3), 586–591. doi:10.1037/0021-9010.90.3.586

Tajfel, H., & Turner, J. C. (1979). An integrative theory of intergroup conflict. In W. G. Austin & S. Worchel (Eds.), *The social psychology of intergroup relations* (pp. 33–47). Monterey, CA: Brooks/Cole.

Taylor, T. S., & Nivens, B. (2011). *The League of Black Women: Risk and reward: Black women leading out on a limb* (Report). Retrieved from http://events.leagueofblackwomen.org/wp-content/uploads/2011/05/Risk-and-Reward-Report1.pdf

Thomas, D. A. (1990). The impact of race on managers' experiences of developmental relationships (mentoring and sponsorship): An intra-organizational study. *Journal of Organizational Behavior, 11*, 479–492. doi:10.1002/job.4030110608

Thomas, D. A., & Ely, R. J. (1996, September–October). Making differences matter: A new paradigm for managing diversity. *Harvard Business Review*, 79–90. Retrieved from https://s3.amazonaws.com/academia.edu.documents/33149013 /MAKING_DIFFERENCES_DIFFERENT.pdf?AWSAccessKeyId =AKIAIWOWYYGZ2Y53UL3A&Expires=1549483527&Signature=9D8Nfzi W1K0n0h%2BlDG3lMky7H9M%3D&response-content-disposition =inline%3B%20filename%3DMaking_Differences_Matter_A_New _Paradigm.pdf

Thomas, K. M., Johnson-Bailey, J., Phelps, R. E., Tran, N. M., & Johnson, L. (2013). Women of color at midcareer: Going from pet to threat. In L. Comas-Díaz & B. Greene (Eds.), *The psychological health of women of color: Intersections, challenges, and opportunities* (pp. 275–286). Santa Barbara, CA: Praeger.

Thomas, K. M., Willis, L. A., & Davis, J. (2007). Mentoring minority graduate students: Issues and strategies for institutions, faculty, and students. *Equal Opportunities International, 26*(3), 178–192. doi:10.1108/02610150710735471

Thomas, K. M., & Wise, P. G. (1999). Organizational attractiveness and individual differences: Are diverse applicants attracted by different factors? *Journal of Business and Psychology, 13*(3), 375–390. doi:10.1023/a:1022978400698

Thompson, J. P., & Suarez, G. A. (2015). *Exploring the racial wealth gap using the survey of consumer finances* (Finance and Economics Discussion Series 2015-076). Washington, DC: Board of Governors of the Federal Reserve System. doi:10.2139/ ssrn.2665627

Ullah, P. (1990). The association between income, financial strain and psychological well-being among unemployed youths. *Journal of Occupational Psychology, 63*, 317–330. doi:10.1111/j.2044-8325.1990.tb00533.x

United States Census Bureau. (2012). *Survey of Business Owners and Self-Employed Persons*. Retrieved from https://www.census.gov/programs-surveys/sbo.html

United States Census Bureau. (2015). *Annual Survey of Entrepreneurs* [Tables]. Retrieved from https://www.census.gov/programs-surveys/ase/data/tables.html

Wilson, J., & Musick, M. (1997). Rater training for performance appraisal: A quantitative review. *Journal of Occupational and Organizational Psychology, 67*, 189–205. doi:10.1111/j.2044-8325.1994.tb00562.x

19

Blacks Leading Whites

How Mutual and Dual (Ingroup and Outgroup) Identification Affect Inequality

LUMUMBA SEEGARS *and* LAKSHMI RAMARAJAN

All my skinfolk ain't kinfolk.

—*Zora Neale Hurston*

As Hurston's quotation suggests, just because one is Black does not mean that he or she also identifies with other Black people. In this chapter, we bring this phrase into dialogue with conversations about Black leadership and attempt to move these conversations beyond simply creating more Black leaders. Specifically, we take seriously the premise that Black representation in leadership positions is a necessary but not a sufficient condition for advancing the welfare of Black people and, in particular, challenging the inequality that results from racial hierarchy and injustice. Therefore, we explore constraints and opportunities that Black leaders face when attempting to challenge inequality, particularly in majority-White organizations.

At the heart of this chapter lies one question: When are Black leaders most able to challenge inequality? Both the popular and the scholarly press suggest that greater representation of Blacks at the top of organizations should result in challenges to inequality, by which we mean using their position to alter organizational practices, structures, and cultures that maintain the current racial hierarchy. Scholars have explored the importance of the representation of subordinate group members in leadership positions (Zweigenhaft & Domhoff, 2006). For example, scholars suggest that greater representation of subordinate group members in leadership positions provides role models and encourages feelings of empowerment among underrepresented group members (Bobo & Gilliam, 1990; Ely, 1995; Lockwood, 2006). However, research also suggests that it is difficult for members of underrepresented groups to actually create change. For instance, subordinate group members can take actions that maintain intergroup inequality because they ascribe to beliefs and ideologies that justify inequality (Jost, Banaji, & Nosek, 2004; Sidanius & Pratto, 1999). Moreover, members of underrepresented groups may actually feel threatened when more members of their ingroup enter organizations and thus choose not to promote or enable the success of others like themselves (Duguid, Loyd, & Tolbert, 2012; Srivastava & Sherman, 2014). These findings suggest that it is important to look more critically at the role racial minorities might play in either reducing or perpetuating inequality once they rise to positions of leadership in majority-White organizations.

Black leaders, who are motivated to enact change, face two hurdles in their ability to challenge inequality. First, they are not seen as prototypical leaders—both in general and particularly in predominantly White organizations (Hogg, van Knippenberg, & Rast, 2012; Rosette, Leonardelli, & Phillips, 2008). This challenge limits their ability to deviate from the status quo in work organizations, which are often associated with structures and practices that perpetuate inequality (Acker, 2006; DiTomaso & Hooijberg, 1996). Second, Black leaders have two groups they must lead, each with its own relationship to inequality: a Black ingroup and a White outgroup. The Black ingroup of the leader is a minority in majority-White organizations but is likely to have high motivation to reduce inequality because of the group's subordinate position in the societal and organizational hierarchy. The White outgroup is a majority within the organization and controls access to organizational resources that can reduce inequality.

Becoming a leader represents a mutual identification process that requires both that the leader claim the leader identity and that the identity be granted by those who follow (DeRue & Ashford, 2010). We argue that Black leaders must build mutual identification with both groups in order to be most effective at challenging inequality. In this chapter, we use the lens of mutual identification to describe how different configurations of mutual identification with both the Black ingroup and the

White outgroup can affect the extent to which Black leaders will challenge inequality. Challenging inequality here consists of both the desire to challenge inequality and the ease of that challenge. We note that Black leaders are not inherently motivated to challenge inequality; rather, the degree to which they are self-identified with the Black ingroup, which has historically been marginalized, relates to the degree that they will be motivated to take measures to reduce that marginality by challenging inequality. Once ingroup identification occurs, the degree to which other Black people and the White outgroup identify with this leader will affect the ease with which he or she can effectively follow through on his or her desire to challenge inequality.

This chapter contributes to our understanding of Black leadership in three ways. First, we elevate the desire and ability to challenge and reduce inequality as a relevant and important dependent variable in judging the success of Black leaders. Second and relatedly, we explore the processes that enable Black leaders to fundamentally restructure the rules of the "tournament" (see Thomas & Gabarro, 1999, for a broader discussion of race-based tournaments for leadership trajectories in work organizations). Finally, we contribute to our understanding of the Black leadership experience by theorizing about the process of leaders establishing mutual identification with two separate groups. Previous literature has demonstrated the importance of mutual identification between followers and leaders (DeRue & Ashford, 2010); however, this chapter extends this work by addressing the conundrum of leaders who have to appeal to multiple groups with different objectives and motivations.

Becoming a Black Leader in a White Organization: Mutual Identification with the White Outgroup

Before we can consider how Black leaders might challenge inequality in majority-White organizations, we must first consider how Blacks become leaders in these organizations. In the mutual identification process, leaders and followers must agree on their respective identities. This agreement is often determined by implicit theories of leadership (DeRue & Ashford, 2010). In particular, the prototypical leader is usually thought to be a White male (Rosette et al., 2008). Because they do not fit the prototype, Black people may be less likely to claim and be granted a leader identity. Therefore, a key challenge Blacks face in gaining leadership positions in predominantly White organizations rests in their ability to overcome intrapersonal challenges and gain acceptance and recognition by their White peers.

One way to overcome this obstacle is to become a more prototypical organizational member and, thus, potential organizational leader through mutual identification with the White outgroup. The concept of identification captures the multilevel process of attachment between the individual and the collective. *Identification* refers both to a sense of connection and shared fate between an individual and a target and to the process by which this connection unfolds (Ashforth, Harrison, & Corley, 2008; Ashforth & Mael, 1989). This process of identification must occur both through the Black member identifying with White members of the organization and vice versa. For example, Black organizational members may manage impressions by signaling that they share qualities of the White outgroup, which may enable White organization members to identify with them (Roberts, 2005). Black organization members may discover over time that they share similar values with White organization members that may lead them to identify more with the White outgroup (Harrison, Price, & Bell, 1998; Phillips, Rothbard, & Dumas, 2009). Thus, as Black people build mutual identification with the White outgroup, they are likely to become more prototypical organizational members and, therefore, leaders. We discuss how this process of mutual identification for Black leaders affects their willingness and ability to challenge inequality next.

Challenging Inequality: The Black Leader's Perspective and Dual Identification

While the mutual identification process with the White outgroup enables the Black leader's personal advancement in a White organization, it does not speak to how the Black leader may challenge inequality. On the one hand, the White outgroup holds greater control over the social, economic, and cultural resources of the organization than the Black ingroup. Thus, the Black leader of such an organization has the ability to challenge inequality. However, the mutual identification process with the White outgroup may constrain the Black leader's motivation and ability to challenge inequality in two ways. First, while mutual identification may enable Blacks to claim and be granted leadership, the fundamental nonprototypicality of Black leaders limits their ability to deviate successfully from the status quo and, therefore, challenge inequality (Hogg et al., 2012). That is, the more prototypical a leader is, the more license he or she has to deviate from group norms and create change. Thus, Black leaders might be constrained by their nonprototypicality to perform successfully as leaders by doubling down on organizational practices and structures that emphasize traditional measures of successful performance, which may be the very same practices that perpetuate inequality. Second, the process of mutual identification is likely to result in strong ties and relationships with the White-majority outgroup that can stymie the possibility of divergent change (Battilana & Casciaro, 2012). To the extent that the White outgroup is motivated not to challenge inequality but rather to preserve the status quo, Black leaders who build strong ties with White outgroup members who are negatively inclined toward change may not be inclined to challenge inequality themselves.

However, a key factor that may moderate Black leaders' motivation and ability to challenge inequality is their level of identification with the Black ingroup. A key aspect of group identification is the advancement of the group's welfare (Blader & Tyler, 2009; Tyler & Blader, 2003). As the minority group at the bottom of the status hierarchy in both society and the organization, the Black ingroup has greater motivation to challenge inequality than the White outgroup. Black leaders who do not identify with the Black ingroup are likely to have a low level of motivation to try to challenge inequality. Therefore, even if they have the access to resources that come with White outgroup identification, the Black ingroup is not likely to experience significant changes in the reduction of inequality due to these individuals' rise to power. In contrast, Black leaders who identify with their Black ingroup are likely to be motivated to advance their group's welfare. This mutual identification with the Black ingroup can alter the Black leader's motivation to access organizational resources, including networks and relationships, decision-making ability, and financial resources, and channel them toward challenging inequality. In sum, we theorize that the Black leader's level of identification with the Black ingroup will moderate the effect of his or her identification with the White outgroup on challenging inequality, such that Black leaders who identify with both groups are the ones who will both want to challenge inequality and have the motivation to access organizational resources in order to implement those changes. In the next section, we explore how being granted the leadership identity by the Black ingroup and White outgroup affects the types of challenges to inequality that a Black leader who already identifies with both groups will make.

Challenging Inequality: The Follower's Perspective—Mutual and Dual Identification

In order for Black leaders to be granted a leadership identity that allows them to effectively challenge inequality, followers from both groups also need to identify with Black leaders. Figure 19-1 zooms in on the other half of this mutual identification process, exploring how Black leaders who identify with both groups are identified with by the Black ingroup and White outgroup, respectively. We discuss four categories of leaders based on their ability to gain follower identification from each target group: factionless, opposition, co-opted, and consensus leaders. We theorize that Black follower identification and White follower identification will differentially contribute to the Black leader's ability to be effective. Black follower identification will provide a power base invested in challenging inequality because of their position in the racial hierarchy. White follower identification will provide a power base that can offer greater security in the face of challenging inequality because of their control of organizational resources. Because each of these types of leaders is motivated to make change and use available resources to follow through on that motivation, they mostly remain capable of challenging inequality; however, the types of change they will be able to implement will be different depending on follower identification from each group. In addition, we provide brief examples of individuals who fit these descriptions. As the real world is often messy, these individuals do not fit perfectly into the categories; however, they are useful illustrations of what these categories look like in reality.

Factionless Leader

The bottom left quadrant represents a leader with whom neither the Black ingroup nor the White outgroup identifies. Because of this, the leader has neither a power base invested in challenging inequality nor a power base that can offer him or her insurance for deviating from the status quo. Thus, this leader lacks the security and support necessary to engage in change, even though the leader might like for it to happen based on his or her identification with the Black ingroup. The factionless leader will be more concerned with business as usual in the short term, even though he or she might hope to engage in change efforts further down the line.

FIGURE 19-1

Typology of Black leaders based on Black and White follower identification

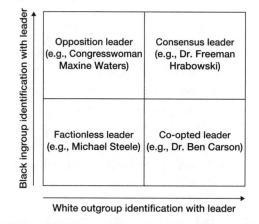

Example: Michael Steele during his tenure as the chairperson of the Republican National Committee. Although Steele attempted to help steer policy in a way that he thought would be useful for reaching out to Black voters and reducing interracial inequality, he was not able to achieve identification from them, as many Black voters remained much more identified with the Democratic Party and the first Black president, Barack Obama. Simultaneously, Steele angered and lost identification from White people as well when he made negative remarks about Rush Limbaugh. Thus, Steele found himself without a substantial power base and only served one term as chairman.

Opposition Leader

The top left quadrant represents a Black leader whom the Black ingroup identifies with but the White outgroup does not identify with as strongly. This is an opposition leader—not accepted by the White outgroup but still accepted by the Black ingroup. The opposition leader has a power base of people who are invested in challenging inequality. The White majority may have identified with this leader enough to allow him or her to rise to power; however, due to the mutual identification with the Black leader's Black ingroup, they might hold reservations about this leader's attempt to challenge inequality and, therefore, may resist change. For example, the White outgroup may withhold access to organizational resources or resist redistribution of those resources. Thus, even though this leader may have ambitions for more divergent change, the resistance from the White outgroup will likely result in more incremental change.

> *Example:* US congresswoman Maxine Waters during her tenure in Congress. Waters has been a vocal critic of President Donald Trump and Republicans, particularly in response to policies and statements that have been noted as disparaging toward the Black community. As an elected member of Congress for over twenty-five years, Waters enjoys considerable support from her district, but also from many members of the Black community beyond her district. Her attempt to use a procedural tactic in order to "reclaim her time" during a congressional hearing of Secretary of the Treasury Steven Mnuchin went viral, and many racial minorities claimed her affectionately as "Auntie Maxine" in order to express their strong support for and identification with her. Yet she has not been able to stop many of the policies of Trump, and, in the same hearing in which she attempted to keep Mnuchin on topic, she later expressed that she still felt that he did not adequately answer her questions. Thus, even though she has considerable appeal and has potentially slowed down some of the harmful effects of Trump's policies to the Black community, she has not been granted power to enact her challenges to inequality from her majority-Republican, and majority-White, colleagues in Congress.

Co-Opted Leader

The bottom right quadrant represents a Black leader whom the Black ingroup does not identify with but the White outgroup does identify with. This is a co-opted leader—one who has been accepted by the White outgroup but is not desired by the Black ingroup for whom he or she ostensibly would be advocating. The co-opted leader has a power base of people who can offer a stable leadership platform; however, this leader does not have a power base of people who are invested in challenging inequality. Thus, the leader is more likely to advocate for the type of changes that the White outgroup will feel comfortable with. As the White outgroup members are more likely to be invested in the status quo, this leader will be more likely to engage in incremental changes that minimize Whites' discomfort but may not have much legitimacy from the Black ingroup.

Example: Dr. Ben Carson in his capacity as the secretary of housing and urban development for the US federal government. Once beloved in the Black community, the *Gifted Hands* author and surgeon eventually lost the identification of many Blacks through a series of statements and policy choices, most notably when he likened former African slaves to immigrants. Yet the majority-White, Republican administration of Trump has identified Carson as a champion of Black progress by putting him in charge of housing and urban development. However, despite his formal authority, he has been unable to create change in housing inequalities.

Consensus Leader

The top right quadrant represents a leader whom both the ingroup and the majority outgroup identify with. The consensus leader has trust and support from both bases of power: the Black ingroup and the White outgroup. This leader represents a pragmatic consensus between both groups and has the ability to integrate both the motivation for change and access to resources into an effective challenge to inequality. Trusted by both groups, this leader has the greatest chance to advance his or her agenda to challenge inequality. This leader is supported by people who want to challenge inequality, as well as by people who can provide security for the leader to take risks. Thus, this leader should feel a greater sense of freedom to push boundaries and change the organization. Similar to those with idiosyncratic credits (Hollander, 1958), the consensus leader can take risks while knowing that he or she will largely be given the benefit of the doubt and not risk complete alienation for thinking and acting outside the box. Thus, this leader can enact more divergent change within the organization and provide a sustained challenge to inequality.

Example: Dr. Freeman Hrabowski in his capacity as the president of the University of Maryland–Baltimore County. Hrabowski has presided over UMBC for over twenty years while also explicitly advocating for the advancement of Black and other minority students.

Through programs such as the Meyerhoff Scholars, Hrabowski has used the resources of his institution to challenge inequalities in higher education and develop future science PhDs from the Black community (as well as other minorities). He has been able to keep the identification of both Black and White members of his university in order to maintain access to resources and use those resources to help the Black community. Thus, he has been able to challenge higher education's disproportionate lack of minorities pursuing advanced degrees and disrupt the current racial hierarchy.

Discussion

A key motivation for this chapter is to expand how we conceptualize the success of Black leaders by moving beyond an understanding of it as simply making it to the top of White organizations and instead looking at the constraints and opportunities that determine how Black leaders may challenge inequality in these positions and, consequently, assessing the degree of difficulty they may face in pursuing this challenge. We argue that Black leaders are most effective at challenging inequality when they achieve mutual identification with both the Black ingroup and the White outgroup. We propose that various types of Black leaders also have varying effects on inequality: factionless leaders are not able to create meaningful change, opposition leaders and co-opted leaders are able to make incremental change, and consensus leaders are able to make more divergent change. The motivation for challenging inequality is affected by how much the leader identifies with the Black ingroup, and the ease with which change can be enacted is affected by how much the Black ingroup and the White outgroup identify with the leader.

One clear path for future research is to further explore the various pathways inductively, as well as test them deductively. First, researchers should engage in qualitative research in order to understand how Black leaders think about inequality in general and their ability to affect it within the firm (i.e., beyond external work, such as sitting on nonprofit boards or donating money). Although there has been considerable work done to explain the trajectory of Black leaders, how these leaders use their positions to challenge inequality is a much more nascent area of research. Thus, this area of research is well suited for inductive work that seeks to explore when and how these leaders consider and enact challenges toward inequality. Second, our emergent model of mutual and dual identification also sets the foundation for testable hypotheses. In the field, researchers can measure both (Black) leaders' and followers' identification with each other by race within majority-White organizations and code actions that the leader has taken from incremental to divergent change. In the lab, researchers can experiment with different configurations of mutual and dual identification and assess the degree to which individuals are willing to challenge inequality.

Future research should also explore how Black leaders balance being simultaneously constrained and enabled in their ability to challenge inequality by their mutual identification with the White outgroup—in particular, the co-opted and consensus leaders. The simultaneous constraining and enabling of Black leaders who want to challenge inequality makes them *sanctioned radicals*. Similar to tempered radicals, whose values and identities are at odds with their organization and, therefore, they attempt to change the organization without destroying it (Meyerson, 2001; Meyerson & Scully, 1995), sanctioned radicals are unique in that they hold formal power granted to them by the organization to challenge inequality. These leaders are both sanctioned by being given permission to exercise leadership and sanctioned by being constrained in how they exercise their leadership. They are radicals to the extent they are engaged in challenging inequality and therefore attempting to create change in their organizations. Thus, they are sanctioned radicals because they are given the authority to challenge inequality, whether it be incremental or deviant. Exploring the tensions built into sanctioned radicalism will aid our understanding of how Black leaders manage constraints embedded within organizational structures.

Additionally, future research can address the spillover effects of this identification process with the Black ingroup to other minority groups. The extent to which Black leaders look at themselves and other minorities in an overarching way (e.g., "Black and Brown people") might affect how they relate to the needs of those groups. In contrast, tensions between minority groups might hinder productive dialogue between groups and stymie policy changes meant to reduce inequality (e.g., a recent lawsuit filed against Harvard by Asian Americans maintaining that affirmative action policies are discriminatory against Asians). Thus, how Black leaders experience mutual identification with other minority groups can also have an important role in how much they will be both willing to and able to challenge inequality effectively.

While this chapter is focused on what Black leaders can do, challenging inequality is not solely the responsibility of Black individuals. The focus on the effects of mutual identification with the White outgroup demonstrates the important role that White organizational members can play in challenging inequality. The more the White outgroup enables Black leaders to take risks and deviate from business as usual, the more these Black leaders will be able to challenge inequality effectively. One way White people can enable this type of behavior is by providing more space for Black leaders to experiment with challenges to inequality that might make White people uncomfortable. While some White people may tend to search for solutions that minimize discomfort, White people interested in helping Black leaders challenge inequality might instead search for optimal discomfort—feelings of unease that encourage reflection and growth—within themselves.

We also note that Black leaders are not monolithic and that there might be important gender, sexuality, class, and other intersecting identities that moderate the model we have laid out. The differing experiences of Black women and Black men have been documented (Crenshaw, 1989, 1991; Rosette & Tost, 2013) and are important to consider as central to the inquiry of understanding Black leadership and challenges to inequality going forward. For example, scholars could examine whether Black women leaders are more or less penalized than Black men for challenging inequality due to their gender and racial nonprototypicality and whether the mutual identification process might differ based on whether they challenge gender or racial hierarchies.

One way to address inequality has been to focus on increasing the representation of Blacks within the leadership ranks of organizations with the hope that this greater diversity at the top could trickle down throughout organizations. Yet, as Zora Neale Hurston cautions, relying on Blackness as an indicator of a desire to help other Blacks will have limited results. We take Hurston's statement seriously and push it further by arguing that not all "kinfolk" can effectively serve their kin either. That is, a desire to challenge inequality is not enough. Even though some Black leaders might intend to challenge inequality, it is their ability to achieve mutual identification with both the Black ingroup and the White outgroup that makes them capable of successfully challenging inequality. While we laud Black leaders who are taking advantage of opportunities that they have been historically denied by making it to the top of White organizations, we hope this chapter also inspires leaders and scholars to think more critically about how Black leaders can challenge inequality within their organizations and society at large.

REFERENCES

Acker, J. (2006). Inequality regimes: Gender, class, and race in organizations. *Gender & Society, 20*(4), 441–464. https://doi.org/10.1177/0891243206289499

Ashforth, B. E., Harrison, S. H., & Corley, K. G. (2008). Identification in organizations: An examination of four fundamental questions. *Journal of Management, 34*(3), 325–374. https://doi.org/10.1177/0149206308316059

Ashforth, B. E., & Mael, F. (1989). Social identity theory and the organization. *The Academy of Management Review, 14*(1), 20–39. https://doi.org/10.2307/258189

Battilana, J., & Casciaro, T. (2012). Change agents, networks, and institutions: A contingency theory of organizational change. *The Academy of Management Journal, 55*(2), 381–398. https://doi.org/10.5465/amj.2009.0891

Blader, S. L., & Tyler, T. R. (2009). Testing and extending the group engagement model: Linkages between social identity, procedural justice, economic outcomes, and extrarole behavior. *Journal of Applied Psychology, 94*(2), 445–464. https://doi.org/10.1037/a0013935

Bobo, L., & Gilliam, F. D. J. (1990). Race, sociopolitical participation, and Black empowerment. *American Political Science Review, 84*(2), 377–393. https://doi.org/10.2307/1963525

Crenshaw, K. (1989). Demarginalizing the intersection of race and sex: A Black feminist critique of antidiscrimination doctrine, feminist theory and antiracist policies. *University of Chicago Legal Forum, 1989*, 139–167.

Crenshaw, K. (1991). Mapping the margins: Intersectionality, identity politics, and violence against women of color. *Stanford Law Review, 43*(6), 1241–1299. https://doi.org/10.2307/1229039

DeRue, D. S., & Ashford, S. J. (2010). Who will lead and who will follow? A social process of leadership identity construction in organizations. *Academy of Management Review, 35*(4), 627–647. https://doi.org/10.5465/AMR.2010.53503267

DiTomaso, N., & Hooijberg, R. (1996). Diversity and the demands of leadership. *Leadership Quarterly, 7*(2), 163–187. https://doi.org/10.1016/S1048-9843(96)90039-9

Duguid, M. M., Loyd, D. L., & Tolbert, P. S. (2012). The impact of categorical status, numeric representation, and work group prestige on preference for demographically similar others: A value threat approach. *Organization Science, 23*(2), 386–401. https://doi.org/10.1287/orsc.1100.0565

Ely, R. J. (1995). The power in demography: Women's social constructions of gender identity at work. *Academy of Management Journal, 38*(3), 589–634. https://doi.org/10.5465/256740

Harrison, D. A., Price, K. H., & Bell, M. P. (1998). Beyond relational demography: Time and the effects of surface- and deep-level diversity on work group cohesion. *Academy of Management Journal, 41*(1), 96–107. https://doi.org/10.5465/256901

Hogg, M. A., van Knippenberg, D., & Rast, D. E., III. (2012). The social identity theory of leadership: Theoretical origins, research findings, and conceptual developments. *European Review of Social Psychology, 23*(1), 258–304. https://doi .org/10.1080/10463283.2012.741134

Hollander, E. P. (1958). Conformity, status, and idiosyncrasy credit. *Psychological Review, 65*(2), 117–127. https://doi.org/10.1037/h0042501

Jost, J. T., Banaji, M. R., & Nosek, B. A. (2004). A decade of system justification theory: Accumulated evidence of conscious and unconscious bolstering of the status quo. *Political Psychology, 25*(6), 881–919. https://doi.org/10.1111/j.1467-9221 .2004.00402.x

Lockwood, P. (2006). "Someone like me can be successful": Do college students need same-gender role models? *Psychology of Women Quarterly, 30*(1), 36–46. https://doi.org/10.1111/j.1471-6402.2006.00260.x

Meyerson, D. E. (2001). *Tempered radicals: How people use difference to inspire change at work*. Boston, MA: Harvard Business School Press. Retrieved from https://books .google.com/books?id=uhoxGytpdXEC&pgis=1

Meyerson, D. E., & Scully, M. A. (1995). Tempered radicalism and the politics of ambivalence and change. *Organization Science, 6*(5), 585–600. https://doi.org/10 .1287/orsc.6.5.585

Phillips, K. W., Rothbard, N. P., & Dumas, T. L. (2009). To disclose or not to disclose? Status distance and self-disclosure in diverse environments. *Academy of Management Review, 34*(4), 710–732. https://doi.org/10.5465/amr.34.4.zok710

Roberts, L. M. (2005). Changing faces: Professional image construction in diverse organizational settings. *Academy of Management Review, 30*(4), 685–711. https:// doi.org/10.5465/amr.2005.18378873

Rosette, A. S., Leonardelli, G. J., & Phillips, K. W. (2008). The White standard: Racial bias in leader categorization. *Journal of Applied Psychology, 93*(4), 758–777. https://doi.org/10.1037/0021-9010.93.4.758

Rosette, A. S., & Tost, L. P. (2013). Perceiving social inequity when subordinate-group positioning on one dimension of social hierarchy enhances privilege recognition on another. *Psychological Science, 24*(8), 1420–1427. https://doi.org/10 .1177/0956797612473608

Sidanius, J., & Pratto, F. (1999). *Social dominance: An intergroup theory of social hierarchy and oppression*. Cambridge, England: Cambridge University Press. Retrieved from https://books.google.com/books?id=ZbCtAQAAQBAJ&pgis=1

Srivastava, S. B., & Sherman, E. L. (2014). Agents of change or cogs in the machine? Re-examining the influence of female managers on the gender wage gap. *American Journal of Sociology, 120*(6), 1–51. https://doi.org/10.1086/681960

Thomas, D. A., & Gabarro, J. J. (1999). *Breaking through: The making of minority executives in corporate America*. Boston, MA: Harvard Business School Press.

Tyler, T. R., & Blader, S. L. (2003). Engagement model: Procedural justice, social identity, and cooperative behavior. *Personality and Social Psychology Review, 7*(4), 349–361. https://doi.org/10.1207/S15327957PSPR0704_07

Zweigenhaft, R. L., & Domhoff, G. W. (2006). *Diversity in the power elite: How it happened, why it matters*. Lanham, MD: Rowman & Littlefield.

20

Managing Diversity, Managing Blackness?

An Intersectional Critique of Diversity
Management Practices

COURTNEY L. MCCLUNEY
and VERÓNICA CARIDAD RABELO

O ver fifty years have passed since the Civil Rights Act of 1964 prohibited employment discrimination on the basis of race. Although
this formal legislation helped to increase racial diversity in the workplace
(Tomaskovic-Devey et al., 2006), particularly for Black people, less progress has been made with respect to *inclusion*, or the extent to which Black
employees gain access to social capital and networks, influence decision
making, and feel that they belong (Mor Barak & Cherin, 1998; Roberson, 2006). Furthermore, Black employees face continued struggles to
be hired, retained, promoted, and included at work. In efforts to reduce
discrimination lawsuits against employers (James & Wooten, 2006), retain Black employees (Allen, Bryant, & Vardaman, 2010), and increase
access to diverse markets (Cox & Blake, 1991), many organizations have
implemented initiatives to "manage" diversity. Cox (1994) defines managing diversity as "planning and implementing organizational systems
and practices to manage people so that the potential advantages of diversity are maximized while its potential disadvantages are minimized"
(p. 11). An increasingly prevalent diversity initiative is the appointment
of diversity and inclusion (D&I) officers, who are typically tasked with
hiring, retaining, and promoting a "diverse workforce." As of 2012, nearly
20 percent of S&P 500 Index firms had appointed a "chief diversity

officer" (Shi, Pathak, Song, & Hoskisson, 2018). D&I officers are increasingly likely to work in academia (Wilson, 2013), as well as government and nonprofit sectors (Williams & Wade-Golden, 2013). Despite the growth of positions centered on D&I over the past few decades, their impact is not readily apparent (Deloitte, 2017). Black employees continue to face sticky floors, glass ceilings, and labyrinthine career paths. Furthermore, their race and gender are often under scrutiny; for example, at the time of this publication, it is legally permissible for employers to rescind a Black woman's job offer for having dreadlocks (*Equal Employment Opportunity Commission v. Catastrophe Management Solutions*).

Why have D&I approaches failed to hire, retain, and advance Black employees at work? Furthermore, how have the past few decades of "diversity management" affected Black employees? In this chapter, we argue that the objective of managing diversity in organizations effectively seeks to *manage Blackness*. We find that D&I officers often adopt an individual approach—whereby they seek to help Black employees "fit" into dominant organizational cultures that reflect and reify the status quo—at the expense of a structural approach, which would seek to eradicate systemic inequality in organizations and communities. Our aim is not to criticize the efforts of individual D&I practitioners; most practitioners are women and/or people of color (Nixon, 2017; Williams & Wade-Golden, 2013) whose leadership skills and strategies are constrained by organizational hierarchies and resources (Leon, 2014). Rather, we call into question the organizational practices that led to the creation and design of D&I roles while also restricting their ability to eradicate inequality.

To move companies beyond "managing" diversity (and, by extension, managing Blackness), we propose that organizations adopt an intersectional (Crenshaw, 1989; Holvino, 2010) approach to justice. Intersectionality is a heuristic that can be used "both as an academic frame and as a practical intervention" (Cho, Crenshaw, & McCall, 2013, p. 807). It helps scholars and practitioners analyze how structures and institutions—including organizations' histories, routines, processes, and networks—affect Black employees as a whole and at the intersections of other social identities (e.g., Elliott & Smith, 2004). Contextualizing diversity management within an intersectionality framework enables us to center the underlying cause of the problems that D&I roles are intended to solve (e.g., White masculine organizational cultures; Rabelo & Cortina, 2016), rather than focusing on "fixing" people harmed by these problems (i.e.,

Black people). Thus, an intersectional (vs. individual) perspective is necessary to identify recommendations for cultivating inclusion that are rooted in social justice (e.g., Opie & Roberts, 2017).

The purpose of our chapter is twofold. First, we use intersectionality to analyze the shortcomings of diversity management, focusing on organizational structures (e.g., routines, networks, processes) that affect the work of D&I officers and, by extension, Black employees. Second, we identify alternative perspectives and practices that D&I officers might adopt to shift their work from an individual to a structural focus. We draw these practices from three different leadership contexts: recent corporate initiatives (e.g., Starbucks' anti-bias training), a phenomenological study of Black clergywomen (McCluney, 2017), and the work of D&I officers in higher education. Collectively, we draw attention to the invisible, embedded aspects of organizations that rely on individualistic approaches to "managing" diversity—at the expense of dismantling underlying power dynamics that privilege particular leaders and groups over others. Doing so is important for ensuring that D&I officers shift away from viewing diversity as a problem to be managed and instead focus on hegemonic Whiteness as the proximal reason for low inclusion among Black employees.

Based on our synthesis of D&I literature and interpretive analysis of the case studies, we identify three mechanisms that contribute to the failure of common diversity management practices and its unintended consequences for Black employees' work experiences: (1) promoting the business case for diversity, (2) holding narrow imaginations of Blackness, and (3) applying a "blanket" perspective of diversity. We discuss how these common diversity practices fail and draw on our examples to illustrate the effectiveness of alternative, intersectional, justice-based approaches to managing diversity.

Mechanism #1: The Business Case for Diversity

Corporate diversity initiatives, including the appointment of D&I officers, have not resulted in substantial improvements with respect to the selection, retention, and promotion of Black employees. One reason for this mismatch between effort and outcomes could be a widespread focus on the "business case" for diversity, which refers to value placed on diversity due to the strategic advantages associated with gaining greater access to, and legitimacy among, diverse markets (Cox & Blake, 1991;

Ely & Thomas, 2001). The business case is at odds with social justice praxis (Edgley, Sharma, & Anderson-Gough, 2016), as it values diversity for its profitability. We argue that the business case commodifies Blackness and objectifies Black people, rendering them valuable only to the extent that they can improve organizational performance. When diversity initiatives are rooted in the business case for diversity, then their success is measured by increased revenue, market share, and customer base (Herring, 2009), rather than by their impact on Black employees (e.g., satisfaction, well-being). The commodification and objectification produced by the business case for diversity can make it difficult for Black employees who already struggle with feeling authentic (Roberts, Cha, Hewlin, & Settles, 2009) and that they belong at work (Ely & Thomas, 2001).

Organizational rhetoric and policies that rely on the "business case" for diversity rarely achieve significant progress with respect to equity and justice, within organizations and their surrounding communities alike. For example, in the wake of civil protests following the murder of Michael Brown by police in Ferguson, Missouri, then-CEO of Starbucks Howard Schultz launched the #RaceTogether initiative (Logan, 2016; McCluney, Roberts, & Wooten, 2017). This strategic campaign included several components, such as dialogues with local police chiefs, opportunities for jobless young people of color, and printing "#RaceTogether" on over one hundred million Starbucks cups. Skeptics wondered whether #RaceTogether would provide material benefits for Starbucks employees, customers, and community members. Critics raised concerns about the increased emotional labor that #RaceTogether would place on baristas (most of whom are people of color), as well as general doubt given the overwhelmingly White and male composition of company executives (Logan, 2019; McCluney, Roberts, & Wooten, 2017). #RaceTogether did achieve success in one realm: fulfilling the promise of the business case, bringing Starbucks increased revenue during the campaign. This is consistent with Schultz's focus on "brand sparks," or marketing rooted in "cultural or humanitarian issues" (Schultz, 2011). Similar rhetoric promoting the business case for diversity permeates the Starbucks website. For example, the Supplier Diversity Program frames diversity as "a smart business decision and business imperative in today's business climate . . . [that can drive] value and economic development in the communities we serve" (Starbucks, n.d.b), with no attention given to the experience of people who live and work in those communities.

Three years and one month after Starbucks initiated #RaceTogether, a Philadelphia branch manager had two Black men arrested for trespassing on April 12, 2018. Starbucks declared the arrests "reprehensible" and responded by closing approximately eight thousand stores in the United States for a daylong anti-bias training for employees (Starbucks, 2018a). Although nearly half of Starbucks baristas in the United States are people of color (Starbucks, n.d.a) and the company generates profits and market share through a global supply chain, its focus on justice was lacking, which both reflected and heightened perceptions of prejudice within the company. Previous efforts by Starbucks to address racial bias were discredited due to the lack of racial representation among senior leaders and reliance on prison labor (NPR, 2018). In light of the arrests, Starbucks leaders demonstrated a desire to address past and present discrimination by forming a new unit titled the Third Place[1] (Starbucks, 2018b). What remains unknown is the extent to which initiatives such as daylong trainings and programming from the Third Place will initiate, and sustain, cultural and structural change.

Mechanism #2: Narrow Imaginations of Blackness

To the extent that the business case commodifies Blackness and values Black people for their adherence to the status quo, it follows that companies seek to hire and retain the "right" kind of Black employees. As members of an oppressed, marginalized social identity group, Black people are perceived to lack individuality and are instead rendered as "representatives of a social group distinguished by a common socio-demographic trait, the repository of a 'true,' essential identity" (Zanoni, Janssens, Benschop, & Nkomo, 2010, p. 13). To appease the hegemonic ideals of organizations, D&I officers are tasked with monitoring and constraining the behaviors and appearance of Black employees. Managers, human resource personnel, and D&I officers often are complicit in "identity regulation" (Zanoni & Janssens, 2007, p. 1375), whereby they impose "desirable," and often White, norms and behavioral expectations. By extension, Blackness is regarded as inherently unprofessional and, therefore, subject to "management" in the workplace. White, Eurocentric organizational cultures regulate Blackness and, in the process, coerce Black employees into monitoring or modifying their identity and appearance (Roberts & Roberts, 2007; Rosette & Dumas, 2007). For example, when Black women chemically straighten their hair (vs. wearing it naturally in an afro or dreadlocks), White people perceive them as more professional and as "fitting in" more with US corporate culture (Johnson, Godsil, MacFarlane, Tropp, & Goff, 2017; Opie & Phillips, 2015). Black employees are keenly aware of the ways they must monitor and possibly modify their bodies to belong and succeed at work. For instance, interviews with prospective job applicants showed that one-third of Black job seekers felt pressured to conceal their race to get a "foot in the door," and over three-quarters felt they needed to assimilate and avoid "sticking out" (Kang, DeCelles, Tilcsik, & Jun, 2016). Maintaining organizational cultures that are rooted in Whiteness and maleness (Liu & Baker, 2014) will further marginalize Black employees as organizational outsiders.

Churches are one organizational context where narrow understandings of Blackness have shaped how D&I practices affect Black employees. Traditionally, churches in Black communities have served as sites of political action and social change (Barnes, 2012), and they thus serve as a valuable field site for informing the social justice praxis needed in organizations. We use an example of one clergywoman within a qualitative study of Black clergywomen to illustrate how Black leaders are often tasked to manage Blackness within organizations, even if it is beyond their purview (McCluney, 2017). Associate Minister Jazmine (a pseudonym) is the first Black clergywoman Episcopal priest of a church with a majority-White congregation and one of the largest endowments of all churches in her state (annual operating budget of approximately $2.5 million). She received her degree from a prestigious divinity school within her denomination that is primarily attended by White men. In her current role as the "downtown missioner" for her church, Jazmine experiences pressure to monitor and modify Blackness to maintain her church's organizational identity. Jazmine is responsible for attracting more "urban" members to the congregation, thereby continuing the church's legacy of "radicals" devoted to the urban poor:[2] "They hired me because . . . my boss wants more young people who live in the city to come to this church." Yet she felt pressure to pursue a specific "type" of city dweller based on the reaction from the other (White) church leaders. She shares, "I could say, 'What about this person over there,' and [the church leaders] are like [gasps], 'Oh no, that's a poor Black person,' even though they would never admit that because they're very good liberals. But when they say 'young . . . urban,' [they] meant people like me . . . educated." Jazmine is subtly directed to diversify the church in ways that accommodate Whiteness by narrowly defining what is acceptable for Black people (in this instance, educational attainment and status) while also using coded language ("urban") to describe Black people. Although not formally a D&I practitioner, Jazmine is expected to assume responsibilities that D&I practitioners often perform. Yet, her ability to authentically engage her community and enact meaningful change is constrained by the more powerful leaders' narrow understanding of Blackness and Black people.

Mechanism #3: Blanket Application of Diversity

An additional mechanism inhibiting D&I is the frequent blanket application of diversity. Many have illustrated how diversity is an ambiguous and "fuzzy term" (Edgley et al., 2016, p. 4) that can encompass all aspects of identities and experiences (e.g., personality traits, eye color) rather than just those that are rooted in historical patterns of exclusion, marginality, and disadvantage. One risk of an overly broad understanding of diversity is the embedding of color-blind ideologies within D&I initiatives, such as diversity statements (Apfelbaum, Stephens, & Reagans, 2016). When organizations do not clearly define diversity, it becomes difficult to acknowledge and address institutional norms and practices that disproportionately exclude, marginalize, or discriminate against Black employees. Moreover, a broad and vague understanding of diversity may not benefit Black students and employees experiencing compounded marginality, including those who are LGBTQ+, undocumented, living with disabilities, or otherwise "nontraditional" (e.g., veterans, caregivers).

An additional consequence of relying on a broad view of diversity is that it contributes to the notion that social groups are homogenous—for example, that all Black people share the same values, beliefs, and career goals. Such a broad, yet simplified, notion of race/ethnicity can contribute to cultural taxation and occupational segregation of Black employees. Organizational discourse often relies on stereotypical and essentialized notions of race (Litvin, 1997; Zanoni & Janssens, 2007). Presuming that Black employees have similar aspirations, competencies, and specialized knowledge may inhibit their career opportunities and development.

Evidence of broad, fuzzy, and blanket understandings of diversity permeate academia. Nixon (2017) characterizes US higher education as a site "of White supremacy, patriarchy, classism, heteronormativity, and other forms of exclusion" (p. 314). Some of the oldest and most prestigious US universities were built by enslaved Black people who were denied admission for several generations to come. Only in the past thirty years have leaders of many higher education institutions begun to think (and act) more intentionally about issues of race, access, and equity (Smith, 2015). Often, students demand institutional change for themselves, with the support of "tempered radical" (Meyerson & Scully, 1995) allies. In response, many higher education institutions have established diversity "initiatives" and appointed diversity "officers" (Nixon, 2017). One study found that 80 percent of postsecondary institutions included "diversity statements" or referenced "diversity" in mission statements and publicity campaigns; however, such rhetoric and initiatives were not correlated with fair and inclusive learning and working environments for students, staff, and faculty (Rowley, Hurtado, & Panjuan, 2002). In this way, diversity often functions "as myth and ceremony rather than having a substantive impact on organizational work or outcomes" (Rowley et al., 2002, p. 16).

We contend that loose understandings of diversity are one reason for these discrepancies between institutional rhetoric and practices. When diversity is conceptualized as every possible axis of difference among humans, then less attention is given to the ways power affects identity, access, and equity. Indeed, the broadening of definitions of diversity enables dominant groups to monopolize power, contributing to underrepresented groups' early departure from postsecondary education institutions (Minefee, Rabelo, Stewart, & Young, 2018). As a result, diversity becomes a project that ought to benefit all institutional members, as opposed to those who have been most severely harmed by historical and institutional injustice. This helps explain why the primary beneficiaries of affirmative action have been White women (Hartmann, 1996).

Essentialist understandings of diversity can also explain why most of the highest-ranking Black employees in universities and corporate settings are D&I officers. On the one hand, these positions may offer pathways to leadership previously unavailable to Black employees. On the other hand, funneling Black employees into D&I may signal that their knowledge is valuable *only* within specific aspects of the organization. Furthermore, D&I work may exacerbate the "cultural taxation" that many marginalized personnel endure at work, particularly if their efforts are not changing the status quo. Finally, appointing Black employees to dedicated D&I roles may alleviate responsibility and accountability for deeper institutional change, "as if being 'just there' is enough" (Ahmed, 2012, p. 23).

Call to Action: From Managing Blackness to Managing Injustice

Black employees, like most people, desire workplace belongingness and opportunities for challenging work, as well as the ability to remain (and advance) within their organizations (Travis, Thorpe-Moscon, & McCluney, 2016). Yet they face disproportionate challenges to securing employment and, once hired, job security, inclusion, and opportunities for advancement. In an effort to address some of these issues, many organizations have created dedicated D&I roles. Given the range of tasks that D&I officers may perform, it is challenging to assess the impact of diversity management. That said, centering Black employees in analyses of D&I discourse and practices illustrates how diversity management often reinforces the status quo by adopting an individual perspective, regulating cultural expression, and enforcing assimilation. We present several recommended strategies for D&I officers to evolve from managing Blackness to managing injustice.

First, an alternative approach to the business case for diversity would ensure that D&I practitioners' work climates are oriented around fairness, equity, and justice, rather than profit maximization at the expense of Black employees' dignity and well-being. D&I leaders drew from Starbucks' mission to take actions focused on encouraging the treatment of everyone with dignity and respect (Starbucks, 2018b). Additionally, Starbucks has implemented hiring programs targeting refugees and youths of color in efforts to mitigate inequality. Its actions emulate a restorative justice approach. Such an approach shifts the attention of D&I officers away from monitoring and managing Blackness and toward eradicating racism (and its denial) in organizations (Opie & Roberts, 2017). Adopting a social justice perspective would include recognizing organizational and societal harm against Black people, including their continuous exposure to racial trauma and violence in society through interactions with police (McCluney, Bryant, King, & Ali, 2017). D&I officers may engage in efforts to redress these harms faced by Black employees by contributing their resources and knowledge to company and community initiatives (e.g., Ruggs et al., 2016).

Second, D&I practitioners must ensure that their work does not result in the control of Blackness (e.g., monitoring and modifying Black people's identities and expressions) but instead focuses on undoing practices that undermine Black employees' satisfaction, inclusion, and performance. Opie and Freeman (2017) posit that assessing employee fit does little to ensure that employers find the right person for their job and instead judges how well individuals fit the current White male–centric organization. Thus, practitioners ought to ensure that their assumptions about appropriate and professional workplace norms and behaviors are not culturally biased (Opie & Freeman, 2017). Further, they must ensure that they are valuing Black employees for their unique ideas, perspectives, and contributions, and not for their representativeness of (or interchangeability with) all Black people, access to certain markets, or adherence to White norms. Taken together, attempts to define "acceptable" behavior and bodies in organizations often narrow and monitor Blackness and pressure Black employees to change, rather than questioning practices that value Black employees to the extent that they "conform to the majority culture" (Opie & Freeman, 2017, p. 4). Further, when bias is acknowledged in the workplace, it is often "disembedded from the greater context of historically determined, structurally unequal access to and distribution of resources between socio-demographic groups" (Zanoni et al., 2010, p. 14).

Third, D&I officers must engage in tangible actions to remove the broad-brush application of diversity to avoid succumbing to managing Blackness. This includes facilitating space for employees to hold difficult conversations. In particular, sharing experiences of inclusion as well as ostracism or undermining can help employees understand how cultural and individual differences shape experiences at work. Research by Catalyst (2016) emphasizes the importance for organizational leaders to engage in dialogue on issues of race and difference. Creating space for honest conversations around areas of difference can begin to address tensions among employees. Also, by adopting an intersectional approach to D&I, practitioners can demonstrate how companies' historical context shapes different groups' access to resources and opportunities. As an example, Georgetown University sought to address historical oppression by offering preferential admission to descendants of the enslaved Black Americans who were sold to subsidize the university's expenses in the nineteenth century (NPR, 2017). Thus, a historical, contextualized, and justice-oriented perspective is necessary if organizations seek to promote inclusion of Black employees. We agree with Opie and Roberts's (2017) assertion "that true diversity and inclusion may be elusive until scholars and practitioners explore the racist history that undergirds contemporary workplace discrimination and subsequently addresses it in ways that encourage actual change" (p. 708). It's challenging, but organizations need to contend with their racist pasts head on and figure out how to move forward.

Conclusion

In this chapter, we have argued that diversity management, while well intentioned, often accomplishes the exact opposite of its goal. We have theorized three mechanisms to explain how, in seeking to manage diversity, practitioners instead manage Blackness by adopting a (1) business case for diversity, (2) narrow imagination of Black people, and (3) blanket (decontextualized) application of "diversity." As an alternative to this traditional approach to diversity management, we instead propose an *intersectional justice* perspective, which focuses on valuing Black employees, accounting for history and social structures, addressing the root cause of inequality, and empowering—rather than commodifying or exploiting—Black communities. We thus problematize current D&I practice by investigating how managing and interrogating Whiteness will enable organizations to increase representation and inclusion of Black people and their experiences in the workplace. Put simply, we advise that practitioners shift away from managing diversity and instead toward managing *injustice*.

NOTES

1. The Third Place (between work and home) policy, implemented through training developed for partners, reflects Starbucks' new commitment to creating "a warm and welcoming environment where customers can gather and connect . . . and use Starbucks spaces . . . regardless of whether they make a purchase" (Starbucks, 2018b).

2. This description of the church is used in secondary documents (e.g., website, brochure) about the church.

REFERENCES

Ahmed, S. (2012). *On being included*. Durham, NC: Duke University Press.

Allen, D. G., Bryant, P. C., & Vardaman, J. M. (2010). Retaining talent: Replacing misconceptions with evidence-based strategies. *Academy of Management Perspectives, 24*(2), 48–64.

Apfelbaum, E. P., Stephens, N. M., & Reagans, R. E. (2016). Beyond one-size-fits-all: Tailoring diversity approaches to the representation of social groups. *Journal of Personality and Social Psychology, 111*(4), 547–566.

Barnes, S. L. (2012). *Live long and prosper: How Black megachurches address HIV/AIDS and poverty in the age of prosperity theology*. New York, NY: Fordham University Press.

Catalyst. (2016). *Engaging in conversations about gender, race, and ethnicity in the workplace*. Practitioner's Tool, Catalyst, New York, NY.

Cho, S., Crenshaw, K., & McCall, L. (2013). Toward a field of intersectionality studies: Theory, applications, and praxis. *Signs, 38*(4), 785–810.

Cox, T. (1994). *Cultural diversity in organizations: Theory, research and practice*. San Francisco, CA: Berrett-Koehler.

Cox, T., & Blake, S. (1991). Managing cultural diversity: Implications for organizational competitiveness. *Academy of Management Executive, 5*(3), 45–56.

Crenshaw, K. (1989). Demarginalizing the intersection of race and sex: A Black feminist critique of antidiscrimination doctrine, feminist theory and antiracist politics. *University of Chicago Legal Forum, 1989*, 139–167.

Deloitte. (2017). *Missing pieces report: The 2016 board diversity census of women and minorities on Fortune 500 boards*. Retrieved from http://www.catalyst.org/system/files/2016_board_diversity_census_deloitte_abd.pdf

Edgley, C., Sharma, N., & Anderson-Gough, F. (2016). Diversity and professionalism in the Big Four firms: Expectation, celebration and weapon in the battle for talent. *Critical Perspectives on Accounting, 35*, 13–34.

Elliott, J. R., & Smith, R. A. (2004). Race, gender, and workplace power. *American Sociological Review, 69*(3), 365–386.

Ely, R. J., & Thomas, D. A. (2001). Cultural diversity at work: The effects of diversity perspectives on work group processes and outcomes. *Administrative Science Quarterly, 46*(2), 229–273.

Equal Employment Opportunity Commission v. Catastrophe Management Solutions, No. 1:13-cv-00476-CB-M (11th U.S. Circuit Court of Appeals 2016).

Hartmann, H. (1996). Who has benefited from affirmative action in employment? In G. E. Curry (Ed.), *The affirmative action debate* (pp. 77–96). Cambridge, MA: Perseus Books.

Herring, C. (2009). Does diversity pay? Race, gender, and the business case for diversity. *American Sociological Review, 74*(2), 208–224.

Holvino, E. (2010). Intersections: The simultaneity of race, gender and class in organization studies. *Gender, Work & Organization, 17*(3), 248–277.

James, E. H., & Wooten, L. P. (2006). Diversity crises: How firms manage discrimination lawsuits. *Academy of Management Journal, 49*(6), 1103–1118.

Johnson, A. M., Godsil, R. D., MacFarlane, J., Tropp, L. R., & Goff, P. A. (2017). *The "good hair" study: Explicit and implicit attitudes towards Black women's hair* (Report). Retrieved from https://perception.org/wp-content/uploads/2017/01/TheGood-HairStudyFindingsReport.pdf

Kang, S. K., DeCelles, K. A., Tilcsik, A., & Jun, S. (2016). Whitened résumés: Race and self-presentation in the labor market. *Administrative Science Quarterly, 61*(3), 469–502.

Leon, R. A. (2014). The chief diversity officer: An examination of CDO models and strategies. *Journal of Diversity in Higher Education, 7*(2), 77–91.

Litvin, D. R. (1997). The discourse of diversity: From biology to management. *Organization, 4*(2), 187–209.

Liu, H., & Baker, C. (2014). White knights: Leadership as the heroicisation of whiteness. *Leadership, 12*(4), 420–448.

Logan, N. (2016). The Starbucks Race Together Initiative: Analyzing a public relations campaign with critical race theory. *Public Relations Inquiry, 5*(1), 93–113.

Logan, N. (2019). Corporate personhood and the corporate responsibility to race. *Journal of Business Ethics, 154*(4), 977–988.

McCluney, C. L. (2017). *Blooming where I'm planted: A phenomenological investigation of Black clergywomen's marginality and leadership* (Unpublished doctoral dissertation). University of Michigan, Ann Arbor.

McCluney, C. L., Bryant, C. M., King, D. D., & Ali, A. A. (2017). Calling in Black: A dynamic model of racially traumatic events, resourcing, and safety. *Equality, Diversity and Inclusion, 36*(8), 767–786.

McCluney, C. L., Roberts, L. M., & Wooten, L. P. (2017). It takes courage: Lessons learned from Starbucks' #RaceTogether campaign case study. In R. Koonce, P. Robinson, & B. Vogel (Eds.), *Developing leaders for positive organizing* (pp. 95–108). Bingley, UK: Emerald.

Meyerson, D. E., & Scully, M. A. (1995). Crossroads tempered radicalism and the politics of ambivalence and change. *Organization Science, 6*(5), 585–600.

Minefee, I., Rabelo, V. C., Stewart, O. J. C., & Young, N. C. J. (2018). Repairing leaks in the pipeline: A social closure perspective on underrepresented racial/ethnic minority recruitment and retention in business schools. *Academy of Management Learning & Education, 17*(1), 79–95.

Mor Barak, M. E., & Cherin, D. A. (1998). A tool to expand organizational understanding of workforce diversity. *Administration in Social Work, 22*(1), 47–64.

Nixon, M. L. (2017). Experiences of women of color university chief diversity officers. *Journal of Diversity in Higher Education, 10*(4), 301–317.

NPR. (2017, April 28). *Georgetown University to offer slave descendants preferential admissions.* Retrieved from https://www.npr.org/2017/04/28/526085106/georgetown-university-to-offer-slave-descendants-preferential-admissions

NPR. (2018, August 21). *U.S. prison inmates to strike over poor living conditions.* Retrieved from https://www.npr.org/2018/08/21/640437993/u-s-prison-inmates-to-strike-over-poor-living-conditions

Opie, T. R., & Freeman, R. E. (2017, July). Our biases undermine our colleagues' attempts to be authentic. *Harvard Business Review,* pp. 2–5. Retrieved from https://hbr.org/2017/07/our-biases-undermine-our-colleagues-attempts-to-be-authentic

Opie, T. R., & Phillips, K. W. (2015). Hair penalties: The negative influence of Afrocentric hair on ratings of Black women's dominance and professionalism. *Frontiers in Psychology, 6,* 1–14.

Opie, T. R., & Roberts, L. M. (2017). Do Black lives really matter in the workplace? Restorative justice as a means to reclaim humanity. *Equality, Diversity and Inclusion, 36*(8), 707–719.

Rabelo, V. C., & Cortina, L. M. (2016). Intersectionality: Infusing I-O psychology with feminist thought. In T.-A. Roberts, N. Curtin, L. M. Cortina, & L. E. Duncan (Eds.), *Feminist perspectives on building a better psychological science of gender* (pp. 179–197). Cham, Switzerland: Springer.

Roberson, Q. M. (2006). Disentangling the meanings of diversity and inclusion in organizations. *Group & Organization Management, 31*(2), 212–236.

Roberts, L. M., Cha, S. E., Hewlin, P. F., & Settles, I. H. (2009). Bringing the inside out: Enhancing authenticity and positive identity in organizations. In L. M. Roberts & J. Dutton (Eds.), *Exploring positive identities and organizations: Building a theoretical and research foundation* (pp. 149–169). New York, NY: Taylor & Francis.

Roberts, L. M., & Roberts, D. D. (2007). Testing the limits of antidiscrimination law: The business, legal, and ethical ramifications of cultural profiling at work. *Duke Journal of Gender Law & Policy, 14*, 369–405.

Rosette, A. S., & Dumas, T. L. (2007). The hair dilemma: Conform to mainstream expectations or emphasize racial identity. *Duke Journal of Gender Law & Policy, 14*(1), 407–421.

Rowley, L. L., Hurtado, S., & Panjuan, L. (2002). *Organizational rhetoric or reality? The disparities between avowed commitment to diversity and formal programs and initiatives in higher education institutions.* Paper presented at the 83rd Annual Meeting of the American Educational Research Association, New Orleans, LA. Retrieved from https://pdfs.semanticscholar.org/9951/c4ac6948736b3c57da637f5832644d7a099d.pdf

Ruggs, E. N., Hebl, M. R., Rabelo, V. C., Weaver, K. B., Kovacs, J., & Kemp, A. S. (2016). Baltimore is burning: Can I-O psychologists help extinguish the flames? *Industrial and Organizational Psychology, 9*(3), 525–547.

Schultz, H. (2011). *Onward: How Starbucks fought for its life without losing its soul.* New York, NY: Rodale.

Shi, W., Pathak, S., Song, L. J., & Hoskisson, R. E. (2018). The adoption of chief diversity officers among S&P 500 firms: Institutional, resource dependence, and upper echelons accounts. *Human Resource Management, 57*(1), 83–96.

Smith, D. G. (2015). *Diversity's promise for higher education: Making it work* (2nd ed.). Baltimore, MD: Johns Hopkins University Press.

Starbucks. (n.d.a). Inclusion at Starbucks. Retrieved from https://www.starbucks.com/responsibility/community/diversity-and-inclusion/aspirations

Starbucks. (n.d.b). Supplier Diversity Program. Retrieved from https://www.starbucks.com/responsibility/sourcing/suppliers

Starbucks. (2018a, April 17). Starbucks to close all stores nationwide for racial-bias education on May 29. Retrieved from https://news.starbucks.com/press-releases/starbucks-to-close-stores-nationwide-for-racial-bias-education-may-29

Starbucks. (2018b, May 29). The Third Place: Our commitment, renewed. Retrieved from https://starbuckschannel.com/thethirdplace/

Tomaskovic-Devey, D., Stainback, K., Taylor, T., Zimmer, C., Robinson, C., & Mctague, T. (2006). Documenting desegregation: Segregation in American workplaces by race, ethnicity, and sex, 1966–2003. *American Sociological Review, 71*(4), 565–588.

Travis, D. J., Thorpe-Moscon, J., & McCluney, C. L. (2016). *Emotional tax: How Black women and men pay more at work and how leaders can take action* (Report).

Retrieved from http://www.catalyst.org/system/files/emotional_tax_how_black_women_and_men_pay_more.pdf

Williams, D. A., & Wade-Golden, K. C. (2013). *The chief diversity officer: Strategy, structure, and change management.* Sterling, VA: Stylus.

Wilson, J. L. (2013). Emerging trend: The chief diversity officer phenomenon within higher education. *Journal of Negro Education*, *82*(4), 433–445.

Zanoni, P., & Janssens, M. (2007). Minority employees engaging with (diversity) management: An analysis of control, agency, and micro-emancipation. *Journal of Management Studies*, *44*(8), 1371–1397.

Zanoni, P., Janssens, M., Benschop, Y., & Nkomo, S. (2010). Unpacking diversity, grasping inequality: Rethinking difference through critical perspectives. *Organization*, *17*(1), 9–29.

21

Uncovering the Hidden Face of Affinity Fraud

Race-Based Predatory Bias, Social Identity, and the Need for Inclusive Leadership

AUDREY MURRELL, RAY JONES, *and* JENNIFER PETRIE

Affinity fraud is often described as exploiting group trust based on shared affiliations or common social characteristics, such as race, religion, ethnicity, age, or professional designation, for the purpose of financial advantage or gain (Perri & Brody, 2012). In affinity fraud, an offender uses identification with a targeted group to gain the trust of group members. Because social identity plays a central role, fraudulent or unethical practices can spread quickly due to positive feelings of affinity among individuals. Some argue that the impact of affinity-based fraud can be more devastating than that of non–affinity fraud or schemes. For example, one estimate over a ten-year period is that there were more than three hundred sizeable Ponzi schemes with combined losses for investors of more than $50 billion. It is estimated that over half of these cases were affinity based (Marquet International, 2011). One of the largest Ponzi scheme offenders in history, Bernie Madoff, relied on his affinity with Jewish clients and wealthy investor circles to scam an estimated $20 billion from clients (Marquet International, 2011). Affinity fraud continues to have detrimental effects on the American consumer; the Federal Trade Commission indicates that an estimated 10.8 percent of all US adults are victims of fraud, with many crimes relying on group trust (Anderson, 2013). Understanding how affinity fraud reflects the negative use of kinship or social identity based on demographic characteristics such as race, ethnicity, religion, or social class is the focus of this chapter. This analysis is important for revealing how the impact of affinity-based fraud is often ignored or mischaracterized as a function of unsophisticated consumers who lack financial literacy. We argue for the need to develop inclusive leadership to help address and ultimately prevent this type of predatory bias and its consequences within business and society.

We focus in particular on race-based affinity fraud targeting African Americans, as it provides a strong example of how negative aspects of social identity characteristics can play a key role in affinity fraud cases. Researchers indicate that marginalized and racialized groups such as African Americans experience more harm from affinity fraud, necessitating more proactive investigation and intervention (Austin, 2004; Federal Trade Commission, 2016). To better understand race-based affinity fraud, our chapter describes three specific case examples of how affinity fraud infiltrated African American groups, as explained by three mechanisms of social identity theory: ingroup favoritism, outgroup derogation, and positive distinctiveness. We then discuss the potential impact of inclusive leadership as a critical intervening factor that can help address race-based affinity fraud. This perspective complements previous literature that advocates for regulatory enforcement, consumer education, and individual behavioral change to combat affinity fraud (Austin, 2004; Bosley & Knorr, 2016; Fairfax, 2003; Federal Trade Commission, 2016; Kramer, 2009). We argue that principles of inclusive leadership can also serve to influence individual, group, and organizational behavior in such a manner as to help reduce predatory biases, such as identity-based affinity fraud, that negatively affect African Americans and other racial/ethnic groups.

This work is important because one of the great dangers of affinity fraud is that it works by undercutting the standard respect for inclusive and ethical practices that should be supported, modeled, and upheld by leadership within organizations (Bucy, Formby, Raspanti, & Rooney, 2008). In legal and public policy assessments of how to prevent affinity fraud, most authors offer technical approaches based on developing awareness of investment practices and recognizing investment opportunities that are "too good to be true." With race-based affinity fraud, a purely technical approach would not address the powerful social and psychological aspects of the fraud that often lead victims to take an active and (even) willing role in the fraudulent activities. This is a leadership challenge that requires far more than just technical knowledge of investments. Thus, we assert that principles of inclusive leadership can play a critical role in preventing and addressing the negative consequences of race-based affinity fraud. This is consistent with previous work that has outlined practical steps for individuals to be vigilant against biases that may render them victims of manipulated trust (e.g., Kramer, 2009). We suggest that while affinity and identity processes within racial and other social identity groups can be manipulated or exploited, these contexts may serve as a unique opportunity for inclusive leadership to have a positive impact in reducing the negative consequences of this type of predatory behavior.

Race-Based Affinity Fraud and African Americans

Previous work shows that affinity fraud disproportionately targets racial identity groups such as African Americans based on community and ethnic connections (Austin, 2004; Federal Trade Commission, 2016; Khasru, 2001). African Americans are more likely to be fraud victims, at 17.3 percent compared with 13.4 percent of Hispanics and 9 percent of non-Hispanic Whites (Anderson, 2013; Federal Trade Commission, 2016). Affinity fraud exacerbates financial obstacles for African Americans, as they already encounter higher rates of fraudulent practices, such as predatory subprime loans, even when controlling for income and risk factors, such as credit score (Fisher, 2009). It is also the case that African Americans are the targets of predatory investment schemes by those who leverage a common group identity within the African American community. These unethical individuals frequently claim solidarity with African Americans and frame their financing as combating the historical racial oppression in mainstream financial institutions (Austin, 2004; Sargsian, 2012). They successfully commit fraud by tapping into the religious social justice beliefs that are highly valued within African American communities, such as a belief in efforts to overcome past injustices or improve the financial condition of the oppressed (Austin, 2004). African Americans are also less likely to report being victims of affinity fraud due to the bonds of ingroup trust and a proclivity to distrust law enforcement and government as the outgroup. The reluctance to report affinity fraud frequently hinders investigation, prosecution, and prevention (Austin, 2004; Bosley & Knorr, 2016; Federal Trade Commission, 2016; Perri & Brody, 2011).

On a macrolevel, affinity fraud renders more harm for African Americans compared with Whites. The negative financial and psychological effects of fraud and betrayal, which all victims experience, are compounded by detrimental and stigmatizing effects specific to African American communities (Austin, 2004; Fink, 2009). As African American communities often self-finance through charitable giving and community investment in local nonprofit organizations and African American churches, affinity fraud erodes both resources and the communal system of trust that brings African Americans together to fund community organizations and missions. Austin (2004) argues that affinity fraud is a crime perpetrated not just on the individual but on the community as a whole. Thus, race-based affinity fraud is a crime against the social fabric of trust that binds African American communities together that can stifle positive community transformation.

Some argue that affinity fraud is particularly egregious to African Americans because of persistent financial vulnerability. African Americans have low rates of proactive investment compared with non-Hispanic Whites at every income quartile (Brown, 2007). At the highest income quartile, 26 percent of African Americans own stocks, compared with 56 percent of Whites (Brown, 2007). At the lowest income quartile, Whites own stocks at a percentage ten times greater than African Americans (Brown, 2007). The affront of affinity fraud perpetuates the reluctance of African Americans to trust and invest in the stock market (Austin, 2004; Bosley & Knorr, 2016). The consequences disenfranchise African Americans from the economic gains available in capital investment even as their rates of discretionary income increase (Austin, 2004; Brown, 2007). The positive growth in African American disposable income has also become an incentive for perpetrators of race-based affinity fraud (Austin, 2004). Across all income and education levels, African Americans remain vulnerable to targeted schemes based on racial group identity.

This targeting has not gone unnoticed, as the high prevalence of fraud among African Americans recently prompted the Federal Trade Commission to enhance prevention and reporting of African American fraud cases (Federal Trade Commission, 2016). In addition, the Federal Trade Commission and academics called for additional research on fraud across race and ethnic groups, specifically regarding schemes targeting African Americans (Austin, 2004; Federal Trade Commission, 2016; Marlowe & Atiles, 2005). Thus, it is essential for us to explore key factors that influence race-based predatory biases, such as affinity fraud targeting African American consumers and communities. In order to accomplish this, we describe three actual cases of race-based affinity fraud and examine how social identity processes operate to explain these types of predatory practices. Harrington (2017) makes the case that Americans are vulnerable to fraud because we shield our children from knowing the negative outcomes of trust and silence discussion of fraud and affinity-based deception. As parents, leaders, and community members, we bypass critical ethical discussions in favor of the flawless American dream narrative (Harrington, 2017). However, in order to combat the negative effects of race-based affinity fraud, we must examine the underlying mechanisms that facilitate affinity-based deception and its negative consequences for African American individuals and communities.

Affinity Fraud: A Social Identity Theory Perspective

Developed by Tajfel and Turner (1979), social identity theory outlines the process and consequences of categorizations of individuals into various social groups. This social categorization significantly influences how individuals evaluate themselves and others in terms of either ingroup or outgroup membership. A key motivating factor is the individual's effort to maintain a positive social identity that is reinforced by positive self-esteem and group distinctiveness. These processes drive how group membership is both defined and valued, as well as the nature of intergroup behaviors and interactions within an organizational context (Ashforth & Mael, 1989).

First, social identity leads to category accentuation in that people often exaggerate or enhance the similarities of people within their ingroup in positive or beneficial ways. This is often labeled as a preference for characteristics of one's own group, or ingroup favoritism. Some argue that rather than a negative perception of non–group members, ingroup favoritism is an enhancement of positive group-based self-esteem (Hogg & Abrams, 1990). Second, a threat to identity creates a need to regain positive ingroup status, which can often be achieved by devaluing other social groups, a process known as outgroup derogation (Turner, 1975). Since outgroup derogation is purely a social process, the criteria for comparison, the evaluation of relative status, and the overall outcome of the comparison process are driven by the individual's subjective belief systems and the strength of his or her own social group identification. Third, when individuals categorize themselves and others into social groups, there are cognitive processes that enhance the differences between social groups in a manner that both defines and maintains one's own positive group identity (Brewer & Gardner, 1996). This positive distinctiveness is a social comparison process in which features and dimensions that define one's ingroup are evaluated more positively than others within the outgroup (Tajfel & Turner, 1979). In extreme cases, positive distinctiveness can drive intergroup discrimination by establishing, maintaining, and maximizing differences between social groups (Brewer, 1991; Brewer, 2007; Pickett, Bonner, & Coleman, 2002).

These three key principles of social identity theory are relevant for helping to explain race-based affinity fraud. Ingroup favoritism, outgroup derogation, and positive distinctiveness can arguably play a role in better understanding how affinity fraud can intensify historical racial barriers that are salient and impermeable within a US context. For example, research on the impact of media in making racial categories salient shows that movies with African American leading actors frequently fail in their appeal to larger, mixed-race audiences (Weaver, 2011). The recent success in 2018 of the movie *Black Panther* is a noteworthy exception (Huddleston, 2018). The marginalized appeal of movies with leading African American actors explains the impact of media as a function of the combined effects of identity salience, ingroup bias, outgroup derogation, and the need to maintain positive distinctiveness associated with racial group status. Thus, it makes sense to explore the ways in which actual cases of affinity fraud can be understood as a function of social identity processes that lead to predatory biases and outcomes based on social category, specifically race.

Affinity Fraud as Ingroup Favoritism: The At-Risk Youth Sports Program

James Brown and Darnell Jones targeted African American athletes in high schools in Aiken, South Carolina (Keating, 2011). They gained credibility within communities with a strong sports culture because of their reputation and fame as professional athletes. In addition, they used stories of previous professional players who were either bankrupt or under financial stress after retirement to provide credibility and appeal to their youth sports program. They especially targeted young athletes and their families, seeing them as highly trusting and most likely to form a bond with Brown and Jones, since the men came from disadvantaged communities yet achieved success in the sports arena. Thus, they positioned the Summit Management Company as a financial service company targeting African American athletes, mostly in high school and all from low-income areas (Keating, 2011).

They wore expensive suits and drove Lexuses to high school sporting events and talked openly about how they used sports to change their social and economic situations, taking their own families out of economic hardship. Their own financial wealth made these appeals very attractive. Thus, they singled out athletes who came from low-income homes and approached each high school athlete with expensive athletic shoes, tracksuits, and gifts to family members. After gaining the athlete's trust, they then promised to help the athlete through the process of turning professional, signing contracts, and managing their finances. They also stayed in contact with each of the athletes and talked with them through the ups and downs of their attempts to play at a high level in professional sports (Keating, 2011). Ingroup favoritism was leveraged by using current clients' families to connect with future athletes and their families so the pipeline of victims was maintained.

All the while, Brown and Jones were using the money from the various professional contracts that they negotiated and the subsequent bonus and contract money that they controlled for the athletes to fund their expensive lifestyles (Keating, 2011). They charged exorbitant fees to clients and moved funds around, often draining the accounts of their young clients. There were no financial accountability measures in place, and many described their actions as nothing more than a pyramid scheme. The power of their scheme was based on the strength of young athletes' identification with these two men as African American athletes from poor backgrounds who became successful. However, stories of the devastating impact of their schemes on these athletes and their families soon became visible. When one victim received notice that his mother's home was in foreclosure, it was explained away by Brown and Jones as simply an "accounting error." However, the reality is that her mortgage had not been paid and the money the athlete earned playing sports was laundered through bogus credit lines, leaving the athlete and his family bankrupt. When reported to the FBI, Brown and Jones went into hiding, and it was several years before the fugitives were found and charged. They were convicted in federal court on fifty-six counts of fraud and money laundering but cut a deal in which Brown would serve twenty-one months in prison and Jones, forty-one months. However, the damage to the victims' savings, reputation, and financial history could not be reversed. Most victims received only meager financial payments because the money entrusted to Brown and Jones was already gone. Jones was ordered to pay a total of $1,817,537.50 in financial restitution at monthly payments of $250. This means that he would finish paying all penalties to their victims in the year 2609 (Keating, 2011).

Affinity Fraud as Outgroup Derogation: The Financial Warfare Club

The Financial Warfare scheme from Marcus Dukes and Teresa Hodge played on the trust and charitable impulses among members of urban African American churches in upper-income areas across Prince George's County, Maryland (Fager, 2002; Rich, 2005). African American churches often encourage their members to give to other African American businesses under the banner of "trust and support." Dukes and Hodge's scheme appealed to African American members' desires to gain access to the investment and entrepreneurship arenas, especially in affluent and well-educated communities. They also used to their advantage the historical and well-documented mistrust within minority communities of the government and especially law enforcement. They promoted being part of the Financial Warfare Club as a necessary protection from the negative effects of the dominant racial group's propensity to take advantage of African Americans in terms of finance and investments. In fact, they used explicit language of outgroup derogation such as ending "economic apartheid" to invoke negative images of being shut out of the benefits of investment opportunities because of racial group membership (Fager, 2002; Rich, 2005). This is consistent with research showing that in situations where mistrust exists, outgroup derogation is enhanced and becomes a self-reinforcing cycle of intergroup bias conflict (Gaertner, Mann, Murrell, & Dovidio, 1989).

While Dukes and Hodge were under investigation, church members were typically unwilling to provide testimony against these fraudulent activities. This reluctance to cooperate with government and law enforcement investigations reflects the traditional distrust of government and law enforcement involvement in the African American community. This point was particularly salient given the fact that the Financial Warfare Club was positioned as a means for church members in the African American community to actively combat a financial system that did not benefit them. Even when Dukes was found guilty of taking more than $1.3 million from at least one thousand African American investors across eighteen states, the overarching points regarding the necessity of combating the government control of wealth in African American communities and distrust of government and law enforcement efforts to prosecute minorities who were trying to create economic opportunity remained a compelling lesson learned from this case (Fager, 2002; Rich, 2005; Securities and Exchange Commission, 2002). When distrust of "others" is high, affinity fraud is more effective in creating barriers between victims of predatory practices and the very systems and individuals meant to provide a protective resource.

Affinity Fraud as Positive Distinctiveness: A Social Capital Investment Program

The notion of positive distinctiveness suggests that when social identity is salient or relevant within the context, individuals will exaggerate the differences between their social groups and others in a manner that favors ingroup membership. In essence, this is the combination of simultaneous processes of ingroup favoritism and outgroup derogation. Individuals will selectively attend to and value information that helps to maintain this positive distinctiveness. For example, research finds that when people read international news articles favoring their own country over another (e.g., the United States versus Germany), they evaluate their country (ingroup) better than the other country (outgroup) and have better knowledge or recollection of the news they read, consistent with the notion of positive distinctiveness (Trepte, Schmitt, & Dienlin, 2018). This can be applied to the case of Ephren Taylor, the son of a minister who targeted African American evangelical churches with a Ponzi scheme that was masked as his Social Capitalist investment program. From 2007 to 2010, Taylor and his wife, Wendy Jean Connor, conducted numerous Wealth Tour Live seminars at evangelical churches in African American communities near Atlanta, Georgia. In the seminars, Taylor presented himself as a successful and "socially conscious" investor who was giving back to the community by working with churches in African American communities to generate economic development opportunities ("Fleecing the Flock," 2012; Wyler, 2014).

Taylor directly focused on the traditional role of African American churches in supporting economic activity in their local communities. His program explicitly referenced ideas that were core to the positive distinctiveness of racial identity that members of churches in African American communities develop with respect to the church's responsibility to support and develop economic benefits within their communities. He connected to members by quoting scripture in an accurate and authentic manner, as the son of a preacher, and tied these references to themes pertaining to economic empowerment and attainable housing within the community. He also made it a point to disparage traditional investment options in the stock market and mutual funds by emphasizing how these investments created no benefit for the African American community (Wyler, 2014). Thus, he enhanced positive distinctiveness based on racial group identity and outgroup derogation among his targeted victims.

In actuality, Taylor's investment program was a multi-million-dollar Ponzi scheme in which churchgoers were encouraged to invest their savings in Taylor's "low risk, high reward" investment opportunities (Wyler, 2014). He emphasized that his investment program was a "no risk sweepstakes machine" that would consistently generate annual gains between 12 and 20 percent by creating and supporting successful inner-city businesses. Taylor was highly successful in convincing church members to invest their savings with him, generating $2 million alone from the New Birth Missionary Baptist Church in Atlanta. In fact, Taylor had no underlying business model or validating financial performance data to substantiate his investment program. He collected money from people and ran a series of laundromats and juice bars that were not profitable. At the same time, he used the money invested to support a luxurious lifestyle for himself and his wife. The Securities and Exchange Commission filed charges, and both Taylor and his wife were convicted and sentenced to prison for multiple counts of fraud (Wyler, 2014). Taylor's investment scheme relied on the positive distinctiveness of African Americans participating in charitable giving to accomplish his fraud.

Affinity Fraud and the Need for Inclusive Leadership

The solutions proposed to prevent affinity fraud cases such as these traditionally focus on legal or procedural efforts yet overlook the role of leadership in creating and sustaining meaningful change. Bosley and Knorr (2016) and Sargsian (2012) cursorily mention the need to educate group leaders on affinity fraud, but they do not include specific strategies or models. While these legal and procedural interventions are necessary, we argue they are insufficient in addressing the economic, social, and psychological consequences of race-based affinity fraud. Mere procedural changes will not affect the social identity processes that enable race-based affinity fraud to have detrimental effects on people, families, and communities of color. We argue that inclusive leadership must play a role in preventing affinity fraud that is based on key demographic categories such race and prevent social identity theory processes from having a negative impact.

Inclusive leadership is often defined as a leader's influence in shaping environments where belongingness and individual uniqueness are respected and where the leader exhibits openness and accessibility and values high-quality interactions among followers (Nembhard & Edmondson, 2006). This type of leadership invites and values diverse input from others that cuts across boundaries such as demographics or social identity group membership. A key benefit of inclusive leadership is its positive impact on perceptions of psychological safety, especially among diverse group members (Carmeli, Reiter-Palmon, & Ziv, 2010). This notion of psychological safety is defined as individuals' perceptions of the consequence of taking interpersonal risks without fear or threat to individual or social group identity (Edmondson, 1999, 2004) and has been related to positive individual, group, and organizational outcomes (Shore et al., 2011).

Psychological safety and inclusion are present when belongingness is strong and value in uniqueness is high. This means that instead of an emphasis on ingroup bias, outgroup derogation, and positive distinctiveness, the dual experiences of belongingness and uniqueness are simultaneously emphasized. This is consistent with research on inclusive workplace cultures that defines them as ones that maintain high acceptance (belongingness) and individual value (uniqueness) (Ely & Thomas, 2001).

One could argue that inclusive leadership creates a superordinate identity through its impact on individual and group outcomes (Gaertner et al., 1989). A key benefit of inclusive leadership for preventing predatory biases such as affinity fraud is the impact of a superordinate identity on perceptions of psychological safety among diverse group members (Carmeli et al., 2010). Inclusive leadership builds a unified social identity that facilitates trust and connectedness among others while valuing individual contribution and diverse perspectives (Nembhard & Edmondson,

2006). This suggests that inclusive leadership can help overcome or correct the negative effectives of ingroup favoritism, outgroup deroga-tion, and positive distinctiveness based on social group membership through enhanced perceptions of group identity, belongingness, and psy-chological safety. This type of leadership at the workgroup, organ-ization, or societal level sends a powerful signal to followers that belongingness and group identity must include and not devalue unique-ness among diverse individuals. The ability to simultaneously support social cohesion and inclusion can build group trust and may offset the negative impact of outgroup derogation and ingroup bias.

Inclusive leadership allows individuals to acknowledge multiple iden-tities and, at the same time, to be wary of identity-based divisiveness or deception. It empowers members to form trust but not blindly follow the herd, and it builds members' capacity to identify and contest affinity-based threats that include perpetrators of fraud. Thus, inclusive leader-ship helps to shape the culture and climate of the work team and workplace to be more supportive, open, and trusting, which yields posi-tive relationships among peers, enhances communication, and builds trust (Randel, Dean, Ehrhart, Chung, & Shore, 2016). These environ-ments would be less susceptible to affinity-based fraud if they were steeped in a culture of inclusivity and inclusive leadership—if the par-ents, school, and church leaders ascribed to a broader conceptualization of leadership. Also, when leaders model the value of inclusion and re-spect to participants and followers, then these organizations may build capacity to resist affinity-based schemes in the future.

A Call for Inclusive Leadership Development

While inclusive leadership sounds promising in theory, a key factor to offset the negative impact of identity-based affinity fraud rests in the need to develop a pipeline of inclusive leadership within organizations and society. Sugiyama, Cavanagh, van Esch, Bilimoria, and Brown (2016) make a similar argument for more relational and identity-based leader-ship development approaches that can address the specific needs of a di-verse and global workforce. They suggest that leadership development programs must explicitly focus on inclusive leadership through the pro-cess of identity work (Ely, Ibarra, & Kolb, 2011) that provides a safe en-vironment for examining, challenging, and transforming traditional identity structures into more inclusive conceptualizations that balance inclusion and uniqueness. This means an explicit focus on identity-based approaches to leadership development that include strengthening the leader's relational competencies in order to build high-quality relationships among diverse social identities (Nishii & Mayer, 2009). An explicit focus on inclusive leadership development also means challenging our definitions of leadership effectiveness to shift toward collective outcomes and away from traditional notions of success, relative gain, and superiority. This type of inclusive leadership development through identity work and collective outcomes is central to feminist approaches to leadership development (Eagly & Karau, 2002). This means that developing inclusive leaders may require a diverse, interconnected social environment in which learning is both personal and reflective while engaging the leader in necessary identity-based work (Vinnicombe & Singh, 2002).

Notions of inclusive leadership are embedded in the common identity model, which is rooted in social identity theory (Gaertner & Dovidio, 2012). This approach emphasizes the value of recategorization, or creating a shared superordinate identity for members of different groups, as a way to address ingroup bias and intergroup conflict (Dovidio, Gaertner, Ufkes, Saguy, & Peterson, 2016). Inclusive leadership based on this model would induce members of different groups to recategorize themselves as members of an all-inclusive social group, thus changing the conceptual representations of different groups from an "us" versus "them" orientation to a more encompassing, superordinate "we" identity. Prior research shows positive benefits of a common identity, such as the reduction of bias between African Americans and the police in response to community-engaged policing efforts (Murphy, Cramer, Waymire, & Barkworth, 2017). This suggests that the presence of inclusive leadership within the youth sports program would have facilitated a common social identity of community-engaged student athletics that could have reduced the vulnerability of at-risk African American high school students to targeted recruitment based on racial group identity alone. A similar impact of recategorization is relevant for the Financial Warfare Club. Leaders cultivated mistrust through outgroup derogation by expanding the differences between African Americans and "others." Recategorization through an inclusive leadership approach would have stressed a common identity supporting social justice, socially responsible investing, and community development that consists of African Americans and other historically disenfranchised communities. The impact of inclusive leadership and recategorization is also relevant to the social capital investment program, especially in terms of encouraging victims of affinity fraud to exercise their voice and take collective action. This is perhaps the strongest benefit of inclusive leadership and recategorization, as followers' voices are often silenced by a notion of misplaced loyalty to the ingroup or mistrust and fear of the outgroup. Some evidence supports this in research that examines the impact a common identity has on facilitating peace in situations of global intergroup conflict (Reysen & Katzarska-Miller, 2017).

Future research should unpack the critical competencies that define inclusive leadership that is able to prevent identity-based predatory biases such as affinity fraud. For example, feminist perspectives argue for a focus on relational competencies, such as social awareness and connectedness, that model identity-based leadership (Day & Harrison, 2007). While this style of leadership focuses on building capacity among diverse individuals and work groups, more field and qualitative research is needed to validate the impact of this type of leader approach on key workplace and organizational outcomes. This should focus on the benefits but also examine the potential consequences of this approach to leadership development, which may include backlash in response to attempts to transform organizations and communities. Making identity and identity work explicit dimensions of leadership development in future theory and practice would be a valuable contribution to attempts to address the ongoing negative consequences of affinity fraud and other race-based predatory practices that affect individuals, organizations, and communities.

REFERENCES

Anderson, K. B. (2013). *Consumer fraud in the United States, 2011: The third FTC survey* (Report). Retrieved from http://ftc.gov/opa/2007/10/fraud.pdf

Ashforth, B. E., & Mael, F. (1989). Social identity theory and the organization. *Academy of Management Review, 14*(1), 20–39.

Austin, D. E. (2004). "In God we trust": The cultural and social impact of affinity fraud in the African American church. *University of Maryland Law Journal of Race, Religion, Gender & Class, 4*, 365–410.

Bosley, S., & Knorr, M. (2016). Pyramids, Ponzis and fraud prevention: Lessons from a case study. *Journal of Financial Crime, 25*(1), 1–15. Retrieved from http://www.emeraldinsight.com/doi/abs/10.1108/JFC-10-2016-0062

Brewer, M. B. (1991). The social self: On being the same and different at the same time. *Personality and Social Psychology Bulletin, 17*(5), 475–482.

Brewer, M. B. (2007). The importance of being we: Human nature and intergroup relations. *American Psychologist, 62*(8), 728–738.

Brewer, M. B., & Gardner, W. (1996). Who is this "we"? Levels of collective identity and self representations. *Journal of Personality and Social Psychologyocial Psychology, 71*(1), 83–93.

Brown, D. A. (2007). Pensions and risk aversion: The influence of race, ethnicity, and class on investor behavior. *Lewis & Clark Law Review, 11*(2), 385–406.

Bucy, P. H., Formby, E. P., Raspanti, M. S., & Rooney, K. E. (2008). Why do they do it? The motives, mores, and character of white collar criminals. *St. John's Law Review, 82*, 401–571.

Carmeli, A., Reiter-Palmon, R., & Ziv, E. (2010). Inclusive leadership and employee involvement in creative tasks in the workplace: The mediating role of psychological safety. *Creativity Research Journal, 22*(3), 250–260.

Day, D. V., & Harrison, M. M. (2007). A multilevel, identity-based approach to leadership development. *Human Resource Management Review, 17*, 360–373.

Dovidio, J. F., Gaertner, S. L., Ufkes, E. G., Saguy, T., & Peterson, A. R. (2016). Included but invisible? Subtle bias, common identity, and the darker side of "we." *Social Isseus and Policy Review, 10*(1), 6–46.

Eagly, A. H., & Karau, S. J. (2002). Role congruity theory of prejudice toward female leaders. *Psychological Review, 109*(3), 573–598.

Edmondson, A. (1999). Psychological safety and learning behavior in work teams. *Administrative Science Quarterly, 44*(2), 350–383.

Edmondson, A. (2004). Psychological safety, trust, and learning in organizations: A group-level lens. In R. M. Kramer & K. S. Cook (Eds.), *Trust and distrust in organizations: Dilemmas and approaches* (pp. 239–272). New York, NY: Russell Sage Foundation.

Ely, R. J., Ibarra, H., & Kolb, D. (2011). Taking gender into account: Theory and design for women's leadership eevelopment programs. *Academy of Management Learning Education, 10*(3), 474–493.

Ely, R. J., & Thomas, D. A. (2001). Cultural diversity at work: The effects of diversity perspectives on work group processes and outcomes. *Administrative Science Quarterly, 46*, 229–273.

Fager, C. (2002, December 9). Fraud: Financial warfare scam targets black churches. *Christianity Today*. Retrieved from http://www.christianitytoday.com/ct/2002/december9/10.18.html

Fairfax, L. M. (2003). The thin line between love and hate: Why affinity-based securities and investment fraud constitutes a hate crime. *U.C. Davis Law Review, 1073*, 1073–1143. Retrieved from http://papers.ssrn.com/abstract=921045

Federal Trade Commission. (2016). *Combating fraud in African American & Latino communities: The FTC's comprehensive strategic plan* (Report). Retrieved from https://www.ftc.gov/system/files/documents/reports/combating-fraud-african-american-latino-communities-ftcs-comprehensive-strategic-plan-federal-trade/160615fraudreport.pdf

Fink, P. J. (2009, February). Fink! Still at large: People who suffer losses as a result of affinity fraud often struggle with the psychological ripple effects of such betrayal. What strategies can we use to help victims move forward? *Clinical Psychi-*

atry News. Retrieved from https://www.questia.com/read/1G1-195148121/fink -still-at-large-people-who-suffer-losses-as

Fisher, L. E. (2009). Target marketing of subprime loans: Racialized consumer fraud & reverse redlining. *Journal of Law and Policy*, *18*, 121–155.

Fleecing the flock: The big business of swindling people who trust you. (2012, January 28). *Economist*.

Gaertner, S. L., & Dovidio, J. F. (2012). Reducing intergroup bias: The common in-group identity model. In P. A. M. Van Lange, A. W. Kruglanski, & E. T. Higgins (Eds), *Handbook of theories of social psychology* (Vol. 2, pp. 439–457). Thousand Oaks, CA: Sage.

Gaertner, S. L., Mann, J. A., Murrell, A. J., & Dovidio, J. F. (1989). Reducing inter-group bias: The benefits of re-categorization. *Journal of Personality and Social Psychology*, *57*(2), 239–249.

Harrington, B. (2017, July 31). Why Americans get conned again and again. *The Atlantic*, p. 7. Retrieved from https://www.theatlantic.com/business/archive/2017 /07/americans-con-fraud-balleisen/535281/

Hogg, M. A., & Abrams, D. (1990). Social motivation, self-esteem and social iden-tity. In D. Abrams & M. A. Hogg (Eds.), *Social identity theory: Construction and critical advances* (pp. 28–47). New York, NY: Harvester Wheatsheaf.

Huddleston, T., Jr. (2018, February 21). An especially diverse audience lifted 'Black Panther' to record box office heights. *Fortune*. Retrieved from http://fortune .com/2018/02/21/black-panther-record-box-office-diverse-audience/

Keating, P. (2011). How to scam an athlete. Retrieved from http://www.espn.com /espn/news/story?id=6408849

Khasru, B. Z. (2001). Affinity scams target religous ethnic investors. *Fairfield Busi-ness Journal*, *40*(34), 1, 20.

Kramer, R. M. (2009, June). Rethinking trust. *Harvard Business Review*, pp. 69–77. Retrieved from https://hbr.org/2009/06/rethinking-trust

Marlowe, J., & Atiles, J. H. (2005). Consumer fraud and Latino immigrant consum-ers in the United States. *International Journal of Consumer Studies*, *29*(5), 391–400.

Marquet International. (2011). *The Marquet report on Ponzi schemes*. Retrieved from https://www.marquetinternational.com/trackpdfs/marquet_report_on_ponzi _schemes.pdf

Murphy, K., Cramer, R. J., Waymire, K. A. & Barkworth, J. (2017). Police bias, social identity, and minority groups: A social psychological understanding of cooperation with police. *Justice Quarterly*, *35*(6) 1–27.

Nembhard, I. M., & Edmondson, A. C. (2006). Making it safe: The effects of leader inclusiveness and professional status on psychological safety and improvement efforts in health care teams. *Journal of Organizational Behavior*, *27*(7), 941–966.

Nishii, L. H., & Mayer, D. M. (2009). Do inclusive leaders help to reduce turnover in diverse groups? The moderating role of leader-member exchange in the di-versity to turnover relationship. *Journal of Applied Psychology*, *94*(6), 1412–1426.

Perri, F. S., & Brody, R. G. (2011). Birds of the same feather: The dangers of affin-ity fraud. *Journal of Forensic Studies in Accounting & Business*, *3*(1), 33–46. Re-trieved from http://esc-web.lib.cbs.dk/login?url=http://search.ebscohost.com /login.aspx?direct=true&db=bth&AN=79819213&site=ehost-live&scope=site

Perri, F. S., & Brody, R. G. (2012). The optics of fraud: Affiliations that enhance of-fender credibility. *Journal of Financial Crime*, *19*(3), 305–320.

Pickett, C. L., Bonner, B. L., & Coleman, J. M. (2002). Motivated self-stereotyping: Heightened assimilation and differentiation needs result in increased levels of positive and negative self-stereotyping. *Journal of Personality and Social Psychology*, *82*(4), 543–562.

Randel, A. E., Dean, M. A., Ehrhart, K. H., Chung, B., & Shore, L. (2016). Leader inclusiveness, psychological diversity climate, and helping behaviors. *Journal of Managerial Psychology*, *31*(1), 216–234.

Rich, E. (2005, June 10). Md. investment club organizer convicted of fraud. *Washington Post*. Retrieved from https://www.washingtonpost.com/archive/local/2005 /06/10/md-investment-club-organizer-convicted-of-fraud/8f41d834-cb80-4b91 -90a2-da0acd561545/?utm_term=.f70d82c4b6ef

Reysen, S., & Katzarska-Miller, I. (2017). Superordinate and subgroup identities as predictors of peace and conflict: The unique content of global citizenship identity. *Peace and Conflict: Journal of Peace Psychology*, *23*(4), 405–415.

Sargsian, K. (2012). A wolf in sheep's clothing: Enacting statutes enhancing criminal penalties for affinity fraud. Retrieved from https://papers.ssrn.com/sol3 /papers.cfm?abstract_id=2006716

Securities and Exchange Commission. (2002, September 5). Commission files injunctive action against Marcus Dukes and Teresa Hodge in affinity fraud. Retrieved from https://www.sec.gov/litigation/litreleases/lr17714.htm

Shore, L. M., Randel, A. E., Chung, B. G., Dean, M. A., Ehrhart, K. H., & Singh, G. (2011). Inclusion and diversity in work groups: A review and model for future research. *Journal of Management*, *37*(4), 1262–1289.

Sugiyama, K., Cavanagh, K. V., van Esch, C., Bilimoria, D., & Brown, C. (2016). Inclusive leadership development: Drawing from pedagogies of women's and general leadership development programs. *Journal of Management Education*, *40*(3), 253–292.

Tajfel, H., & Turner, J. (1979). An integrative theory of intergroup conflict. In J. A. Williams & S. Worchel (Eds.), *The social psychology of intergroup relations* (pp. 33– 47). Belmont, CA: Wadsworth.

Trepte, S., Schmitt, J. B., & Dienlin, T. (2018). Good news! How reading valenced news articles influences postive distinctiveness and learning from news. *Journal of Media Psychology*, *30*(2), 66–78.

Turner, J. C. (1975). Social comparison and social identity: Some prospects for intergroup behaviour. *European Journal of Social Psychology*, *5*(1), 5–34.

Vinnicombe, S., & Singh, V. (2002). Women-only management training: An essential part of women's leadership development. *Journal of Change Management*, *3*, 294–306.

Weaver, A. J. (2011). The role of actors' race in White audiences' selective exposure to movies. *Journal of Communication*, *61*, 369–385.

Wyler, G. (2014, September 17). Ephren Taylor's disastrous megachurch Ponzi scheme. *Vice*. Retrieved from https://www.vice.com/en_us/article/nnq9mq/the -black-bernie-madoff-000442-v21n9

THE FUTURE

*Lessons for the Next Generation
of Leaders*

22

Ujima

Lifting as We Climb to Develop the Next Generation of African American Leaders

LYNN PERRY WOOTEN, SHANNON POLK,
and WHITNEY WILLIAMS

> Our goal is to create a beloved community and this will require a qualitative change in our souls as well as a quantitative change in our lives.
>
> —*Dr. Martin Luther King Jr.*

The term *beloved community* was coined by the American philosopher Josiah Wright to conceptualize the goal of an inclusive community where we bring our best selves to work collaboratively to improve humanity. In the 1960s, Dr. Martin Luther King Jr. popularized the term when he spoke about the civil rights movement and the need for all people to share in society's wealth. Fifty years later, we believe there is still a need to persevere in the creation of the beloved community, and as members of the academy who are committed to the mission of educating leaders, we have become particularly mindful of the investments needed for African American millennials to thrive.

Millennials are defined as the generation born between 1980 and 2000. For African Americans of this generation, their leadership journey has involved opportunities and challenges as they experienced the first Black president, navigated life in a "postracial" society, and lived

TABLE 22-1

The lived experiences of Black millennials

	Black (%)	White (%)	Latino/a (%)
Unemployment rates (age range 25–34; collected second quarter of 2015)	10.8	4.5	6.7
College enrollment status, 2013 (two-year and four-year colleges)	38.5	42.8	38.8
Average college graduating rates for 2002–2006 entering cohorts	20.4	41.0	27.7
Postcollege student loan debt burden, 2009—$35,000+	35.7	23.3	22.1

Source: Rogowski & Cohen (2015).

with movements such as Black Lives Matter, bans on affirmative action, and the economic shifts associated with a digital economy. Moreover, the lived experiences of Black millennials are different from those of other millennials, as reported in research conducted by the Black Youth Project and summarized in table 22-1 (Rogowski & Cohen, 2015). Black millennials are more likely to live below the poverty line and have higher unemployment rates than white and Latino millennials. Although college attendance has increased among Black youths, there is still a significant disparity between the college attendance of white youths and that of young people of color, and graduation rates are substantially higher among white youths, resulting in sizable racial disparities for millennials receiving college degrees. Moreover, Black youths who attend college experience higher debt burden, and this affects their long-term financial well-being.

These statistics speak to our desire to work continuously toward the creation of the beloved community for Black millennials and future generations, and to support this vision, we propose four specific actions. First, we argue that education systems and especially universities should develop the infrastructure for nurturing and developing their African American students. Second, we propose that an entrepreneurial mindset is a necessity for their success. Third, we contend that to advance issues of justice and equality, we must empower African American millennials with the tools to challenge the status quo and engage in collective action for positive change. Fourth, we emphasize the importance of instilling the principles of living an integrative life.

Institutions of Higher Learning and the American Dream

Throughout America's history, a college education has been a pathway for socioeconomic mobility and a key for launching young adults in their pursuit of the American dream. American colleges are viewed as the institutions responsible for empowering young adults to mature by developing their organizational, problem-solving, technical, analytical, and communication skills while exposing them to diverse groups of people and thoughts (Immerwahr & Foleno, 2000; Immerwahr & Johnson, 2007). Given the important role of colleges in our society, it is not surprising that research conducted by the National Center for Public Policy and Higher Education indicates that 87 percent of Americans believe a college education has become as important as a high school diploma used to be and that American families are willing to make an investment to ensure their young adult has opportunities associated with a college education.

Given the significant role of higher education in our society, it is important that we create the infrastructure for African American college students to not only graduate within a reasonable time but also experience personal growth while attending college and thriving after college. Research by Gallup (2015) has identified factors contributing to thriving college experiences that produce long-term well-being outcomes. Interestingly, when Gallup researchers analyzed the data for African Americans in the sample, they found that those who attended historically Black colleges and universities (HBCUs) were more likely to recall the support of professors and mentors and to have participated in engaged learning through internships, long-term projects, and extracurricular activities, as summarized in table 22-2. Furthermore, the African American HBCU graduates in this study were more likely to agree that their university prepared them for life after college and for thriving— being strong, being consistent, and progressing—particularly in their financial, purpose, and social well-being, as presented in table 22-3.

The results of the Gallup study call to our attention the essential role that higher education plays in supporting and developing African

TABLE 22-2

Different experiences for Black HBCU and non-HBCU grads

% Black US college graduates who strongly agree

	HBCUs (%)	Non-HBCUs (%)	Difference (pct. pts.)
My professors at my university cared about me as a person.	58	25	−33
I had at least one professor at my university who made me excited about learning.	74	62	−12
While attending my university, I had a mentor who encouraged me to pursue my goals and dreams.	42	23	−19
Felt support	35	12	−23
While attending my university, I had an internship or job that allowed me to apply what I was learning in the classroom.	41	31	−10
While attending my university, I worked on a project that took a semester or more to complete.	36	30	−6
I was extremely active in extracurricular activities and organizations while attending my university.	32	23	−9
Experiential learning	13	7	−6

Source: Gallup-Purdue Index, 2014–2015, Gallup.

Americans and the positive deviance outcomes (i.e., extraordinarily positive outcomes) of HBCU students and graduates. Even with limited resources, HBCUs have mastered a formula for transformational learning environments and instilling the self-efficacy necessary for building a rewarding career and life. Institutions and individuals committed to the development of African American millennials and the generations after millennials can learn from the practices of HBCUs. We believe HBCU professors, administrators, and staff, through their mission-centric behaviors, take co-ownership for ensuring that their students succeed by helping them navigate the complexities of academics, identity formation, and career preparation. Moreover, HBCUs con-

TABLE 22-3

Black HBCU graduates more likely to be thriving in financial and purpose well-being

% Black US college graduates who are thriving in each element of well-being

	HBCU (%)	Non-HBCU (%)	Difference (pct. pts.)
Purpose well-being	51	43	−8
Social well-being	54	48	−6
Financial well-being	40	29	−11
Community well-being	42	38	−4
Physical well-being	33	28	−5
Thriving in all five elements of well-being	7	7	—

Source: Gallup-Purdue Index, 2014–2015, Gallup.

vey their commitment to reinforcing the stance that Black lives do matter by creating welcoming and safe spaces for students. In these spaces, students are not ignored, marginalized, or stereotyped and have a learning environment where they are valued for their intellect and considered the heart, soul, and hope for a better future (Green, 2015).

An Entrepreneurial Mindset and Economic Equality

Although African American millennials are more educated than previous generations, economic inequities still persist, and it is predicted that it will take 228 years to close the wealth disparity gap between Black and white families (Asante-Muhammad, Collins, Hoxie, & Nieves, 2016). Suggested remedies for reducing these economic inequities include changes in monetary, collective bargaining, and employment discrimination policies. In addition to these policies, we advocate for educational programming that focuses on developing an entrepreneurial mindset—a state of mind oriented toward entrepreneurial activities and outcomes that produce opportunities, innovation, and value creation (*Financial Times Lexicon*, n.d.).

Educational programming that focuses on developing the entrepreneurial mindset of African American millennials should begin with the premise that entrepreneurial activities come in many forms. For example, this education should inform them of how to act as entrepreneurs in a "gig economy," where organizations hire freelancers and independent contractors for contingent employment. This may entail directing them to educational experiences that are competency based and develop skills that are in high demand and aligned with industry trends. In addition to managing gigs, young African American entrepreneurs need to know how to create their own businesses by identifying market opportunities, analyzing competitive dynamics, and understanding consumer behavior, and they need the accounting skills to recognize the drivers of profitability and the ability to manage human capital. Hence, for an entrepreneurial mindset to play a major role in our beloved community, we must provide our youths with an educational foundation that opens up multiple pathways to achieve economic security and exposes them to entrepreneurs through activities such as internships, co-ops, apprenticeships, and job shadowing.

Challenging the Status Quo through Collective Action

The African American community has a history of its young adults challenging the status quo for positive social change. To continue this trajectory, we must remind them that challenge is the crucible for greatness and that accepting the status quo breeds societal stagnation, mediocrity, and injustices (Kouzes & Posner, 2014). Challenging the status quo calls for African American millennials to "rise up" and realize they can lead from any position by knowing themselves and collectively working with others who embrace ideals of the beloved community. From our perspective, "leaders as learners" is the central tenet of this approach, which is achieved by inspiring young leaders to do great things, have an openness to the contributions of others, make sense of systems, and view leadership as service (Preskill & Brookfield, 2009).

For African American millennials to develop the capacity to engage in purposeful leadership activities that will result in positive social change, we believe our beloved community must encourage them to have a strong consciousness of self and to pursue areas where they can challenge the status quo that are aligned with their values, identities, and interests. This entails reinforcing the notion that they are citizens of an ecosystem and we all are responsible for the care of each other and stewardship of resources (Komives & Wagner, 2017). Also, to groom African American millennials for this citizenship behavior, we must provide them with the opportunities for planned and grassroots civic engagement within their communities.

Living an Integrative Life

Parker Palmer, author of *A Hidden Wholeness* (2009), espouses the theory that an integrative life begins with the deep exploration of one's soul to uncover strengths and fears so that a person may utilize this knowledge to embrace the entirety of his or her being. Millennials should be encouraged to spend significant reflection time in a process of transformational development in which they identify their core values and motivations. Equipped with this knowledge, millennials can align their professional interests with their personal values and transition from simply meeting occupational benchmarks to achieving vocational fulfillment. Identifying the employment or entrepreneurial spaces where their career aspirations and their personal values strongly align allows millennial leaders to spend less energy covering and code-switching and increases their freedom to engage more authentically in the workplace. Essentially, millennials want to work in environments where they can bring their whole selves to that space.

However, one's whole self may be composed of multiple identities for millennials, which, according to the US Census, is the most ethnically diverse generation to date (US Census Bureau, 2018). In addition to race, ethnicity, and gender, salient identities for African American millennials may include sexual preference, religion, and level of physical ability. Utilizing the tool of intersectionality can assist millennials with embracing any (perceived or experienced) paradoxical inconsistencies in their identities. In a *Harvard Business Review* article (Caza, Ramarajan, Reid, & Creary, 2018), the authors emphasize the importance of helping millennials recognize how existing in spaces where they may simultaneously experience majority privilege and the bias of otherness strengthens their emotional quotient and expands the versatility of their leadership skills. Thus, millennials should be encouraged by knowing their professional success will likely be bolstered by embracing their varied identities and deploying the unique behavioral skills learned from living in intersectional and marginalized spaces to navigate their work environment.

It is critical that in a world fueled by (seemingly) perfect social media photos and narratives that portray everyone's highlight reels, millennials are given permission to experiment in living authentically. On the journey of achieving congruency between work, family, home, and community, Stew Friedman (2014) of the Wharton Business School encourages the process of integration through experimentation. A person must be willing to overcome the temptation to abandon the process too early because of the difficulty in finding the right personal strategy for work-life integration. It may take several attempts to learn what an individual needs in order to bring his or her life into congruency. Additionally, millennials should expect to repeat the process of experimentation several times as they move into various stages of their professional and personal lives (Dutton, Roberts, & Bednar, 2010). This process of growth, self-acceptance, and self-transparency in the journey will help solidify their leadership.

REFERENCES

Asante-Muhammad, D., Collins, C., Hoxie, J., & E. Nieves. (2016). *The ever-growing gap: Without change, African-American and Latino families won't match white wealth for centuries.* Washington, DC: Corporation for Enterprise Development and the Institute for Policy Studies.

Caza, B., Ramarajan, L., Reid, E., & Creary S. (2018, May 30). How to make room in your work life for the rest of yourself. *Harvard Business Review.* Retrieved from https://hbr.org/2018/05/how-to-make-room-in-your-work-life-for-the-rest-of-your-self#comment-section

Dutton, J. E., Roberts, L. M., & Bednar, J. (2010). Pathways for positive identity construction at work: Four types of positive identity and the building of social resources. *Academy of Management Review, 35*(2), 265–293.

Financial Times Lexicon. (n.d.). Entrepreneurial mindset [Def. 1]. Retrieved from http://lexicon.ft.com/Term?term=entrepreneurial-mindset

Friedman, S. (2014). *Leading the life you want: Skills for integrating work and life.* Cambridge, MA: Harvard Business School Press.

Gallup. (2015). *Gallup-USA Funds minority college graduates report.* Retrieved from http://9b83e3ef165f4724a2ca-84b95a0dfce3f3b3606804544b049bc7.r27.cf5.rackcdn.com/production/PDFs/USA_Funds_Minority_Report_GALLUP-2.pdf

Green, A. (2015, November 19). Do historically Black colleges provide the safe spaces students are after? *The Atlantic.* Retrieved from https://www.theatlantic.com/education/archive/2015/11/are-hbcus-necessary-racial-sanctuaries/416694

Immerwahr, J., & Foleno, T. (2000). *Great expectations: How the public and parents—white, African American and Hispanic—view higher education.* San Jose, CA: National Center for Public Policy and Higher Education.

Immerwahr, J., & Johnson, J. (with P. Gasbarra, A. Ott, & J. Rochkind). (2007). *Squeeze play: How parents and the public look at higher education today.* San Jose, CA: National Center for Public Policy and Higher Education.

Komives, S. R., & Wagner, W. (Eds.). (2017). *Leadership for a better world: Understanding the social change model of leadership* (2nd ed.). San Francisco, CA: Jossey-Bass.

Kouzes, J., & Posner, B. (2014). *The student leadership challenge: Five practices for becoming an exemplary leadership.* San Francisco, CA: Wiley.

Palmer, P. (2009). *A hidden wholeness: The journey towards an undivided life.* San Francisco, CA: Jossey-Bass.

Preskill, S., & Brookfield, S. (2009). *Lessons from the struggle of social justice.* San Francisco, CA: Jossey-Bass.

Rogowski, J., & Cohen, C. (2015). *Black millennials in America.* Chicago, IL: University of Chicago, Black Youth Project.

US Census Bureau. (2018, January 19). Millennials outnumber baby boomers and are far more diverse. Retrieved from https://www.census.gov/newsroom/press-releases/2015/cb15-113.html

Conclusion—
Intersections of Race, Work, and Leadership

Lessons in Advancing Black Leaders

LAURA MORGAN ROBERTS *and* ANTHONY J. MAYO

The twenty-first century has demonstrated that African Americans, when given the opportunity, are capable of leading at the highest levels—politically (in the White House and Cabinet), in educational institutions, in corporations, and in nonprofits and foundations. As an exemplar, Americans chose former US president Barack Obama as the top president in their lifetime (Pew Research Center, July 2018). Though he is a political leader, not a corporate leader, Obama engineered one of the most dramatic economic turnarounds in US history, taking the helm during the recession that began in 2008.

Yet advances in black leadership—especially those that involve taking strategic control over economic resources—were met with resistance in the nineteenth and twentieth centuries. Thriving black economic communities were destroyed by white supremacists (e.g., the Tulsa, Oklahoma, race massacre of 1921; the Wilmington, North Carolina, insurrection of 1898), showing how vehement the opposition can be toward black business leadership. Even in the twenty-first century, there remains a pervasive, organized impetus to "undo" the strides that black leaders have made over the past fifty years in shaping and growing inclusive, high-performing organizations. The numbers of African Americans earning bachelors and graduate degrees continue to rise, but the number of black senior executives in those large corporations, which heavily influence the global marketplace, is waning.

We began this book with a fundamental question: Why do we need a volume on race, work, and leadership, and especially one centered on the black experience? The chapters in this volume dispel the notion that we live in a postracial society. While there has been undeniable progress, we are far away from principles of equal opportunity, access, and meritocracy. As Arthur P. Brief asserts in his commentary in chapter 3, the United States has had to confront a resurgence of both overt and subtle racism in the last few years. The insidious growth of overt racism has found traction in the highest echelons of American society, and the resultant backlash against diversity has challenged the very foundation of our nation's fundamental beliefs about fairness and equality.

In many ways, now more than ever, we need to understand the reality of the black experience, and we need to embrace and champion policies, practices, and programs that help to level the playing field but also, more importantly, allow organizations and society to benefit from the collective experiences, knowledge, and skills of all, not just a few. This volume on race, work, and leadership provides both a conceptual understanding of the current contextual landscape for black professionals and a series of recommendations and action plans to enable individuals and their organizations to collectively benefit from diversity.

By centering on the black experience, the chapters in *Race, Work, and Leadership* unearth several key insights about engagement, development, advancement, and leadership impact. While the focus of this volume is on the black experience, the lessons are applicable for any underrepresented or marginalized individual trying to deliver his or her best, and they are especially valuable for organizations that seek to leverage and optimize their full talent pool. While we cannot do justice to the richness of the compelling perspectives in the twenty-two other chapters of this volume, we have tried to distill some of the lessons into five core insights.

Insight #1—(Still) Unique: Differentiating the Black Work Experience

Recent years have brought widespread interest in employee experiences and advancement. The Gallup Institute has been collecting "employee engagement" data from millions of global twenty-first-century workers and documenting its impact on performance. *Race, Work, and Leadership* presents findings from groundbreaking empirical investigations of racial differences in engagement—as measured by a sense of connection to work, to employing organizations, and to colleagues. Detailed analyses in chapter 3 (Mayo & Roberts), chapter 4 (Wilkins & Fong), chapter 5 (Washington, Maese, & McFeely) and chapter 7 (Blake-Beard, Roberts, Edgehill, & Washington) show that black workers report lower levels of engagement than nonblack respondents on multiple dimensions, including

- lower assessments of coworkers' commitment;

- less perceived importance of their role in light of the mission or purpose of the company;

- fewer opportunities to learn and grow in the past year;

- lower levels of overall satisfaction with the workplace; and

- lower intent to stay at their current employer.

Moreover, chapter 6 (Hewlin & Broomes) and chapter 7 (Blake-Beard, Roberts, Edgehill, & Washington) indicate that black professionals experience an authenticity tension, in which they feel constrained in their ability to express their values or bring their whole selves to work, because they are navigating unwelcoming cultural and interpersonal contexts. W. E. B. DuBois purported that the same phenomenon of "double consciousness" would define race relations in the twentieth century; this volume asserts that these race-related authenticity tensions have carried forth into the twenty-first century.

- Chapter 6 (Hewlin & Broomes) shows that African Americans in the legal profession are particularly susceptible to conformity pressure and respond by donning facades of conformity.

- Chapter 9 (Roberts, Blake-Beard, Creary, Edgehill, & Ghai) highlights that African Americans in health care face similar challenges.

- Chapter 10 (Sims, Toigo, Allen, & Cornelius) illustrates the authenticity tensions faced by African Americans in financial service firms.

The aforementioned engagement challenges are correlated with higher intent to leave. Thus, instead of experiencing deepened commitment and long-term investments in organizational leadership development, black managers (who are less engaged than white and Hispanic managers), are prone to seek external opportunities to grow and develop outside their current firms.

- As reported in chapter 3 (Mayo & Roberts), even black Harvard Business School alumni experience more career plateaus, more job changes, and less interest in pursuing senior executive positions in *Fortune* 500 corporations than their white counterparts.

- As highlighted in chapter 4 (Wilkins & Fong), these same trends are also apparent among black Harvard Law School alumni (especially black women).

Chapter 18 (Thomas, Robinson, Provolt, & Brown) documents the considerable costs that organizations bear when they lose high-potential black leaders to other firms or entrepreneurial ventures. Millennials, who value engagement to a greater extent than baby boomers, are less likely to embrace conformity and detachment in order to climb the corporate ladder. This pattern raises questions about younger workers' tolerance for the disengagement that black professionals reported in our volume. As organizations pursue racially diverse talent, they should look to the experiences of black employees as a signal about the broader context, attending to varied experiences of engagement and the disparate impact on retention and leadership advancement among historically underrepresented group members.

Insight #2—Taking Charge: Conveying How Black Leaders Navigate Contested Authority

For any leader, regardless of race, the ability to establish credibility, take charge, and motivate others is critical to both initial and ongoing success. All leaders are confronted with the need to fulfill the expectations of a diverse set of stakeholders, but black leaders face a number of documented challenges with taking charge, due to

- divergence from the white male leadership prototype;

- deficit-based thinking that associates blackness with disadvantage, risk, unintelligence, and disinterest in challenging and complex intellectual tasks;

- territorial power dynamics that reinforce disparate access to resources among racial and class groups; and

- implicit biases that lead people to doubt the legitimacy and credibility of black (and other nonprototypical) leaders, and to fear those black leaders who exercise authoritative leadership.

The data reported in *Race, Work, and Leadership* reveals similar patterns of contested authority across educational, corporate, and community organizing settings. Chapter 11 (Macchia & Porcher) details examples of black instructional coaches whose authority was questioned or challenged by K–12 teachers, and chapter 13 (Shockley & Holloway) describes how college students often challenge the authority of black female professors. Chapter 15 (Berthoud, Taylor, & Green) presents a nuanced, intersectional scaffolding for theorizing about active, unconscious resistance toward black leaders' exercise of authority. The authors reflect on their experiences as facilitators of a conference focused on racial issues ("On the Matter of Black Lives"), during which white men "took cover" or "claimed traditional hierarchical roles" by saying nothing and detaching, attempting to speak for black participants, and announcing themselves as overseers who were surveilling the group dynamics to ensure the black facilitators "didn't mess up."

Black leaders, on the other hand, tread lightly while exercising power; in health care (chapter 9, Roberts, Blake-Beard, Creary, Edgehill, & Ghai), they report trying to lead in a disarming (i.e., friendly and nonthreatening) manner because their passion and enthusiasm for work have been perceived as threatening. This disarming approach is consistent with research showing that black leaders are evaluated more favorably when they appear less threatening (see chapter 18 by Thomas, Robinson, Provolt, & Brown for a focused discussion of this dynamic). In some cases, the opportunity to take charge is limited to extremely difficult or crisis situations, where expectations of success are low (see chapter 17, L. P. Wooten & James).

Insight #3—Strength in Action: Portraying How Black Leaders Positively Affect Organizations and Societies

The chapters of this volume present a sobering picture of racial disparities, barriers, and obstacles. Simultaneously, they are punctuated with a melodious chorus of agency and resilience. *Race, Work, and Leadership* reveals how black leaders successfully navigate the tightrope of tenuous engagement, constrained authenticity, and contested authority. Chapter 18 (Thomas, Robinson, Provolt, & Brown) articulates how black leaders bring "unique positionalities to offer novel perspectives, ideas, and analyses that enable institutions to better serve and lead diverse stakeholders." Specifically, black leaders positively affect organizations by

- redefining norms of leadership, actively mentoring professionals of color, and serving as role models who enhance institutional and organizational images (chapter 18);

- drawing on cultural resources to serve as ambassadors who close the gap of cultural divides and champion diversity initiatives (chapter 10, Sims, Toigo, Allen, & Cornelius);

- challenging inequality in (white) organizations (chapter 19, Seegars & Ramarajan); and

- taking on high-stakes "glass cliff" roles to lead organizations through sustained crises (chapter 17, L. P. Wooten & James).

Chapters that focus specifically on black women's experiences, using womanist theorizing and relational cultural theory, conclude that the strength of black leadership is inextricably tied to the ability to develop a robust sense of self (chapter 13, Shockley & Holloway). Referencing hooks, Shockley & Holloway describe how black women activists in the academy use the margins as sites of radical possibility, resistance, openness, and nourishment to transform the disciplinary and organizational hierarchies in which most students are socialized. Black CEOs often confront tough challenges with a growth mindset, seeing both risk and opportunity in crisis and using their knowledge of business, agility, resourcefulness, and resilience to shape their organization's future and their career using an open-systems approach (chapter 17, L. P. Wooten & James).

Through the lens of the black experience, the researchers in this volume highlight a number of practices that could enhance the vitality and impact of black leaders, including the following:

- Challenging inequality in "stealth mode" to protect from stereotyping (chapter 10, Sims, Toigo, Allen, & Cornelius)

- Challenging inequality through mutual identification with in-groups and outgroups (chapter 19, Seegars & Ramarajan)

- Being aware of the tendency for pigeonholing into diversity-related fields that don't position managers for senior leadership roles (chapter 9, Roberts, Blake-Beard, Creary, Edgehill, & Ghai)

- "Start[ing] where you are, do[ing] what you can, . . . speak[ing] your truth, even if it is spoken quietly at first," and participating in small causes, local needs, support, and one-on-one conversations to build allyship (chapter 12, Fraser & Samuels)

- Resting, refueling and refusing to bear the weight of the world despite the pressure of the strong black woman syndrome (chapter 12, Fraser & Samuels; chapter 13, Shockley & Holloway; chapter 14, Davis)

Insight #4—Co-Creating the Beloved Community: Forging Relationships That Nurture Black Leaders' Best Selves

Black leaders develop themselves and affect society through healing connections. Often surrounded by people from diverse racial groups, many current and aspiring black leaders experience isolation and doubt (chapter 3, Mayo & Roberts; chapter 10, Sims, Toigo, Allen, & Cornelius) and yearn for communities in which they can "drop the masks . . . and breathe deeply into their true selves" (chapter 13, Shockley & Holloway; see also chapter 6, Hewlin & Broomes). Humans are hardwired for connection, but they must acknowledge racial and cultural dissimilarities to experience meaningful relationships (chapter 12, Fraser & Samuels). Forming these authentic encounters with managers, coworkers, mentors, and even subordinates can be challenging. *Race, Work, and Leadership* offers rich examples and evidence-based suggestions for doing the hard work of forming the beloved community (chapter 12, Fraser & Samuels; chapter 22,

L. P. Wooten, Polk, & Williams), in which people learn across differences and form multifaceted alliances.

Chapter 14 (Davis) presents a case example of Soul 2 Soul, through which the impactful, transforming, liberating work of fighting racism is catalyzed by black female facilitators but is carried out by the whole. Importantly, black women are no longer tasked solely with the burden of consciousness raising and execution; rather, through healing connections, they equip and invite other invested community members to take up the mantle of liberating society. Chapter 12 (Fraser & Samuels) presents a case example of the authors' work with Mission United, in which a similar process of consciousness raising and social change occurred through interracial facilitation—modeling how black women and white women can share power in more generative ways. Both of the featured examples of powerful, cross-race alliances occurred in community organizing settings. The findings on cross-race relationships at work indicate that more commitment, consciousness, and healing needs to take place to strengthen connections between black workers and their managers (chapter 5, Washington, Maese, & McFeely; chapter 7, Blake-Beard, Roberts, Edgehill, & Washington; chapter 10, Sims, Toigo, Allen, & Cornelius).

The research featured in *Race, Work, and Leadership* points to several possible tactics for strengthening cross-race developmental relationships at work:

- Increasing access to and effectiveness of mentoring for black workers and executive coaching for black leaders (chapter 3, Mayo & Roberts; chapter 5, Washington, Maese, & McFeely; chapter 7, Blake-Beard, Roberts, Edgehill, & Washington; chapter 9, Roberts, Blake-Beard, Creary, Edgehill, & Ghai)

- Training managers on techniques for delivering (rather than avoiding) performance feedback, and helping managers to communicate the meaning and purpose of daily work tasks, as they connect to a broader organizational mission (chapter 5, Washington, Maese, & McFeely)

- Hiring more diverse managers and executives, especially black leaders (chapter 8, Wingfield)

- Addressing discomfort with learning about race and bias (chapter 5, Washington, Maese, & McFeely)

- Normalizing "optimal discomfort" so that black leaders can challenge inequality without losing leadership credibility (chapter 19, Seegars & Ramarajan)

- Preparing nonblack leaders to take initiative with promoting diversity and inclusion, relieving black leaders of diversity fatigue (chapter 12, Fraser & Samuels; chapter 14, Davis; chapter 16, Purdie-Greenaway & Davidson; chapter 19, Seegars & Ramarajan)

Insight #5—Leading Change: Reimagining the Intent and Impact of Diversity Initiatives

According to Rowley et al. (2002), "[D]iversity often functions as 'myth and ceremony rather than having a substantive impact on organizational work outcomes.'" Wingfield (chapter 8), Purdie-Greenaway and Davidson (chapter 16), and McCluney and Rabelo (chapter 20) present sharp critiques of increasingly popular diversity initiatives that have fallen short in developing and advancing black leaders. Black employees tend to be more aware of workplace racial discrimination and are more likely to leave firms that do not offer inclusive diversity climates (see chapter 18, Thomas, Robinson, Provolt, & Brown, for discussion of turnover). Paradoxically, the needs of black employees have been decentered—and most remain plateaued in middle-management roles—even while the diversity industry has increased in size and popularity. Instead of being actively developed for leadership roles, black workers report experiencing less growth at work (chapter 3, Mayo & Roberts; chapter 4, Wilkins & Fong; chapter 5, Washington, Maese, & McFeely) and less access to gateway positions for senior executive pathways (chapter 3, Mayo & Roberts; chapter 8, Wingfield; chapter 9, Roberts, Blake-Beard, Creary, Edgehill, & Ghai).

Researchers argue that diversity initiatives focus more on managing blackness than eradicating racism (chapter 20, McCluney & Rabelo), cultural competence training than executive leadership development (chapter 8, Wingfield), and philosophical statements of inclusion than concrete steps for advancing black inclusion (chapter 8, Wingfield; chapter 16, Purdie-Greenaway & Davidson). By consequence, there is a widening gap between the way that organizations market and promote diversity and the realities of day-to-day work life (chapter 10, Sims, Toigo, Allen, & Cornelius).

Race, Work, and Leadership details key features that could strengthen alignment between diversity initiatives' espoused aims and corollary impact for black leaders. While recruitment and retention are the most basic levels of diversity initiatives (chapter 10, Sims, Toigo, Allen, & Cornelius), these recommendations focus on creating inclusive climates that welcome black leaders' full range of experiences, skills, and aspirations:

- Using data analytics to assess the degree to which an organization's climate is fair and inclusive (chapter 5, Washington, Maese, & McFeely; chapter 20, McCluney & Rabelo)

- Promoting psychological safety, especially in the form of interpersonal risk taking, and reevaluating organizational values that promote bias in order to liberate diverse, authentic self-expressions (chapter 6, Hewlin & Broomes)

- Creating a culture of inquiry around race and promoting "race-intelligent inclusion" that involves acknowledging inequity, equipping workers to manage their own psychological reactivity, and facilitating flourishing even in the headwinds of racism (chapter 16, Purdie-Greenaway & Davidson)

- Recognizing, valuing, and rewarding the leadership roles black professionals take on in the absence of formally acknowledged roles (e.g., mentoring, diversity and inclusion committees, "lumpy citizenship") (chapter 8, Wingfield)

- Avoiding the purely instrumental rhetoric of the "business case," narrow imaginations of blackness, and "blanket" perspectives of diversity, instead focusing on social justice for those who have been harmed most severely by racism and its denial (chapter 20, McCluney & Rabelo)

New Beginnings: Fostering Leadership Legacies

We began this volume with a return to the zenith of the civil rights movement. In the wake of the assassination of Dr. Martin Luther King Jr., a world-renowned black leader, young black students empowered themselves to advocate for the creation of a more just, safe, and inclusive society. On the manicured lawns and in the austere halls of an elite, Ivy League institution, a handful of black students were courageous enough to raise consciousness and increase access for hundreds of equally talented students who had been denied fair consideration simply because of their race. In essence, these twentysomething black students took up the mantle of leadership that fell when Dr. King was murdered, and refused to let the cause for which he fought die with him, Malcolm X, Medgar Evers, and so many other men and women who died while fighting for freedom. The Harvard story is not unique; young, ambitious, passionate black leaders across the country promoted justice and freedom on college campuses, in workplaces, and throughout communities.

Have we now entered into a new age? Is the emphasis on black leadership development still warranted? Many have argued that the twenty-first century has borne evidence of a "postracial society," in which citizens of all backgrounds and hues supported the first African-descended president, first lady, and first daughters of the Obama family. The findings of this volume suggest otherwise. In fact, the need to develop black leaders strategically is as important as ever. We thus conclude with a life-stage model (table 23-1) for developing black leaders that addresses their changing needs at various stages of their careers (as recommended in chapter 16, Purdie-Greenaway & Davidson).

Our hope is that this volume and its contributions will fuel the career paths and prospects of black professionals and other underrepresented groups; will enable organizations and their leaders to adopt new practices and programs that support the advancement of all, not just the few; and will encourage academics and thoughtful practitioners to build a vibrant stream of additional research that helps to normalize black leadership throughout organizations, across industries, and in society as a whole. We cannot and should not continue to tacitly accept the revolving door faced by high-potential black leaders. For far too long, black leaders have been too few. Rather than looking to black leaders as exemplars of exceptionalism who must beat the almost insurmountable odds (see Roberts, Mayo, Ely, & Thomas, *Harvard Business Review*, March–April 2018) to advance to senior levels, we must leverage the insights, perspectives, and recommendations in this volume to encourage and cultivate a robust pipeline of black talent.

TABLE 23-1

Life-stage model for developing black leaders

Early stage	**Aims:**
	• Building a robust sense of self (chapter 13, Shockley & Holloway) that strengthens young adults with the agency, openness, self-awareness, and humility to do the following:
	  ◦ Critically question stereotypes and lowered expectations of black leaders (foreword, Bell & Nkomo; chapter 15, Berthoud, Taylor, & Green)
	  ◦ Embrace their unique strengths and cultural resources (chapter 10, Sims, Toigo, Allen, & Cornelius; chapter 18, Thomas, Robinson, Provolt, & Brown)
	  ◦ Recognize their psychological reactivity (e.g., ego-defensive routines) toward microaggressions and identity-related obstacles (chapter 16, Purdie-Greenaway & Davidson)
	  ◦ Meet failure with resilience through growth mindsets (chapter 17, L. P. Wooten & James)
	  ◦ Lessen the likelihood of falling prey to affinity-based fraud through affirmation of inclusive leadership (chapter 21, Murrell, Jones, & Petrie)
	• Equipping young adults for vibrant careers in the new world of work
	  ◦ Develop the credibility, network, and capabilities to thrive in competitive, high-engagement, low-commitment labor markets (i.e., the "gig economy")
	  ◦ Align cultural resources (chapter 10, Sims, Toigo, Allen, & Cornelius) with opportunities in the "experience economy"
	  ◦ Promote entrepreneurial mindsets to build more inclusive, high-performing organizations (chapter 22, L. P. Wooten, Polk, & Williams)
	
	Facilitators:
	• Safe spaces to grow and develop in which black men and women can experience authentic failures and successes without being subsumed in narratives of racial oppression and limitation, including the following:
	  ◦ Historically black colleges and universities (commentary in chapter 3, M. Wooten; chapter 22, L. P. Wooten, Polk, & Williams)
	  ◦ Race-inclusive leadership development programs (chapter 16, Purdie-Greenaway & Davidson)—for example, the Partnership (chapter 7, Blake-Beard, Roberts, Edgehill, & Washington; chapter 9, Roberts, Blake-Beard, Creary, Edgehill, & Ghai), the Toigo Foundation (chapter 10, Sims, Toigo, Allen, & Cornelius), INROADS, Management Leadership for Tomorrow, and national Panhellenic Greek organizations
	  ◦ Black churches and civic engagement organizations (chapter 14, Davis)
	  ◦ Same-race peer-mentoring relationships (chapter 10, Sims, Toigo, Allen, & Cornelius)

(continued)

TABLE 23-1 *(continued)*

Life-stage model for developing black leaders

Middle stage	**Aims:**
	• Refining "race-savvy" techniques for enacting authority (chapter 15, Berthoud, Taylor, & Green)
	• Creating vibrant networks that position one for new opportunities (chapter 9, Roberts, Blake-Beard, Creary, Edgehill, & Ghai)
	• Fostering mindful practices for reflecting on key transitions—identify core values and motivation, align professional interest with personal values—from occupational benchmarks to vocational fulfillment (chapter 16, Purdie-Greenaway & Davidson)
	• Clarifying personal commitments for leading change (chapter 12, Fraser & Samuels; chapter 14, Davis; chapter 19, Seegars & Ramarajan)
	• Collectively organizing to mobilize changes that promote inclusion (chapter 12, Fraser & Samuels; chapter 14, Davis; chapter 22, L. P. Wooten, Polk, & Williams)
	Facilitators:
	• Healing connections and cross-race alliances (chapter 12, Fraser & Samuels)
	• Providing significant line or general management experiences and creating opportunities for global assignments (chapter 3, Mayo & Roberts)
	• Enabling mentorship and sponsorship that provide candid feedback and positioning in order to actualize black leaders' potential (chapter 3, Mayo & Roberts; chapter 5, Washington, Maese, & McFeely)
Late stage	**Aims:**
	• Exercising strategic organizational and industry leadership at senior levels that promotes organizational success through inclusive practices (chapter 2, Gates; chapter 10, Sims, Toigo, Allen, & Cornelius; chapter 17, L. P. Wooten & James; chapter 18, Thomas, Robinson, Provolt, & Brown; chapter 19, Seegars & Ramarajan)
	• Strengthening one's legacy by developing a cadre of black leaders who are positioned to advance steadily toward senior levels of leadership (chapter 22, L. P. Wooten, Polk, & Williams)
	• Safeguarding against ethical breaches and abuses of power that take advantage of vulnerable communities (e.g., blacks targeted for affinity fraud—chapter 21, Murrell, Jones, & Petrie)
	Facilitators:
	• Passing the baton through storytelling and transferring connections and endorsements (chapter 10, Sims, Toigo, Allen, & Cornelius) and sharing power across generations (chapter 15, Berthoud, Taylor, & Green)
	• Creating opportunities for the next generation to assume leadership (chapter 22, L. P. Wooten, Polk, & Williams)
	• Increasing visibility and impact through board governance

REFERENCES

Pew Research Center, U.S. Politics & Policy. (2018, July 11). *Obama tops public's list of best president of their lifetime, followed by Clinton, Reagan.* Retrieved from http://www.people-press.org/2018/07/11/obama-tops-publics-list-of-best-president-in-their-lifetime-followed-by-clinton-reagan/

Roberts, L., Mayo, A., Ely, R., & Thomas, D. (2018, March–April). Beating the odds. *Harvard Business Review,* 126–131.

Rowley, L. L., Hurtado, S., & Panjuan, L. (2002). *Organizational rhetoric or reality? The disparities between avowed commitment to diversity and formal programs and initiatives in higher education institutions.* Paper presented at the 83rd Annual Meeting of the American Educational Research Association, New Orleans, LA. Retrieved from https://pdfs.semanticscholar.org/9951/c4ac6948736b3c57da637f5832644d7a099d.pdf

Index

Acknowledgments

The contributors to this volume represent a dedicated community of scholars, executives, and activists who have conducted groundbreaking research on race, work, and leadership for decades. We extend our gratitude to each of them for generously sharing their keen insights and for bringing the black perspective to the forefront of a much-needed conversation about what it means to be black in various professional settings. A work of this magnitude could not have been completed without the thoughtful and diligent support our editorial assistants, Serenity Lee and Libby Quinn. They were instrumental in supporting the overall production process for each chapter and the edited volume as a whole, and we appreciate their enthusiasm, can-do spirit, and energy.

This volume was inspired by and developed in conjunction with the research and programming for Harvard Business School's 2018 commemoration of the fiftieth anniversary of the founding of the African American Student Union (AASU50). For their leadership of the AASU50 initiative, we thank the core planning team members: Taran Swan (Project Director), NaDaizja Bolling (Staff Assistant), Serenity Lee (Research Associate), Cara Mathews (Program Manager), and Bennie Wiley (Adviser). We are indebted to Harvard Business School's Division of Research and Faculty Development and the Gender and Leadership Initiatives, which sponsored the overall AASU50 commemoration activities, including this volume. We sincerely appreciate the support, encouragement, and counsel of Harvard Business School dean Nitin Nohria, Professor Robin J. Ely, and Professor Linda A. Hill.

This volume also benefited from various HBS colleagues who provided research, outreach, and programmatic assistance, including those in Admissions, Baker Library Special Collections, the Dean's Office, External Relations, Marketing and Communications, and the Registrar's

Office. In particular, we appreciate the support of Colleen Ammerman of the Gender Initiative and Letty Garcia and Karina Grazina of the Leadership Initiative. We are also grateful for the research support we received from Antioch University's Graduate School of Leadership and Change, Georgetown University's McDonough School of Business, and Morehouse College.

We also wish to acknowledge the HBS Gender and Work Symposium presenters and participants in 2017 and 2018, who enthusiastically joined us in centering black experiences of race, work, and leadership in ways that stimulated our thinking and shaped our framing of this volume. Several of the symposium participants have authored chapters in this volume; we include the entire list here for full acknowledgment of their collective contributions. 2017 Race, Work and Leadership mini-conference participants: Modupe Akinola, Colleen Ammerman, Rachel Arnett, NaDaizja Bolling, Arthur Brief, Heidi Brooks, Lindsay Cameron, Stephanie Creary, Brook Dennard, Robin Ely, Rayshauna Gray, Charlice Hurst, Aida Hurtado, Elizabeth Johnson, Robert Livingston, Tony Mayo, Courtney McCluney, Tsedal Neeley, Tina Opie, Lakshmi Ramarajan, Joan Reede, Laura Morgan Roberts, Ashleigh Rosette, Nancy Rothbard, Lumumba Seegars, Taran Swan, David Thomas, Melissa Thomas-Hunt, and Alexis Smith Washington. 2018 Race, Work, and Leadership symposium presenters: Doyin Atewologun, Arthur Brief, Drew Carton, Stephanie Creary, Sreedhari Desai, Tracy Dumas, Sandra Finley, Diane Forbes, Kyra Gaunt, Zachary Green, Oscar Holmes IV, Tony Mayo, Courtney McCluney, Shira Mor, Cindy Pace, Addie Perkins, David Porter, Elena Richards, Aspen Robinson, Steven Rogers, Ashleigh Rosette, Lumumba Seegars, Rebecca Shaumburg, Alexis Smith, Ron Sullivan, Flora Taylor, Melissa Thomas-Hunt, Adia Harvey Wingfield, and Melissa Wooten.

The success of these symposia relied on the dedicated contributions of the HBS Gender and Work Symposium planning team members: Lauren Moran and Serenity Lee of the Division of Research and Faculty Development and Bethany Harris, Rayshauna Gray, Liz Johnson, and Colleen Ammerman of the Gender Initiative. We thank them all for their careful planning, attention to detail, and thoughtful follow-up.

We sincerely appreciate the enthusiastic support and visionary guidance of our editorial team at Harvard Business Review Press, especially Melinda Merino, editorial director and associate publisher. We also thank Alicyn Zall, editorial coordinator; Stephani Finks for the cover design; and Ashley Moore for copyediting assistance.

Finally, we thank our families for their love, support, and encouragement. They are the extended members of the village who made this important work a reality.

About the Contributors

MAURA ALLEN has led Segesta Communications for more than twenty years, providing market strategy, client engagement initiatives, and C-suite content to top investment, venture, consulting, and nonprofit organizations. She has worked with the Toigo Foundation for more than fifteen years, providing strategic program development, market strategy support, and content for thought leadership initiatives. Maura believes in the power of story as a way to connect and communicate and advises organizations on ways to leverage their unique narratives in order to deepen client relationships. Her client roster includes JPMorgan Chase, Khosla Ventures, Kleiner Perkins, Charles Schwab & Co., Stanford University, University of California–San Francisco, Saint Mary's College, Ernst & Young, and more. A Telly Award winner, Maura holds a BA in classical studies and Latin from Stanford University. After authoring *Write Now: Essential Tips for Standout College Essays*, she was selected as a Khan Academy coach, providing a powerful platform for the Bay Area native to share creative writing advice with thousands of rising high school seniors worldwide as they apply to college and embark on their careers.

ELLA L. J. EDMONDSON BELL is a professor at the Tuck School of Business at Dartmouth College. She is also an author, managerial consultant, nationally recognized researcher, and advocate on women's workplace issues. She is the coauthor of *Our Separate Ways: Black and White Women and the Struggle for Professional Identity*. Her second book is *Career GPS*. As a nationally respected managerial consultant, Ella has shared her expertise and knowledge on discriminatory barriers in the workplace, strategic leadership, managing inclusion, and work-life balance with corporate leaders across the country. Ella's scholarly work has been reported in the *Wall Street Journal*, the *Boston Globe*, the *Los Angeles Times*, the *Charlotte Business Journal*, the *Christian Science Monitor, Newsweek, Working Women, Business Week, Black Enterprise*, and *Essence*. She is considered by industry and the academy to be one of the leading experts in organizational change and the management of race, gender, and class in organizational life. In addition, Ella appeared on CNN's *Democracy in America '96* as a nationally recognized expert of race relations in the workplace.

DIANE FORBES BERTHOUD is the Assistant Vice Chancellor for Equity, Diversity, and Inclusion at the University of California, San Diego, where her responsibilities include strategic planning, advancing institutional effectiveness, serving as liaison to human resources, and leading diversity-focused and campus-wide initiatives. She is affiliate faculty of the George Washington School of International Affairs in Leadership Studies and faculty emeritus for the RISE San Diego Urban Leadership Program, which trains and empowers urban leaders to take effective and sustainable action to transform San Diego's urban communities. Diane's research on gendered, raced, intersectional processes of organizing has been published in *Management Communication Quarterly, Journal of Applied Communication Research*, and the *Journal of International and Intercultural Communication*. She has presented her work on black women's leadership, intersectionality, and organizational discourse at national and international conferences, most notably the 2016 International Fulbright Conference. One of her recent works (2017) appears in the International Leadership Association's book series, Women and Leadership: Research, Theory, and Practice. Diane earned her BA in Communication and a certificate in Spanish translation and interpretation from Barry University in Florida and her MA and PhD in organizational communication and social psychology from Howard University.

STACY BLAKE-BEARD is the Deloitte Ellen Gabriel Professor of Women and Leadership at the Simmons University School of Business. She is also faculty affiliate at the Center for Gender in Organizations at Simmons and visiting faculty at the Indian School of Business in Hyderabad, India. Before joining Simmons, Stacy was a member of the faculty of the Harvard University Graduate School of Education. She has also worked in sales and marketing at Procter & Gamble and in the corporate human resources department at Xerox. Stacy holds a BS in psychology from the University of Maryland at College Park and an MA and PhD in organizational psychology from the University of Michigan. Her research is on the challenges and opportunities offered by mentoring relationships, with a focus on the impact of increasing workforce diversity. She has published research on gender, diversity, and mentoring in several publications, including the *Academy of Management Executive*, the *Academy of Management Learning and Education*, and the *Psychology of Women Quarterly*.

ARTHUR P. BRIEF is the George S. Eccles Chair in Business Ethics and Presidential Professor, Emeritus at the University of Utah. His research focuses on the moral dimensions of organizational life (e.g., ethical decision making, race relations, and worker well-being). In addition to having published more than a hundred journal articles, Art is author or editor of several books, including *Attitudes In and Around Organizations* (1998) and *Diversity at Work* (2008). He is a past editor of the *Academy of Management Review* and cofounding editor of the *Academy of Management Annals*. Art now coedits *Research in Organizational Behavior*. He is a fellow of the Academy of Management, the Association for Psychological Science, and the American Psychological Association. Art has been a Fulbright Fellow in Lisbon, a Batten Fellow at the Darden Graduate School of Business at the University of Virginia, and the Thomas S. Murphy Distinguished Research Professor at the Harvard Business School. His research has been reported on by ABC's *Good Morning America*, CNN's Headline News, *USA Today*, the *Wall Street Journal*, the *New York Times*, and various other news outlets.

ANNA-MARIA BROOMES is an English-as-a-second-language teacher and master of counseling student in the Werklund School of Education at the University of Calgary. Her main research interests focus on the integration of multicultural counseling competencies with diverse theoretical approaches in counseling settings. She is currently conducting research on authenticity and facades of conformity in work environments. Anna-Maria holds a BA in psychology from McGill University, where she led and facilitated interactive seminars in organizational behavior.

B. LINDSAY BROWN is a doctoral candidate in the industrial-organizational psychology program at the University of Georgia. She has published several book chapters and presented research on workplace discrimination, diversity management practices, and underrepresented workers in both practitioner and academic outlets. Lindsay is currently a doctoral fellow in the J. W. Fanning Institute for Leadership Development at the University of Georgia, where she provides consultation and evaluation services for nonprofits and community groups, including Goodwill of North Georgia, Athens Land Trust, Advantage Behavioral Health Services, and the Athens-Clarke County Police Department.

TONI CORNELIUS is President of TamarindTree Consulting, a firm that assists individuals and organizations to move "beyond the numbers" of traditional diversity initiatives to a focus on developing sustainably inclusive work environments. With more than thirty years in the field of corporate human resources and organizational development, Toni has driven both traditional human resource functions and the development and implementation of strategies that promote an inclusive workplace. Toni introduces stylized approaches through a variety of methods, including workshops and panel facilitation, leadership assessment and development training, needs analysis, and program development to guide clients to their "best fit" approach. Toni holds a BA from Creighton University and an MS in industrial relations from Loyola University. She is a certified instructor of the Hogan Level I Leadership Assessment Program and the Hay Group Emotional and Social Competency Inventory, as well as a qualified instructor of the Myers-Briggs Type Indicator. Toni currently works with the Toigo Foundation on the expansion of the foundation's APEx leadership curriculum.

STEPHANIE CREARY is an Assistant Professor of Management in the Wharton School of the University of Pennsylvania. She is also an affiliated faculty member of Wharton People Analytics and a senior fellow of the Leonard Davis Institute of Health Economics. Her research program is motivated by understanding how multiple identities, perspectives, and experiences are managed in organizations to promote learning and growth. She investigates how individuals and groups minimize the conflict that can ensue when their differences become more salient; how they navigate pressures to conceal, reveal, or downplay valued aspects of themselves at work; and the organizational features and relationship qualities that enable and constrain these dynamics. Previously,

Stephanie was a research associate at Harvard Business School and the Conference Board. She has also worked in the health-care industry. Stephanie has earned BS and MS degrees from the Boston University Sargent College of Health and Rehabilitation Sciences; an MBA degree from Simmons School of Management; and MS and PhD degrees from the Boston College Carroll School of Management.

MARTIN N. DAVIDSON is the Johnson and Higgins Professor of Business Administration at the University of Virginia's Darden School of Business. He currently serves as Senior Associate Dean and Global Chief Diversity Officer for the school. His thought leadership has changed how global leaders approach inclusion and diversity in their organizations. His scholarly research appears in top academic and practitioner publications and his book, *The End of Diversity as We Know It: Why Diversity Efforts Fail and How Leveraging Difference Can Succeed*, introduces a research-driven road map to help leaders effectively create and capitalize on diversity in their organizations. Martin teaches leadership in Darden's MBA and Executive Education programs and consults with numerous *Fortune* 500 firms, government agencies, and nonprofit organizations, including Bank of America, Massachusetts General Hospital, and the US Navy SEALs. He has been featured in many media outlets, including the *New York Times*, *Bloomberg Businessweek*, and the *Wall Street Journal*. He served on the faculty of the Tuck School at Dartmouth College before joining the Darden faculty in 1998. He earned his AB at Harvard College and his PhD at Stanford University.

TAWANA DAVIS, a lifetime member of the NAACP and a retired itinerant elder in the African Methodist Episcopal Church, is a cofounder/consultant of Soul 2 Soul, a black Woman–led, faith-based racial justice nonprofit organization. Tawana has a bachelor of science degree in human resources management from the State University of New York Empire State College, a master of divinity from Interdenominational Theological Center (Turner Theological Seminary), project management certificate from New York University, and human resource professional certification from Cornell University, and she is currently pursuing her PhD at Antioch University's Graduate School of Leadership and Change (her expected graduation date is 2020). Tawana has held leadership positions in corporations, churches, and the community. She serves on several boards, including the Institute for Racial Equity and

Excellence, the Stomp Out Breast Cancer Foundation, and the Interfaith Alliance of Colorado. She is currently in active treatment for HER2+ metastatic breast cancer, a mother of two educators, and a grandmother.

BEVERLY EDGEHILL is an accomplished organizational development (OD) professional who guides leaders and their teams in managing complex and large-scale change to support existing and emerging business priorities. For the past twenty-five years, Beverly has enjoyed working inside retail and financial services companies, and in the position of President and CEO of the Partnership, Inc., a Massachusetts-based leadership development organization. Beverly, also a former regional selection panelist for the White House Fellows program, completed her doctoral studies at Teachers College, Columbia University and teaches graduate level courses in leadership, OD, and change management. She is a sought-after speaker at conferences and workshops and has published several articles on the topic of career success.

BRYON FONG is the Research Director of the Center on the Legal Profession at Harvard Law School. He manages the center's institutional research activities, including its flagship Globalization, Lawyers, and Emerging Economies project, research on lawyer career paths, and initiatives on innovation in the legal profession. He is also the managing editor of the center's digital magazine, *The Practice*. Since 2016, he has served as a lecturer on law at Harvard Law School, teaching the Legal Profession Seminar with Professor David B. Wilkins. His publications on the legal profession include *The Women and Men of Harvard Law School: Preliminary Results from the HLS Career Study* (with David B. Wilkins and Ronit Dinovitzer), *Mapping India's Corporate Law Firms* (with David B. Wilkins and Ashish Nanda), and *The Harvard Law School Report on the State of Black Alumni II: 2000–2016* (with David B. Wilkins). Bryon earned his BA from Georgetown University and his MSc and PhD from the London School of Economics and Political Science.

KATHRYN FRASER is a licensed psychologist and behavioral medicine coordinator in the Halifax Health Family Medicine Residency Program in Daytona Beach, Florida. For the past twenty-four years, she has been teaching, consulting, and doing research in various areas in behavioral health and physician professional development. She is the Director of the Behavioral Science/Family Systems Educator Fellowship, a nationwide mentoring program for early-career behavioral medicine faculty. She is a founding member and Vice President of Community Outreach for Prevention of Eating Disorders, a grassroots, nonprofit organization dedicated to informing the public about eating disorders and positive body image. She spearheaded the cultural competency and health disparities curriculum in her residency program and has presented regionally and nationally on these topics. In collaboration with several members of the Minority and Multicultural Health Collaborative of the Society of Teachers of Family Medicine, she published an article in the *Journal of Family Medicine* based on their 2016 STFM Annual Conference workshop on teaching about racism in health care.

HENRY LOUIS GATES JR. is the Alphonse Fletcher University Professor and Director of the Hutchins Center for African and African American Research at Harvard University. An Emmy Award–winning filmmaker, literary scholar, journalist, cultural critic, and institution builder, Henry has authored or coauthored twenty-one books and created fifteen documentary films, including *Black in Latin America*, *Black America since MLK: And Still I Rise*, *Africa's Great Civilizations*, *Reconstruction: America after the Civil War*, and *Finding Your Roots*, his groundbreaking genealogy series now in its third season on PBS. His six-part PBS documentary series, *The African Americans: Many Rivers to Cross* (2013), which he wrote, executive produced, and hosted, earned the Emmy Award for Outstanding Historical Program—Long Form, as well as the Peabody Award, Alfred I. duPont–Columbia University Award, and NAACP Image Award. Having written for such leading publications as the *New Yorker*, the *New York Times*, and *Time*, Henry now serves as Chairman of TheRoot.com, a daily online magazine he cofounded in 2008, while overseeing the Oxford African American Studies Center, the first comprehensive scholarly online resource in the field. The recipient of fifty-five honorary degrees and numerous prizes, he earned his BA in English language and literature, summa cum laude, from Yale University in 1973 and his MA and PhD in English literature from Clare College at the University of Cambridge in 1979.

SAKSHI GHAI is a research coordinator at the Wharton People Analytics of the University of Pennsylvania. Previously, she worked as a research assistant at the Wharton School and the School of Arts and Sciences at Penn. She has also worked as an advertising executive at

Ogilvy & Mather and as a program lead at Vedica Scholars, a unique women-only management program in India. Sakshi earned her BA (Hons) in philosophy from Lady Shri Ram College for Women, Delhi University, and her MS in behavioral and decision sciences from the University of Pennsylvania. She also pursued the Young India Fellowship from Ashoka University.

ZACHARY GREEN is a Professor of Practice in Leadership Studies at the University of San Diego and lead faculty for the RISE Urban Leadership Fellows Program. A clinical psychologist by training, Zachary teaches courses on human development, organizational behavior, dialogue, negotiations, mindfulness, and love. As a practitioner, Zachary's clients include multinational corporations, government agencies, nongovernmental organizations, universities, religious institutions, and nonprofits. He has coached top leaders at the World Bank for the better part of two decades. His most recent venture, through IMAGO Global Grassroots, involves a cocreative model of international development in South Asia, sub-Saharan Africa, and South America. Zachary frequently offers training on integral and unconscious psychological dimensions of leadership and conducts consultations with organizations on diversity, equity, and inclusion. Zachary received a doctorate in clinical psychology from Boston University and completed advanced clinical training at Cambridge Hospital/Harvard Medical School and Georgetown University. He began his career as an associate of the Wharton Center for Applied Leadership.

PATRICIA FAISON HEWLIN is an Associate Professor of Organizational Behavior and Associate Dean of Undergraduate Programs at the Desautels Faculty of Management, at McGill University. She conducts research on how organization members and leaders engage in authentic expression, as well as factors that impede authenticity in everyday work interactions. Her research has centered on employee silence and the degree to which members suppress personal values and pretend to embrace those of the organization, a behavior she terms "creating facades of conformity." Patricia's research also includes gaining insight on how members make sense of and cope with organizational value breaches in values-driven organizations. She received her BA in English rhetoric and literature, and Spanish language and literature from Binghamton University. She holds an MBA in finance and a PhD in organizational behavior from the Stern School of Business, New York University. She is published in leading academic journals and her work has been featured in several media outlets including *Harvard Business Review, Huffington Post, The Times (UK)*, and *Globe and Mail*.

ELIZABETH L. HOLLOWAY is a Professor of Psychology in the Graduate School of Leadership and Change at Antioch University. She is a fellow of the American Psychological Association and diplomate of the American Board of Professional Psychology. She has over thirty-five years of experience as an educator, researcher, and international consultant in clinical supervision, relational practice, and respectful cultures in higher education and health-care organizations. She also serves on the faculty of the American College of Healthcare Executives conducting workshops on the impact of toxic behaviors on organizational culture. Her most recent publications are in qualitative methodologies for inclusion and diversity research, and relational practice in teaching and learning in graduate education. Her most recent books are *Essentials of Supervision for a Systems Approach to Supervision* and *Toxic Workplace! Managing Toxic Personalities and Their Systems of Power*. She received her PhD in Counseling Psychology from the University of Wisconsin-Madison, MA in counseling at University of California, Santa Barbara, and her Honors Psychology BA from the University of Waterloo, Canada.

ERIKA HAYES JAMES is the John H. Harland Dean of Goizueta Business School at Emory University. An award winning scholar, she had published numerous academic articles in such journals as *Academy of Management Journal, Organization Science, Strategic Management Journal* and *Journal of Applied Psychology*. Her scholarship has been featured in media outlets including *Wall Street Journal, Washington Post* and *NPR*. She is coauthor of the book *Leading under Pressure: From Surviving to Thriving Before, During and After a Crisis*. In addition to her scholarship, Erika is a passionate educator and consultant with expertise in diversity and inclusion and crisis leadership. Before joining Goizueta, she served as the Senior Associate Dean for Executive Education at the University of Virginia's Darden Graduate School of Business, and was an assistant professor at Tulane University's Freeman School of Business and a visiting professor at Harvard Business School. Erika is active in the community serving on several nonprofit boards and as a member of the Board of Directors for SurveyMonkey. She received her undergraduate degree in psychology from Pomona College and her PhD from the University of Michigan.

RAY JONES teaches introductory undergraduate courses in business ethics and organizational behavior, as well as advanced undergraduate courses in gender and diversity in management and governance at the University of Pittsburgh. In the MBA program, he teaches the required organizational behavior core course. For the past several years, he has served as coordinator of the Certificate Program in Leadership and Ethics, in which more than sixty undergraduate students work toward the completion of the certificate as an enhancement of their undergraduate major. In addition to teaching, he plays a variety of advisory roles in a number of different student activities and pursuits in the College of Business Administration.

SERENITY LEE is a research associate at Harvard Business School. She is interested in the interpersonal and organizational factors that cultivate workplaces in which all employees, including those with marginalized identities, have the capacity to thrive. Serenity received her BA (Honors) in psychology from the University of Michigan.

MICHELLE SMITH MACCHIA is an Assistant Professor of Professional Practice at the Rutgers University Graduate School of Education. As a PK–12 education practitioner, Michelle helps preservice teachers improve their pedagogical practice, which, in turn, improves learning outcomes for students. She codesigned the Early Reading Matters program, an inquiry-based professional development initiative for elementary teachers. Her research interrogates systemic inequities influenced by policy and educator mindset within traditional, public school systems in the United States. She earned her doctorate in teacher leadership from Rutgers University; her master's degree in educational administration from Teachers College, Columbia University; and her bachelor's degree in French and linguistics from the University of California, Los Angeles.

ELLYN MAESE, MA, is a research analyst with Gallup's Workplace Analytics and Research team. She conducts both quantitative and quantitative research related to organizational policies and employee experience, providing empirical evidence to guide Gallup's data-driven advice and practices. As a doctoral candidate of developmental psychology at University of Nebraska Omaha (UNO), Ellyn specializes in statistical and methodological issues related to the cross-cultural study of social development, with expertise in psychometrics, structural equation modeling, and multilevel analysis. She has also served as an adjunct instructor at UNO, where she taught courses in psychological research methods and statistics; provided consultation on research methodology and statistics for faculty in the UNO College of Business Administration, at the University of Nebraska Lincoln, at Fudan University, and at Universidade Federal do Parana; and served as managing editor for the *Journal of Latino/Latin American Studies*.

COURTNEY L. MCCLUNEY is a postdoctoral research fellow at the Darden School of Business and Academic Strategic Partnerships for Interprofessional Research and Education in the School of Nursing at the University of Virginia. She received her PhD in psychology (personality and social contexts) at the University of Michigan and BA in psychology and interpersonal/organizational communication from the University of North Carolina–Chapel Hill. Courtney investigates how marginalized employees are surviving and thriving at work, and the organizational structures and processes that create these conditions. She primarily centers black women's workplace experiences and uses interdisciplinary frameworks to examine how they cultivate resources to navigate inequities in organizations. Her most recent work, which was funded by the Batten Institute for Entrepreneurship and Innovation at the University of Virginia, explores black women's entrepreneurship in resource-constrained environments. For more information about her research, visit www.CourtneyLMcCluney.com.

SHANE MCFEELY, PhD, is an organizational researcher at Gallup. He conducts research and consults with clients on topics most important to human capital management with the goal of making the workplace more productive, more positive, and, ultimately, more profitable. Among other workplace topics, Shane has expertise in the areas of program evaluation, employee selection, workplace effectiveness, research methodology, data visualization, and advanced analytics. Before joining Gallup, Shane was an administrator for the Omaha Public Schools' Research Division, where he implemented research methodology to evaluate the effectiveness of programs and other educational initiatives in the largest school district in Nebraska, serving over fifty-two thousand students. He analyzed district performance and program data, evaluated the effectiveness of teacher professional development, aided in the strategic planning process, and managed the district's 360-degree principal evaluation system.

AUDREY MURRELL is currently Associate Dean of the College of Business Administration and Associate Professor of Business Administration at the University of Pittsburgh, School of Business. She received her BS from Howard University and PhD from the University of Delaware. Audrey conducts research on mentoring, careers in organizations, workplace and supplier diversity, and social issues in management. Her work has been published widely in management and psychology journals, as well as in several books: *Mentoring Dilemmas: Developmental Relationships within Multicultural Organizations* (with Crosby and Ely), *Intelligent Mentoring: How IBM Creates Value through People, Knowledge and Relationships* (with Forte-Trummel and Bing), and her recent book entitled *Mentoring Diverse Leaders: Creating Change for People, Processes and Paradigms* (with Blake-Beard). Audrey frequently serves as a consultant in the areas of mentoring, leadership development, and workforce and supplier diversity. She teaches courses at the undergraduate, graduate, and executive education levels in the areas of organizational behavior, leadership, ethics, and cross-cultural management. Her community service activities include having served on and chaired a number of nonprofit and community boards.

STELLA M. NKOMO is currently a Strategic Professor in the Department of Human Resource Management at the University of Pretoria, South Africa. She is a former scholar-in-residence at the Bunting Institute of Harvard University and a visiting scholar at the Tuck Business School of Dartmouth College. Her internationally acclaimed research on race and gender in organizations, leadership, and managing diversity and management in Africa has been published in numerous journals and books. She is coauthor of the critically acclaimed Harvard Business School Press book *Our Separate Ways: Black and White Women and the Struggle for Professional Identity.* Stella serves on the editorial board of several management journals and is currently coeditor of a special issue of the *Academy of Management Review* focused on diversity in the workplace. She is the recipient of several honors, including the 2009 Academy of Management Gender and Diversity in Organizations Award for Scholarly Contributions. Most recently, she received the International Leadership Association 2017 Lifetime Achievement Award.

JENNIFER PETRIE is a postdoctoral fellow at the David Berg Center for Ethics and Leadership at the University of Pittsburgh's College of Business of Administration. She received her EdD from Ohio University in 2015. At the University of Pittsburgh, she researches global competency, service learning, ethics education, and African education policy. In Ghana, Jennifer's current project focuses on improving policy, outcomes, and resources for senior high school education. Jennifer has also performed dance as a member of Azaguno, a multicultural African performing arts ensemble, for the past eight years.

SHANNON POLK is the principal consultant for Leadership Solutions, LLC. She recently completed a doctor of ministry degree at the Assemblies of God Theological Seminary at Evangel University, where her research focused on racial and ethnic clergywomen ministering in predominantly white denominations. She is a graduate of Western Michigan University's Cooley Law School (JD) and Michigan State University (BA).

KISHA PORCHER is an Assistant Professor of Professional Practice at Rutgers University, Graduate School of Education. She also serves as a senior educational consultant at Teaching Matters, Inc. in New York City, and is the cofounder of Equity Consulting Group. As a consultant, she coaches in the areas of race, social justice, culturally responsive pedagogy, literacy, assessment, and teacher leadership. She was an Advanced Placement English Language Arts, College Summit, and International Baccalaureate educator in Prince George's County for four years. She also served as the International Baccalaureate Coordinator in Prince George's County for two years. She obtained her bachelor of arts degree in English and secondary education from Spelman College; her master of arts in curriculum and instruction from Teachers College, Columbia University; and her doctorate of education in teaching and teacher education, with a specialization in education policy. Her professional interests include urban teacher preparation, curriculum design, urban education research, education policy, and instructional strategies.

LAURA PROVOLT is a doctoral candidate in the University of Georgia's industrial-organizational program and is currently working to complete her dissertation. Her dissertation research addresses the role of informal social networks as a mechanism of systematic hiring discrepancies among mothers reentering the workplace. Her master's research addressed the cognitive awareness and intentional control of unconscious racial and gender bias in the context of applicant evaluation. Other current research projects include an examination of the ideologies regarding diversity in science, engineering, technology, and mathematics fields. Before coming to the University of Georgia, Laura earned bachelors degrees in psychology and business administration and finance at Humboldt State University, California.

VALERIE PURDIE-GREENAWAY is Associate Professor in the Department of Psychology at Columbia University. Valerie has authored numerous publications that have appeared in journals such as *Science*, *Psychological Science*, and the *Journal of Personality and Social Psychology*. She has been awarded grants from the National Science Foundation, Russell Sage Foundation, Spencer Foundation and William T. Grant Foundation. In 2013, Valerie was awarded the Columbia University RISE (Research Initiative in Science and Engineering) award for most innovative and cutting-edge research proposal for her proposal titled, "'Cells to Society' Approach to Reducing Racial Achievement Gaps: Neuro-physiologic Pathways Involved in Stereotype Threat and Social Psychological Interventions." Previously, Valerie served on the faculty of Yale University. She completed her doctoral work in psychology at Stanford University in 2004 as a student of Claude Steele.

VERÓNICA CARIDAD RABELO (she/her/hers; they/them/their) is an Assistant Professor of Management in the College of Business at San Francisco State University. She received a PhD in psychology (gender and feminist psychology) and women's studies from the University of Michigan and a BA in psychology (with concentrations in Latin@ studies and Africana studies) from Williams College (Williamstown, MA). Her research examines how dignity, health, and mistreatment in the workplace are shaped by race and ethnicity, gender and sexuality, and social class. She researches these topics from the perspectives of people who are underrepresented or silenced in research. She also researches strategies to make teaching, research methods, and workplace environments more inclusive and accessible. Her honors include a Student Scholar Latina Award from the American Psychological Association and the inaugural Diversity Research Award from the University of Michigan's Department of Psychology. For more about her research, teaching, and consulting, visit www.VeronicaRabelo.com.

LAKSHMI RAMARAJAN is the Anna Spangler Nelson and Thomas C. Nelson Associate Professor of Business Administration in the Organizational Behavior Unit at Harvard Business School. Her research examines how people can work fruitfully across social divides, with a particular emphasis on identities and group boundaries. Her research addresses two broad questions: (1) How does the work environment shape people's experiences as members of particular groups and of their multiple identity groups? (2) What are the consequences of multiple identities and group differences in organizations? She investigates professional and work identities alongside other identities that are important to people, such as those pertaining to ethnicity, community, and family. She examines consequences in areas such as employee engagement and commitment to work, career success and satisfaction, quality of interpersonal and intergroup relations, and performance. Lakshmi earned her BA (Honors) in international relations from Wellesley College, her MSc in international relations from the London School of Economics and Political Science, and her PhD in management from the Wharton School of Business.

ASPEN J. ROBINSON is a doctoral candidate in the Industrial and Organizational Psychology Doctoral Program at the University of Georgia. Her research interests include workplace discrimination, the experiences of people of color at work, and the impact of organizational diversity messages on individual outcomes. Aspen has published an article about black lives in organizations and has coauthored a book chapter focused on diversifying STEM. She also has presented research on sexual minority employees' diversity climate perceptions, diversity ideologies in organizations, and on the relationship between gender and leadership self-efficacy. Aspen is currently an intern on the Workforce Analytics team at Johnson & Johnson. Aspen received a bachelor's degree from the University of Georgia and a master's degree from the University of North Carolina at Charlotte.

KAREN SAMUELS is a licensed psychologist in Ormond Beach, Florida. Her career has been dedicated to empowering women and other forgotten populations through her community involvement, psychotherapy practice, and lectures and consultation. She is the founder and President of COPE: Community Outreach to Prevent Eating Disorders, a nonprofit since 2001. She is a consultant to the Halifax Health Family Medicine Residency Program, training physicians in interprofessional treatment teams. She is also an affiliate and key contributor to the Jean Baker Miller Training Institute, Wellesley Centers for Women. Utilizing relational cultural theory, she spearheaded media literacy programs for middle schools in two entire school districts, as well as conducted eating disorder groups with midlife women. She has published widely, highlighting eating disorders and related health concerns in midlife and beyond. She serves as the resident psychologist and body image specialist, promoting size acceptance and diversity with online videos and blogs, on the wellness platform OneOEight.com. Karen received the 2014 National Eating Disorders Association Westin Family Award for Activism and Advocacy in recognition of her community and social justice work.

LUMUMBA SEEGARS is a doctoral student in organizational behavior, a joint program with Harvard Business School and the Department of Psychology. He studies how individuals' values and identities affect how they experience, enact, and react to changes in organizations meant to address inequality. He has work experience in education, the performing arts, political campaigns, and ministry. Lumumba completed his undergraduate studies in social studies at Harvard College.

MURIEL E. SHOCKLEY is the Director of the Undergraduate Studies Program at Goddard College. She has over twenty-five years of experience as a faculty member and administrator in colleges and universities. Her work centers on the impact of intersectional identities on individuals, communities, and systems. Muriel has deep experience working with community collaborations that address issues of service and access to diverse populations and as a consultant and researcher supporting progressive organizations in program design, implementation, evaluation, and training.

NANCY SIMS is President and CEO of the Toigo Foundation, a national leadership program supporting underrepresented professionals within finance throughout the arc of their careers. Nancy brings nearly thirty years of service in the financial services industry to her leadership of the nonprofit, offering solutions-based engagement with organizations through programming and collaboration. Her entrepreneurial leadership style has advanced Toigo's work from a small, grassroots organization to a high-impact partner extending its reach today to a broad mix of industries from technology and media to government. During Nancy's twenty-year Toigo tenure, the organization has become a staunch advocate for diversity, including coverage in business and industry publications, thought leadership, and speaking engagements. In 2008, Nancy testified before the US House Financial Services Oversight Committee, reporting findings from the foundation's Retention Returns Survey that highlighted the viewpoints of diverse professionals on inclusion practices within their employer organizations. In 2016, her leadership in stewarding the challenges of the financial crisis of 2008 was chronicled in the *Case Research Journal* and is now a case study available for use in MBA and executive education classrooms.

FLORA TAYLOR is an organizational development consultant, executive coach, educator, and group dynamics specialist. Her practice areas include team development, meeting effectiveness, and large and small group facilitation. Flora passionately advocates for the benefits of experiential learning. She has designed, directed, and staffed many experiential conferences, simulations, and retreats for executives on the dynamics of organizational life using social systems (Power Lab), and group relations methodologies. Flora has worked for associations including the Center for Applied Research and Praxis, both boutique consulting firms specializing in psychodynamic approaches to organizational development. Flora brings significant teaching experience to bear in the areas of leadership, power authority, and group development, including engagements at the School of Social Policy and Practice at the University of Pennsylvania, Teachers College of Columbia University, and Ashoka University (Haryana, India). Flora earned her AB cum laude from Harvard University and her PhD from the University of Pennsylvania. She is a fellow of the A. K. Rice Institute for the Study of Group Relations and a licensed psychologist.

KECIA THOMAS is a Professor of Industrial/Organizational Psychology at the University of Georgia and the founding Director of the Center for Research and Engagement in Diversity. Kecia currently serves as the Senior Associate Dean in the Franklin College of Arts and Sciences at the University of Georgia. Kecia is an expert in the psychology of workplace diversity. Her scholarship and institutional engagements focus on the issues of strategic diversity recruitment; supporting diversity in science, technology, engineering, and mathematics workplaces; and understanding the career experiences of high-potential women of color. She is the author of numerous peer-reviewed articles and book chapters, as well as the textbook *Diversity Dynamics in the Workplace*; editor, *Diversity Resistance in the Workplace*; and coeditor, *Diversity Ideologies in Organizations*, as well as of special "workplace diversity" journal issues. She is an elected fellow of both the Society for Industrial and Organizational Psychology and the American Psychological Association, and a recipient of the Janet Chusmir Award for Distinguished Service from the Gender and Diversity in Organizations division of the Academy of Management.

SUE TOIGO, through Fitzgibbon Toigo & Co, provides access for emerging investment managers to the global institutional investment community. A principal in Goldmine Consulting, she provides career and business research and advice to minority investment professionals. Sue cofounded the Institute for Fiduciary Education in 1985 to provide investment education through global seminars for over three thousand fund sponsors and consultants. Sue spent sixteen years as the lobbyist for the California Children's Lobby and fourteen years on the Columbia Business School Board of Overseers. She was a Woodrow Wilson Fellow at universities in Texas, Nebraska, and Indiana, and she has spoken for the US State Department in Australia, New Zealand, Syria, and Chile. In 1989, she and her late husband, Bob Toigo, founded the Toigo Foundation to support minority MBA students pursuing careers in finance. She is in the Berkeley Women's Hall of Fame for founding child care centers at University of California, Berkeley.

ELLA F. WASHINGTON is an organizational psychologist providing subject matter expertise in leadership, diversity, and inclusion. Her research and client work focus on women in the workplace, barriers to inclusion for diverse groups, and working with organizations to build inclusive cultures. Ella has conducted inclusiveness audits, learning workshops, and strategic planning sessions with clients in order to support their goals of building a more diverse and inclusive workplace. She has partnered with Gallup clients across the retail, manufacturing, banking, higher education, technology, government, and nonprofit industries. Before joining Gallup, Ella was a talent management consultant at Ernst & Young. Earlier, she worked at the Federal Reserve Bank of Chicago as a diversity and inclusion consultant. She has extensive teaching experience in business schools in the area of organizational behavior. She earned her PhD in organizational behavior from the Kellogg School of Management at Northwestern University. She was a Phi Beta Kappa scholar at Spelman College, where she graduated summa cum laude with a bachelor's degree in psychology.

DAVID B. WILKINS is the Lester Kissel Professor of Law, Vice Dean for Global Initiatives on the Legal Profession, and Faculty Director of the Center on the Legal Profession at Harvard Law School. He is also a senior research fellow of the American Bar Foundation and a faculty associate of the Harvard University Edmond J. Safra Foundation Center for Ethics. David has given over sixty endowed lectures at universities around the world and is a frequent speaker at professional conferences and law firm and corporate retreats. He is the author of over eighty articles on the legal profession in leading scholarly journals, as well as a coeditor of several books, including *Diversity in Practice* (2016), *The Indian Legal Profession in the Age of Globalization* (2017), *The Brazilian Legal Profession in the Age of Globalization* (2018), and *The Chinese Legal Profession in the Age of Globalization* (forthcoming 2019). He is a coauthor of *Problems in Professional Responsibility for a Changing Profession* (6th edition 2016), one of the leading casebooks in the field. David was elected to the American Academy of Arts and Sciences in 2012 and the Spanish Royal Academy of Doctors in 2014 and most recently was the recipient of the Harvard Law School Association Award in 2016. His major research interests include the legal profession, legal ethics, diversity, and globalization.

WHITNEY WILLIAMS is the Senior Project Manager in Faculty Development at the University of Michigan Medical School where she is responsible for the oversight and execution of facilitating the advancement and development of early-career and women leaders; fostering impactful and influential relationships through mentoring, coaching, and sponsorship; and creating positive cultures. She also serves as the Board

President at the Women's Center of Southeastern Michigan, a nonprofit organization dedicated to the economic and emotional self-determination of women and families. She received her MSW, with particular interest in maternal and infant mental health, and a Bachelor's of Science in neuropsychology with a minor in women and gender studies from the University of Michigan. She is currently pursuing her graduate studies in organizational development from Eastern Michigan University.

ADIA HARVEY WINGFIELD is Professor of Sociology at Washington University in Saint Louis. Her research examines racial and gender inequality in professional occupations and has been published in *Social Problems, Gender & Society*, and other leading peer-reviewed sociology journals. She is the author of several books, most recently, *Flatlining: Race, Work, and Health Care in the New Economy*. Adia has served as President of Sociologists for Women in Society and is a regular contributor to *Slate*, the *Atlantic, Fortune*, and *Harvard Business Review*. She is also the 2018 recipient of the American Sociological Association's Public Understanding of Sociology award, which honors exemplary contributions to advancing sociological research and scholarship among the general public.

LYNN PERRY WOOTEN is the David J. Nolan Dean of the Charles H. Dyson School of Applied Economics and Management of Cornell University. Previously, she served as Senior Associate Dean for Student and Academic Excellence and Clinical Professor of Strategy, Management, and Organizations at the University of Michigan's Ross School of Business. Lynn's current research bridges theory and practice and focuses on positive organizing routines, diversity management practices, and crisis leadership. Lynn is an alumna of the University of Michigan (PhD). She received her undergraduate degree from North Carolina A&T State University and her MBA from the Fuqua School of Business at Duke University.

MELISSA E. WOOTEN is an Associate Professor of Sociology at the University of Massachusetts, Amherst. Her research lies at the theoretical intersections of organizations, race, and education. Her book, *In the Face of Inequality: How Black Colleges Adapt*, uses historically black colleges as an empirical context to investigate how the social structure of race and racism affect an organization's ability to acquire the financial and political resources it needs to survive. She is currently working on a project that traces how twentieth- and twenty-first-century entrepreneurs get involved in philanthropic causes related to black education. Public commentaries on her research appear in the *Conversation*, in the *Academic Minute*, and on the website of the African American Intellectual History Society (www.AAIHS.org).

About the Editors

LAURA MORGAN ROBERTS is a Teaching Professor of Management at Georgetown University's McDonough School of Business. She previously served on the faculties of Harvard Business School and Antioch University's Graduate School of Leadership and Change. Laura has also taught courses in organizational behavior, psychology, negotiations, group dynamics, and leadership and career development as a faculty affiliate of the University of Michigan; the Wharton School of Finance; the Tuck School of Business; Georgia State University; the University of California, Los Angeles, Anderson School of Management; and AVT Business School (Copenhagen). She is currently a visiting scholar of Harvard Business School's Gender Initiative, researching the influence of African American business leaders. Laura is also a cofounder of RPAQ Solutions, Inc., a research and consulting firm that brings strength-based practices to leaders who seek extraordinary performance and personal fulfillment.

Laura's research examines how leaders cultivate positive identities in diverse work organizations. She has published research articles, teaching cases, and practitioner-oriented tools for strategically activating best selves in workplaces and communities. Her publications, "How to Play to Your Strengths" and "Creating a Positive Professional Image," are among the most popular articles from *Harvard Business Review* and have been featured in several media outlets. Laura is an editor of *Positive Organizing in a Global Society: Understanding and Engaging Differences for Capacity-Building and Inclusion* (with Lynn Perry Wooten and Martin Davidson) and *Exploring Positive Identities and Organizations: Building a Theoretical and Research Foundation* (with Jane Dutton).

Laura earned a BA in psychology (highest distinction and Phi Beta Kappa) from the University of Virginia and an MA and PhD in organizational psychology from the University of Michigan.

ANTHONY J. "TONY" MAYO is the Thomas S. Murphy Senior Lecturer of Business Administration in the Organizational Behavior Unit of Harvard Business School. He currently teaches Leadership and Organizational Behavior and Authentic Leader Development in the MBA program. Previously, he was the course head of FIELD (Field Immersion Experiences for Leadership Development), a required experiential, field-based course in the first year of the MBA program that is focused on leadership, globalization, and integration. Before his work on FIELD, he cocreated and taught the elective course Great Business Leaders: The Importance of Contextual Intelligence. In addition, Tony teaches extensively in leadership-based executive education programs.

He recently coauthored the second edition of the textbook *Management*, which features a new approach for teaching the core principles of management courses to undergraduate students based on the integration and dynamic interaction of strategic management, organizational design, and individual leadership. His previous coauthored works include *In Their Time: The Greatest Business Leaders of the 20th Century*, which has been translated into six languages; *Paths to Power: How Insiders and Outsiders Shaped American Business Leadership*; and *Entrepreneurs, Managers and Leaders: What the Airline Industry Can Teach Us about Leadership*. These books were derived from the development of the Great American Business Leaders database that Dean Nitin Nohria and Tony created (see https://www.hbs.edu/leadership/20th-century-leaders/Pages/default.aspx).

Tony served as the Director of the Leadership Initiative from 2002 to 2018, and in this capacity, he oversaw several comprehensive research projects on emerging, global, and legacy leadership and managed a number of executive education programs on leadership development. He was a cocreator of the High Potentials Leadership Development, Leadership for Senior Executives, Leading with Impact, Maximizing Your Leadership Potential, and Leadership Best Practices programs and has been a principal contributor to a number of custom leadership development initiatives. He launched the executive coaching component for the Program for Leadership Development.

Before his current role, Tony pursued a career in database marketing, where he held senior general management positions at the advertising agency Hill Holliday, the database management firm Epsilon, and the full-service direct marketing company DIMAC Marketing Corporation. Most recently, Tony served as the General Manager of Hill Holliday's

Customer Relationship Management Practice. At Epsilon, he served as Acting Chief Executive Officer and had full responsibility for the delivery and management of strategic and database marketing services for *Fortune* 1000 companies and national not-for-profit organizations.

Tony completed his MBA from Harvard Business School and received his bachelor's degree, summa cum laude, from Boston College.

DAVID A. THOMAS took office as the twelfth President of Morehouse College on January 1, 2018, ushering in a new era of leadership for the school, the nation's largest and most prestigious liberal arts college for men.

His appointment in October 2017 ended a six-month period of leadership transition at the college, which began in April when the board announced its national search for a new Morehouse president. Members of the Morehouse College Board of Trustees selected David for many reasons, including his visionary leadership as a business school administrator and his proven track record in fund-raising, which includes a capital campaign that raised more than $130 million in five years for Georgetown University's McDonough School of Business.

David has thirty years of higher-education experience. He holds a doctorate in organizational behavior studies and a master of philosophy degree in organizational behavior, both from Yale University. He also has a master's degree in organizational psychology from Columbia University, and a bachelor of administrative sciences degree from Yale College.

David is the former H. Naylor Fitzhugh Professor of Business Administration at Harvard Business School and the former Dean of Georgetown University's McDonough School of Business. As Dean of Georgetown McDonough, David led 250 employees and more than two thousand students through a period of growth, which included a redesign of the MBA curriculum, the launch of the school's first online degree program, and a $130 million capital campaign. He enhanced academic and professional opportunities for the school's undergraduate and graduate students, including adding the Global Business Experience and an Office of Professional Development for undergraduates. He also increased the diversity of faculty and staff, launched new research initiatives, and boosted the school's research funding.

Before Georgetown, David served for two decades as a professor and administrator at Harvard University. He returned in 2017 as the H.

Naylor Fitzhugh Professor of Business Administration at Harvard Business School. He is also a former Assistant Professor of Management at the Wharton School at the University of Pennsylvania.

In addition to his work as an educator, David serves as a member of the Board of Directors of DTE Energy, the American Red Cross, and the Posse Foundation. He was the recipient of the *Washington Business Journal*'s 2014 Minority Business Leader of the Year award and the National Executive Forum's Breaking Through: 2020, Beacon Award, among other honors. He has also worked as a consultant on issues relating to organizational change, diversity, and inclusion for one hundred of the *Fortune* 500 companies, as well as major governmental and non-profit organizations.

David is nationally renowned for his research on managing diversity in the workplace. He has written numerous case studies and academic articles on the subject. He is also the coauthor of two related books: *Breaking Through: The Making of Minority Executives in Corporate America*, one of the first in-depth studies to focus on minorities who have made it to the top; and *Leading for Equity: The Pursuit of Excellence in Montgomery County Public Schools*.